Shifting Contexts

Medieval & Renaissance Literary Studies

Shifting
Contexts

Reinterpreting Samson Agonistes

Joseph Wittreich

DUQUESNE UNIVERSITY PRESS
Pittsburgh, Pennsylvania

Library of Congress Cataloging-in-Publication Data

Wittreich, Joseph Anthony.
    Shifting contexts: reinterpreting Samson Agonistes / Joseph
Wittreich.
        p. cm. — (Medieval and Renaissance literary studies)
Includes bibliographical references and index.
    ISBN 0-8207-0331-1 (hardcover)
    1. Milton, John, 1608–1674. Samson Agonistes.   2. Samson (Biblical
judge) — In literature.   3. Judges in literature.   4. Bible — In
literature.   I. Title.   II. Series.
    PR3566   .W56 2002
    822'.4 — dc21
                                                                        2002001653

∞ Printed on acid-free paper.

for **Stuart Curran**

"things through thee take nobler form"

— *Ralph Waldo Emerson*

the story survives its immediate occasion and the loss of some of the senses it originally carried. It enters a future wherein it bears a burden of meanings not necessarily independent of the old, but more accessible and more necessary. Such, at any rate, is the history of interpretation not unduly constricted by an institutional scholarship so repressive as to propose for its sole hermeneutic aim the "single correct interpretation."
— *Frank Kermode*

the Hebrews will write their own version of Samson's story. In that version, he will be the innocent hand of God's vengeance, and I will be a lying, avaricious seducer; at best a tool for fulfilling the words of their prophets. Truth may be written by poets, but history is written by the victors. And it looks like the Hebrews are going to win this one.
— *Dorothy Bryant's Delilah*

But there are evidently for Milton other bonds with other texts and other traditions; there are other cultural systems to which he seems sometimes to be no less engaged. . . . In the end what we have is a case of "radical translation," of a brave attempt to "resituate the text within an alien conceptual framework."
— *Harold Fisch*

Contents

Illustrations viii

Preface xi

ONE Reinterpreting *Samson Agonistes* 1

TWO Justifying Samson's Ways 67

THREE "Glorious For A While" 101

FOUR Several Texts in One 145

FIVE Thought Colliding with Thought 193

SIX From Political Allegory
to an Allegory of Readings 243

Notes 287

Index 345

ILLUSTRATIONS

Figure 1. Dustjacket and Frontispiece: Illustration
No. 18, "Sword-players and gymnic
artists," from *Samson Agonistes.*
A Dramatic Poem by John Milton.
Illustrated by Robert Medley
(Norwich, 1979). ix

Figure 2. Preface and Chapter Ornaments: Nos. 3
("The cutting of Samson's Hair"), 11
("The pain of grief"), 17 ("Image for the
Hero"), 7 ("Image for the fallen state of the
Hero"), 14 ("Fame if not double-fact is
double mouthed"), 20 ("The Destruction"),
and 22 ("Samson's Destiny"). xi

Figure 3. The "Frontispiece" and Title Page for
Paradise Regain'd. A Poem. In IV Books.
To which is added Samson Agonistes
(London, 1671). 15

Figure 4. The Separate Title Page for *Samson
Agonistes* (1671). 17

Figure 5. The Tail Pieces: *Omissa* and *Errata*
(1671). 21

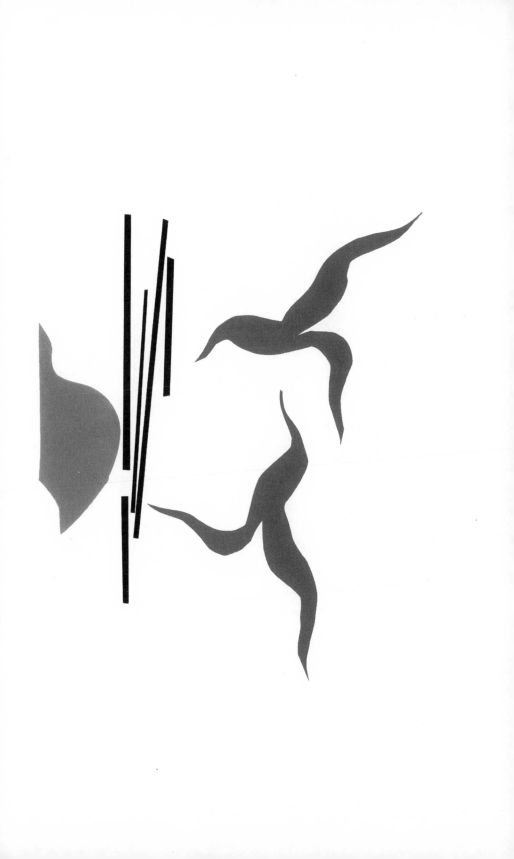

Preface

The matter is too big for any mortal man
who thinks he can judge it.
—*Athene in Aeschylus's* The Eumenides

It's hard to judge or understand
A case like this until we've heard both sides.
—*The Leader in Euripides'* The Heracleidae

Here are two sides, and only half the argument.
—*Athene in Aeschylus's* The Eumenides

Criticism is cumulative and, as it accumulates, assumes a corrective function, emending both a critic's own errors, as well as the mistakes of others, in the process setting the record straight. That is a first imperative when criticism, in this instance of Milton, risks coming to a standstill, largely through its resistance to theory when, in fact, Milton's practice of insisting upon the generic purity of tragedy, as John Penn reports, is less "at war with theory"[1] than an element in its formation and when, even within the context of existing theory, Milton's attitude seems to be (as with his refurbishing of the Chorus in *Samson Agonistes*) that because something has never fully succeeded does not mean it has no possibility for success. In the instance of *Samson Agonistes*, the problem is also magnified when, in the face of contrary evidence, it is said that no one, at least in Milton's time, ever questioned Samson's election and redemption, when such questioning is implicit in the debate over the perseverance of the saints and in the Arminian theology subtending it, and finally in the interrogative casting of so much biblical commentary (Christian and Jewish) in the Age of Milton. If Milton criticism has been in need of a jump-start, it has recently been given one by the nearly simultaneous appearance of new books by Stanley Fish, Barbara K. Lewalski, John T. Shawcross, and Derek N. C. Wood.[2]

This book is not for those who equate received doctrines with "the truth," or for those who believe there is only one truth, and it is complete. Rather, it is addressed to those who understand with Milton that poets are truth-tellers who, nonetheless, tell the truth just partially because part of the truth is all they know. If Milton leaves indefinite what actually happens in *Samson Agonistes*, he does so because there are finally no means of knowing the answers to the questions that his retelling of the Samson story poses. What this new book on *Samson Agonistes* aims to develop and document are the propositions that there are various Samsons, together with different *traditions* of interpretation wheeling around his story and, hence, that the task of a new criticism, examining the Samson story in its seventeenth century formations, will involve, first, the unearthing of new texts (at least texts new to the map created by F. Michael Krouse),[3] which, in their turn, yield competing Samson traditions. A second task for a new criticism involves, if not inventing, certainly appropriating a critical vocabulary including terms like *critical inquiry, contradiction, interrogation, double reading*, not to mention *traditions*, as well as adoption of a point of view toward Scriptures, one which sees them more as commentary than as dogma and hence interpretation of them not as a fixed but rather as an ongoing process. One of the most remarkable features of biblical commentary in the Age of Milton is the instability of its own texts. Sermons and prophesyings, scriptural interpretations both direct and oblique, are regularly — sometimes silently, sometimes just quietly — modified. A comment is added here, deleted there (as we will see in chapter 2 of this study), occasionally to ambush conventional interpretations, but more often (as with Robert Sanderson and James Ussher) to create a snugger fit between their interpretations and those of orthodoxy.[4] We are reminded by one of the most recent–and acute–receptions of Milton that, whatever else, the poet of *Paradise Lost* (and I would add, *Samson Agonistes*) was, often startlingly so, an experimental theologian.[5] This is precisely the proposition that some Miltonists, denying their poet authorship of *De Doctrina Christiana*, would bury.

One of the oddities of Milton criticism, duly noted by John Carey as its perversity, is that Milton "to whom orthodoxy was little more than a starting point for dissent, has been made the preserve of orthodoxy himself."[6] Improving the fit of *Samson Agonistes* with Christian orthodoxy and, in the process, diminishing its enquiring spirit, its interrogative element, have been principal objectives of much criticism of Milton's tragedy belonging to the last century. Once William Riley Parker minimizes its Euripidean context, for instance, Samuel S. Stollman proceeds to extinguish any legendary content, Jewish or Christian, from a poem in which Milton is said to borrow nothing of significance from the Rabbis who, faulting Samson for his pride, sometimes saw divine justice in his downfall. Muting the Jewish interrogation, Milton, Stollman thinks, is bent upon elevating Samson to the plane of the elect and, by making him a prophet of freedom, aligns Samson with the Christian Messiah. Thus hinting at a typological connection, Milton, it is thought, both christianizes and spiritualizes Samson.[7]

These are the broad outlines of a *Samson* criticism that this book, after challenging, redraws and, in its redrawing, shows Classical and Christian, Christian and Hebraic traditions, both generic and interpretive, often bleeding into one another, with the emphasis falling upon the plurality of traditions and shifting contexts intersecting within Milton's poem and on the conflicted nature of each of them. As Jeffrey Shoulson has demonstrated through a citation of the Palestinian Talmud, a sequence of rabbinic statements often has the effect of each undermining the other, while rabbinic commentary itself constitutes "only one stream of Judaic traditions regarding Samson" so that "Josephus's Samson constitutes a parallel, rather than subordinate, tradition to the rabbinic accounts of the biblical judge."[8] Christian traditions are no less fraught — and certainly no less multifaceted — in their perspectives. Contradictory impulses are as evident in its traditions as they are in Milton's poetry itself, in each instance yielding conflicting readings. Thus Barbara Lewalski reports that *Samson Agonistes* "has elicited a cacophony of interpretations," owing in part to the emphasis Milton gives to "the ambiguous signs and events of the Samson story," even as she turns from classical to scriptural paradigms as both more interesting and more apt.[9] What also needs attention is their fusion.

Perhaps better than any of Milton's poems, *Samson Agonistes* illustrates the proposition invoked by the subtitle of this book (and the title of its introductory chapter), that interpretation (whether one's own or another's) provokes reinterpretation. "Interpreting" *Samson Agonistes*, as I once did, within the context of scriptural traditions presupposes "Reinterpreting" *Samson Agonistes* in the light of traditions both classical and scriptural: their correlative genres, their allied myths, and their interfacing ideologies. And the pressing question for Milton criticism now, whether reinterpretation is focused upon *De Doctrina Christiana* or *Samson Agonistes*, is with whom do we sort Milton, with whom does he fit: the upholders of received opinion, the messengers of orthodoxy, or those like Hugo Grotius, John Goodwin, and John Lightfoot, no slaves to dogma or tradition, for whom the meanings of

Scriptures are still to be settled. Which critics, ultimately, are the better representatives of Milton's achievement: those for whom his poetry is an inscription of the common glosses of theologians, or those who would place Milton in the vanguard of modern biblical science? those who intertwine his poetry and polemics, his politics and theology, or those who would hold them distinct? those who situate Milton within a national conversation — or an international debate, in which through "liberties defence" he has, as he reports in "Sonnet 22," "all *Europe* talk[ing] from side to side" (*CP*, 245).

Reinterpretation is an urgent enterprise when the very scriptural texts from which the Samson story is taken are the ones that during the seventeenth century sometimes provoke commentators into developing a new vocabulary for biblical hermeneutics. That vocabulary would address the need for "diligent inquiry" (John Trapp), including "double reading" and "interrogation" (John Weemes), especially in the jarring parts of Scriptures — in those sites of contradiction, engendered by confusingly complex abridgments or disruptions of chronology (Richard Simon) and fostering both the need for laboriously sifting the truth and the sense not of one but of many (occasionally competing) scriptural traditions, especially those "certainly once in the Church, but now utterly lost."[10] To emphasize (as does Milton) the spirit over the letter, the spirit within, is not "*deifying* the Light within" Scriptures, nor setting them "above" or even making them "equal to . . . the Light or Spirit" that brought forth the Scriptures. Rather, as George Whitefield makes plain, inflecting the spirit within *is* to promote ongoing interpretation and to create rival interpretive authorities; it is less an affirmation of established readings than an invitation to be led by an inner light into pathways of newly emerging understandings.[11]

Much of the language given currency by now-established theoretical discourses was already in play during the seventeenth century as is amply illustrated by one aspect of the poetics here ascribed to *Samson Agonistes*: its preoccupation with different Samson *traditions*, hence with *different* interpretations, and thus with their relevance to and circulation within Milton's poem. The rhetoric of biblical hermeneutics in the seventeenth century intersects, sometimes locks arms, with that of literary theory today. As one seventeenth century translator and hermeneut proposes concerning the tendency to blur and blot differences: difference will always be difference, however much we try to trim it under "a disguise of Conformity."[12] Typologies may still be at play, but they are not always flattering: they are now sometimes devised to inflect disparities.

If, in the age of Milton, the new philosophy calls all in doubt, new exegetical presuppositions ensure that the biblical texts would not be exempt from this enquiring spirit, one effect of which was the unsettling of received interpretations, even occasional uprooting of them, sometimes through the tendency evident in Hugo Grotius, John Goodwin, and John Milton to "Arminianize" theological discourses. Indeed, opponents of Arminius might, like John Owen, imagine themselves as "another Samson," having "received strength from God, . . . [to] pull downe the rotten house upon the head of those *Philistims* who would uphold it."[13] Not only figured as an avenging Samson in his own time, or (as some would have it) so figuring himself in *Samson Agonistes*, Milton was represented even more often as a Philistian interpreter of scriptural texts, especially in the attention he gives not to monologic but to dialogic reading, not to fixed but to emerging interpretations of each of them.

Still, within ten years of Milton's death, one commentator, examining different Bibles, with their manifest diversity, writes also of their various interpretive traditions, some written, some oral; apostolic interpretation, as well as interpretations emerging from conversations with people who knew the apostles and, from those conversations, collated their thoughts; subsequent interpretive traditions deriving from the church fathers, both Greek and Latin; and the flood of commentaries inspired by them, sometimes affirming, other times assailing their positions. Sensitizing us to the plethora of scriptural interpretation, as well as its variety, fixing on "contradictions, or contrarieties," this commentator, Simon Patrick, argues that *Scriptures* are *Traditions*, this pluralization sanctioned by 1 Thessolonians 2.15 where we find the exhortation: *"stand fast, and hold the Traditions, which ye have been taught, whether by word, or . . . Epistle."* If we reject traditions, Patrick contends, they should be *"unwritten Traditions,"* extra-biblical ones; for those enshrined within Scriptures constitute the "several ways of bringing us . . . [in touch] with the same Christian Truth; not with different parts of that Truth."[14] Translated into the underlying proposition of this book, any poem faithful in its rendering of the scriptural sources for the Samson story will be not one text but several: it will be an *intertext*. It will be, as Dayton Haskin would say, an interpretive performance founded upon the "manifold contradictions" of Scriptures; and, if not as well understood in the twentieth as in the nineteenth century, such tensions in Milton's poetry, such "disproportion and even disorder," are marks of the poet's "disordered times," as well as a way of poeticizing both her "uncertainties" and those of his age.[15]

For much of the last century, Milton criticism had been satisfied with one interpretation in defiance of the Nietzchean proposition, recently reasserted by Thomas M. Gorman, that "One is always wrong, . . . but with two, truth begins." But as the twentieth rolls over into the twenty-first century, new critical propositions are on the ascendancy: first, that *Samson Agonistes* is uncertain in its meanings, a deeply ambiguous text; second, that it is informed not by one but a multiplicity of traditions, each of them often in conflict, each of them just as often conflicted; and third, that if Milton's tragedy is inexplicable "in isolation from its scriptural source[s]" and their "dialogic interplay" in the poem, as Gorman also concludes,[16] those scriptural contexts are, as has not always been recognized, inextricably involved with the classical tradition of tragedy, especially in its Euripidean and Senecan modes. Whether we are to view Samson as going to the temple with divine commission, or of his own accord, has long been a topic of debate within scriptural commentary but is just now being accepted as a crucial matter of uncertainty in Milton's poem — as James Holstun views the matter, whether in Milton's tragedy those rousing motions come from within or from above — that is now the pressing matter.[17] And not just in Milton's poetry, but in Milton criticism as well.

Take, for example, Toni Morrison's novel whose notions of paradise seem to be founded upon a critique of Milton's own conceptions and whose overriding ethic may be construed as a critique not so much of *Samson Agonistes* as of most of its twentieth century critics. If the lost paradise is ever to be regained, by Morrison's reckoning, that will happen only after dreams begin to outstretch the people who have them, and only when our theologies, instead of crediting those who claim "God at their side" in murder, take aim at such; at those who act as God's instruments and think themselves the executioners of his justice. "How are you going to be His instrument if you don't know what He says," one character asks in an earthy version of Samson's "the contradiction / Of their own deity, Gods cannot be" (898–99).[18] If anything is dead in the new Milton criticism, it is the proposition, set forth so famously by Walter Raleigh just over a century ago, that Milton's poetry (he is speaking of *Paradise Lost*) "is a monument to dead ideas."[19]

Criticism of *Samson Agonistes* has a new look as we enter another century and a new millennium, and it is a look fashioned by some fifteen years of rethinking interpretation of this poem. Judging from Shawcross's recent study, though, interpretation still remains Janus-faced: alongside the new certainties, first, that *Samson Agonistes* is a critique of its culture and, second, that, forcing a distinction between this poem and its author, Milton "asks the reader to read *it*, not him," are those old chestnuts, which continue to insist that the command Samson follows at the end of the poem "comes from God"; that the "renovation of Samson seems certain . . ., as does God's part in the resulting act of that renovation."[20] The last of these propositions is now repudiated, almost as often as it is affirmed, with Shawcross's reaffirmation coming as a surprise, though not completely so in view of the contending currents in recent criticism, no less evident in Shawcross's own book where, as we have just seen, the chief *certainty* in the *uncertain* world of *Samson Agonistes* is its protagonist's renovation, if not regeneration. More important, though, Shawcross also rides free of the clichés of an earlier Milton criticism by acknowledging within this poem a critique of certain forms of the politics this poet had embraced during the Civil War years — and I emphasize with Shawcross: a *critique*, not a repudiation.

Orthodox readings of Milton's tragedy continue to have their spokespersons less in Shawcross, however, than in J. Martin Evans, the late Philip J. Gallager, Anthony Low, and Alan Rudrum, the last of whom, while "know[ing] himself to be in the right," is still compelled to mount a new "case for traditional interpretation of *Samson Agonistes* . . . as the drama of Samson's regeneration." Rudrum is certain that, because he was "not our contemporary," Milton "did not participate in the historical consciousness of modern times" — its resistance to violence or its ethic of charity — but was rather a representative of a seventeenth century culture and consciousness that, even if not documented, can be easily surmised and that, according to Rudrum, reinforces Samson's "regeneration" and "rehabilitation."[21] It is not so much the interpretation of critics like Rudrum as the suppositions on which their interpretations rest that my own book brings under scrutiny, including the notions that there is a single correct interpretation of scriptural texts, with the function of criticism being the elucidation and elaboration of their authentic reading; and that history can be written without accounting for oppositional movements and voices, one of which (as it happens) is Milton's own.

The real difference between Milton's critics is not between those who accept and those who question Samson's regeneration. Both positions are represented within recently emerging criticism of the poem, much of which, like Shawcross's project (and my own for that matter), is "interpretively vexed."[22] Instead, the real difference is between those who embrace or resist what is now the conclusion of many critics, which, in the eloquent formulation of one of them, is that Milton's tragedy "inscribes within it a conventionalized interpretation of its protagonist and his story, then radically subverts without completely destroying that interpretation."[23] All too often Milton remains a star who dwells apart, and even if his poetry is no longer segregated from his prose writings, his writings are studied, again too often, in splendid isolation from those of his age, even from some of his own writings. Thus, when a prose work like *De Doctrina Christiana*, obviously heterodox, and sometimes heretical, becomes threatening to received interpretation, its place in Milton's canon is challenged before interpretation of the poetry, allegedly orthodox, can be modified by it. We are told that this "questionable" work no longer has a place in interpretation of Milton's "genuine" works.[24]

Even some who persist in advancing the orthodox reading with its regenerative, heroic Samson have newly empowered those readings by accommodating theory and, simultaneously, affording sometimes unexpected contexts. Notable examples are David Loewenstein and Michael Lieb, both of whom maintain a close connection between Milton's prose works and his poetry, each of which is imbued with the politics of the other. For Loewenstein, Milton's "turbulent," often "fiercely iconoclastic" drama, with its "militant saint" and "elect hero," is full of liberating gestures, "profoundly violent" ones, and brimming, too, with images of "destructive renewal," themselves forming "a poetics of regenerative iconoclasm," in what is a "moment of . . . intense vision" for Samson.[25] Lieb registers no doubts concerning Milton's emulation of his contemporary culture of violence and thus puts no brakes on Samson as "a model of heroism," whose actions Lieb applauds as "the mark of a hero," even though Francis Barker, writing about this same culture, affords a devastating critique of it as if to say that literature, though mirroring, does not necessarily mimic the violence of a culture. Certain that Milton's motives are otherwise, Lieb advances, in two other essays, arguments intended to corroborate his position. The first of his arguments is that the theological outlook of Milton's poem, "harsh and uncompromising in its violence," indeed exulting in that violence, is summed up in the shorthand of "the theology of dread," with the deity here "portrayed in its most archaic and terrifying form" as is "befitting a drama that culminates in mass destruction." The second of Lieb's arguments is that "violence assumes its most virulent form in *Samson Agonistes*" and receives its most ringing endorsement in the line, "A thousand fore-skins fell" (144), not to mention the line cited in Lieb's previous essay, "of my own accord" (1643), this idiom, according to Lieb, belonging to gods, not humans, and belonging, furthermore, to the Hebrew, not the Christian Bible.[26]

It may be that Barker, instead of Lieb, gives us the better handle on *Samson Agonistes*, especially if we come to see Milton's poem as representing the crisis of the tragic text, or tragedy at a crossroads where, "not necessarily stand[ing] in humane opposition to political power . . ., but . . . profoundly in collusion with it," violence is an aspect of culture, one of its "seductive strategies," "achieved in the very spectacles of the text's own strange savagery." For Barker, the text thus offers no "antidote to generalised violence," with criticism itself sometimes participating in the process by occluding, or possibly even sanctioning and celebrating, "the violence which is culture."[27] Alternatively, a tragic text like *Samson Agonistes* may offer not an occlusion but a focalization of the violence in a culture whose underpinnings are often found in stories, like Samson's, sabotaged by new versions, newly inflected tellings of old tales. The issue for criticism now is whether Milton, through *Samson Agonistes*, condones or criticizes, underwrites or undermines, his own culture of violence. No recent criticism of *Samson Agonistes* presents a starker vision of Milton's poem than Lieb's, nor a sharper summary of the perennial concern over where the heart of this poem is to be found — in the Hebrew Bible or its Christian counterpart? And no recent theorization of tragedy affords so strong a challenge to Lieb as does Barker's, nor opens up such startlingly new directions in which criticism of *Samson Agonistes* may now move.

The new Milton criticism reveals how, far from evading politics, Milton's last poems, especially *Samson Agonistes*, have an inlay of political commentary as well as a sharp political edge. No longer seen as divorced from his polemics, Milton's last poems are regarded as irrevocably involved with and illuminated by his prose writings, and as having moorings in the very times — the 1660s and 1670s — during which these poems were completed and published, if not initially written. According to Laura Lunger Knoppers, "Historicizing Milton in the 1660s and 1670s . . . helps to account for the radical, complex, and distinctive nature of his three long poems," to which Dennis Kezar gives telling definition: "*Samson Agonistes*'s invalidation of the interpretive conventions it dramatizes attains ironic significance as a Restoration publication. For this self-consuming drama recapitulates a drama of construction and deconstruction that an audience in 1671 would have recognized as recent history"[28] — indeed, by the lights of some recent critics, as history not just recent but reaching back into the 1640s and 50s as well.

If the new Milton criticism takes its life blood from any

"movements," they are new historicism and revisionist history; and if it advances through dialogue with enabling critics,
it is, in the case of *Samson Agonistes,* the voices of Stanley
Fish, John Guillory, Christopher Hill, Barbara K. Lewalski,
Mary Ann Radzinowicz, and John T. Shawcross who made
possible the new wave of Milton criticism in the 1990s as it is
represented by the important books of Michael Lieb, David
Norbrook, Annabel Patterson, David Quint, Ashraf Rushdy
and Nigel Smith — and the stunning essays on *Samson Agonistes* by Lana Cable, Ann Baynes Coiro, Richard S. Ide,
Victoria Kahn, Laura Lunger Knoppers, David Loewenstein,
and Janel Mueller. Evident in all this work is a deep alliance,
an interdependency, between history, literature, politics, and
theory. The old admonitions — let's historicize, let's context-
ualize — are now writ large in a criticism that, doing both,
theorizes each. It is not so much the "enterprise" as the
"surprise" of contextualization that is remarkable in the best
recent criticism,[29] no place more evident than in a new anthology of essays on *Samson Agonistes,* where philosophy and
psychology, international law, economics, ethics, legal and
gender theory, aesthetics and biblical hermeneutics (indeed
opposing hermeneutical systems), the laws of genre and generic
transformations, republican politics, comparative religion, the
paganizing of Judaism and the Arminianizing of Christianity —
all come into play.[30]

Among the best recent criticism is David Quint's reading
of *Samson Agonistes* as "a reversal or undoing" of the Restoration and as an expression of "militant Protestantism." The
"surprise" is not in Quint's reading of this tragedy as Milton's
"final blow against his political enemies," his "dream" of laying low the Restoration government, but in Quint's assertion
of a "typology that made Samson . . . into an antithetical or
'good' version of Guy Fawkes" and then in his invocation of a
"tradition that read the destruction of the Philistines' temple
as a figure of the divine retribution for the Gunpowder Plot, a

punishment in kind that turned the evil that God's enemies sought to perform back upon themselves."[31] For another instance, take David Norbrook who, however conventional in pointing to "Samson groping the temple's pillars" as "a stock-image for post-Restoration dissenters, . . . especially appropriate to Milton," or in proposing that *Samson Agonistes* may invoke the "fate of regicides like Vane," already "a republican martyr," is amazingly acute in his realizations, first, that tragedy in the seventeenth century is a genre of both studied irony and increasingly ambiguous heroism; and second, that tragedy, the genre in which England excels, as well as the genre of the Civil War years, is also that in which *Paradise Lost* originates. Tragedy, in sum, is still the center of gravity in Milton's poetry. With Norbrook, the moments of astonishment come as he proceeds "to open up [Milton to] different traditions" through a close look at republican literary culture (important inspiration for which comes from George Buchanan and Hugo Grotius) and in Norbrook's suggestion that, whether or not *Samson Agonistes* was drafted between 1645–49, a possibility Norbrook allows for, it is Euripides who really matters to Milton and whose impact registers, within Milton's tragedy, in its "disturbing, questioning generic instability."[32] If, in the words of Harold Skulsky, *Samson Agonistes* is an experimental, subversive tragedy, "a playhouse of the mind," in this mental theater it stages the crises of its culture — of Renaissance humanism, of Catholic, Calvinist, and Puritan theology, of the politics of the Revolution — and on this stage, "courting scandal," it makes "the defendant at the bar . . . no less than Justice itself."[33] Richard S. Ide is right, therefore, to urge upon us a Euripidean/Senecan model for Milton's tragedy — a topic (in its Euripidean dimension) on which Mark R. Kelley is now leading the way.[34]

One feature of seventeenth century radical Protestantism, laid bare by Norbrook and earlier by both Frank Kermode and Dayton Haskin,[35] is its unblocking of scriptural interpretation, its commitment to open reading, to interpretation not as a fixed but as an ongoing process. If terms like "critical inquiry," "interrogation," and "double reading" are popularized by post-modernism, they are nonetheless part of the idiom of seventeenth century biblical commentary. Indeed, these terms are especially applicable to the jarring parts of Scriptures — those sites of contradiction, engendered by confusingly complex abridgments or disruptions of chronology and fostering both the need for sifting the truth and the sense not of one but of many (occasionally competing) scriptural traditions. The Samson story in the Book of Judges is crucially important in this context. Yet, the way to write a scriptural drama, Grotius's theory and examples make clear, is to create an intertext out of all the places in the Scriptures where a given story is told, alluded to, or interpreted, in the case of Samson starting with Genesis 49.16–18, Judges 13–16, Hebrews 11.32, and Revelation 7, and then to take into account different traditions of interpretation as Grotius does with the Joseph story.

Obviously, Milton's is not the first encounter with Samson in the genre of tragedy, nor the only one struggling to translate stories from Judges into Christian tragedy. It is, though, in the words of Skulsky, "The bravest, the most tormented — and the most compelling" of such examples; among them, the most daringly experimental; and finally bearing comparison with so many existing models of tragedy not because of "mutual influence" but owing to "mutual illumination."[36] The new starting points for criticism of *Samson Agonistes* are the understandings, first of all, that Milton's poem is more Euripidean and Senecan and also more of a piece with early modern biblical tragedy than previously admitted and, second, that Milton, like the Scriptures themselves, attaches not one but a range of senses to the Samson story, an obvious enough procedure for a dissenting poet of the Protestant tradition, who, as Frank Kermode remarks, "abhor[s] the claim of the institution to an historically validated traditional interpretation."[37]

Furthermore, in its various and sometimes unnerving encounters with scriptural texts, as Jeffrey Shoulson shows, *Samson Agonistes*, indebted not just to the Hebrew Bible but to rabbinical literature, figures as a misrashic poem with attention now given to multiple possible interpretations within which there is an agon of invention and textual fidelity.[38] As the text moves away from fixity and determination, it becomes a scene for correction, with the correction itself often resisting a totalizing typology and with the emergent interpretation often effected by the midrashing of Christian readings and the Arminianizing of Christian theology.

In the last decade, a cadre of critics has been rewriting the Renaissance in ways that relocate Milton within the early modern period and revitalize *Samson Agonistes* as a token of that culture. *Milton Quarterly* has provided one forum for revisionary thinking. Noam Flinker was quick to see that seemingly commendatory allusions, even typologies, as "double-edged for Samson" as they had been for Satan, make his "heroic status . . . no longer as clear as in the past" with Flinker himself eventually charting a perspective from which "Samson's slaughter [of the Philistines] . . . can be seen as a deranged act of an ancient Terrorist."[39] Others would also dub Samson a terrorist and, simultaneously, would foreground Milton's tragedy as our most fully elaborated paradigm of the Miltonic relations among politics, religion, and gender. In quick succession, still others shift attention from matters of gender to questions of genre where the uncertainty of rhyme in *Samson Agonistes* emblematizes the uncertainty of its world; where, in turn, its uncertainty is magnified within a genre lacking authorial presence and possessing the dialogic character of closet drama; where at the same time taking on the concerns of tragicomedy but handling them problematically, "Milton unsettles rather than reassures us about the kind of redemption available for his hero and ultimately for those who take that hero as a model for their own reawakening to action"; and where, finally, much of this generic uncertainty is owing to misreadings — and misapplications — of Aristotle in a poem that, because so "highly encoded," forces us to be "careful about its conclusions." After Stanley Fish's intervention, pressure mounts to rethink orthodox readings of *Samson Agonistes*, quite compellingly in the work of Ashraf H. A. Rushdy, for whom Milton's poem "highlights . . . ambivalence" but also finds an interpreting context in *Paradise Regain'd*. This pressure intensifies in Jane Melbourne's effort to decipher and explain biblical intertextuality in Milton's poem and then in Skulsky's rejection of all readings, which either "anoint or condemn" Samson as Milton's "hero."[40] It climaxes in Stanley Fish's claim that "Milton finds in Samson a figure of deep hermeneutic trouble, and in his play troubles are not removed but multiplied."[41]

Yet another forum for revisionary thinking has been *Milton Studies*, and for our purposes a special issue of this annual publication, *The Miltonic Samson*, edited by Albert C. Labriola and Michael Lieb, where, in addition to the essay by Lieb cited above, is Norman T. Burns's subtle foray into Milton's and Samson's antinomianism. Burns has a fine eye for Milton's transgressive maneuvers, observing that "Though Samson in the Judges narrative shows no concern about idolatry, Milton adds to Samson's character two traits that are never far from Samson's consciousness: shame for having encouraged idolatry by his failure, and zeal to sanctify the divine name." Burns reaches toward the conclusion that "in Samson Milton created . . . a man ready to follow commands that he believes to be divine without knowing whither he is going." Other keen eyes in this collection are Janel Mueller and John T. Shawcross. Mueller decodes Milton's versification in *Samson Agonistes*, finding therein "pointers for interpreting" this poem, "both through what it offers by way of stable connotations and through what it signals as irresolvable sites of indeterminacy or of outright violation within the drama's shifting sequence of local contexts." Shawcross, on the other hand, supremely sensitive to the ambiguities of characterization in *Samson Agonistes*, forces us to think twice, and then again, about what we call "misreadings" in the poem, about its multiplying versions of god, its complications of plot, the different faces the poem gives to both Samson and Dalila, even about whether this poem is an accommodation or interrogation of its scriptural source books. In an earlier essay, differently inflected from Shawcross's, but also anticipatory of some of his conclusions, Laura Lunger Knoppers considers what writings on women and marriage Milton engages in his tragedy, and what changes he makes, in the process showing that "Milton draws on and significantly reworks the depictions of Solomon's harlot to demonstrate the need for male discipline, not of the transgressive female, but of the self." In this way, Knoppers concludes, Milton "provides the solution to the threat of foolishness and harlotry — both of male and female, Samson and Dalila."[42]

Work by Knoppers, along with that by Lana Cable and Victoria Kahn, affords a particularly valuable perspective on this book. Seizing upon the documents of religious controversy, especially oppositional voices typically neglected by the self-styled new historicists, Knoppers continues the recent effort, spearheaded by Christopher Hill, of shifting attention from "how Milton makes history" to "how history makes Milton," thus situating herself within the double irony that in *Samson Agonistes* "the people are self-enslaved, and Samson's act of violence cannot set them free"; and that "Samson's act of iconoclasm against the Philistines enhances the tendencies toward idolatry in his own people." For Knoppers, "the true threat" to Milton is not just the Philistine or papist or even Dalila but, more crucially, the Samson within — Milton here questioning "the martyrdoms of the regicides by pointing to the tendencies for idolatry in God's chosen people."[43] No less invested in Milton's iconoclastic enterprise, Lana Cable

comprehends that one consequence of its "radical ambivalence," of its "iconoclastic attack on the heroic image of
Samson ... promulgated during the ... Civil War," is that
Samson, as well as *Samson Agonistes*, "lies beyond the capacity of any to interpret"; is that "what interpreters most seek
in the final scenes of *Samson Agonistes* ... is that which
Samson's words and gestures most pointedly display only to
overturn."[44] At the end of tragedy, here and in the Book of
Judges, Israel awaits not liberation but fresh subjection, while
the Danites are ready to be written out of the Book of Life.

Theology and politics are intimately involved in the seventeenth century and in Milton's last poems, which are just as
unmistakably their product. Especially in *Samson Agonistes*,
the exceptions in jurisprudence find their analogies in the
miracles of theology, with both Milton and Samson, as Victoria
Kahn suggests, "attempt[ing] to think the exception in the
realm of politics and theology." Kahn knows full well the usual
associations between the violence exercised in the founding
of new political orders and supposed acts of divine violence;
and she knows too that, in Milton's tragedy, "the norms of
conscientious action and the sanctions for violence are themselves the subject of debate." For the Milton of *Samson
Agonistes*, Kahn argues, political theology involves "the ambivalent human experience of the divine, an experience which ...
had come to seem irreducibly tragic," with the genre of tragedy,
in turn, "dramatiz[ing] the tensions and ambiguities of human
decision-making ... in relation to the divine." In this light,
then, we are urged to re-view Samson's tearing down of the
temple, an act that for Kahn is "notoriously available to conflicting interpretations," thus forcing the question of "whether
Samson's political act is an expression of divine authority or
of merely human violence" and, doing so, using "the surplus
of possible meanings" to dramatize "the lack of sure coincidence between politics and theology, human action and divine
authority."[45] No one has defined more acutely the intellectual

dilemmas in *Samson Agonistes* nor the daunting challenges now before its critics than Kahn, whose own voice is now supplemented by those voices heard within *Altering Eyes: New Perspectives on "Samson Agonistes."* This book is best read in concert with this new anthology, especially the essays by Stephen B. Dobranski, John Rogers, Mark R. Kelley, Blair Hoxby, and Abraham Stoll and, more, in terms of that title's invocation of William Blake's wise injunction that "the Eye altering alters all."[46]

This book had many readers during the years it was in progress, beginning with William Kerrigan and Edward Tayler, both of whom were skeptical, and John T. Shawcross, always encouraging, who was already at work on his own recently published study of *Samson Agonistes*. The reading given the book manuscript, the careful attention accorded it by David Loewenstein, reached far beyond both the obligations of duty, as well as authorial expectations at their most demanding. In consequence, Loewenstein gave shape to an argument he himself would probably never make, and strengthened its underpinnings in ways too numerous to document but deserving open declaration and repeated thanks. This book has also had its listeners, who became contributors, chief among them my Milton students at The Graduate Center of The City University of New York: Henry McDonald, Hope Parisi, Peggy Samuels, Desma Polydorou, William Moeck, Mark Kelley, Lynne Greenberg, Erin Henriksen, Zachary Davis and Chih-ping Alex Ma (in chronological order). There were also those to whom I listened: first of all, my colleagues at The Graduate Center — Jackie DiSalvo, Will Fisher, David Greetham, Tom Hayes, W. Speed Hill, Gerhard Joseph, Richard McCoy, David Richter, James Saslow, Michael Sergeant, Jacob Stern, and Scott Westrem; plus my colleagues around the City, especially Joseph Conners, Tom Craviero and Shari Zimmerman; and finally my colleagues-at-large, chief among them, John Carey, Stanley Fish, Dayton Haskin, Christopher Hill, Barbara Lewalski,

Michael Lieb, Annabel Patterson, Mary Ann Radzinowicz, John Rogers, and John Rumrich.

Others provided occasions for presenting parts of the book either in seminar format or as lectures: Susanne Woods at a meeting of The Milton Seminar at Brown University (even at Wheaton College when I had to say "no"), Albert Labriola at a later meeting of the same seminar at Duquesne University, and Peter Stallybrass at The Book Seminar at the University of Pennsylvania. I owe special thanks to Alan Fishbone for providing me with an authoritative translation of *Christos Paschon* (referred to in the preface to *Samson Agonistes* as *Christ Suffering*), for his expert translations throughout of Grotius's observations on both the Old and New Testaments — and finally for his own welcome suggestions, often unsolicited, yet always valuable. Fishbone reminds me repeatedly that translators with his gifts invite the question not of what is lost but of what is recovered in the act of translation.

Throughout this book, unless otherwise indicated, quotations of Milton's poetry are from *The Complete Poetry of John Milton*, 2nd ed., rev., ed. John T. Shawcross (Garden City, N. Y.: Doubleday, 1971) and quotations of his prose from *The Complete Prose Works of John Milton*, ed. Don M. Wolfe et al. (8 vols.; New Haven and London: Yale University Press, 1953–83). When identification of these editions might not be clear, I use *CP* for Shawcross's *Complete Poetry* and *YP* for the Yale edition of Milton's *Complete Prose Works.* Moreover, when quoting from Milton's last poems, with the obvious exception of preliminary matter to them, I have embedded citations to book and line numbers, and in the case of *Samson Agonistes* just line numbers, within the text of the separate chapters. Quotations from the Bible, unless otherwise indicated, accord with the King James Version. All illustrations are reproduced with permission from The Henry E. Huntington Library and Art Gallery, San Marino, California, except for the illustrations to *Samson Agonistes* by Robert Medley, the photographic work for which was done at the Huntington Library with permission to publish them coming from Susie Medley, the Executrix of The Robert Medley Estate.

Completion of my book is owing to several fellowships, including PSC Grants from The City University of New York and a timely award from the Henry E. Huntington Library and Art Gallery, whose Director of Research, Dr. Roy Ritchie, prodded me on with the regular reminder that Wittreich's Samson was still under challenge. (Marie Davidson and Brit Kirwin taught me how to respond when under any challenge.) The resources of various libraries, at different stages of the project, were indispensable to its writing and completion: the Libraries of The City University of New York, The New York Public Library, The Library of The Union Theological Seminary, Van Pelt Library of The University of Pennsylvania, as well as The Library of Penn's Center for Judaic Studies, The Folger Shakespeare Library, The Library of Congress, The University of Maryland Library at College Park, The University of Louisville Library at Belknap Campus, The Henry E. Huntington Library, and The British Library.

Yet my largest debt, unpayable because so immense, is to Stuart Curran for whom this book was written, without whom it would never have been conceived, let alone completed, hence to whom it is dedicated: *you saw us through.*

Santa Fe, New Mexico
Joseph Wittreich
25 December 2001

ONE

Reinterpreting
Samson Agonistes

The seventeenth century was fiercely concerned
and one might even say dominated
by the problem of how to interpret sacred texts,
but as the art (or imperatives) of reading evolves,
ways of reading the Bible elide themselves
into ways of construing the canon.
— Balachandra Rajan[1]

The history of criticism is partly the story of changes and choices in both focus and methodology, some of which, the outcome of new discoveries, force both a reconceiving and a rewriting of tradition and, simultaneously, its pluralization. If criticism of *Samson Agonistes* has stressed the Greek tradition of classical tragedy, the partial change in the focus of a new criticism of the poem will shift the accent to Euripidean models, to the Romanizing of such models by Seneca, and then to the mutation of both Euripidean and Senecan

1

models into Christian tragedy, the chief examples for which are afforded by the biblical books of Genesis, Judges, Job, and Revelation. Tragedy modeled on Euripides and Seneca, plus these scriptural books, is not so much a purveyor of traditions, literary and mythological, as their interrogator — a phenomenon that is powerfully evident in the historical sequence of plays beginning with *The Bacchae;* embracing the drama of uncertain date and authorship, *Christos Paschon* (alluded to in the preface to *Samson Agonistes* as *Christ Suffering*); and concluding with Milton's tragedy.

Reaching from Euripides into the eleventh or twelfth century imitation of his *Bacchae* entitled *Christos Paschon* (initially published in Rome during 1542, in both Louvain and Paris in 1544, and in 1550 in Antwerp), this sequence includes, as importantly, Hugo Grotius's *Christus Patiens* (1608) and George Sandys' translation of it (1640). It also comprehends in the early modern period George Buchanan's *Jephthes* (1554), as well as *Baptistes* (1577), Grotius's *Sophompaneas* (1635), plus Milton's *Samson Agonistes* (1671), together with the first early modern tragedies founded upon divine revelation, some early examples of which are provided by "Zieglerus, who wrote two Latin tragedies, Protoplastis and Samson Agonistes, published in 1550."[2] Moreover, Milton's notebook jottings include the titles "Baptistes" and "Christus Patiens," both of which situate him within this line (*YP*, 8:558, 560, 594). But it is the tragedy he actually writes that is both the culmination of this sequence and the climax of the traditions it charts, with Joost van den Vondel's *Samson, of Heilige Wraeck, Treurspel* (1660) setting forth, rather unexpectedly, the critical propositions underpinning my own argument: "ambiguity gives scope for choice. . . . We differ only in interpretation."[3]

Not just a recapitulation of the historical record concerning Samson, subsequent chapters in this book are more exactly an elaboration and extension, especially of seventeenth century representations of Samson, as well as a sorting out of the politics of competing portraits by different writers or, as is sometimes the case, competing representations from different times by the same writer. The eclectic character, though, of Milton's representation acts as a dissuasion to source-hunting; Milton's text sometimes hints at analogues with the most unlikely and even most politically alien texts. In this proliferation of viewpoints, the Samson tradition, once pluralized, is redrawn and rewritten in such a way that Milton's theology now rules over, indeed determines his politics, rather than vice versa. That is, Milton achieves the integration of theology and politics that Grotius attempted. But Grotius is exemplary in other ways as well, not least of which is presenting a hero whose great work actually is deliverance.

In a prefatory note to *Sophompaneas* (the title in the Latin Vulgate means "the Saviour of the World"), Grotius observes that the "History" for this work "is recorded by *Moses, Gen[esis]*," with other contexts afforded by Philo and Josephus, by Justin and Astapanus, Demetrius and Eusebius.[4] Then offering his play as a modeling of tragedy according to the theory of Aristotle and examples established by George Buchanan, Grotius signals the importance of examining the biblical source of a story, other scriptural references to and contexts for it, plus the diversity of interpretation that over time accrues to the tale, in the understanding that the poet himself is formulating yet another interpretation. If not, why bother with a new rendering of an old tale?

Yet, once bothering, Milton finds in Grotius's elaborate agenda for contextualizing *Sophompaneas*, not only generic paradigms for biblical tragedy, but ways of mapping his own efforts, which, beginning with Scriptures, always seem to center in the ground of contestation occupied by competing interpretations of any given story whether it be Creation and Fall, or Jesus tempted in the wilderness, or Samson imprisoned at Gaza, then hurling down the temple/theater. But more than generally indicating the importance of creating an intertext of scriptural stories, Grotius, as we will see in subsequent chapters, offers an elaborate articulation of the scriptural contexts adjoining the Samson story, setting them forth in his own *Opera Omnia Theologica* (1679) and then, within this work, in cross references to the third edition of *De Jure Belli Ac Pacis* (1631). In these writings, by reverting to Euripides and Seneca as his authorities and later by translating some of their plays, Grotius underscores the pertinence of Euripidean and Senecan models to Milton's project as well.

It is as models for Milton's interrogations that Euripides and Seneca, together with the books of Judges and Revelation, plus early modern biblical tragedy, should now figure in Milton criticism. If earlier criticism of *Samson Agonistes* has studied the Christian tradition of tragedy (in its broadest sense), the choice here involves refocusing attention, first, on the Book of Judges as a series of deepening tragedies and, then, on the pressures exerted by the Revelation model and the trans-formational changes in Christian tradition, both literary and theological, effected by it. The Book of Judges, along with the books of Joshua and Kings, in the seventeenth century was supposed to have been written by the very first of the prophets. The Apocalypse, on the other hand, the culmination of various traditions of prophecy, is a radically new form of literature that "prescribes, calls for, and demands a new religion";[5] that glimpses an improved age of humanity. Tragedy founded upon the Apocalypse, together with the Book of Judges, is tragedy with both a politics — and a purpose — each of which comes under review, then undergoes mutation during the Civil War years when, as Nigel Smith remarks, "The prevelant mode of perception was tragic; the dominant mode of representation, tragedy"[6] and when, as Milton reports in *An Apology Against a Pamphlet*, the imperative is to remember tragedy, and use it, as a genre that "ought to . . . strike high, and adventure dangerously at the most eminent vices among the greatest persons" (*YP*, 1:916). The study of politics, as Milton explains in *Of Education,* is the "next remove" from tragedy; indeed, "tragedies of statliest and most regal argument" are irrevocably allied with "Politicall orations" (*YP,* 2:398, 400–01). It should come as no surprise if we find, folded into *Samson Agonistes,* the many sophistries fomented by the English Revolution. Nor is it accidental that, in the stunning formulation of Stephen Goldsmith, "Milton knits together the history that matters most to him and the text's formal dimensions. It can hardly be coincidental, for instance, that the stanza describing Samson's self-destructive heroics ('He tugg'd, he shook, till down [the pillars] . . . came') begins at line 1640, the year of the 'Long Parliament,' and ends at 1659, the year before Charles II resumed the throne."[7]

Neither is it sufficient to say that tragedy was the dominant mode of representation only during the Civil War years, for it would also become the dominant mode for representing those years. Cromwell and his army, both from the viewpoint of the Royalists and the disillusioned radicals, were part of the problem, hence the players in a tragedy of history. In the words of one of Milton's contemporaries, *"Cromwell* though he snatch'd at a Crown in the Comedy, could not expect to gain one by the Tragedies acted over three Nations"; indeed, his successes, in the eyes of some, not only made him a traitor to his own cause but showed him playing the role of the Devil for God's sake. The tragedy, at least for the aforementioned critic, belongs to Cromwell and his army; the comedy, to Charles II and the Restoration years: "God appear'd not in the thunder and lightning of War; but in the soft whisperings of Peace for the most happy Restaurations."[8] The same point is epitomized in the title of Walter Aston's play, *The Restauration of King Charles II. Or, the Life and Death of Oliver Cromwell. An Histori-tragi-comi-ballad opera* (1733). As for Cromwell, he gets swallowed up in tragedy within titles belonging to his own century: the anonymous, *Cromwell's conspiracy. A tragy-comedy, relating to our latter times* (1660), Edward Howard,

The usurper. A Tragedy (1668), Thomas Porter, *The Villain, A Tragedy* (1670), the anonymous *The Religious-Rebell, or the Pilgrim's Prince. A Tragedy* (1671), and Gerolamo Graziani, *Il Cromuele tragedia* (1671).[9] The emphasis, as in Euripides and Seneca, is on high vices in people occupying exalted places.

If among Royalists, the emphasis is on diatribe and ridicule, with the Revolutionaries it falls upon acute critique, simultaneously broad-ranging and judicious and sparing no parties, including one's own. If all that survives on both sides is a propensity for revenge, a nation of barbarians, a culture of violence, then as Nicodemus explains in Sandys's translation of Grotius's *Christus Patiens*, "The minds Disease" shows itself most completely in the rhetorical questions:

> . . . Who censures his own deeds?
> Who not anothers? These accusing Times
> Rather the men condemne, then taxe their Crimes.
> Such is the Tyrany of Judgement; prone
> To sentence all Offences, but our owne.[10]

The tradition of biblical tragedy, with *Samson Agonistes* as its culminating example, turns the tables, sets the record straight, in a poem of double vision and multiplying perspectives, in which personal tragedy is a prelude to public disaster and the defeat of the hero forecasts the demise of his nation.

With the accent thus falling on the vices of heroes in Euripides and Seneca and simultaneously shifting from divine retribution to human revenge, once heroic figures, now the doers of dreadful deeds, become the villains of tragedies often concluding in horrible ruin.[11] Or if not altogether villains, former heroes, historic and legendary, are shown in their villainous moments — in sports of cruelty transacted within tragedies of blood that culminate in what the Messenger of *Samson Agonistes* calls "this so horrid spectacle" (1542), the emphasis here as in Seneca falling upon the *horror*. In comparison with Hercules, in the visual arts and certainly in

Milton's poetry, Samson, depicted in scenes of violence, seems the more savage figure, the one more compromised in his heroism, with sculptors and painters alike often capturing him in uncontrolled moments of rage and sometimes in scenes of mass destruction.

In the first instance, one may think of the huge sculpture in the first courtyard of the Palazzo Vecchio in Florence where Samson, with the jaw bone of an ass, executes a Philistine as he also does in the painting, *Samson Killing a Philistine*, by Andrea Schiavoni, hanging in the Galleria Palatina of the Pitti Palace. Or, as in the de'Medici tapestries, Samson is shown amidst scenes of carnage, "with a great quantity of dead bodies," E. H. Gombrich will not allow us to forget.[12] Comparisons with his pagan counterpart Hercules are inevitable, as well as ubiquitous, in literary and pictorial traditions no less than in Milton's poetry, where Samson is usually the more one-dimensional figure, violent rather than noble, haughty not humble in his conquests and where Milton's cautionary point, emphatically so, is that Samson is no Hercules the Second. Even if the reference to *Christ Suffering* in the preface to *Samson Agonistes* is construed as an allusion to the typological Samson such as the one depicted by Palma il giovane (1544–1628) in the Venetian church of Santa Maria della Salute, Milton's intention, it would seem, is to restrain, even repudiate, the tradition Palma means to promote. In Palma's *Sansone*, the Judges figure, in a rose tunic, is shown carrying away the gates of the city, this panel of painting, in turn, finding its counterpart in the parallel panel of *Giona profeta*, where Jonah is shown leaving the mouth of the whale.

In his poetic volume, Milton reverses the usual sequence that Palma observes, by deepening Samson's tragedy while, simultaneously, relocating the Son's triumph from the cross to the desert. Indeed, a comparison of their respective Samsons has the effect of underscoring that what resemblance there may be, in both instances, is with the tragic Christ of the

Crucifixion, not the triumphant Christ of the Resurrection, with Milton himself casting a dubious eye even on the former comparison. Indeed, as both Erin Henriksen and Jeffrey Shoulson demonstrate, it is in parallelisms drawn between their respective passions that the Samson typology "founders on the vast differences," or as Shoulson also says, Milton's poem "tempts us to follow such a typological reading only to undermine it."[13] This point gets reinforcement through Milton's pairing of *Samson Agonistes* with *Paradise Regain'd* in a poetic volume where, through calculated avoidances and strategic silences, the poet does all he can to ignore the typological Samson, thereby repudiating Samson's place in the very tradition Palma promotes. If no Hercules in Milton's poetry, Samson is no type of Christ either, not at all of Christ triumphant and only ironically of Christ suffering.

In the perusal of these various traditions, both classical and Christian, an interdisciplinary approach has been too much a stranger to Milton studies where often it is forgotten that what is distinctive about this author is his taking all knowledge for his province. Matters of methodology can no longer be eschewed by Milton's critics and, as they involve the study of *Samson Agonistes*, are raised most provocatively by titles such as *Milton and the Christian Tradition, Milton and Scriptural Tradition, "Paradise Lost" and the Genesis Tradition, "Paradise Regained": The Tradition and the Poem, Milton's "Samson" and the Christian Tradition*, and then by Milton who, instead of representing tradition, is a purveyor of truths; who, indeed, eventually rejects tradition as an opponent, as a suppressor and silencer of truths. In each of the aforementioned studies, the inflection falls thumpingly on tradition; and the tradition under scrutiny (for the most part) is the Christian tradition for which Milton's last poems allegedly act as a conduit. Christopher Hill sounds the warning note: "It is . . . quite wrong to see Milton in relation to anything so vague and generalized as 'the Christian tradition'. He was a radical Protestant heretic. . . . His great theological system, the *De Doctrina Christiana*, arose by a divorcing command from the ambiguous chaos of traditional Christianity. . . . He cannot reasonably be claimed as 'orthodox'."[14]

Hill's warning would replace a diachronic with a synchronic history of biblical interpretation (in this instance of the Samson story), even as it hints at the current phenomenon, which has those for whom Milton is fundamentally orthodox challenging his authorship of *De Doctrina* in the same fashion that others, troubled by its heterodoxy, once challenged the Apocalypse as part of canonical Scriptures. With Francis Barker, Hill comprehends that tradition, finally, "is historicist but not historical"; that it operates by suppression, effecting exclusions; that traditions are not how cultures remember but, instead, how they forget; and, finally, that they become historical, as Barker observes, by "a certain sedimentation through imposition over time which makes it *now* a part of the history of the present."[15]

Several reminders are thus in order. First, as a formulator of Christian doctrine Milton is his own church, belonging to a sect of one. Hence his published views, as he himself avows in *De Doctrina*, are frequently "at odds with certain conventional opinions" (*YP*, 6:121) and with what Milton thinks of as other commentators' distortions of Scriptures. Second, although Milton has been praised for being "So exact . . . in all the particulars of the [Judges] story,"[16] it is more to the point that, as a biblical poet, through repeated transgressive maneuvers, he regularly breaches the decorums others expected him to observe, in this way if not improving certainly expanding upon his source book. Third, heterodoxy and transgression are not necessarily marks of originality. For, in the process of directing Milton studies "away from the classics and the Church Fathers to Milton's contemporaries and immediate predecessors,"[17] Hill reveals how dependent Milton's ideas and aesthetics are upon a newly emerging understanding of the Scriptures as a site of conflict and sponsor of radical culture-critique. Milton may not lift his interpretations from this or that commentator, or even cobble them together from assorted commentaries; but the diligent inquiry he brings to Scriptures, plus his readings of scriptural stories for their bearing upon his own times, are both debts owed by Milton to seventeenth century biblical hermeneutics as are his dwelling upon moments of disrupted chronology — and dwelling in places of calculated contradiction. Doubtless, criticism will continue to address the topic of Milton and tradition, one hopes with a new sensitivity to questions like: Milton and *which* traditions? In *which* of their manifestations? With what *new* inflections?

I

During the age of Milton, Scriptures became a vehicle for ongoing revelation, which, in itself, may make seventeenth century thinking, in a progressive mode, far more immediately relevant to Milton's writings than the traditions and customs he usually associates with tyranny and error. Milton's poetry, though informed by, is never ruled by the common glosses of theologians. Scriptures are also for Milton the source books for a poetics not normative but revolutionary. Moreover, to privilege contemporary thinking, especially its controversies, over settled opinions and received traditions, may not be to banish the Classics from Milton studies after all but, instead, to turn from Aeschylus and Sophocles to models of greater contemporary relevance — namely, Euripides and Seneca, both of whom are molding influences on early modern tragedy and its Italian theorists and each of whom also highlights the paradox that, while early modern dramatists may cite the Greeks first, their debt to Seneca predominates. These two poets were particularly influential in mapping Christian tragedy founded upon scriptural stories; so much so that in conjunction with the Judges's redactor and John of Patmos, they showed Milton the way, no small part of which was to write tragedy (rather like the plays of Euripides and Seneca) that is, again in the words of Nigel Smith, "capable of radically

different political interpretations."[18] Indeed, the defining features of Euripidean and Senecan tragedy are their dramatiza-
tion of competing viewpoints, their creation of deep hells
within the human soul, and, above all, their challenge to
theodicies where vengeance is attributed to divine providence
and the avengers, in their turn, claim to be God's agents.

These latter are the misconceptions that a tragedy like
Euripides' *Heracles* is meant to expose; though that said, it is
equally important to remember with William Empson that,
as "the reverberation after the fall of human sacrifice," Greek
tragedy, in its theology, is at once "adventurous and rather
confused." On the other hand, Milton is less imprisoned than
his critics in the propaganda of Christianity, especially its
atonement theories; and where he does invoke those theories,
however cryptically, he aligns himself with the adventurous
thinking of those like Grotius and, before Grotius, what Milton
presumed to be the work of Gregory Nazianzen. Milton seems
to remember as early as "The Passion" and differently, yet
emphatically, in all three of his last poems that Christianity
is the one religion, again in Empson's words, "which ratted
on the progress, the only one which dragged back the Neolithic
craving for human sacrifice into its basic structure,"[19] which
is exactly where Milton places it, in the case of *Paradise Lost*
at the poem's structural center (and later, historical climax),
on the way to expunging it from his last poems. In these poems,
Milton, like Grotius, moves toward an "atonement" theology
grounded in love, mercy, and forgiveness. It is a theology, as
becomes manifest in *Paradise Regain'd*, in which God's power
modulates into mercy, His terror into meekness and peace,
"reconciling all to one another," and (to appropriate the words
of George Sandys) "Man-kinde to Him-selfe."[20]

After Thucydides and Virgil, the largest number, plus the
longest of the classical allusions in *De Doctrina Christiana* (where such allusions are rare) come from Euripides.[21]
Here Euripides is cited as an authority unrivaled even by

contemporary biblical commentators, with such admiration clearly stemming from the striking relationship Euripides displays (albeit unconsciously) with the revealed truths of Scriptures and the audacity he displays in challenging received opinion. Euripides is similarly cited in the preface to *Samson Agonistes* as *the* classical tragedian worthy of representation and quotation in Holy Scriptures. Moreover, in his 1801 variorum edition of Milton's poetry, representing the scholarship of an entire century, Henry John Todd's annotators, together with Richard Cumberland, invoke Euripides' *Philoktetes*, plus Aeschylus's *Prometheus Bound* and Sophocles's Oedipus plays, as models for *Samson Agonistes*.[22] Yet not *Philoktetes*, and not Prometheus and Oedipus, but instead Euripides' Heracles is the most obvious counterpart to Milton's Samson: "Heracles tied to a fallen column among the corpses,"[23] in the posture of the vengeance hero, bound not free, surveying the dead bodies of all his victims.[24] At the same time, various annotators tabulate some fifteen allusions to Euripides within Milton's poem (more than to Aeschylus and Sophocles combined), two of which, coming early in Samson's soliloquy and then in the epode to his tragedy, act as a framing device. Nor is Milton alone in his citation of Euripides or preference for him among the Greek tragedians: Euripides is in the margins of commentaries by Erasmus, Peter Martyr, and Grotius; and if Milton bothers to annotate his Euripides, in addition to Erasmus, his principal precursors in biblical tragedy, Buchanan and Grotius, translate Euripides as well.

The annotations accompanying Todd's edition of Milton come on the heels of two separate works by Richard Paul Jodrell, which together document that Milton himself regularly imitates Euripides; that his poetry, both beginning and late — the Nativity Ode and *Ad Patrem* no less than *A Mask, Paradise Lost*, and *Samson Agonistes* — is saturated with Euripides' influence; and that in his imitations and borrowings, plus marginalia to Euripides, Milton, both critic and interpreter, excels in "poetic criticism" marked by "ingenious conjecture."[25] In a preliminary study of those marginalia, moreover, John K. Hale has isolated some salient features through which we can take leads concerning how Milton read Euripides, as well as why this dramatist so mattered to him, especially when, with Hale, we note that, "alert to context," Milton resisted readings that produced "tame platitude" and, simultaneously, engaged in "inspired correcting of false text," as well as judicious alteration of "received tradition."[26] Very tellingly, a poem that seemingly withholds prophetic status from Samson, nevertheless credits the tradition by having Manoa accept his son's words as prophetic (472–73) just moments after rejecting Samson's claim to have married with "Divine impulsion prompting" (422). This Euripidean confusion over — and questioning of — divine inspiration, coming into play in the course of *Samson Agonistes*, mounts as the poem nears catastrophe with Samson claiming that "Some rouzing motions" (1382) compel him to go to the temple/theater.

But most telling of all, in "Sonnet 8," Milton analogizes his own situation with that of Euripides in a way that distances both poets from the likes of Samson: "sad *Electra*'s poet had the power / To save th'*Athenian* walls from ruin" (*CP*, 197). The poet as creator will eventually confront Samson as destroyer by way of saying that poets are retainers of the walls Samson tears down. If it can be said that "a Euripidean subtext governs the . . . shape" of Milton's first major poem, "On the Morning of Christs Nativity,"[27] it should also be allowed that, in *Samson Agonistes*, Euripides not only effects the shape of and representations in the poem, as well as its spirit of interrogation, but through his Heracles poems offers subtexts for Milton's own tragedy.

A poem's paraphernalia — in the case of *Samson Agonistes*, the book's title page of which this poem is one of two parts (see fig. 3), its own separate title page with epigraphs (see fig. 4), the poem's preface (or "Epistle"), its appended "Argument" and "Omissa," along with "Errata" (see fig. 5) — all harbor clues for reading *Samson Agonistes*, many of which have eluded Milton's readership and some of which invoke contexts subsequently forbidden to that readership. The most startling feature about the front matter for this volume is the presentation on what might otherwise have been the frontispiece page — indeed, is a frontispiece page with portrait in *The History of Britain* (1670), *Artis Logicae* (1672), and *Paradise Lost* (1674) — of the information, centered with bars above and below, that the book was "**Licensed, / July 2, 1670**" (see fig. 3).

Not even on the title page to *Areopagitica* (1644), where "Licensing" is an issue, is the stipulation given such prominence, although in this instance it does appear as the title of the work on the page where printing of it commences: "For the Liberty of unlicenc'd Printing." Moreover, as a fact of publication, licensing is sometimes (though in Milton's writings, rarely) acknowledged as a discrete entry somewhere on the title page: thus in 1645 in *Colasterion* ("the Licencer conferr'd with") and, again, in *Poems of Mr. John Milton* ("Printed and publish'd according to ORDER") and, years later, on four different states of the early title pages for *Paradise Lost* (1667), always in the same formulation: "Licensed and Entered according to Order."

On the other hand, however common such acknowledgments were in Milton's time, they remain an oddity in his own publications. None accompanies *Accedence Commenc't Grammar* (1669), *The History of Britain* in either 1670 or 1671, *Artis Logicae* in either 1672 or 1673, *Poems, &c. Upon Several Occasions* (1673), *Of True Religion* (1673), nor the second edition of *Paradise Lost* (1674). Nor in 1674 is there mention of licensing on the title pages either of *A Declaration*, or *Letters Patents*, translated by Milton, or of his *Epistolarum Familiarum* (1674). If an oddity in the 1671 poetic volume, the device is also unusual in publications of the early 1670s where an "Imprimatur" appears opposite the title page, in analogy

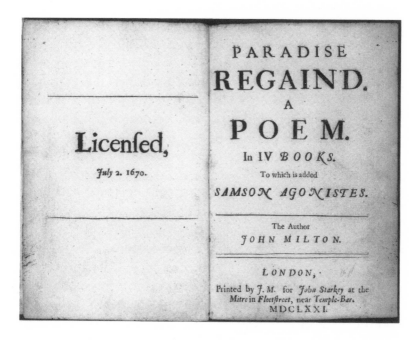

PARADISE
REGAIND.
A
POEM.
In IV BOOKS.
To which is added
SAMSON AGONISTES.

The Author
JOHN MILTON.

LONDON,
Printed by J. M. for John Starkey at the
Mitre in Fleetstreet, near Temple-Bar.
MDCLXXI.

Licenfed,
July 2. 1670.

Figure 3

with the licensing order for Milton's volume, in just two publications I have seen from 1670 and 1671: one by the ejected minister Giles Firmin, and the other by the nonconformist John Tillotson.[28] The 1671 poetic volume bears the civil stamp for publication but not, like these other publications, the ecclesiastical seal of approval — an imprimatur (one supposes) that would not be given readily to either poem: the first because of its disturbing theology, and the second owing to its seemingly terrorist agenda.

Paradise Regain'd and *Samson Agonistes*, alone among Milton's writings published between 1669 and 1674, bear the licensing order (along with date), albeit ostentatiously, in the space to the left of the title page sometimes used for a frontispiece portrait or illustration. It is as if this initial page of print is there to protest against the very kinds of readings the poems themselves are about to invite. What does it say about these poems that, the exception among all Milton's writings, the fact and date of their licensing is what we learn first about the contents of the book? Is the separate and special prominence given to the "Licensing" of the 1671 poetic volume an immediate attempt to forestall the questions, which were bound to be raised, *which were raised*, concerning Milton's most politically charged and theologically adventurous poems: *how did they ever get by the censor*? Certainly the tradition of biblical tragedy invoked by Milton's title and inscribed within his poem would seem to be reinforced by Milton's subtitle ("A Dramatic Poem"), which, once recalling Milton's projected plans for biblical tragedy (and for British history plays), together with the plays already written by Buchanan and Grotius, also underscores the heavy inlay of politics often placed under the covers of biblical stories and of older history. With such issues in mind, it is important to remember — indeed this recollection is forced by the 1670 date — that these early years of this decade saw a "crack-down against nonconformists" and a new resistance to religious pluralism, at which time, "July 1670," as John Spurr reports, "L'Estrange's men raided John Streater's printing-house with warrants to search and arrest suspects, but twenty people 'fell into an uproar, and begin crying out that they were freeborn subjects, and not to be meddled with by such a warrant'. . . . Intimidation and insinuations . . . were part and parcel of the political process."[29] Indeed, a sense of intimidation may well prompt a poetics of insinuation within Milton's poems of 1671, which, far from representatives of complacency, are harbingers of crisis.

With its increasing sense of a government in crisis and profound sense of an Eden gone to ruins, with a growing reaction against "the misguided zeal and the 'enthusiasm' of mid-century and the hypocrisy of contemporary pretenders to godliness," with its kaleidoscopic politics and literature of

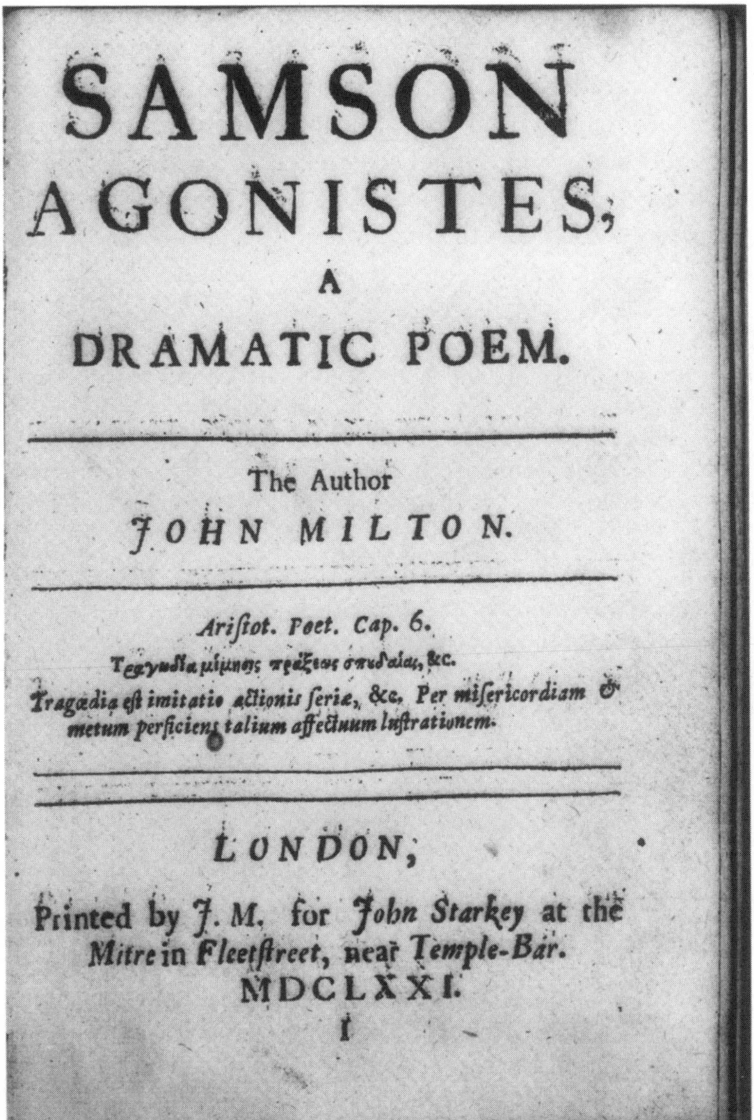

SAMSON
AGONISTES;
A
DRAMATIC POEM.

The Author

J O H N   M I L T O N.

Arifiot. Poet. Cap. 6.

Τϵγγωδία μίμησις πϱάξεως σπυδαίας, &c.

*Tragædia eſt imitatio actionis ſeriæ, &c. Per miſericordiam &
metum perficiens talium affectuum luſtrationem.*

LONDON;

Printed by *J. M.* for *John Starkey* at the
Mitre in *Fleetſtreet*, near *Temple-Bar.*
MDCLXXI.

Figure 4

heroism, the early 1670s is, paradoxically, a time in which, having bestowed his mercies, God is now unleashing his chastisements, in part directed against national leaders who should have inspired a nation — but did not; who broke a nation's expectations by failing to fulfill their appointed roles. An age of heroic poetry (epic and dramatic) is devoid of heroic action, as Spurr avers; and its craving for heroes bespeaks a lack of heroism, which, in its turn, raises "moral questions about heroism" and results not in heroism celebrated but heroism contested. As Spurr writes:

> In the 1670s England badly needed heroes and yet the English could not bring themselves to trust heroism. It is not simply that all heroes seemed flawed, nor that recent heroism had too often served dubious or false causes. . . . No, it is rather that the English had lost their bearing as to what counted as heroic.[30]

While Spurr may underestimate the extent to which Samson is involved in this contestation, he nonetheless admits it as a factor and understands that interpretations of the Samson story may, at this time, be differently inflected: "Milton presented a human hero and a more ambiguous message about activism. Obviously Samson is a flawed hero and his final act in destroying the Philistines and himself has been seen as vengeful," even if more usually Samson is regarded as "a man chosen by God, a man whose self-sacrifice is a response to a divine call to action."[31]

The title, *Samson Agonistes*, foregrounds a protagonist whose actions, by the standard of Aristotelian poetics, are held up for imitation but, by the theological discourse of Milton's age, are often exempted from it. In this connection, the citation of Gregory Nazianzen in the preface to Milton's poem is revelatory; for Daniel Heinsius, who wants to credit Gregory with authorship of *Christos Paschon*, also counts him as one of "the best two writers in the patristic age [who] defiled tragedy," not by introducing biblical subject matter to "profane writings," but by imitating (as Milton may be said to have done) what is to be avoided in imitation and, further, by displaying a license, indeed a certain rashness, that introduces politics to poetry (again, as Milton seems to do in *Samson Agonistes*).[32]

The very presence of a preface and an "Argument" as parts of the front matter to his tragedy invokes the examples and traditions of Euripides and Seneca, as well as of Grotius and Heinsius, both of whom Senecanized tragedy in Holland as their plays *Adamus Exul* (1601) and *Auriacus* (1602) illustrate.[33] Indeed, if repetition means anything in this poem, *Samson Agonistes* is emphatically, insistently a tragedy — an historical and political tragedy — with Milton here bent upon writing a drama that will "vindicate" as well as illustrate the genre, especially as it mutates into Christian tragedy. In the two-paragraph preface he calls an "Epistle," Milton uses the word *tragedy* in its different forms twelve times. Furthermore, *tragedy* is the penultimate word in Milton's "Argument" to this poem. Like Euripides before him, Milton lets tragedy turn back upon itself in such a way that he writes tragedy that is meta-tragedy.

As importantly, though, Milton's preface and argument signal that *Samson Agonistes* is a reading not an acting text, with reading texts having their own conventions, one of which going back to Euripides and Seneca (and still very much in evidence within the plays of Buchanan, Heinsius and Grotius, not to mention the earlier *Christos Paschon*) is the spirit of interrogation. The interrogative mode of closet drama is the very tradition that, until recently stifled by his critics, Milton invokes in his preface as he explains, first of all, that acts and scenes are here omitted (as they were in *Christos Paschon* presumably) because they refer to "the stage" for which *Samson Agonistes* "never was intended" and then declares his wish that this tragedy "not [be] produc't beyond the fift Act" (*CP*, 574). As Francis Goldsmith explains in an annotation to Grotius's *Sophompaneas*, "after the fifth Act" comes the judgment or "sentence," which, if rendered by the Chorus, thus forcing the play *beyond* its fifth act, limits interpretive options instead of maintaining their availability.[34]

As if to drive the point home still further, Milton omits from the poem proper, but then sequesters at the end of the 1671 poetic volume, the lines that give sharpest definition and fullest expression to both the political content and enquiring spirit of *Samson Agonistes* (see fig. 5). Those lines, containing "the poem's most urgent and violent images for the revitalization of the Good Old Cause," as Stephen B. Dobranski observes, also emphasize this poem's status as "a political allegory,"[35] thus allowing for (without necessarily advocating) a reading of this poem as Milton's revenge fanatsy or, better, as his hope for a political miracle, with the poem itself envisioning a restored Samson and a newly flourishing nation, but doing so as a possible — not certain — outcome of the poem's action. The "omissa" lines, that is, present views we are meant to entertain, not necessarily adopt, and are printed in conjunction with an errata list as if to remind us that writing, like interpretation, is a continuous revisionary process such as that described by Milton in *Areopagitica* as he asks: "what if the author shall be one so copious of fancie, as to have many things well worth the adding, come into his mind after licencing, while the book is yet under the Presse, which not seldom happ'ns to the best and diligentest writers; and that perhaps a dozen times in one book" (*YP*, 2:532). The omissa lines, then, are as much peripeteia as their overturning and contain not so much *the* truth as what Dobranski describes as "a roller coaster of possible truths."[36] Correspondingly, the various items on the errata list achieve interpretive importance because, as Henriksen smartly observes, "they contain typological mistakes and show characters in error and, in this way, are both thematically and textually erroneous."[37] With the

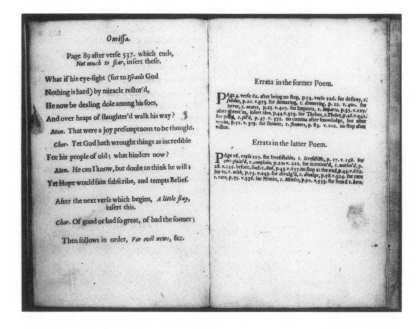

Figure 5

emphasis achieved through its enforced re-readings, the errata list forces correction, reinterpretation.

Now we may wish to look again at the title pages for both the 1671 poetic volume and *Samson Agonistes*. Titles "always look back to their past," Anne Ferry remarks, "imitating, modifying, questioning, rebelling against it."[38] The separate title page to *Samson Agonistes* (see fig. 4) is itself revelatory with the name of its protagonist, both in type size and boldfacing, overwhelming all other features and, simultaneously, diminishing in importance the title's epithet, almost as if to say that the Samson (or biblical) tradition predominates over generic (or classical) tradition when it comes time to interpret this poem. "Samson" is given as much prominence here as "Regain'd" receives on the title page to the 1671 poetic volume (cf. figs. 3 and 4), where, in comparison with *Paradise Regain'd,* "To which is added / *Samson Agonistes,*" the latter poem, emphasizing actor, not action or event, takes on the appearance of a mere afterthought as if it were a footnote to (or an episode in) history, but not a decisive or climactic moment therein.

With the accent falling so heavily upon Samson, Milton seems to fix attention upon SAMSON's agon in comparison with — and as distinct from — that of other tragic heroes even as he appears to question, simultaneously, Samson's worthiness as a tragic hero. When we remember with Dobranski that the lines of poetry constituting the "Omissa" are "something . . . we readers need to insert,"[39] when we then examine those lines and find in them the hard questions concerning the Samson story — is Samson's "eye-sight . . . / . . . by miracle restor'd" (1527–28)? has God "wrought [these] things . . . incredible" (1532)? — then the omitted lines themselves both signal and accentuate the interrogative spirit of the poem. The poem with which *Samson Agonistes* is paired forces the questions: does Samson participate in the process of deliverance, and to what extent? is he to be numbered among the saviors of the world, with the restorers of the lost paradise?

In the "Omissa" questions, Manoa acknowledges a God who could do these things, but "doubt[s] to think he will" and, so far as these questions are concerned, thinks "Hope . . . tempts Belief" (1534–35). In his turn, Milton the dramatist frontloads the catastrophe with question marks, not just here but earlier when he converts Samson's initially declarative statement into an interrogation by substituting a question mark for a period: "Can they think me so broken . . . / . . . that my mind ever / Will condescend to such absurd commands?" (1335–37) To avoid further humiliation — "Because they shall not trail me through thir streets / Like a wild Beast, I am content to go" (1402–03) — Samson proceeds to the temple anyway. Moreover, even as we say Milton does "this" we need to admit the possibility that the printer, who could have interfered in order to adjust and alter authorial intention, may have intruded on this occasion in order to accentuate the interrogative element. Finally, though, in this poem loaded with question marks, the interrogation centers in the temple catastrophe. As much as Lehi, where Samson slays a thousand men with the jawbone of an ass, the scene of the temple/theater catastrophe should be remembered as "Agon," a point of reference for the poem's epithet, *Agonistes*, where, as St. Ambrose remarks, "still . . . not content . . . with what he had done in revenge," Samson slaughters thousands "in a great orgy of bloodshed."[40]

Indeed, this catastrophe is thrown into relief (literally, punctuated) by question marks and their proliferation so that by the eighteenth century certainly, one suspects owing in part to Milton's example, interpretation of the Samson story moves increasingly into the interrogative mode (as illustrated by Augustin Calmet) and eventually becomes locked there by the *Woffenbutteler Fragmente*:

> Ought Samson to have put himself to death? And should he have sought revenge for the loss of his eyes?
> . . . Was this strength constantly resident in him, in the same superlative degree? . . . May *one* virtue only be given by inspiration . . .? or, *must* we suppose, that the Spirit of the Lord coming on an individual, filled him with *every* grace and virtue at the same time, not withstanding the failings of Samson?[41]

The focus of interpretation is now, as in Milton's poem, emphatically on the temple/theater catastrophe and the destruction wrought by it.

In addition, the Aristotelian epigraphs, appearing on the separate title page for *Samson* (see fig. 4), are, within the context of *Paradise Regain'd*, doubly ironic. First of all, it is an Aristotelian Satan who observes the generic hierarchy that the Son upsets as he moves prophecy to the summit of the literary genres (4.261–66; cf. 288–92, 334–63), thus reducing tragedy to the status of one of nature's fallen forms — a form that, enacting, Satan founds. Second, the one matter that

Milton's contemporaries disputed, yet *generally* could agree upon (whether they regarded Samson as hero or villain or somewhere in-between) is that Samson's actions, even if warranted by God, are not commendable and thus are best not imitated. To be sure, Samson is invoked as a model at the portal to the pocket Bible for the New Model Army, but here the exemplary Samson is a figure at prayer. Otherwise, he affords John Lilburne a sanction for vexing his enemies "with as much earnestness as *Sampson* prosecuted the *Philistems*," in this instance Lilburne comparing his own attack on new tyranny of Cromwell and Ireton to Samson prosecuting the Philistines. Tearing down the pillars, killing God's enemies — whatever Samson does, however horrific his acts, and however much such actions are lauded by extremists at either end of the political spectrum, whether Robert Sanderson on the right or John Lilburne on the left — the horrors were owing, it would seem, to "the special *secret direction of Gods* holy Spirit," for whom Lilburne's Samson, like Sanderson's Phineas, is the supposed warrior, dispatching his errand and "leav[ing] the event to the Providence of God." To the extent that God's laws, which still circumscribe man, are violated in the process, the question eventually becomes one of whether the seemingly "*extraordinary motion* and peculiar secret instinct . . . prompting . . . [Phineas or Samson] to this *Heroicall Act*" is "no sweet *impulsion* of the holy *Spirit of God*, but a strong *delusion* of the lying *spirit of Satan*."[42] In his choice of a protagonist for his tragedy, Milton breaches the protocol, established by Grotius, that the hero of a biblical tragedy should be illustrious, exemplary — *imitable*. Rather, in choosing Samson, Milton advances as his protagonist one of those figures, even if acting with a divine warrant, whom Grotius (and many others) thought should never be invoked as a precedent. Indeed, writing from the left as it happens, Milton uses the same rhetoric of inspiration and interrogation for Samson that Sanderson, also in a publication of 1671, refers to Phineas.

One enduring line of thinking concerning the Samson story goes back to Peter Damian for whom Samson is an example of those who "engage the enemy eagerly and bravely," in the process dramatizing the proposition that "it is glorious to act boldly."[43] Yet another line of thinking, complicating the first, even questioning it, emerges in the early modern period, and, fully encompassing the age of Milton, extends from Peter Martyr (1583) to Thomas Wood (1682). According to Martyr, Samson's prayer may seem "not to be verie godlie":

> for he praieth, that it might be granted him to take revenge upon his enimies; bicause they put out both his eies. In verie truth, if he had ment to fulfill his wrath, we might not iustlie allow his praier: for he should no more haue beene allowed of God, than if he had said expreslie; I beseech thee Lord to prosper either my theft or my adultrie. . . . And surelie, it was not lawfull for him, as a private man, to reuenge iniuries; but as a magistrate, both he might, and should doo it. But . . . in a publike cause, the magistrate, by the commandement and authoritie of GOD, must reuenge the iniurie doone unto him: for he is Gods deputie upon the earth.[44]

Milton lets private and public hang together in his poem, yet also here withholds from Samson the title of judge.

A century later, through the voice of Reason, Thomas Wood, translator of Abraham Cowley, as well as nephew and defender of Anthony á Wood, will contend, with eyes fast fixed to David, Samson, and Phineas, "That you ought to be zealous for God, that your Zeal will excuse you . . . I answer, That you ought to be zealous for God in a good cause, not in a bad one; that your Zeal can then justifie you, not otherwise." In each case, says Reason, "'tis a Question whether he did well or no":

> I shall answer . . ., That men of Heroical Spirits and Gifts, such as . . . *Sampson* . . . &c., especially at such a time as they were imployed for the Service of Almighty God; were exempt from the Common Rules of Life, and did many things with a secret Motion of a powerfull Spirit, which Motion of the Spirit was as

good to them as a special command from God's mouth. But
those acts ought not to be allowed by others, without a particular and certain assurance of the like Instinct. But if any of
you should pretend to this Motion of the Spirit, we'll tell you,
as our Saviour did his Disciples, . . . with indignation, that *you
know not what manner of spirit you are of.*[45]

In a long discussion of Jephthah, Martyr makes clear what is
at issue both in representing and interpreting the Samson story:
even if Jephthah vows (and Samson destroys) by divine inspiration and warrant, each is "a particular example" and thus
"ought not to be extended to imitation."[46] If there is a divine
warrant for Samson's actions of which some commentators
are absolutely certain, then Samson's actions, if lawful for him,
are still not for imitation by others and all the worse when
those motives are pretended to by others. If imitation *is* extended to Samson, apparently it will be done so within a
tragedy, huge in its compass, where imitation is conceived,
rather as Paul Sellin summarizes it in Gerard Vossius's
Poeticarum Institutionum (1647), as involving characters not
necessarily "more excellent than," but "like, or inferior to
ourselves."[47]

Milton problematizes the Samson story enormously, outside
Samson Agonistes hesitating over whether Samson acts by
divine warrant or human instinct and, within his tragedy,
equivocating on whether Samson prays or not. The prayer itself
is a fixture in the tradition of Samson plays resurrected by
Kirkconnell where, in one notable instance, Samson "rumi-
nated" *and* then prays and, not as in *Samson Agonistes*, prays
or "some great matter in his mind revolv'd" (1637–38).[48] In
this poem, Milton never mentions Samson's judgeship per se;
yet in dialogue, while allowing Samson to slide from his private
to his public role, Milton also lets him insist that he acts of
his own accord, which, within the context of biblical idiom,
as we shall see, implies that he is not now overruled or commissioned by God. In the emphasis Milton's epigraphs give

to *imitation*, they turn attention to plot (the very soul of tragedy) and to the quality of its action (determined by character and thought), with the inflection on the climactic action. If character reveals an individual's purpose in tragedy, purpose itself is revealed by what a character says and does, embraces or resists. The gist of Aristotle's *Poetics*, chapter 4, is focused here, that is, and now in the foreground of Milton's poem hints at the very terms by which Samson will undergo interrogation and the place in the poem where judgment finally will fall upon him: the temple/theater catastrophe.

The preface to *Samson Agonistes* begs for attention, first of all because, as Milton himself says, it allows for "self defence" and "explanation." By now a routine feature of Greek drama, the hypothesis or *argumentum* is the place for an apologia, as well as a site from which to set forth interpretive clues. We have been reminded by a work, in which Milton's hand can be seen, of how one of his adversaries prided himself on "'omitting reference to . . . Euripides, Sophocles, and other pagan authors, for a Christian simply has no need to resort to the pagans.'"[49] With St. Paul as his authority, Milton here follows an alternative course for which he had the precedents of Erasmus, Peter Martyr, Grotius, and others.

However, if *Samson Agonistes* in the presentation of its front matter recalls any seventeenth century example, apart from the general Greek example, it is Ben Jonson's *Sejanus*, which contains (putting aside the dedication) both a preface ("To the Readers") and an "Argument," the former including an explanation that this is a reading, not an acting, version of the play, as well as a listing of models and sources like Tacitus and Seneca, who write in tongues other than English. If there are these marks of identity between the prefaces of Jonson and Milton, there is also a distinction; for Jonson wants to be excused for "the absence of . . . *Formes*" like the Chorus in tragedy, now newly conceived, where there is no need for "the ould state, and splendour of *Drammatick Poemës*."[50] Milton, on the contrary, defends the presence of the Chorus "here introduc'd after the Greek manner, not ancient only *but modern*" (*CP*, 574; my italics) as older forms, now revived and reconstitued, assume a conspicuous presence in his tragedy.

Secondly, the preface is crucial not only because of its bonds with the poem's epigraphs, which theorize tragedy according to Aristotle, but because in exemplifying tragedy with reference to "*Aeschulus, Sophocles,* and *Euripides,* the three Tragic Poets unequall'd yet by any" (*CP*, 574), it enforces an important inflection. Mentioned just once before by Milton, Aeschylus had previously come in for little attention in comparison with Sophocles and Euripides, Milton occasionally citing the latter two together. Even as it twice invokes Aeschylus, Sophocles, and Euripides, Milton's preface roots interest (emphatically so) in Euripides, reportedly (along with Homer and Ovid) one of Milton's three favorite poets. The preface does so, initially in its recollection that St. Paul "inserts a verse of *Euripides*" into 1 Corinthians 15.33 ("evil communications corrupt good manners") as part of its warning, "Be not deceived";[51] and then in its citation of "a Tragedy . . . entitl'd, *Christ suffering*" (*CP*, 574). "*Whether by* Gregory Nazianzen, *or* Apollinaris *of* Laodicae," each of whom is identified by Gerard Vossius as a model for "sacred Dramatiques both Comicall and Tragicall,"[52] this play, which sometimes reads as if it were an extended quotation from Euripides, owing to this distinctive feature, has been described as "a piece of Byzantine Euripidean pastiche,"[53] a "curious mosaic,"[54] through which, as it happens, the lost pages at the end of Euripides' *Bacchae* are often restored by modern editors.[55] If it bears the imprint of Euripides, *Christos Paschon* is given its generic identity and definition in Latin versions of that play's title: *Christus Patiens, Tragoedia Christiana.*

It is Euripides as tragedian, then his tragedies as Romanized by "*Seneca* the Philosopher," and finally the Euripidean play *Christos Paschon,* together with John of Patmos's Revelation — works specifically cited in Milton's preface — that resonate most powerfully within *Samson Agonistes*. This point is folded into the shorthand of Milton's prefatory observation that in the "modelling . . . of this Poem, . . . the Antients and *Italians* are . . . follow'd" (*CP*, 574) — folded into the preface, that is, in order to prompt the recognition that Euripides and Seneca together were the dominant influences on *both* the emerging tragedy in Italy and the theorizing inspired by it. For good reason, then, Euripides and Seneca are likewise, indeed predictably, conspicuous classical influences on Milton's tragedy.

Since (and owing to) William Riley Parker's study, now over 60 years old, Euripides and Seneca have been a curious area of silence in criticism of *Samson Agonistes*, despite the fact that, invoked repeatedly in the preface to the poem, Euripides is alluded to again in its epilogue where the initial words of the final Chorus recall the concluding lines to *Alcestis, Andromache, Bacchae, Helen*, and (with some variation) *Medea* and despite the fact that, as we have just noted, Euripides and Seneca are principally comprehended in the references to Italian tragedy and theory. They are also major influences, declared to be so, by the charters of the newly emerging tradition of biblical tragedy. When it comes to Euripides, Parker cannot avoid the obvious: that "*before* the time" of *Samson Agonistes* Euripides is Milton's "personal favourite" among the Greek tragedians and his influence, along with Sophocles's, predominates.[56] *Before* the time of *Samson Agonistes*, depending upon the poem's date, involves very different stretches of time: half a life — or virtually a lifetime.

Moreover, given the premise that this poem is a drama of regeneration, featuring a hero who is never "sub-heroic," Parker must also suppress (by denying) the obvious. Thus he argues that, "wisely or unwisely," in *Samson Agonistes* Milton "borrowed little from his favourite tragedian" in consequence of which this poem registers "no 'debt' . . . of really major importance" to Euripides; and then that, while Harapha and Dalila are "essentially Euripidean portraits," Samson is "a more idealized figure" than the heroes of Euripides, whatever his faults never displaying their kind of blemishes. Although Parker does not miss the ethical content of *Samson Agonistes*, he does exhibit a persistent insensitivity to its ethical bent and nuance. If he judges the ethical purposes of Sophocles to be "deeper, and more profound, than those of Euripides" and hence more in accord with those of Milton, he also misjudges Milton's Samson, a figure of once celebrated but now compromised heroism. Pushing all the contrary evidence aside, Parker judges Euripides (not just Samson) differently from Milton, dismissing as "over-stressed" and "negligible" the influence that most matters in Milton's tragedy.[57]

Parker gives the wrong answers concerning Milton and, unlike Moses Hadas and John Harvey McLean, never asks the right questions of Euripides: "what was the dramatist to do who not only disbelieved, but in many cases actually hated and despised the hoary old legends to which he was compelled to repair for the themes of his drama?" — to which they respond:

> He might present the old myths as if they were true. He might invest them with all the circumstances of reality, all the embroidery of orthodoxy. But from the start his plan would be *to tell the stories badly*, to lay the emphasis in all the wrong places, to tell them in a way that would bring out and underline all that was morally revolting and intellectually absurd in them. Euripides did take that line. He did more than spoil many a good old story; he ruined them beyond . . . repair.[58]

Milton may be less irreverent than Euripides, which is not to say that he does not bring a healthy suspicion and sometimes ruinous touch to the stories he tells. Like Euripides, he takes considerable liberties with inherited materials as if, through revision, to wring from his newly told tale a higher truth.

Indeed, the very combination that Roger Ascham finds in

George Buchanan's *Jephtha* is there, equally so, in *Samson Agonistes*: "*Aristotles* preceptes and *Euripides* examples"; and of *Jephtha* it also needs to be remembered that this play, however Euripidean, has been "completely Senecanised."[59] No less than *Samson Agonistes*, *Jephtha*, for the sake of its argument, seems to allow with Thomas Aquinas for the possibility that its protagonist "*probably repented his evil*" and is thus "placed in the catalogue of the saints [in the Epistle to the Hebrews]." Indeed, unlike Milton, Buchanan makes the point explicitly: "her father who for long had appeared bloodthirsty and more savage than a tigress, was suffused with Tears and covered his eyes with his garment, and condemned both himself and his rash vow." Yet *Jephtha* also presents a character with "troubled mind" in anticipation of Milton's devils with "restless thoughts" in *Paradise Lost* (2.526), as well as his Samson with "restless thoughts" rushing upon him (19–21), with tormenting thoughts (623), "The tumors of a troubl'd mind" (185), and, again like *Samson Agonistes*, turns finally on the questions of God's supposed dispensing with his laws and man's propensity for "attributing . . . [his] own sacrilegious deed[s] to heaven," as if "God takes joy in bloody victims." For Jephtha, "the law descended from heaven bids us fulfill what has been once vowed to God," although, according to the Priest, "You have no excuse here by which you can defend your deed." Those who bind themselves to "carry out unspeakable crime" do so of their own accord, and thus, "whatever that vow of yours," says the Priest, "cease to associate God with your cruelty." This is a play that condemns rather than condones barbaric customs, uncontrolled savagery, lunatic stupidity, placated cruelty, the produce of which is carnage cloaked fields and the justification for which comes from "attributing the sacrilegious deed to heaven."[60]

The issues in Buchanan's plays, as well as in Milton's *Samson Agonistes*, are more tangled than usually allowed. They have as their base line the propositions that only one law is to be observed, that nothing contrary to the law is lawful, that one lays down a life, expiates with blood, in order to compensate for others, in order to save their lives. Each drama is concerned less with God's ways to man than with man's ways to God; and Milton is ultimately concerned with mankind's participation in his own deliverance. As John says in *Baptistes*: "[mankind] spurns God's commands, rejects the reins of the laws, and rushes headlong into every crime. He measures justice by wantonness, and weighs law by violence." As aptly as Buchanan's plays, *Samson Agonistes* might bear the subtitle: "Calumnia Tragoedia" or "Votum Tragoedia."[61] Nor is Milton's poem less Euripidean than the plays by Buchanan either in its questioning of the truth of the usual presentations, as well as interpretations, of a story; or in its humanization of the hero and suggestion that God cannot be as he appears within typical tellings of inherited — and regularly redacted — tales.

   Samson Agonistes also bears comparison with the Heracles/ Hercules plays of both Euripides and Seneca, but first and most obviously with the *Heracles* of Euripides, which "centers on conflicting concepts of heroic *aretê*, opposing a new, modernized heroism, adopted by Herakles at Theseus's urging, to the traditional model of violence and force."[62] It is difficult to imagine that a poem published in a sequence with *Paradise Lost* and *Paradise Regain'd*, both of which poems (like Euripides' tragedy) are similarly engaged in overthrowing the old for the new, now a pagan for a Christian conception of heroism, does not follow suit. It seems to be Milton's way as well as the way of Euripides, indeed Milton's way not just in *Samson Agonistes* but in his epics, to invert, correct, and refine traditional standards of heroism founded upon war and violence. Otherwise, the Copernican revolution Milton effects in the history of epic poetry becomes, in his tragedy, a Ptolemaic reversion.

   When one remembers with Ann Pippin Burnett that Euripides' Heracles appears, "as the vengeance hero should, among the corpses of his victims," and then with Milton's Chorus recalls that scene in *Samson Agonistes* where, with "Ruin, destruction at the utmost point" (1514), Samson is imagined as "dealing dole among his foes, / And over heaps of slaughter'd walk[ing] his way" (1529–30) — in these moments (the latter of which is represented by "omissa" lines), as the characters of Heracles and Samson begin to blur into one another, we may wonder if Milton does not mean (as much as Euripides) to reject this culture of violence, its heroes as destroyers, for what Burnett calls a new "heroic humanism."[63] That Samson is dead should give us a clue: that instead of surveying the slain like the Hercules of Euripides, he lies slain, "Soak't in his enemies blood" (1726). In this newly imagined heroism, people are saved, not slain, and civilizations are built up instead of torn down. It seems as if Euripides and Seneca showed the biblical tragedians of the early modern period, Milton included, the way.

In the instance of Euripides and Milton, it is in their skeptical attitudes toward, as well as in the daring, virtuosity and license, which both exhibit in their respective handlings of received myths and legends, in the changes each makes in representing (and the challenges each poses to interpreting) them that these poets lock arms. But there are numerous other links as well:

(1) in their tendency to unfurl the nonsense in both legend and myth and in paralleling both with modern history;

(2) in their impatience with fanaticism, no less than with traditional religion, and in their sometimes heretical religious positions;

(3) in their displacement of normal tragic structure with a fractured edifice and their tilting of tragedy itself toward mental theater;

(4) in their choice of characters who inspire not so much compassion as wonder;

(5) in their humanization of traditional heroes, often through the destructive power and fury those heroes exhibit, especially in their passion for vengeance and their spectacles of horror;
(6) in their respective Choruses who, far from ideal spectators, both vacillate in their beliefs and are sometimes numbingly conventional in their separate articulations of those beliefs;
(7) indeed, in the Choruses' promotion of beliefs the poet means to prosecute and adherence to precepts he never condones;
(8) in these poets' vacillations between the extremes of feminism and misogyny;
(9) in the long-term uncertainty on the part of their different audiences/readers concerning whether they are spokesmen for pagan and Christian orthodoxy respectively, or underminers of each;
(10) in their historicizing as well as politicizing of tragedy, while centering it in the miseries, disasters and insanities of warring cultures;
(11) in their mountings of critiques of cultures, both their own and alien, and in their steady protest against and insistent questioning of cultural commonplaces.

In these features especially, including a shared liberalism, as well as a propensity for multiplying ironies, while turning tragedy into meta-tragedy, Euripides and Milton find their common ground as playwrights. Yet it is also ground that each shares with Seneca, that taking from Euripides Seneca yields to Milton.

Itself a feature of Senecan tragedy, Milton's "Argument," by its very presence, places *Samson Agonistes*, literarily, in the tradition of closet drama and, philosophically, in the line of Senecan tragedy, which is yet another site toward which the preface gestures. Indeed, the Euripides-Seneca connection, the pairing of the two in Milton's mind and in his tragedy, is further reinforced by the Hercules myth encoded within both poems in the 1671 poetic volume. Hercules and Samson are initially yoked together in book 9 of *Paradise Lost*: "So rose the *Danite* strong / *Herculean Samson*" (1059–60) — the very book in which Milton momentarily abandons a narrative of epic heroism for the darkening vision of tragedy. Hercules and Jesus are again joined through simile in *Paradise Regained* (4.563–68), while, in *Samson Agonistes*, the earlier "harmony" between pagan and Christian mythology, once submerged, is finally broken. The Hercules plays of Euripides and Seneca afford an illuminating perspective as well as an unexpected analogy.

It has been said that "The Greek Heracles is a heroic figure whose life is blasted by the intervention of a vindictive divine force, and he becomes even more deeply a hero by understanding the nature of the force that has crushed him and by resolving to endure the pain." On the other hand,

> Seneca's Hercules . . . has become a savage who considers himself strong enough to break the laws of nature and force his way to divinity. Juno's threat to turn Hercules against himself is a metaphor for the moral war within the great but arrogant hero. He has lost piety and virtue. He regains them when he rejects his arrogance by subjecting himself to the will of his father.[64]

In Seneca's play the will of the earthly and the will of the heavenly father are in accord; in Milton's poem, Samson rejects the will of his earthly father as he lays claim to being motioned to the temple/theater by, and thus submitting to the will of, his heavenly father: "I begin to feel / Some rouzing motions in me" (1381–82). For some interpreters, though, there remains the lingering doubt over whether Samson executes what the heavenly father wills; over whether what He is said to will accords with Hebrew law or with Christian ethics.

Samson's final action reads as if it were the fulfillment of

Lycus's curse: "The woods on heapes together cast, let all their temples burne / Even throwne upon theyr heads" — an action that is also reminiscent of Hercules's envisioning the fall of Lycus's palace: "Let shake both here, and there the house, with all stayes overthrowne, / Let breake the poasts: and quight let shrinke the shaken piller downe: / Let all the Pallace fall at once."[65] But most of all, the catastrophe in *Samson Agonistes* recalls the imagined suicide and death of the protagonist in *Hercules furens*:

> . . . al at once with their all housen I
> And with the Lordes therof the roofes with goddes of Thebes all
> The Thebane temples even uppon my body will let fall:
> And wyl be hyd in towne upturned: if to my shoulders might
> The walles themselves all cast theron shall fall a burden light.[66]

Yet *Hercules furens* is also a play in which we hear complaints concerning Hercules's cruel countenance and bloody slaughters and in which, moreover, Theseus urges rulers to forgo the sports of cruelty and blood, to overcome their furious rage, and, thus sparing their souls, "to heaven . . . find the wayes."[67]

Samson Agonistes displays an asymmetrical relationship not just with *Hercules furens* but with all the classical models customarily invoked as context or paradigm. Unlike Samson, Hercules quits a life of bloody slaughter and eventually surrenders his wish for death. If Samson's emblems, owing to Jacob's prophecy in Genesis, are the serpent/dragon and viper (49.16–18), if the image of the evening dragon (or serpent) is reattached to Samson as the first item in the triple simile at the end of *Samson Agonistes*, these are also, in *Hercules furens*, the images of the kingdom, the civilization, that Hercules tames, having first subdued those same savage impulses within himself in a play which, like *Samson Agonistes*, moves toward the conclusion that, contrary to the claims of some characters in each work, the gods are not the problem: *man* is. If Seneca's play displays "the audacity and violence of the destructive hero" as he moves toward a new value system and eventually attains virtue,[68] Milton's poem reveals a protagonist with unaltering ways. The two value systems vying within Hercules, and within Seneca's play, vie with one another, however, in Milton's 1671 poetic volume.

The trio of Greek tragedians invoked at the beginning and end of the prefatory epistle to *Samson Agonistes*, in their works most frequently cited as models for Milton's poem, display the same sort of disjunctive relationship with it, particularly in their conclusions. In *Prometheus Bound*, despite the apt conceptual analogy it affords for Milton's mental theater, the hero keeps rather than publishes his "secret" and, initially motivated by petty acts of vengeance, finally endures his *agon* out of newly found love for the human race. In *Oedipus at Colonus*, despite the parallel between the blind men and their guides at the beginning of the play, grief gives way to joy in the transfiguration of Oedipus at the end of the play, and there is now a disjunctive relationship between the burial sites in the two poems. The comedic ending of Sophocles's play, the joy and exhilaration of its conclusion, has no counterpart in Milton's tragedy where the body of a defeated Samson lies mangled in the ruins and where, as with Thomas Fuller, the only reason to behold Samson's sepulchre is "that therein [we] . . . may bury all our vain thoughts of eternity."[69]

Most striking of all is the radical disjunction evident in the juxtaposition of Euripides' *Heracles* and Milton's *Samson* and nicely reinforced by a hero who, instead of slaying a lion, tames the lion of his rage and whose ambition to deliver his people into freedom and equality, "to civilize the world" (in the words of Amphitryon), gains credibilty as he acquires perseverance and patience.[70] In the process, Heracles, unlike Samson, through a tragedy of hope, through its loss, comes to hope for things possible, as becomes evident, first of all, in the evolving conception of deity within the play — "how dark are all the ways of god to man!"; yet how just in the way "they raise the good and scourge the bad," and how "perfect, lacking nothing," as Heracles comes to understand — and, finally, in the guiding hands also at the end of the play.[71] After Theseus, now anointed as surrogate son of Heracles, offers a guiding hand — "Give your hand . . . I shall lead you" — and thereafter Heracles and his father embrace — "*Heracles*: I long for it, yearn to embrace my father. *Amphitryon*: My arms are waiting" — the Chorus concludes that any man who prefers strength to love "is diseased of soul" (1426). This concession comes in a play where the hero, initially choosing suicide, recoils from a path that will lead to inevitable death and who, though he could destroy a city, refuses to do so.[72]

Just as *Samson Agonistes* gathers into itself different scenarios for and movements of tragedy — Samson pursophorus or Hybristes . . . Dagonalia (*YP*, 8:556) — both *Heracles* by Euripides and *Hercules furens* by Seneca show "the agony of Heracles . . . surmounted in apotheosis."[73] That is, the first movement in the Hercules plays, what might be called "Hercules hybristes," is followed by a second movement of "Hercules furens or agonistes" and a concluding movement of "Hercules triumphans." The first two movements, with the heavy accent falling upon the second, are subsumed by *Samson Agonistes*, while the third movement, very much a part of the 1671 poetic volume, finds its counterpart in the climax of *Paradise Regain'd*, where in epic simile the triumphant Jesus is likened to the victorious Hercules. The inclusion of the Hercules comparison here, the withholding of it from the climactic moment in *Samson Agonistes*, speaks volumes.

What is said of Heracles in *Heraclidae* is more likely to be credited to Milton's Jesus than his Samson — "I knew . . . your son to be no ordinary man but one of true heroic stamp . . .; I can give him only praise" — and this in a play that pits generations against one another, an earlier one exacting vengeance and a later one responding with generosity. And not just generations vie with one another, but heroes like Heracles of noble heart, and Eurystheus, a man of vengeance — and value systems, one of which marked by violence, revenge, and barbarism, by a people swollen with arrogance and pride, is about to be extirpated by those like Demophon who come to understand that "I must act justly to be treated justly." But perhaps the better example is the daughter of Heracles, his "god-like spirit . . . living on in his offspring," who, "ready to die," offering "willingly," "freely" to do so in order that others might live, knows that the sublimest act is to put another before her. She understands the sanctity of human life, the "magnanimity" of self-sacrifice: "Who in the world could speak or act more nobly than this?"[74] Milton's surest counterparts to such heroism are the Christ of *Paradise Lost*, book 3, and the Eve of book 10.

Which of Milton's heroes in the 1671 poetic volume, one may ask, is the more just measure of such heroism, both here in *Heraclidae* and in *The Bacchae*? How deeply does the parallelism run between Dionysus and Samson, their "holy" hair chopped off, both prisoners in chains, each subject to mockery, especially when one remembers the message Dionysus would teach: it is better not "to invite violence by using it."[75] If Milton's purpose, like that of Euripides, is "to rouse [people] into new awareness," and if that awareness involves wisdom superseding strength, if it is love not strength that finally matters, it is no small irony that what we see in *The Bacchae* ("I want the whole of Thebes to laugh / as I parade him through the streets") and what remains at the end of the play, the mutilated, scattered body of Pentheus ("we captured this beast of prey and ripped it limb from limb")[76] is what in *Samson Agonistes* its protagonist fears he will experience ("they shall not trail me through their streets / Like a wild beast" [1402]), together with both what Samson promises — "to tear thee joint by joint" (953) — and what both he and the Philistines get — "horrible convulsion" (1649), "thunder / Upon the[ir] heads" (1651–52), his mutilated "body . . . / Soaked in his enemies' blood" (1725–26). *The Bacchae* and the Book of Judges explicitly, and *Samson Agonistes* implicitly, end in images of hacked, riven bodies, including Samson's own. The still pressing question is whether Milton, like Euripides and like the redactor of the Judges stories, deplores the culture of violence he depicts.[77]

II

Criticism's evasion of Euripides may be owing to, first, some modern editors' conviction that the lines Milton attributes to him in his preface to *Samson Agonistes* belong to Menander, when actually the lines are attributed to both writers in early modern editions of their works; and second, to the fussing of modern commentators over the authorship of *Christos Paschon*, while ignoring its Euripidean pedigree, along with the huge infusion of allusion to and quotation from this playwright in that work. The crucial issue for Milton studies is not whether Milton is guilty of mistaken attribution but, rather, recognition of the special authority he gives to Euripides as a Greek tragedian speaking through Holy Scripture. The essential questions are, first, why, given the precedent set by Erasmus of naming no one,[78] Milton mentions Euripides but not Menander in his citation of 1 Corinthians 15.33? Second, why Milton insinuates a play like *Christos Paschon*, through notation of it in this preface, as a context for his tragedy even as he shies away from the usual seventeenth century attribution of the play to Apollinarius, and what may be inferred from this gesture? And, last, why should Milton invoke the Apocalypse, as presented and perceived by David Pareus, as a literary model?

Initially, we should remember that, although the verse from 1 Corinthians (as Milton implies) is attributed to Euripides in some early modern editions of this tragedian's work, it is not usually attributed to him in scriptural annotation. Milton is thus able to bring new knowledge to the fore and, through it, to hint at revisionary interpretation. Moreover, by ignoring Menander for Euripides, Milton purges from his preface a poet associated with the "comic stuff" he here prefers to ridicule and also avoids invoking the memory of Menander's suicide — a notion which, with reference to Samson, if not the preface, certainly the "Argument" to *Samson Agonistes* seeks to suppress. Indeed, when we remember that Menander allegedly committed suicide and that Samson, sometimes thought to have done the same, is being excused from such action in Milton's "Argument" to the poem — when we remember these facts, it makes sense that Milton should use learned authority to attribute the biblical verse not to Menander but to Euripides. As much a prophet of Christianity as a philosopher profoundly in tune with Christian ethics, Euripides is to Milton what Seneca is to Grotius:

> the language of Seneca approaches very near to the perfection of Christian morals. He calls revenge, in its usual and proper acceptation, a term of inhumanity, differing from injury only in degree. For retaliation of pain can be considered as nothing better than excusable sin . . . the pleasure of a little and infirm mind. . . . punishment cannot justly be inflicted from a spirit of revenge.[79]

In a similar vein, Milton's attribution of *Christos Paschon* to Gregory Nazianzen is as curious as it is illuminating: curious because its authorship, much disputed in the early seventeenth century, was assigned by Protestants and, reluctantly, by Catholics to Apollinarius. Not "*all* his contemporaries," as Merritt Y. Hughes reports, not even most of them, believed *Christos Paschon* was the work of Gregory Nazianzen.[80] Rather, as Jean Le Clerc explains, "the Tragedy which is at the end of . . . [Gregory's] *Poems*, and is entitled *Christ's Sufferings*, was made by *Apollinaris* of *Laodicea*" or, as some thought, if initially made by Apollinarius, was revised by Gregory, or as still others believed was placed there fraudulently.[81] "Whoever else may have written it, St. Apollinaris, Tetze, Prodomus, or some other," it became abundantly clear, says W. S. M. Knight, that most probably Gregory did not, although George Sandys (for one) thought that the discrepancies between this and Gregory's other poems — its rebellious poetry, its theological unorthodoxy — being used to discount Gregory's authorship, could be explained by the fact that this poem alone is written in heavy imitation of Euripides.[82] It should be noted here as well that there is no real orthodoxy, no one established theory, when it comes to explaining the Atonement.

In any case, Sandys attaches to Grotius's poem a succinct summary of the controversy over authorship and attributions of the earlier *Christos Paschon*:

> The Tragedie of CHRIST'S PASSION was first written in Greek by *Apollinarius of Laodicea*, Bishop of *Hieropolis*: and after him by *Gregory Nazianzen*; though this, now extant in his Works, is by some ascribed to the former: by others accounted supposititious, as not agreeing with his Strain in the rest of his Poems; which might alter in that particular upon his imitation of *Euripides*. But *Hugo Grotius*, of late hath transcended all on this Argument: whose steps afar-off I follow.[83]

It is a summary that answers to Robert Cooke's elaboration of the argument that "*Tragedia*, Christus patiens, *falsò adscribitur Greg. Nazianzeno*."[84] Moreover, for Sandys, Apollinarius and Gregory together have produced a poem that, in its "*truth*," is "*a Pattern to all History*" and, in its "*strangenesse*," a pattern for "*all Fables*."[85] The movement from Gregory to Grotius to Sandys is one of shifting accents where the resurrection, receiving long and imposing treatment in Gregory's poem, is skirted except for the Messengers' prophecies of it in Grotius's tragedy, along with Mary's cryptic notation of it as, remembering that Jesus now gives mankind a pathway to heaven, she

envisions worldly kingdoms and scepters of tyranny laid down
and a "reformed world" in which the just "injoy perpetuall
Day." Likewise, the Crucifixion itself is a far more immediate
presence in Gregory's poem than in that by Grotius where
Mary, her heart breaking, alludes to it in the shorthand of "side
gor'd" and "feet pierc'd."[86]

In Gregory's as well as Grotius's poem, the Crucifixion is
there less as theology than as a way of focusing, as well as
affording a critique of, the violent impulses within a culture,
although even here the tendency is, as in Gregory's poem, to
look beyond the Crucifixion to the Resurrection, or as in
Grotius's poem to the new Jerusalem in history and the Last
Judgment. Grotius's poem begins with Jesus and ends with
Mary speaking; Gregory's begins with the Mother of God
speaking. In Grotius's poem, the hero is named Jesus; in
Gregory's, Christ. Within the gaze of both poems, the Crucifixion is present; in Gregory's tragedy, in the form of prophecy,
in the Mother of God's imaginings, in the words of the Messenger; and in Grotius's tragedy, anticipated by Jesus and
alluded to by Mary, it is prophesied by messengers, just as
Milton's *Christus Patiens* would have done had the play ever
been written. Gregory's play may proceed differently from
Grotius's. Indeed, given those differences (often exaggerated)
between their plays, it has been proposed that "the *Christos
Paschon* was entirely unknown to Grotius when he wrote his
Christus Patiens," though subsequently he must have been
drawn into discussion of Gregory's poem given the stance of
the Leyden group on the question of its authorship, together
with the furor over what this group seemed uniquely able to
tolerate — a poem so unusual both in spirit and form and with
a "theology . . . so unorthodox."[87] On the other hand, Sandys,
as we have seen, claims that Grotius observes the examples
of Apollinarius and Nazianzen whose footsteps, though from
afar, he himself will follow.

It is as if two cultures, two systems of values, are opposed

within the speaking voices of the Mother and her Son in
Christos Paschon; she repeatedly crying out for her son's
avenger, unable to believe such horrid deeds will stand without
retaliation, imaging both an avenging Father and her Son (as
does the Theologian) as his own avenger; her Son, on the other
hand, uttering no words about revenge, but speaking instead
of forgiveness and deliverance, resurrection and hope. In their
"theologies" of atonement, the poems by Gregory and Grotius,
while emphasizing the Son now in his divine, now in his
human aspect, may not be fully congruent. Yet the first poem
beats a pathway toward the second where the Son explains
the Crucifixion as God's decree, a way of appeasing his "Fathers
wrath," but, more important, as part of the "ordered Course
of things to come," with all history tending toward fulfillment
of the prophecy concerning the bruising of "th' infernall
Serpents poysnous Head." If Jesus here imagines his crucified
body, with "purple sweat," his "entrailes beat" and "a showre
/ Of bloud, rain'd from my wounds" and is described by others
with "entrails bare . . . / And from that wide-mouth'd Orifice,
a floud / Of water gusht, mixt with a stream of bloud," his
defeat is prelude to the cultural disaster of Jerusalem beseiged,
the temple destroyed, the landscape littered with mangled flesh
and unburied corpses. These are images of the calamities
inflicted by "Divine Vengeance" upon the Jews in a world
where retaliation is met with retaliation, horror with horror,
tragedy with tragedy.[88] As in *Christos Paschon,* so in Grotius's
poem: the malice of the crowds is fronted by Jesus's face of woe;
the people's mendacity, with the humility of Jesus; His father's
wrath, his mother's and Peter's pleas for revenge, with his own
cry for forgiveness; and their rage and anger with his generosity
of spirit. These passion plays each depict a world in which
humanity seems exiled — except in the person of Christ/Jesus.

Only in the Grotius circle was the attribution to Gregory
generally preserved,[89] which fact, given Milton's own ascrip-
tion of authorship, might suggest that inscribed within the

allusion is some hint at the sway Grotius held over Milton. Their titles *Adamus Exul* and *Paradise Lost* have been linked over the centuries. Grotius and Milton alike (each a devotee of Euripides, each with Arminian tendencies, each with spiritual ancestry in sects and schisms, each with books on the Index, and each fascinated by the story of paradise lost) would revolutionize the world of theology from which Gregory, as its emperor, would ban dissent — in reputation if not in this one poem. Even as Grotius and Milton would harmonize the laws of nature with those of nations, they would, likewise, privilege divine law over both, Milton more agilely than Grotius; and each would reflect provocatively on such matters as Atonement and Antichrist. *Sophompaneas* and *Samson Agonistes*, moreover, will converge on the exclamatory questions: "what a man is this!" and "what is man!"[90] — yet part company in their endings, the apocalyptic promise of Grotius's poem fronting the eschatological despair in Milton's. If Grotius tended toward the comedic, Milton turned such notes back to tragic, in *Samson Agonistes* scrutinizing not the apocalyptic murmurings in the biblical story but its "deeper horror,"[91] albeit with a finely calibrated sense of ethics so that, as Primo Levy might say, the story cannot be told without the heart eventually cracking in the breast.[92]

It is, of course, odd that a preface to a poem so evasive of traditional typology should refer openly (on the one hand) and obliquely (on the other) to Christ in his First and Second Comings: to Christ suffering at the time of his Passion and to his judging in what, in *The Reason of Church-Government*, Milton calls the "high and stately Tragedy" of the Book of Revelation, the genre wherein previously "*Sophocles* and *Euripides* raigne" (*YP*, 1:814–15); to the anguished Christ at the time of his Crucifixion and the apocalyptic Christ at the fall of Jerusalem. It is doubly odd that, until recently, these references have received so little and, in the instance of *Christos Paschon*, still such unfocused and unilluminating commentary, in part because the Crucifixion story is a shadow text not only for *Samson Agonistes* but in Milton's two epics as well and especially in view of the fact that one of Milton's many projected titles for a biblical tragedy is "Christus patiens" (8:560, 594), along with "Samson pursophorus or Hybristes, or Samson marriing / or in Ramath Lechi Jud. 15 / Dagonalia. Jud. 16" with "Hybristes" usually translated as "Violent . . . wanton, licentious, insolent" (8:556, 562).

Bearing the following description — "The Scene in ye garden beginning from ye comming thither till Judas betraies & ye officers lead him away ye rest by message & chorus. his agony may receav noble expressions" (*YP*, 8:560) — Milton's "Christus Patiens," in its very title, would become one in a sequence of plays, which comprehends the eleventh or twelfth century imitation of Euripides, *Christos Paschon*, plus the more recent tragedy, *Christus Patiens or Christs Passion. A Tragedy*, written by Hugo Grotius and subsequently translated and annotated by George Sandys whom Lord Falkland calls "the *English Buchanan.*"[93] The headnote to *Christos Paschon* is remarkable both for what Milton's own description shares with, and for what Milton's omits from it: "The verses of Gregory the Theologian concerning the passion of salvation of our lord Jesus Christ and concerning his disciple Judas, how, with a treacherous kiss, he betrayed his Lord."[94] Moreover, had Milton's projected poem been written, it would have served historically as a pivot between these earlier tragedies and René Rapin's *Christus Patiens: Carmes Heroicum.*

On the other hand, the tragedy Milton does write, albeit with Samson as its protagonist, in a move that parallels Milton's description of his own *Christus Patiens*, commences with Samson coming from the prison house and centers upon betrayals (Samson's betrayal of his vows, and others' — including the Israelites' — betrayals of him), while all the while pressing toward the moment when the Public Officer leads Samson away, with the rest of the tragedy now reported "by

message & chorus." In both poems, their respective catastrophes are seen from a distance: the Chorus in what Milton
supposes is Gregory's poem reports that it will situate itself
"where we will see it from afar" (500), and the Messenger in
Milton's tragedy explains that "I among these aloof obscurely
stood" (1611; cf. 1631). And the two tragedies, if not repetitions
of one another, do rhyme within an ongoing pattern of history
where retaliation follows upon retaliation; where, in the words
of the Theologian in *Christos Paschon*, "bloodthirst and evil
heedlessness" (1776) are irrevocably a part of the course of
history, the chief aspect of its tragic design, as they still are in
history as it is envisioned by Grotius and Sandys where Peter
attacks the "bloud thirsty" people as foes of peace and fomen-
ters of sacrifice yet also complains, contrary to Jesus, that the
atrocities of history should not go "unrevenged." Mary complains about such "unrevenged" atrocities as well, the work
of "Ungrateful Man," which, meanwhile, are not likely to go
away if this is a world (as described by the Jews) in which
"celestiall Vengeance" continues to fall upon and disperse their
race or in which (as with Mary and Peter) minds are so gripped
by revenge and people still so willing to execute it.[95]

The tragedy Milton does write, then, in certain details and
emphases resembles, first of all, *Christos Paschon* — for
example, in the description by the Mother of God of evil
following upon evil in a series of betrayals by seeming friends,
as well as in the description of Jesus by his Mother, "You have
come into chains . . . and are led, / You, the liberator of the
race, in chains" (446–47), and in their respective representations of "suffering" protagonists, both seen from a long perspective, the one "Soaked in . . . blood . . . / The clotted gore" (1726,
1728), the other a "crucified corpse" (894). In the one instance,
Samson dies as an avenger; and in the other, Christ dies at the
hands of avengers. In each case, both "sons" are returned to
their fathers for burial in striking contrast to *Christos Paschon*
and *Paradise Regain'd* alike, wherein each protagonist returns

to his mother's home in triumph. Also, like the earlier play, *Samson Agonsites* is written, emphatically, "along the lines of Euripides" (3). Furthermore, as Watson Kirkconnell demonstrates, Milton's poem takes its place in a long line of tragedies, designated "new" and "sacred," that both precede and follow *Samson Agonistes*.[96] And it is a line of tragedies perfecting upon, not wavering from, the Euripidean ethic that judges "wisdom . . . / of all the God-given gifts / . . . more beneficial to man / than the power to hold / an enemy powerless at bay"; that faults "the arrogant man / who brazenly worships / his own image as God / and not the Gods themselves" and that holds as its highest "Law" mankind's "lov[ing] each living particle" and coming to know love as its "only strength."[97]

Debora Kuller Shuger affords a crucial perspective on *Samson Agonistes* when she explains that the early modern period was unique in its witnessing to a Christ who becomes what he beholds: Christ judged becomes the judge, and Christ the victim of violence becomes a minister of violence.[98] In the words of Thomas Pierce, "An *injur'd Saviour* will become a most *angry Judge*" in which role the Mother of God imagines her Son in *Christos Paschon* (as does the Theologian) and prophetic Mary envisions Jesus in the final lines of Grotius's play.[99] These are the very roles, as judge and avenger, that the Samson typology, in the first half of the seventeenth century, was used to reinforce, with Henry Smith declaring that "*Sampson* . . . a figure of Christ . . . glorified God at his death, more than all his life, in killing so many of Gods enemies" and with Edmund Staunton proposing that the biblical judges be seen as "the executioners of divine judgements."[100] In contrast, Samson the judge is never acknowledged to be one in Milton's poem and, while not usually a target of violence, is repeatedly an agent of violence toward others: when he kills the 30 men at Askalon, then 1,000 with the jawbone of an ass, and finally many thousands more as the temple/theater falls. Milton's point is obvious: evil is imputable to man, not God. Man's will, not God's (and here Milton would have no problem following Thomas Pierce), is the "Author of *all* the *Evil* which he *committeth*, and of the *Evil* which he *suffereth* for such *commissions*." Or in the words of Sandys, "no evil proceeded from God; . . . Vertue and Vice were in our own Arbitrements."[101]

These events achieve special prominence in Milton's retelling by virtue of insistent repetition through which, apparently, Milton means to remind us, with Richard Baxter, that men are godly or ungodly to "the bent and course of their lives, and not by a particular act," although the particular act of pulling down the temple/theater especially matters in both the Book of Judges and *Samson Agonistes* because it is of a piece with Samson's life, consistent with its "bent and course."[102] Samson's slaying here sets him at odds with Christ's saving, thus encouraging a typology of difference that, as with George Sandys,[103] will distinguish Samson the Nazarite from Jesus the Nazarene, as well as Hercules from Samson, and that, by the middle of the seventeenth century, will mark how very far the antitype exceeds the type, which for some is so far that Samson is no type at all. Not of Christ. Not even of Hercules. What we see in Milton's last published major poem, if I may borrow the words of James Shapiro from another context, is "typology run amok," as it seems to be doing in the strainings of an earlier commentator like Irenaeus for whom "The little boy . . . who guided Samson . . . pre-typified John the Baptist" and Samson's retaliation against a thousand men is nominally with a jawbone but actually with the body of Christ.[104] Christ is singular, unparalleled in dying "for his Enemies, and the ungodly" and altogether unique in that, as Grotius puts it, "all Christ's Actions were indeed full of Virtue" and are ones, unlike Samson's, "which we may laudably imitate."[105] Throughout his treatise, in honing fine ethical distinctions, Grotius repeatedly invokes (as Sandys will also do) the authority of Euripides. Or as the Chorus says in *Christs Passion*,

"While thus they hung, none could the doubt explain, /
Whether He more had sav'd then They had slain," and then
the Chorus of Soldiers proclaims, "Not [even] Hercules so
many Monsters slew," with Sandys thereupon explaining:

> Hercules, *saith* Seneca, *travelled over the world, not to oppresse
> it, but to free it from Oppressors; and by killing of Tyrants and
> Monsters to preserve it in Tranquillitie.* But how much more
> glorious were the victorie of *Christ;* who by suffering for Sinne,
> subdued it, led Captivity captive, was the death of Death; tri-
> umphing over Hell, and those Spirits of Darknesse.[106]

Without ever acknowledging so, Grotius and Sandys here use
language that invokes the character of Samson and the Judges
coda to his story — "So the dead whom he slew at his death
were more than those whom he had slain during his life"
(16.31) — as well as the language frequently used to differen-
tiate Samson, who in death slays, from Jesus who, dying, saves.

According to Sandys, "the acts of *Samson*, . . . [his] force and
fortune, are said to have given to the Poets their inventions of
Hercules, who lived not long before him."[107] According to
Fuller, "the *Pagan-Samson* . . . may seem, by the luxury of
Poets wits, to *ape* this *Jewish Hercules.*" Yet this tradition of
similitude based on their being lion-slayers, each ruined by
women — in the words of Fuller, "Both . . . very like for their
valour, and too like for their wantonness"[108] — and each
delivering the world from monsters, in the seventeenth century
collapses into a typology of difference with Milton's poem,
then, invoking not *a* tradition but traditions of interpreting
the Samson story. More a type of Christ than Samson ever is
in Milton's poetry, even in that of Grotius and Sandys, Hercules
and Jesus, Hercules and Samson, when elided, are terms in
comparisons acting as vehicles for moral instruction,[109] and
in the latter comparison Hercules is advantaged. Take as just
one example the fact pointed out centuries ago by William
Massey: Hercules is "translated into Heaven . . . [for] ridding
the Earth of many mischievous *Serpents* and *Dragons*";[110] yet

these images remain among Samson's insignia in the triple simile with which Milton's poem concludes as if to suggest that, unlike Hercules who overcomes his passions, Samson is overcome by them. It is time to dispute the claim that, in his exuberant energy, Samson is the very essence of the Herculean hero. At best Hercules is a hidden presence in *Samson Agonistes*, available in the poem proper only (as Christ is) through cryptic allusion.

Where others had seen an affinity between Hercules and Samson, Samson and Christ, Milton perceives differences, like those made evident by Sandys in his implied contrasts between the hill to which Samson carries the gates of Gaza and Mount Calvary; then between the "Summite of the hill" with "the ruines of huge arches sunk low in the earth," fabled by the Jews "to have bin the theater of *Samson*, pulled down on the head of the *Philistims*"[111] (there is another temple of Dagon near by), and the temples standing in Jerusalem. Here, Sandys lets different topographies figure typological difference. Such difference is figured, resoundingly so, by Grotius as well: first of all, in *Christus Patiens* where revenge, raging within the human mind, is the way of Caiaphas, Judas, and Pontius Pilate, but not of Jesus of whom it is said that "He more had sav'd then They had slain"; that instead of inflicting death, he is "the death of Death." More like Milton's Samson than Jesus, Peter (in Grotius's play) wishes he were "the Minister of Fate," in which case, pursuing revenge, he would curse his foes and, tearing down the buildings, drown the ruins. In a very different sense than Jesus, Samson and Peter are "to destruction borne."[112] And that sense gets underlined not just in *Christus Patiens* but in *De Jure Belli Ac Pacis*, where Grotius assembles an arsenal of passages from Scriptures to make his points, first, that Christ died *for* his enemies, not revenging them; and, second, that anyone who kills with, will be killed by, the sword, which subverts the law that war and arms both silence. When Grotius gets around to asserting the importance of eschewing war even when it is lawfully undertaken, which is, he says, especially the duty of Christians, therein imitating "the exact Pattern of *Christ*, who laid down his Life for us, dyed for us, *while we were* yet Enemies to him," he cites as other examples not Samson but Hercules and Praxithea.[113]

If in Germany, *Christus Patiens* had been "proposed as the model of perfect Tragedy," in its role as model it would eventually be displaced by *Sophompaneas*, which was described by Vossius as "the most perfect thing in its kind the age has produced."[114] Indeed, Milton's own resistance to the Crucifixion story may be explained, in part, by some of the prefatory material (drawn from Vossius) in Grotius's *Sophompaneas*, where poets are warned that "it agrees not with the majesty of sacred things to be made a play and fable":

> [indeed, it is] of very dangerous consequence to mingle humane inventions with things sacred; because the Poet adds uncertainties of his owne, sometimes falsities; which is not onely to play with holy things, but also to ingraft in mens minds uncertaine opinions, and now and then false.[115]

For the latter reason especially, biblical dramatists should avoid God, Christ, and the mysteries of religion, concerning themselves with sacred stories where the "argument is civill" such as "David *flying from* his Sonne Absalom *or* . . . Joseph *sold by his Brethren*," with Grotius's own "*Tragedy* . . . set[ting] . . . a pattern to him that would handle an argument fetcht from the holy Scriptures" — a pattern, according to Francis Goldsmith, "*excellent and admirable . . . not onely for Poetry . . . but all Divine and humane learning.*"[116] Within such a perspective, Samson agonistes, not Christus patiens, is the better choice for a tragedy, with *Sophompaneas*, then, providing the masterpiece of decorum observed by Milton in his writing of a tragedy for his 1671 poetic volume.

With this example in mind, it is revealing to see how, just five years after Milton's death, the figures of Joseph and Samson are portrayed, in this instance by someone who, though he seems to have believed in the perseverance of the saints, was sometimes taken for an Arminian. Here is Thomas Pierce:

> how much safer 'tis to *fly*, than to *incounter* such Allure-ments, . . . we may illustrate by the examples of *Joseph*, and *Sampson*, who were as *various* in their *Behaviours*, as they were *different* in their *Success*. *Joseph fled from his Mistress* by whom he was tempted *day by day* . . . Whereas *Samson* (on the contrary) was no sooner come to *Gaza*, then *he saw there an Harlot*; nor did he onely *See* but *he went unto her*. . . . Again, no sooner was he come to the Valley of *Soreck*, where he adventur'd to converse with another *Woman* . . . but one of the next Things we read of, is *His telling her all his heart*. . . . And the very next to That, is *His sleeping upon her knees*. . . . And the consequent of This, *the loss of his Liberty, and his Eyes.*[117]

The differences noted here are accentuated when we ask whether Milton's Samson is, like Grotius's Joseph, an exem-plary "leader of the people . . ., provident for the future, un-broken in evils, a maintainer of justice, observing moderation in all things, . . . [and] set[ting] himself no other copy, next to the divine Commandements, by which to order his actions"? And ask the questions, too, if both men are equally by God inspired and if each fits with the other as an interpreter and deliverer — as men "unto whom secrets are revealed" and as "Saviour[s] of the World?"[118]

Could Milton announce in *Samson Agonistes* what Grotius's translator Goldsmith proclaims to be the case in *Sophom-panaes*: "Here no . . . / Hercules *the Stage with horror fils*"?[119] Would Milton celebrate Samson as enthusiastically as Grotius does Hercules:

> *Hercules* is so highly extolled by the Ancients . . . for having freed the Earth of *Antaeus, Busiris, Diomedes*, and such like Tyrants, *whose Countries*, says *Seneca* of him, *he pass'd over not with* an *ambitious Design of gaining for himself, for the sake of vindicating the Cause of the Oppressed*; being as *Lysias* shews, the Author of great good to mankind, by punishing the Unjust.[120]

Or would Milton say of Samson what Grotius says of Joseph: that among his "glorious titles" is "Great Saviour" of his people; that "To follow the strict rules of Law he sought" and "close he keeps to justice and the Laws!"[121]

Both Joseph and Samson may inhabit worlds in which every man is his own law, but Samson revels in the world from which Joseph provides release. For a while, both may be quartered in dark and loathsome prison-houses, Joseph by another's fault, and Samson by his own; but when each is outside the prison, Samson is still sorrowing, while Joseph is replete with joy. Both these poems, finally, are ironic inversions of their own claims, "Night follow[s] night without a glimpse of day" from Grotius's poem, while, according to Milton's tragedy, day breaks, the "breath of Heav'n" is now "fresh-blowing."[122] Ironically, Grotius and Milton afford descriptions of one another's play worlds, not of their own. Moreover, when the Samson/Jesus analogy collapses into a typology of difference, other typological schemes involving Samson and David, as well as Samson and Joseph, in addition to Samson and Elias, crumble too.

In the first instance, David, unlike Samson, lives in accordance with the law and, instead of destroying a kingdom, limits himself to proportionate measures. In the last of these instances, an epigraph once used by Lancelot Andrewes as he brooded over Samson and Elias as types of Christ — an exegetical site to which we will return later — makes the point forcefully:

> And when his disciples James and John saw this, they said, Lord, wilt Thou that we command that fire come down from Heaven, and consume them, even as Elias did?
>
> But He turned, and rebuked them, and said, Ye know not what manner of spirit ye are of.
>
> For the Son of man is not come to destroy men's lives, but to save *them*. (Luke 9.54–56)[123]

Skilled typologist that he was, who continually reinforces inherited analogies in his epics, Milton, both in his juxtaposition of poems within the 1671 poetic volume and in his preface to *Samson Agonistes*, gestures toward typological analogies and structures that, instead of exploiting, he ultimately denies.

In other words, this juxtaposition of poems implies the typology that their placement (the inverted order of the stories of the Son and Samson) resists. If *Paradise Lost* and *Paradise Regain'd* ring changes on the received typology, in his tragedy Milton extends to Samson the counter-typology previously enveloping Satan. At the center of *Paradise Lost*, as well as the centerpiece to Milton's final trilogy of poems, the Son continues to be (as in "The Passion") the "Most perfect *Heroe*" (*CP*, 78) against whom all other heroes are judged. However, if in "The Passion" Milton stresses the parallel between Christ and Hercules, in the 1671 poetic volume he settles, instead, on the discrepancies first between Satan and the Son and then between Samson and the Son. To the extent that Hercules is a presence (explicitly or implicitly) in Milton's final poetic volume, he exhibits a moral bearing, as well as heroic character, superior to Samson's and always more of a piece with that of Jesus.

The early modern period marks a significant moment of transition in the Crucifixion no less than in the Samson story. As its ethical substance comes under review, the story itself modulates from comedy into tragedy as one set of terms, the Passion and Resurrection, is displaced by another set, the Passion of Christ and the Fall of Jerusalem, so as to imply a correlation between the defeat of an individual and the demise of a nation. This is the same sort of correlation that, in the seventeenth century, would be used to explain the disrupted chronology of the Book of Judges and its consequent pairing of Samson's tragedy with the story of an entire nation falling into idolatry. The supplementary annotations to Matthew Poole's Bible make the point twice, succinctly: the episode in Judges 18, "which though placed after this History [of Samson], was done before it"; "*Sampson's* time was long after."[124] Two panels of narrative, then, pose Samson defiled against his tribe defeated, both of which occurrences (again, the point is twice repeated) belong to "those days" when *"there was* no king in Israel, *but* every man did *that which was* right in his own eyes" (Judges 17.6, 21.25; cf. 18.1, 19.1). Moreover, the series of biographies and the episodes in history related in Judges culminate in the redactor's injunction:

> all that saw it said, There was no such deed done nor seen from the day that the children of Israel came up out of the land of Egypt unto this day: consider it, take advice, and speak *your minds.* (19.30)

The Book of Judges climaxes in this summons to judgment even as, by implication, it is written during the time of kingship made necessary by the failure of judgeship.

As with the saga of Samson, so with the Christ story (as it is explained by Shuger): what was a story of "redemptive sacrifice" metamorphosed into one of "crime and punishment" in the very moment that what had functioned as "a dominant cultural myth" loses it "normative values and ontological solace."[125] What had been presented as the divine comedy of Christ's triumphant descent into hell for its harrowing becomes a tragic descent into the agony of the cross and desolation of the grave. What had been Samson's apotheosis at the pillars emerges as the moment of his defeat prognosticating the eventual disappearance of his tribe from history. In Milton's 1671 volume, indeed in the white space between the preface and "Argument" to *Samson Agonistes* and the poem proper, the "tragedy" of Christ is transferred to Samson just as, earlier in this same volume, the Crucifixion had been displaced by the story of Jesus in the wilderness, into himself descending, and eventually reascending into the epiphany on the pinnacle, where, having already discovered his manhood and determined his earthly roles, Jesus now apprehends his divinity. In 1671, Milton invokes two vastly different scriptural tales, each, in Shuger's words, "to brood over the outcome and implications of the Civil War."[126]

Milton's own discomfort with the Crucifixion story, evident in his evasions of it both early ("The Passion") and late (*Paradise Regain'd*), together with his unexpected — and usually ignored — foregrounding of the topic in the preface to *Samson Agonistes*, should remind us that, encoding "cultural disturbance," early modern retellings of the Passion story "draw into themselves a wildly problematic and complex range of cultural issues"; that revealing discontinuities and ruptures, as well as clarifying by problematizing and limning interpretation with political resonance, these retellings dwell on what Shuger describes as the "half-lit recesses of biblical narrative." The "ethical opacity" of many such stories "opens a space for interpretive maneuvering — for using narrative to discern meaning rather than merely enforce it," says Shuger, and for mounting critiques of obviously sanitized readings of legendary biblical tales.[127] In their retellings, moreover, stories like the Crucifixion and that of Samson acquire simultaneously tragic form and psychological complexity. The tragic form and characterization of such stories is, finally, a distinctly early modern emplotment of these biblical narratives, with poets like George Buchanan, Hugo Grotius and John Milton all writing across the grain of majority opinion that in the sixteenth and seventeenth centuries was strongly resistant to dramatizing matter from the Bible and each of them, in the process, challenging theological clichés concerning both Antichrist and the Atonement.

In a poem like *Samson Agonistes*, the gesture of rebellion is doubly subversive with Milton, first, recasting the biblical narrative as a drama and, then, reinflecting (and sometimes revising) the inherited story in order to wrest from it new meanings. In this strategy, Milton has the precedent of Jerome Ziegler, who proclaims: "base it were / Merely to parrot what was said before," for even what is taken from Scriptures

deserves recasting "in another form."[128] What matters finally
is not the biblical nature of the story per se, but instead what
Ziegler here calls the "re-edit[ing]" — how the materials are
selected from these inherited stories and how they are
conveyed. So far as Milton's coupling of the Samson and Jesus
stories is concerned, it occurs in the aftermath of Grotius's
explosively controversial treatise on atonement theology, *De
Satisfactione Christi* (1617), at a time when atonement theology becomes increasingly a matter of dispute, and in the
aftermath, too, of *Dissertatio de Antichristo* (1640), in that
decade of the seventeenth century when apocalyptic fervor is
running at high pitch. Yet, if Grotius uses the example of the
Apocalypse, coupled with select plays by Aeschylus and
Euripides and thereupon worries whether "Some perhaps will
find fault, that this Tragedy hath not a sad conclusion,"[129]
Milton, emptying the Apocalypse of comedy, distills from it
pure tragedy, complaining in the preface to *Samson Agonistes*
of "the Poets error of intermixing Comic stuff with Tragic
sadness and gravity" (*CP*, 574). Here Milton embodies the
theory that more than a century later John Penn will enunciate:
the practice of intermingling comedy and tragedy is a violation
of decorum; these genres should be joined in neither a simple
nor a double plot.

Instead of drifting backward, Milton's preface is "extraordinary" in anticipating newly emerging opinions on tragedy,
the theory of Gotthold Ephraim Lessing and the Germans for
whom comedy mingling with tragedy produces "a mons-
trosity" and the practice, we should go on to say, of Byron and
Shelley whose mental theaters are scenes less of instruction
than of interrogation.[130] But if his preface is anticipatory,
Milton's poem is even more so, forecasting the issues, indeed
the very critique of Christianity, that will emerge a century
later with the publication of the *Woffenbutteler Fragmente*
(and later still in plays like Byron's *Cain* and Shelley's *The
Cenci*). Those fragments, like Milton's last poems, are much

more questions than answers, founded upon the notion that
there has been a radical corruption of Christ's ethical teachings,
which, once restored, will establish again that God does not
contradict himself and that, if revelation occurs at all, it "can
only occur on rare occasions to particular individuals, in whose
testimony other men put their trust." Certainty of their election is always a delicate affair, all the more so when their claims
to inspiration belong to the distant past and when murderers
of mankind are being represented as the bearers of divine
revelation. When accounts disagree concerning circumstances,
the facts themselves may be mistaken.[131] It is precisely these
issues that the embedded narratives in *Samson Agonistes* bring
to the fore, apocalyptically so, in such a way that ethical discrepancy yields moral insight within a poem where "Samson's
Admonitory Fall" (in a broader sense than Clement of
Alexandria ever intended) "is to be hated and abominated by
those who fear God."[132]

The point should not be lost that, invoking the Book of
Revelation, as understood by David Pareus, as a model for tragedy, Milton is, in effect, saying that this book about the
tragedy of Antichrist, with its scenes of destruction and theme
of deliverance, following upon a history of faked deliverances,
has significant bearing on *Samson Agonistes*. For Pareus, the
Apocalypse is "truly Tragicall. For it representeth Tragicall
motions and tumults of the adversaries . . ., and at length the
Tragicall end also of the wicked themselves."[133] In thus choosing to cast Samson's rather than Christ's story as a tragedy,
thereby placing in juxtaposition a true and false apocalypse,
Milton owes a debt not just to Grotius, as well as Buchanan,
but (he thinks) to Gregory Nazianzen for tragic models as
well as the precedent of embracing controversial atonement
theology and still more highly charged thinking on the nature
and person of Antichrist. Yet the debt to Grotius, because unspecified, has proved particularly elusive, at least until one
detects within the different apocalypses contrasting heroes of

deliverance: one, who himself saved, saves his people; the other who, slaying his enemy, also slays himself, in the end soaked in the blood of those enemies. *Samson Agonistes* presents an image of the horror: of death and destruction at their utmost point. *Sophompaneas*, on the other hand, envisions the promised end: sorrow ebbs, joy returns, there is a reign of peace.

Or if instead we turn to *Christ's Passion*, in its vision of the Son's destiny, a long way down the corridor of history, He comes in judgment and, in his triumph over death and then in the general resurrection, all earthly scepters are surrendered to him. There is a lasting reign of peace. In the short term, however, *Christ's Passion* and *Samson Agonistes*, like the Book of Judges, are darkened by similar visions of horror: the destruction of a temple; a play-world strewn with dead, mutilated bodies; in the words of Sandys, in the destruction of the temple, in the delight of spectators with bodies "torne in pieces by wild beasts in the *Amphitheater*."[134] Milton is not the first to represent the end of Samson's story as "a mound of wreckage and of men" and his world as now an "utter ruin," a scene of "carnage," where presumably "severed feet and fingers lie apart."[135] It is in their respective catastrophes, it is not often enough allowed, that the stories of *Samson Agonistes* and *Christs Suffering* converge. Similarly, the temple scenes converge, in order to contrast the stories of Moses and Samson, with the Rabbis, as Shoulson remarks, using this juxtaposition to mark "the pinnacle of Israel's cultic experience, on one side, and one of the most dubious episodes in pre-monarchic Israelite history, on the other . . ., the entire sweep of Israelite history, its peaks and valleys, triumphs and tribulations" thus captured within these contrasting typologies.[136]

Milton's own coupling of the Son and Samson, accomplished through the juxtaposition of *Paradise Regain'd* and *Samson Agonistes*, is reinforced both through explicit reference to *Christs Suffering* in the preface to *Samson Agonistes* and cryptic allusion to the "ransom" theory of Atonement in the

"Argument" to this poem. Through the atonement theory founded upon the two Adams and the two trees, Samson himself, because locked within the intervening system of types (as C. A. Patrides reports),[137] is implicated in a theory that could be challenged by challenging typology itself and that became downright gruesome in its typological unfurling where, in a ransom paid to Satan, the tree of the cross becomes a mousetrap in which the blood of Christ is placed as bait. This was one area of controversy from which Gregory Nazianen did not stand aloof, nor even the anonymous author of the play *Christos Paschon* once attributed to Gregory — "Now is the time to pay the hateful penalty," Christ declares (736). In a corresponding moment in *Christs Passion*, the Chorus of Soldiers declare with relish: "For Sin, what greater Ransome can we pay? / What worthier Offering on thy Altar lay?" Or in the earlier words of Caiaphas: "Let him redeem his Nation with his Death."[138] Nor need these poets stand aloof, since no theological explanation is binding when it comes to this mystery at the core of the Christian religion. This was also a controversy (owing to Grotius) very much alive in Milton's own time. It was Gregory Nazianzen, after all, who, asking about the cause and cost of the ransom theory, denounced it, recoiling in horror at the thought of God's paying a ransom to Satan: "If to the Evil One, fie upon the Outrage."[139]

Indeed, from the very beginning (and their beginning comes relatively late, it seems), passion plays, as James Shapiro remarks, were "revenge" dramas "deeply enmeshed . . . in theological conflict,"[140] the revenge motif underscored by those plays culminating in the harrowing of hell. But, in the early modern period, this genre was fast becoming "a theological quagmire" (this phrase is also Shapiro's)[141] as the typology of trees was displaced by contract theory from the law, where the ransom, still paid, now goes into God's till and where God as Judge, a god of fury, exacts punishment by crushing his enemies to pieces. Theology may say so; theologians, as in

Christos Paschon, may think this way: "The Father will not allow the son to suffer these things. / . . . Indeed, he may punish them; for he will not cease / From anger; and he said clearly that he would burn the city. / The just, defending eye of the Father / May do this to enemies who are not friends" (1194, 1196–99). But this is also a "theology" that some playwrights, like the author of *Christos Paschon* and later like Grotius and Milton, put under challenge.

No wonder that some would move atonement theory away from divine justice, then segregate it from the idea that by faith alone mankind participates in salvation through the Passion; and that some like Grotius would use their atonement theory to reinforce the notion of divine forgiveness and thus involve mankind cooperatively in the process of redemption. Milton's 1671 poetic volume is, simultaneously, a critique of atonement theology and a relocation of redemption, moving it from the cross onto the desert and then actively engaging people in the process of redeeming themselves. No longer accomplished by divine fiat, redemption now involves both divine cooperation and human participation. Emphasis now shifts from the death of the body to the resurrection of the spirit.

Not only an aspect of Aristotelian theory, as well as a particularly prominent feature in the Euripidean and Senecan branches of classical tragedy with which Milton aligns his poem, interrogation is also the driving force in seventeenth century scriptural exegesis where, among others, John Weemes would seem to advocate reading by "interrogation."[142] In the case of classical tragedy, what Sophocles did implicitly, Euripides, with his deepened skepticism toward both myth and prophecy, does quite explicitly so that his heroes, instead of being enmeshed in external forces they cannot control, supply the immediate cause for their own destruction. Milton's Arminian theology, with the check it places on the perseverance of the saints, with its insistence that what we do is of our own accord and that our destruction, if that be our fate, is *per accidens*, is a perfect fit with the principles and ethics of Euripides. Euripides, as well as Sophocles, as Rebecca W. Bushnell remarks, "shared a culture that respected and yet questioned prophecy," with Euripides bringing "the kinds of questions that Sophocles implicitly raised about the abuse of prophecy . . . to the surface in his plays," thereby creating a huge disjunction between received explanations and revisionary interpretations.[143] These are plays in which inherited stories, less plot than framework, invite improvisation, not repetition, and in whose upside-downings expectations are dashed, while things unexpected are accomplished. The same sort of interrogation of prophecy, coupled with a critique of inspiration, that emerges in the writings of Grotius, whose rationalism allows for only a limited adherence to inspiration; the same emphasis on Christian charity, the same progressive and humanitarian elements — all are powerfully evident in Milton's 1671 poetic volume as well.

Not Aeschylus and Sophocles, but Sophocles and Euripides is the coupling within the great triad of Greek tragedians that Milton himself emphasized and to which Milton criticism should now turn, even as it encourages other groupings — Euripides and Seneca, for example, as well as both dramatists and the author of *Christos Paschon*, the author of this poem and Grotius, and Euripides and John of Patmos — each of these pairings secured within and sanctioned by the preface to *Samson Agonistes*. Euripides' *Iphigenia* and Seneca's Hercules plays, for example, and the *Christus Patiens* plays of Gregory and Grotius had already been clustered together by Vossius[144] — and with good reason. These are the rebel poets, who dared to ask questions and who, in their daring, capture Milton's allegiance and with whom, in the very act of contemplating (even if never writing) a play called *Christus Patiens*, he does align himself, emphatically so. In turn, Milton brings the same enquiring spirit, the same kind of rigorous interrogation, to Christianity that Euripides and later Seneca bring to pagan mythology.

It is Samson's god, not Milton's, who is flawed; and his flaws are ones perpetrated by Samson and some of his people, with Milton's authorial voice probably finding both its clearer and finer tones as well as ethical affinity not in Samson's utterances, but in those of Euripides' Heracles:

> I do not believe the gods . . . / . . . bind each other in chains. / I never did believe it. I never shall; / nor that one god is tyrant of the rest. If God is truly god, he is perfect, / lacking nothing. These are poets' wretched lies. (1341–46)[145]

Not just in *Paradise Lost* and *Paradise Regain'd*, but in *Samson Agonistes*, Milton's project is not the promulgation of heroic norms but instead, as Ann Norris Michelini writes of Euripides' *Heracles*, "the construction of an ethic that inverts and corrects the traditional standard of heroism."[146] It is the Danites in Milton's poem, together with Samson, who at times represent a god unworthy of belief by a civilized people. Milton, on the other hand, as if joining his voice to that of Euripides' Heracles, exposes Samson and his people, as well as a host of other poets, in their "lies."

Rebellious writings provoke rebellious readings. Everyone knows that the shapers of a canon tell us what to read, but they also try to control how we read — in what sequences and combinations — in the process, erecting forbidden contexts, which, in the case of *Samson Agonistes*, are both classical and biblical. Aeschylus and Sophocles are "in," Euripides (and Seneca apparently) are "out"; similarly with Judges and Hebrews (on the one hand) and Genesis in conjunction with Revelation (on the other hand). In this connection, it is too often forgotten that all of Seneca was translated into English by 1581; the complete Sophocles, not until 1759. The very poets in the vanguard of the emerging tradition of biblical tragedy, especially George Buchanan and Hugo Grotius, were the early translators of Euripides. Nor should the fact be lost that the seventeenth century is the great age of commentary on the Book of Revelation; that never before or since has the book enjoyed such popularity, nor been the occasion for the kind of ground-breaking interpretations provided by David Pareus, Joseph Mede, Henry More, and the young Isaac Newton. So intellectually daring in both its aesthetics and politics, Mede's commentary (and Mede, it should be remembered, was Fellow at Christ's College, Cambridge, during the period when Milton was a student there) was not translated until 1643, nor published in England until that year. David Pareus's commentary, in turn, though dating back to 1618, was not translated until 1644.

It is, of course, the most influential, as well as the highly volatile, texts that typically come under siege and for which there are always acceptable as well as unacceptable yokings, the function of which, as Eve Kosofsky Sedgwick explains, is to "insulate and deform the reading of politically important texts."[147] Whatever the forced decouplings — Milton and Euripides, Milton and Seneca, Milton and the poet of *Christos Paschon*, Milton and Buchanan, Milton and Grotius, or Milton and the Genesis-Apocalypse connection — the effect, in the case of *Samson Agonistes*, is to divert attention from theological and political audacity, from volatile theorizings of the Atonement and Antichrist, from thinly veiled allegorizations of current history, and also from end-time and end-myths, as well as from those forms of tragedy in which individual failings are harbingers of cultural dissolution. Euripides and Seneca, John of Patmos and Milton are the great poets of apocalypse, each of them calling for a revival of the human spirit, each understanding that the human heart has not corrupted institutionalized religion but that the prevailing religious orthodoxies have, instead, corrupted the human heart.

Everything that complicates and ambiguates, questions —
or casts suspicion — is, by those orthodoxies, shunted to the
side. The spirit of interrogation at the core of the Euripidean
project, as well as the Senecan tradition in early modern drama,
is equally prominent in the collocation of scriptural texts
telling (or alluding to) the Samson story, especially so in the
Book of Revelation, and, more, is at the center of seventeenth
century biblical exegesis, not just Christian but Rabbinic, and
not just liturgical traditions but secular ones, including
especially the long tradition of biblical drama of which *Samson
Agonistes* is a remarkable representative.[148] It is a tradition
that, prizing controversy with or without resolution and dramatizing debate involving all sides of an argument, presents a
full panoply of the questions that debate engenders and answers
it provokes, even mutually exclusive ones. Doing so, it makes
clear that tragedy is less an affirmation than a disavowal of
proverbial wisdom.

Biblical tragedy is also a tradition that, in its advocacy of
interrogation, urges reading any text by what is there parenthetically, or in its margins — Judges 13–16 in terms of Genesis
49.16–18, Hebrews 11.32, Revelation 7.7, and their adjoining
contexts — thus producing, in any work faithful to its tradition,
double, triple, or even quadruple readings.[149] *Samson Agonistes*
is not one but many texts, all circulating at once and each
bracketing the others with question marks. Not a poem that
propounds an interpretation, Milton's tragedy arrays alternative possibilities for interpretation as if to say that only those
who do not want to know ask no questions, and those who
ask no questions receive no answers.

Two

Justifying
Samson's Ways

. . . by and large there are two lines of approach: those who
see in Samson a religious hero with tragic elements, and
others who make an essentially negative evaluation of him,
as an example not to be imitated, the opposite of the true hero.
— J. Alberto Soggin[1]

For some it is a fact, now indisputable, that the Samson of the
Epistle to the Hebrews — a Samson sanitized and sainted —
is Milton's Samson. While Gladys J. Willis would trace Milton's
Samson, a "Saint," to Athanasius (d. 373), even as she questions, then dismisses "the Biblical Samson" as "a bad choice"
(that is, an irrelevant context) for Milton's poem; in the more
tempered judgment of Leland Ryken: "Although Judges is the
source for the story in *Samson Agonistes*, the essential character of Milton's Samson is illuminated more when placed into
a context of . . . the encomium to faith in Hebrews 11."[2] When
the "essential character" of Samson is thus construed, the

usual supposition is that, given the Hebrews text (not to mention the apocryphal book in its background), how could Milton's Samson be otherwise?

This supposition, insofar as it concerns the Hebrews account of Samson, had been encouraged by Erasmus:

> With the support of God's help he performed many, well nigh miraculous deeds against the Philistines on behalf of his people, deeds which could not be performed either by a multitude of men in concert or by the physical strength of any human body.
> . . . Although all these have not yet obtained the reward promised for godliness, which will occur in the resurrection of the body, nevertheless they have earned everlasting praise for their steadfast confidence.[3]

The sainted Samson of Hebrews also finds a counterpart in the sanitized Samson of Ecclesiasticus (or what is sometimes called The Wisdom of Ben Sira):

> The judges, too, each when he was called, all men whose hearts were never disloyal, who never turned their backs on the Lord — may their memory be blessed! May their bones flower again from the tomb, and may the names of those illustrious men live again in their sons. (46.11–12)[4]

Readers of and commentators on Ecclesiasticus have been quick to notice, however, that certainly here the praise of the judges is hyperbolic and, insofar as it is meant to comprehend Samson, downright misleading. In the words of one of them, "Samson was deceived by Delilah . . . and Yahweh did abandon him."[5] Not Samson but Samuel is the illustrious, hence illustrative, judge through whom all of them are exalted in just those terms that would seem to exclude Samson from the list. For unlike Samson, Samuel pledged and kept his vows and was consecrated with a prophetic voice so that, when he "called upon God," the Lord would "thunder from heaven," so honoring Samuel that he was allowed "from the grave" to raise "his voice as a prophet, to put an end to wickedness" (46.16–17).

Erasmus's supposition, perhaps fueled by the Ecclesiasticus portrait, may even seem to be reinforced by *Samson Agonistes* where Milton's protagonist enrolls himself among the heroes of faith: "Of such examples add me to the roul" (290). Yet, having here numbered himself with those who later would be catalogued as the worthies of Hebrews — the "matchless *Gideon*" and "*Jephtha*" (280, 283) — Samson proceeds to cancel his own name from the roll: "Nor am I in the list of them that hope" (647), nor as the Chorus then explains is Samson's name listed in those books "Extolling Patience" (654). The Samson of *Samson Agonistes*, it would appear, is not to be elided with, but distinguished from, the Samson of both the Epistle to the Hebrews and Ecclesiasticus, as well as Christ in *Christos Paschon*, for the very reasons the Ecclesiasticus representation raises eyebrows. If Samson is an example to us, from Milton's point of view, it is apparently as a "mirror of our fickle state" (164). In the words of the Chorus,

> Since man on earth unparallel'd!
> The rarer thy example stands,
> By how much from the top of wondrous glory,
> Strongest of mortal men,
> To lowest pitch of abject fortune thou art fall'n. (165–70)

In his dialogue with Dalila, Samson confirms the point that he is "to Ages an Example" (765) of what *not* to be — or do.

Moreover, Milton's own views from *De Doctrina Christiana* seem pertinent here: "Hope has its origin in faith." To be without the one presupposes a lack of the other: "Hope differs from faith as effect from cause. It also differs in its object, for the object of faith is the promise, the object of hope, the things promised." It seems clear that, for Milton, the true heroes of faith are steady, not "wavering," in their hope (*YP*, 6:476); that for them to surrender the things promised is for them to surrender the promise itself, which, according to the Hebrews text, figures like Samson never had anyway: "And these all, having obtained a good report through faith, *received not* the promise: God having provided some better thing for us, that they without us should not be made perfect" (11.39–40; my italics). A "story of regeneration" committed to the "rehabilitation of Samson's heroism" — these are clichés of Milton criticism that *Samson Agonistes* prosecutes rather than promotes.

Thus, if in the Argument to *Samson Agonistes* Manoa is described as, in the end, "full of joyful hope" (*CP*, 575) and even if, in the conclusion to Milton's drama according to some critics, "Samson is pronounced to be the faith hero of Hebrews,"[6] the pressure from interrogation intensifying throughout the poem invites us to question, not acquiesce in, such pronouncements and simultaneously to wonder, as Milton repeatedly urges us to do, whether in drama a character's viewpoints actually match with and express those of the author. If the promise was that Samson would begin the deliverance of his people, that promise is unrealized in both the Book of Judges and *Samson Agonistes*. Moreover, Judges exalts not Manoa but his wife as a hero of faith. In *Samson Agonistes*, Manoa's role in this story may be enlarged, but Manoa himself is never aggrandized. Rather, in seeking to pay a ransom to the Philistines, with his "joyful hope" stemming from feelings of success, Manoa, in the words of the poem's "Argument," ironically seeks "*Samson's* redemption," the cost of which will be Samson's surrendering his public life and, with it, the promise that his will be the pioneering work in the redemption of the Israelites. As *Paradise Regain'd* teaches: "hope" and "joy" are returned to history by Jesus (2.57), whereas in *Samson Agonistes*, in the words of Manoa, "Hope" strains, even "tempts Belief" (1535).

The usual supposition begs for modification: *Samson Agonistes* contains, but is not contained by, the Hebrews Samson — just one of several Samsons inscribed within Milton's poem. It is also a corollary of the usual argument that, while another Samson may pertain and even prevail in our own cen-

tury, this Samson's lineaments are owing to the higher criticism of the nineteenth century or to neo-Christians today or,
more whimsically, to those still traumatized by the Vietnam-
war experience — and hence irrelevant to Milton and his century. On the contrary, Samson as a divided image, complicated
in his character and ambiguous in his heroism, is traceable
to Milton's own time. Indeed, this Samson emerges not from
a hermeneutics and poetics of consensus but of conflict.
Moreover, this Samson has been hidden from history by those
who continue to believe that during the early modern period
nothing changes in biblical interpretation, because its commentators remain loyal to readings they derive from — and
refer back to — the Church Fathers.

The Miltonist-turned-theorist, Harold Fisch, has brought
our understanding of biblical hermeneutics and poetics to
a new plateau of sophistication, requiring us to exchange
the old language of "transmission" and "transfusion" for one
that both allows and accounts for a poet's transformational
acts and transgressive maneuvers.[7] The poet who admitted to
the corrupt, damaged status of the New Testament and
acknowledged the chronological disruptions within the
Hebrew Bible was committed to unloosing the spirit of Scriptures. The poet who, in the proem to *Paradise Regain'd*, promises "to tell of deeds / . . . in secret done / And *unrecorded*
left through many an Age, / Worthy t' have not remain'd so
long *unsung*" (1.14–17; my italics) will be averse neither to
reinterpretation nor new interpretation of Scriptures. Nor
would he oppose representations or augmentations of scriptural figures and tales.

Presumably, Milton would have little patience with those
who described *his* "tradition" as "treating the Bible as one
inspired book *without internal contradictions.*"[8] Milton's
habit of reading Scripture by Scripture, as becomes evident in
Tetrachordon, taught him otherwise. Thus, it may be right to
say with James H. Sims that "Milton . . . shaped his poetry

according to his understanding of . . . Scripture"[9] so long as
the inflection falls on *his* understanding — an often fluctuat-
ing understanding owing to newly emerging revelations and
revisionary interpretations. Milton's understanding is also
lodged in paradoxes and rife with complexities. Another
Miltonist writing as theorist, but without ever asserting a connection between the biblical hermeneutic she describes and
Milton's poetics, gets the point exactly: conflicts and contradictions are keys to, not occlusions of meaning in Scriptures (and
in Milton's writings).[10]

As in the Bible, so in Milton's poetry: there is imagination
and distrust of it, a sense of both pattern and its shiftiness,
and of closure, sometimes where none exists. Images dissolve
in the very moment they seem to have been affirmed. Characters merge into their opposites. Theological commonplaces,
cultural clichés, received interpretations — each is counte-
nanced only to be challenged. The tensions in Milton's poetry,
their attendant contradictions, exist within the hermeneutical
traditions informing it, which, in their turn, replicate those
within the Bible itself. It is on these very tensions and contradictions that we should focus: "Here, it may well be," says
Fisch, "is the specific determinant of biblical poetics."[11] As
Fisch goes on to explain, the biblical stories are not seamless:
they are composed of different layers of texts, each with a
different authorship, and then often filtered through the con-
trolling consciousness of a later redactor. If in the resulting
tale there are cracks and fissures, conflicts and collisions, it is
plausible to assume they are there by plan, not accident. Moreover, what we say of such scriptural stories, in this regard, we
should credit to Milton's poems both informed by those stories
and teasing such complexities from them.

It is an obligation of criticism to notice that, in his last
poems, Milton has chosen stories, Old as well as New Testament, particularly laden with contradictions. Each story, in
turn, has been a magnet for contending interpretations. The

jarring accounts of Creation in the Book of Genesis, by Milton's time, had produced competing hermeneutics: patriarchal, misogynist, and feminist. *Paradise Lost* inscribes each hermeneutic, maps each discourse: "Hee for God only, shee for God in him" (4.299); "Out of my sight, thou Serpent, . . . / . . . false / And hateful" (10.867–69); "O fairest of Creation, last and best / Of all Gods works" (9.896–97). Whose sentiments did Milton (and thus are we to) privilege: those of the narrator installed in the fallen consciousness of Satan and reporting what "the Fiend / Saw" (4.285–86)? those of fallen Adam or of Adam in a still unfallen state? Or should we privilege no character, no state of consciousness, no interpretation? *Paradise Regain'd* derives from similarly conflicting accounts of Jesus tried in the wilderness; and these competing accounts, again by Milton's time, had given rise to different hermeneutics: one reading the story literally, the other figuratively; the one interpreting this tale as a drama of knowledge and the other as a visionary experience, unfolding a drama of expanding consciousness?

Samson Agonistes is a still more exaggerated example of a poem founded upon conflicted and conflicting texts and producing rival interpretations from them. As the first task of a new *Samson* criticism, then, we need to re-view the Samson story under the general hermeneutical hypothesis articulated by Frank Kermode:

> The story survives, but its original interpretative freight may at any time be unloaded into oblivion. The tradition preserves some interpretations, loses others, and acquires new ones instead. We are always having to explain not the story, but why it counts. Of course one reason is that it has always been the vehicle of urgent but mortal interpretation.[12]

This is only to say that different interpretations, at different times, get attached to the Samson story: they are evidence of the hermeneutical potentiality of the tale. Then, one interpretation gets privileged over another: there is a superimposition of orthodoxy and a consequent stalling of interpretation. The seventeenth century, through the increasing rigor of its inter-rogations, restores hermeneutical potentiality to the Samson story; and *Samson Agonistes*, in its turn, is a representation of that potentiality and a crediting of recovered interpretations, as well as newly emergent ones. This chapter, and the two immediately succeeding it, are concerned chiefly with esta-blishing the hermeneutical potentiality of the Samson story. Two final chapters will examine the extent to which these conflicting — and conflicted — interpretations resonate within Milton's poem.

Start with the modern-day Samson as he is figured in Protes-tant exegesis on Hebrews; then scan backward. Here are three representative portraits:

> 1. We have no idea why the author chose these examples which are not really in keeping with his idea of faith.
> 2. Gideon, Barak, Samson, Jephthah — . . . They were not men of special virtue. *Gideon* was hesitant and timid. *Barak* had to be shamed into action. *Jephthah* is known chiefly for his rash oath. And *Samson* was a physical giant with the weakness of mind and conscience that such men often embody. . . . If the phrase *through faith* is in keeping with the usage in other parts of this chapter, it can mean only that these heroes were relying on the promises of God, that they "did not receive what was promised" (vs. 39). . . .
> 3. Samson can hardly be credited even with patriotism; his exploits were those of the individualist, and his value to his own nation as a champion against the Philistines was negligible.[13]

Nor is there any notable discrepancy between the essentially negative portrait of Samson here and that etched by modern-day commentators on the Book of Judges.[14] If such discrepan-cies exist (and they do), they belong to an earlier era of biblical interpretation.

The Janus-faced Samson remains in place as late as 1880:

> The enrolment of his name by an apostolic pen (Heb. xi, 32) in the list of the ancient worthies . . . warrants us, undoubtedly, in a favorable estimate of his character on the whole, while at the same time the fidelity of the inspired narrative has perpetuated the record of infirmities which must forever mar the lustre of his noble deeds.[15]

And it is made evident by John M'Clintock and James Strong that this divided image, by no means the invention of their own time, reaches back into the eighteenth century. They then trace the view that, whatever arguments "may palliate," none can "excuse the moral delinquencies into which . . . [Samson] was betrayed, and of which a just Providence exacted so tremendous a penalty in the circumstances of his degradation and death" to Jesaias Friedrich Weissenborn (1705) and Daniel Maichel (1739).[16]

Furthermore, M'Clintock and Strong also document their supposition that "this wilful and rough hero of the olden times, judged by the moral law, is unworthy of comparison with Christ" with references to August Hermann Niemeyer (1775) and Mr. Hauke (1740), even as they acknowledge that the "Wolfenbüttel Fragments (according to the specimens in Bayle and others) would simply degrade Samson."[17] Doubtless, there were times when not too scrupulous views were accorded the Samson story in either its Old or New Testament representations; when, therefore, through typological fiat Samson could be counted among the elect, the chosen, the saints, who "won glory by their faith"; when there seemed no cause for explaining, much less defending, this Hebrews listing of sainted military heroes.[18] These were times when Samson, the last and certainly not the worthiest of the judges, was, nevertheless, "the greatest hero of the period and, except Goliath," Louis Ginzberg reports, "the greatest hero of all times."[19] But even before the nineteenth century, the cords of this positive interpretation become frayed and are loosened: the typologies spun around the Hebrews text come under scrutiny and, with them, the unexamined adulation by which Samson had been vaulted into a pantheon of heroes.

The times of adulation had not completely passed in the eighteenth century. Witness James Peirce who concludes, "surely *Samson* cannot be blamed," although what seems more remarkable is Peirce's insistence that "It is . . . necessary here to consider *Samson's moral* character, since the apostle reckons him to be one of those who have *obtain'd salvation*, whereas some can hardly think, he was at the last qualified to be made partaker of it," and it must be "own'd, that he had very great defects and blemishes." Clearly Peirce recognizes that Samson is now a much disputed character even if he himself would silence such dispute with the argument that "it cannot be proved, that he did not repent of . . . [his sins] before his death."[20] Nor, as others argued by way of advancing the contrary thesis, could it be proved that Samson *did* repent.

What seems clear from Peirce's defensive observations is that the eighteenth century inherited a fully problematized Samson story, the product of competing traditions of interpretation, and that any representation of this story entailed a tabulation of those problems: "whether Delilah was a woman of Israel or one of the daughters of the Philistines . . .; or whether she was . . . [Samson's] wife, or a harlot only"; "whether Samson's hair was the physical or only moral cause of strength"; and "whether Samson ought to have died in this manner, with a spirit of revenge and self murder"? Such questions may have been focused, even fostered by "casuists and divines" of the seventeenth century; but they also have venerable tradition behind them: St. Augustine excuses Samson, St. Bernard censures him; and still "others maintain, that without having recourse to this supernatural motive," Samson's actions "might be vindicated from his office, as being the judge and defender of Israel." It is remarkable, given the attention this scholiast gives to what is "expressed in

Scripture," and a just measure of the power of nonscriptural to overrule scriptural traditions, that he should then inform us of Delilah: "she cut off his hair."[21] The Book of Judges says otherwise.

Interrogation of the Samson story is well underway in the last decades of the seventeenth century — "*What are we to think of the salvation of* Cain, Eli, Sampson, Uzzah . . .?" — in the writings of Mary Astell and John Dunton, where the interrogation is wrapped in a polemic of faith, and in the writings of Andrew Marvell and William Walsh where, unencumbered by such a polemic, the interrogation is plausibly engendered by the scrutiny Milton gives this story in *Samson Agonistes*.[22] It remains a crucial question whether *Samson Agonistes* is simply a redaction of the Samson tradition as delineated by F. Michael Krouse — or whether it is a point of convergence for separate, contending traditions, thus making of Milton's poem a mental theater, trafficking in multiple traditions and containing several texts in one. Krouse's Samson tradition survives into the seventeenth century in writings (among others) of Simon Westall, Joseph Hall, Thomas Taylor, Thomas Lushington, Paul Knell, Thomas Wilson, and Henry Hammond where the Samson of Hebrews, quelling violence and exhibiting righteousness, is a saint properly numbered in "the *Catalogue* of the *faithful*," because "the effects of *faith* [are not] wanting in him," and where, acting by a warrant from God, he is a divine avenger, a type of Christ, one of the worthies.[23] But this is also the Samson tradition that others — sometimes unwittingly but more often deliberately, deftly — were putting under review.

More typically, the Samson of the Hebrews text is approached with a guarded questioning such as David Pareus displays when he says, though not with specific reference to Samson, that "the failings of the Saints . . . must not too peevishly be canvased . . .; but prudently, according to the rule of Charity"; that they "are to be deplored, rather then censured."[24]

Indisputably, the hesitations and misgivings of the Hebrews commentators — their interrogations — are *sometimes* wrapped in a polemic of faith or, as here, in an appeal for charity. But since the interrogation has usually been an ellipsis in reporting the Samson tradition as it evolves from the Hebrews text, the interrogation is what matters now. But let me emphasize: an interrogation is not an inquisition, nor is it necessarily a repudiation; it is rather a way of registering reticences, uncertainties, hesitations, and misgivings; and misgivings, let me further emphasize, are not doubts, but inclinations toward doubting.

Often the nature and extent of an interrogation has something to do with a writer's theology — the fear, in the case of Pareus, that to question the saints too mercilessly may exclude one from being numbered among them; or the belief, again to instance Pareus, that there is no reprobation, only election; or the ethic affirmed by Hugo Grotius that *"Charity* teaches us not to judge any one rashly to be a *Reprobate."*[25] Take as an example William Gouge (1655), a Samson enthusiast, who records no less than twenty ways in which this hero is like Christ. Despite Samson's "strange dotage on strange flesh," despite the fact that his "scandalous crimes" do not "pass unpunished," that he manifests an "impure, disobedient and rebellious disposition against God," Samson is regarded as one of God's dearest children, a great man, a sun among the stars of his people, "more excellent than any of them," whose last act was his "greatest, and best" with Samson, by "special warrant," playing God's avenger and dying "as a type of Christ."[26] It is true that as here, or for that matter as in Samuel Bird (1598),[27] a polemic of faith can silence the interrogation; but it is also true that, as in the cases of William Perkins (1608) and David Dickson (1635), the interrogation can survive — and stand apart from, even when it is overruled by — such a polemic.

Perkins employs a question/answer format, which suggests

that there are questions to be asked of Samson, answers to which are then forthcoming: "Now touching *Samson*, this question may well bee asked, How he can be iustly commended for his Faith, seeing it may seeme hee killed himselfe"? The question is silenced by the declaration that, in fact, "*Samson* did not kill himselfe" but rather responded to his calling by "taking just reuenge vpon his enemies, and the enemies of God." Indeed, Perkins here anticipates what will be said of Samson in the early years of the Puritan Revolution by John Lilburne, for example, and accounts for why Samson will figure as poster-boy for the New Model Army:

> hee prayed first vnto God: and so did no more then the Souldier in the field ought to doe; who, bearing a louing minde towards his Countrey, is content to aduenture his owne life for the destruction of his enemies.[28]

Thus "Gods champion," Samson evidences "great zeale for Gods glory, and . . . singuler loue to his people."[29] Yet, from another point of view, when it is remembered that the law of Moses allows for the killing of Jewish people if they forsake God and his laws, thereby leading others into idolatry, in the end Samson is an example of what Grotius will call "the *Judgment of Zeal*."[30]

Perkins leaves no doubt that Samson holds his place in "this Catalogue of most worthy beleevers": "*Gedeon, Barac, Samson,* and *Jephte.*" But he also concedes that at just the point on the list where Samson's name appears the list becomes problematical, in part because of the disruption of chronological sequence — Samson judges after Jephthah but is named before him. *Confusing chronology* — "This the holy Ghost would neuer doe, without some speciall cause," says Perkins, who thereupon alerts us that an "order of *dignitie*" operates here: "the most worthie and excellent is named first" with Samson taking precedence over Jephthah because of "this grace of Faith" but others like Gideon who is named first taking precedence over him.[31] We do not doubt that Samson is called but, despite (or perhaps because of) Perkins's insinuations, may continue to wonder whether he is really chosen. Here Samson is a hero of faith, responding to his calling; but elsewhere in Perkins he is one who "went out of his calling, by breaking the vowe of a Nazarite" and the "commandment, that hee should be a Nazarite to the end" with Samson, on at least one occasion, figuring those who, betraying secrets, overthrow themselves.[32] In balance, however, Perkins's representations of Samson and uses of his story are highly favorable; and Perkins makes it clear that, while others may think differently about Samson, he would silence their questioning, in part by insisting that God's calling remains sure and so requires no repentance and in part by countering the tendency (encouraged by commentators on Genesis 49 and Revelation 7) to align Samson through Dan with idolatry.[33]

When Perkins asserts that "Idolatrie, and Adulterie, . . . are ioyned together" and then continues, "Adulterie is the punishment of Idolatrie; and Idolatrie the punishment of Adulterie. Spirituall Adulterie is punished with bodily adulterie," it is easy to think of Samson's tribe and even of Samson himself. But Perkins does not name Samson. Why he does not, why he finally disallows this line of questioning, is indicated in a reflection on David who "sometimes prayes for the finall destruction of his enemies":

> . . . but this is not giuen ordinarily, no not to gods ministers. The iudgement of charity is that which binds a man to iudge the best of another: and herein be two degrees. First, touching the vnregenerate, charitie binds vs, not to despaire of such as yet liue profanely; but to hope that God will in good time call them. And touching the regenerate, . . . charitie binds vs to be persuaded without doubt that they be the children of God.[34]

Very simply, Samson is of the class called the elect, so Perkins must silence his own questioning, in one instance as we will see in chapter 4 by turning a piece of negative Samson typology back into a complimentary cliché. He must also silence others' questionings. The inflection upon interrogation, so light in Perkins that he does not here get caught up in the controversy over the perseverance of the saints, is registered more strongly by Dickson, yet eventually disowned by both men.

This is Dickson's comment whole:

> [*The diversitie of those that are heere recorded, TEACHETH VS,* That albeit there bee difference of Believers;] some stronger, as DAVID, some weaker, as the rest; some base Bastardes, as IEPHTHAH; some of better sorte; some of them notable in holinesse, and conversation; some of them taynted with notorious falles in their lyfe; [Yet are they enrolled by GOD, in a Catalogue of Honour, amongst His Sayncts.][35]

I have bracketed the polemic in order to sequester the interrogation, which, admittedly, Dickson sandbags, perhaps because he knows so well that some interrogations can have the force of repudiation and denial,[36] while others merely register hesitations and misgivings.

Still, it should be clear that Dickson would number Samson with the weaker sort whose lives are tainted with notorious falls. In fact, if we are to judge by his annotation for Hebrews 11.33 where, once having listed representatives of the faithful, St. Paul is said to "reckoneth . . . [their] works" though he "suppresseth" their names, Samson is among those who stop the mouths of lions and wax valiant in fight.[37] The heroizing of Samson (in Hebrews) for his encounter with the lion (in Judges) required some whitewashing of the latter text such as we find in a sermon by John Bramhall: "When Sampson, without any weapon in his hand, set upon a lion as though it had been a kid, the reason is intimated . . . for the safeguard of his 'father and his mother.'"[38] Samson's parents, in turn, emblematize his tribe, his people who are under his protection.

Such whitewashings allowed Dickson and others to do no more than register certain reticences. For whatever reasons (they are not explained), Dickson's interrogation is dropped from a different and later version of this commentary, where he is nonetheless emphatic: the ultimate test of these heroes of faith, the chief evidence both for their approval and justification by God, is that they are themselves "preserved from the destroying Angel."[39] Dickson may evade addressing this issue in terms of the Samson story but also must have known that others were addressing that issue and had already observed that Samson is singular among these heroes in *not* avoiding that angel — that Samson is avenged in the very act of avenging.

Indeed, in this later version of the commentary (1659), Dickson does a turnabout. In place of the interrogation is this comment: "to question . . . is impious, when the Holy Ghost is the Author . . . so that there remains no place for doubting, or curious enquiring from what History hee fetched those things, seeing wee know this very Narration to bee beyond all exception." But then comes another turnabout; for in the same year, in yet another commentary on Hebrews, this demurral is deleted and the earlier interrogation restored, now with the assurance that "All these [mentioned in Hebrews 11.32–38] died in the Faith of Christ, and were justified."[40] Dickson's intention, all along, has been to correct faults and mistakes in earlier representations of his sermons, using the occasion to crystallize points of doctrine. And his preoccupation with Hebrews obviously derives from his own (and others') opinion that this is one of the truly hard parts in Scriptures. Even if we conclude that Dickson's polemic has simply subdued his interrogation, both may still stand as reminders that, one, Dickson would silence the questioning which he himself may have helped to foster and which, at any rate, is still going on in other quarters; and that, two, there are devices of containment, which, historically, have facilitated appropriations of the Samson story. The Judges narrative is an early — and obvious — attempt to contain, even under pressure, what is marginal, even explosive, in a civilization. The Hebrews verses are another such attempt, as is Dickson's comment on them.

That the interrogation matters to Dickson (or once mattered), and why it matters, is best evidenced in another treatise where the question is asked: "do not the *Puritans*, (I do not mean the *old Non-conformists*) *Antinomians, Anabaptists*, and many *Quakers* . . . err, who maintain, *That all the saints of* GOD *are free from every spot, and blemish of sin?*" The answer is "Yes," with Dickson thereupon explaining that "the best of saints" have a hamartia: "We see it from the grievous falls of the most eminent Saints, as *Noah, Lot, Abraham, Jacob, David, Solomon, Asa, Jehospaphat*, and the disciples of Christ."[41] At least here Samson is not numbered among *the best of saints*, or *most eminent* of them, which is not to say that Samson, for Dickson, is excluded from the faithful, the elect, the predestined, *who are the only men called*, although Dickson obviously remembers that Samson is a Danite and that his is a tribe of idolaters.[42] Dickson simply straddles the fence on the question of whether or not the anointed saints manage to persevere in their sainthood.

Dickson, along with Perkins, is no more than a starting point in such a discussion, here anchored in the seventeenth century. They are early but by no means stern interrogators of the Hebrews Samson. It is finally the entire sequence of interrogations that matters; and the sequence reaches backward from Perkins to Martin Luther, John Calvin, and Richard Hooker — and forward from Dickson to John Trapp, Hugo Grotius, Thomas Goodwin, John Lightfoot, John Goodwin, William Twisse, and apparently John Milton. After Dickson, the sandbagging polemic diminishes, then disappears, as if to remind us that hermeneutic potentiality is restored to the Samson story by the gradual erosion of the reigning structure of interpretation, not by a ball and crane knocking down of its walls, and by here questioning and there challenging external authorities as does Thomas Ager: "To believe as the Church believes is not the rule to understand the Scriptures by, for the Church may erre, and when she erreth . . ., her interpretation

is private, and not to be received."[43] *Gradually*, orthodox interpretation becomes muddled by emerging interpretations that
are incompatible, incongruent with it. In this history, *Samson
Agonistes* is a crucial text, enabling us to lay down the old
question of the Bible's influence on Milton and to take up the
new — and equally interesting — one of Milton's influence
on the Bible. Not only Milton's epics but this tragedy are
involved in the charting of new hermeneutics, with Milton's
indebtedness traceable to no one, not even political allies
always, but evident in a highly imaginative (yet sometimes
quirky) eclecticism.

Dickson's polemical wrapping is still there in Trapp's commentary (1647), although in abbreviated form:

> Here the names only of sundry Worthies of old time *per praete-
> ritionem conglobantur*, are artificially wound up together, for
> brevity sake. All these were not alike eminent, and some of
> them such, as, but that we finde them here enrolled, we should
> scarce have taken them for honest men; yet by faith, & c., Christ
> carries all his of what size or sort soever, to the haven of heaven:
> as a ship does all the passengers that are therein to the desired
> shore.[44]

Trapp's concluding simile resonates powerfully with *Samson
Agonistes*, underlining its typology of differences with Christ
(as a ship) saving and Samson (as a ship) wrecking.

Later, Trapp will focus on the figure of Samson himself:

> *Sampson* fell so farre, and (twenty years after he loved the
> *Philistim*-woman, . . . when certainly he had repented of that
> sinne) he returned to *Gaza*, and went in to a harlot, that we
> should hardly take him for a godly man, did we not finde his
> name in the list of those Worthies, *Heb.* 11. But, like a tame
> Hawke, though he flew farre, yet he came to hand again. So
> will all that belong to God: recover they shall of their relapses,
> though with difficulty, yet *sometimes* with advantage. . . .[45]

Earlier Trapp had remarked: they do evil "by meditating
revenge"; thus, those ruled by the "devil of anger," must "pray
it down." Later he says: "Some good souls have so farre

declined, as *Solomon, Samson, Asa,* others, that it might be said of them . . . *He is dead, some evil beasts hath devoured him.*"[46] Even if it may be said that "Gods Spirit in his servants is heroick," as in the instance of Samson, let us say, such an observation should not prevent us, as it did not prevent earlier interpreters, from "a more diligent search, *a more diligent enquiry*" (my italics). Trapp may be impressed by Samson's breaking the cords, then saddened by the Philistines who, putting out his eyes took from him "the *key of knowledge*"; yet he also recognizes that, if Samson is not one of those "silly soules," after succumbing to Delilah, this hero's shame was that he became an ordinary man.[47] Moreover, if in the tradition Trapp represents, Hercules, as well as Nisus, is a deformation of Samson, Milton implies otherwise, thus turning such a tradition on end.

Like Dickson before him, Trapp will remember with a typical collocation of scriptural texts (Genesis, Judges, Revelation) that "*Dan* [is] cut out of the roll [Rev. 7.7] for his shamefull recidivation, and revolt from the true religion, *Judg.* 18. This, *Jacob* fore-saw and bewailed." And Trapp will say this in full knowledge of what had been said by the Jewish Kabbalah, Rabbines, and Onkelos. Still, Trapp regarded the fable of Antichrist coming from the tribe of Dan as a "thin . . . devise," though he also knew that, while the other tribes constituted the elect, Dan was Samson's tribe, the tribe of idolatry, and knew too that by others Jacob's prophecy concerning Dan was often construed (see John Diodati, for example) as a fearful prophecy relating generally to the entire tribe of Dan and specifically to Samson.[48]

This is Jacob's prophecy as it appears in the penultimate chapter of Genesis:

> Dan shall judge his people, as one of the tribes of Israel.
> Dan shall be a serpent by the way, an adder in the path, that
>   biteth the horse heels, so that his rider shall fall backward.
> I have waited for thy salvation, O Lord. (49.16–18)

According to Diodati, one of Trapp's usual sources, this prophecy refers either to the whole tribe or to "Sampson, the Danite, who judged." Its serpent imagery, especially the adder (or sometimes viper) in the path, suggests that the tribe or person proceeds "more by deceits, than by open strength"; and the prophecy concludes with a Jacob who, remembering Dan and reproaching him, "trembleth with horror, and rageth, fore-seeing that in that Tribe should be created the generall idolatrie . . . from whence should grow their ruine."[49]

Jacob foresees the defection of Dan and this tribe's subsequent miseries, according to Trapp, who knows "that *Justice, justice* . . . is, pure justice, without mud, run down as a mighty torrent" and who says of Dan's adder that "He shall subtily set upon his enemies, and suddenly surprize them . . . as *Sampson* . . . did the *Philistims.*" At other times, though, Trapp seems to attach different significances to Samson as the serpent and adder in Genesis. Here the association is positive, with the serpent image figuring "the parts and points of an excellent warrior," and there it is negative with the same serpent and adder being remembered for the "methods or way-layings" by which it "biteth the heels of passengers, and thereby transfuseth his venome to the head and heart."[50] Commenting on *turning away* and *turning aside* in the second chapter of Amos, a prophecy that had been interpreted as referring to the Samson story, Diodati explicates thus: "A terme taken from serpents; as Gen. 49.17. *Turne aside*] by their windings, like to the Serpents; doe overthrow good mens Rights, who are stiled in the Scripture, men humble, and meeke";[51] and in his general remarks upon the same idiom, John Goodwin will contend that *turning aside* refers to God's children embracing Satan and "that by means of their turning aside," in a "*total defection*" or "a total Declining in the Saints," to their becoming "*Slaves of Satan.*"[52] Or as Trapp says elsewhere: "Gods people tread so hard upon the Devills head, that he cannot but turne againe, bite them by the heeles, with *Dans* adder in the path."[53]

Whatever else they remembered (and said) about Samson, these and other seventeenth century commentators had to confront "Samson of kicking Dans Tribe," if not in their meditations on Hebrews, certainly in their reflections on Genesis 49 and Revelation 7. And even if they subscribe to elements in the usual Samson typology, as does Henoch Clapham whose phrase I have just quoted, they still remember, along with Clapham, that Judges is a book of miscreation and degeneration: creatures depart from their creator, and the creator withdraws from creation; sin yields to death and deathful deeds with Judges thus producing an image of "the whole World upside down."[54]

There seem to have been two approaches taken by the commentators. One is represented by the Anglican divine Henry Hammond who sees in Hebrews 11.32 the greatest champions of God's people, fighting battles, winning conquests, and "by faith liv[ing] godly and righteous lives," yet who recognizes as well that Dan is omitted from the catalogue of twelve tribes in Revelation because this tribe "was either destroyed or brought very low."[55] Nevertheless, Hammond avoids linking Hebrews and Revelation and thus evades the implications that reading Samson as Dan (in the Book of Revelation) might have for an interpretation of the Hebrews text. On the other hand, he speaks cautiously (albeit catechistically) when he encounters the climactic scene in the Judges narrative and then addresses its crucial issue. The question, *"What is to be said of* Sampson, *who killed so many by pulling away the pillars, and involved himself in the same destruction,"* elicits this answer:

> He was a judge in Israel; and such those days (and particularly him) did God ordinarily move by his Spirit to do some extraordinary things: and it is to be imagined, that God encited him to do this; or if he did not, he were not to be excused in it.[56]

This answer prompts a further question — *"What is to be said of those that . . . did kill themselves, and remain still upon record for* Martyrs"? — a question eliciting this additional response:

> If the same could be affirmed of them which was conceived of *Sampson*, that God incited them to do this, they should by this be justified also: but having under the Gospel no authority to justifie such pretence of divine incitation, it will be safest to affirm, that this was a fault in them. . . .[57]

The New Testament disallows what, in the case of the Samson story, the Hebrew Bible permits, with Milton, in his turn, rendering the question of Samson's suicide moot in an "Argument" contending that Samson perished "by accident" (*CP*, 575), and in the poem proper where the Chorus describes Samson as "self-kill'd / Not willingly, but tangl'd in the fold" (1664–65).

A second — increasingly more common — approach is represented by Trapp who reveals what those like Hammond evade, allowing Samson as Dan in Genesis and especially Revelation to produce an interrogation of the Samson in the Hebrews catalogue.[58] Trapp seems acutely sensitive to the fact that Hebrews and Revelation are competing texts in the New Testament, each implying a different judgment of Samson. The former text is an emblazoning of "Christs worthy warriours, who by faith, (and yet by force of arms too) . . . *fought the Lords battles"*; the latter, on the other hand, while it implies that those not rejected from the list, however afflicted, "are counted blessed" and thus numbered with the elect and redeemed, implies equally a censure of the entire tribe of Dan, including (if not in Trapp's reckoning, certainly in that of others) Samson himself.[59]

Blame, of course, never falls simply on Samson. The purpose of seeing Samson in Dan, and vice versa, is to implicate each in the fall of the other; and the importance of Amos 2 (a prophecy sometimes referred to the Samson story)[60] is that it implicates the Danites in the fall of Samson, even sometimes blames them for it. As Trapp remarks of Amos 2.12, "they corrupted his young *Nazarites* . . . and silenced his *Prophets*, or enjoyned them at least to meddle with *toothlesse truths* only, to preach *placentia*. . . . This God heavily here complaines of, as an horrible Ingratitude. To render good for evill, is divine, good for good is humane; evill for evill is brutish, but evill for good is divelish."[61] On such a scale of judgment, Samson is not devilish, but he *is* brutish.

Trapp may never let go of a polemical wrapping, using the Samson story repeatedly as illustration for the propositions that "whom the Lord loveth, he chasteneth," and that his chastisements exist in order to move us toward repentance. Yet allowing for the larger polemic, we find within it a Samson story being used now positively, now negatively: Samson is both afflicted and an affliction. "God afflicts his own deare servants," like Samson, in order to stop them from being "foolish, and froward . . . wilde and wicked. . . . How far," asks Trapp, "would not *Sampson* have run, being once out, if God had not stopt him with the crosse?" Samson's sins are the father of the cross he was made to bear; and while that cross is lighter for lesser offenders, for others God can load on punishments, "not temporall onely . . . but spirituall also . . . punishing one Sinne with another," as he indubitably did with Samson, "deliuering . . . [him] up to *Spirituall wickednesses*, to be lasht and buffetted," until he repented and returned at the end. We learne from Samson, no less than from his people, of the power of prayer; for "up goe their hands and hearts and all, when they suffer'd for their Sinne."[62]

If afflicted himself, Samson is also, like Dan's adder in the path, *our* affliction, one of our injurers, who, as we wrestle through a life of spiritual warfare, are continually biting at our heels and laming us. Only fools think they can escape such afflictions and so tread upon God's cross or, as did Samson, "runne away with it." To forsake the Lord is to be forsaken by him; and when God leaves, the evil spirit comes in as "we may see in *Sampson, Joash, Asa,* and others": we are then betrayed into "the hands of the Devill, as *Dalilah* did *Sampson* into the hands of the Philistines," thus risking death "Temporall, Spirituall, and Eternall."[63] Trapp is unrelenting yet delicate in his interrogation, whatever the polemic he is prosecuting, and acutely conscious, it seems, that Samson's story is as much a riddle as Samson's own riddles — and still too bound to the letter by Philistian interpreters.

What proves liberating for the Samson story in the seventeenth century is practices (such as Trapp displays) of free and open questioning, of diligent inquiry. The extent of his inquiry is amply illustrated by the running judgments Trapp imposes upon the Samson story in his annotations to the Book of Judges. One of the "Ill guides" in Scripture ("How much better *David*"), "Sampson cannot be altogether excused" for his licentiousness or for his marriage choices in which "one can err but once." Nor can Samson be excused for not heeding the counsel of his parents, for his "mulierosity" or "uxoriousness," for his "presuming upon his strength, and therefore [being] justly deserted and foiled," for being "besotted" by whoredom, or for being a commander who by woman is commanded. Trapp may move for final acquittal of Samson, but not before diminishing Samson as a deliverer (he begins what David perfects and Christ completes) and later, showing Samson as "he meditateth revenge, which is the next effect of anger" and then analogizing him with the reprobate who, as "the vassals of Antichrist," bring the house upon their own heads.[64]

Within a single volume, Trapp arrays various interpretive possibilities: that bound down by Delilah to "fleshly pleasure," Samson eventually "divorce[s] the flesh from the world" so that the devil cannot hurt him; that this greatest of martialists is himself finally conquered and commanded; that this "*young Saint*" is at the end of his life "*an* old *Angel*" or that having once gone "crooked," try as he may, he can "never be set streight again"; that in the end he responds to God's "*summons for sleepers"* and is finally cured of his lusts but also, engaging in "a dangerous peice of businesse," is "crusht in the ruin."[65] Trapp thought that Samson's story is a tragedy out of which his admirers would make a comedy and his enemies a farce, yet seems to have thought, as well, that any interpretation of the story altogether canceling its tragedy is an enemy of truth. Milton goes a step further, canceling the comedic from his own version of the story as an all-consuming tragedy.

What is particularly telling about the status of the Samson story in the seventeenth century, when we review its different representations in the writings of Perkins, Dickson, and Trapp, is the amount of erasure in biblical commentary itself — not the instability of the biblical texts but rather the instability of the commentary surrounding them. Here are some of those erasures: in Perkins, a piece of negative typology is displaced by a typology of similitude; in Dickson, the invitation to questioning the Samson story is withdrawn with the insistence that such questioning should be halted; and in the case of Trapp, the commentary is revised, curiously, so that Samson can be analogized with the reprobate. If there are erasures in, there are likewise (as here) intrusions upon biblical comment- ary, suggesting a measure of discomfort with the Samson story and consequent dis-ease in interpreting it. It is this unsettling of normative interpretation that liberates the Samson story for the interrogations we find in Grotius's writings and later in Milton's tragedy.

An extraordinary instance of intruding the Samson story as both an afterthought and an elucidation occurs, this time, not in biblical commentary but in the third edition of a treatise on international law, *De Jure Belli Ac Pacis* (1631).[66] No sooner does Grotius publish his monumental work for the first time (1625) than he begins revising and expanding it. In July, 1628, he writes to his brother: "My books concerning the Law of War and Peace have been revised by me in many places" and, later the same year, refers to his "not inconsiderable additions."[67]

It is this enlarged edition, first published in 1631, to which Grotius later refers in his effort to explain and supplement his scriptural annotations. Thus, his interpretation of Judges 15.3 ("And Samson said to them, 'This time I shall be blameless in regard to the Philistines, when I do them mischief'") contains the citation: "Vide . . . de Iure Belli ac Pacis, libro II. cap. XX. [sect.] 8." In the Latin Vulgate, the concluding phrase in Judges 15.3 reads, "for I shall do you evils."[68]

Regarded as the crucial chapter in this treatise, "the climax and essence of Grotian doctrine,"[69] chapter 20, with its eventual citation of the Samson story in section 8, details as well as deepens, reviews but also revises, earlier references to the Hebrews Samson as an illustration that the *"battails of God . . .* [are] pious and just" and previous citation of those Hebrew commentators who invoke "*Samson*'s example," on the one hand, to argue for the legitimacy of killing oneself "as an honorable *exit*" and, on the other hand, to insist upon the legitimacy of the Philistines having Samson "deliver[ed] up . . . to them as an Evil-doer." What makes Samson's case different from that of Ehud, to take but one example, is that Scripture "plainly witnesseth [of Ehud], He was raised by God himself, and sent as an Avenger, to wit, by special command."[70] When it comes to Samson's case, Scripture equivocates as Grotius eventually will do in his revised version of chapter 20.

In Judges 15.3, Grotius argues, Samson makes his case against the Philistines, declares his innocence as it were, by citing his "*Natural Right*" to injure those who "first injured him" and, once doing so, "justifies himself with the same Reason, saying, *As they have done to me, so have I done to them.*" Grotius then cites a host of commentators from Plutarch to Thucydides, to Demosthenes, to Sallust, to Aristides, to St. Ambrose as authorities for taking revenge, deploying violence, and expatiating blood with blood. But precisely because "we are apt to be *Partial* in our own Cases, and to be hurried on too far by Passion," judges were appointed, which leads Grotius, citing Quintilian, to question *"Private Revenge . . .* [as] *an Enemy to Peace. . . . Hence sprung the sacred Reverence of Laws, that no Man might revenge himself by his own Hand."*[71] Milton, of course, lets the issue of private slide into that of public revenge.

Yet Grotius's larger point is that things permitted by natural or civil law may be *"forbidden* by the *Divine* Law, that being the most *perfect* of all Laws."* Hatred of one's neighbors is wrong; and even when they are enemies, some good should be shown them. By the rule of the Gospel, which is also the rule of charity, "An Eye for an Eye . . . is the Justice of the Unjust." Indeed, it is a philosophy overruled and negated by the Gospel, which is "to be understood as much more strictly prohibiting *Revenge;* because it quite abrogates the *old Indulgence* as only suitable to the time of a more imperfect Dispensation: *not that a just Revenge is evil, but that patience is much better."* Samson is not evil by such a system of accounting, his acts may even be a strange amalgamation of private and public motives; yet he does represent a scheme of values superseded by Jesus who, *"eradicat*[ing] Revenge," commands patience and teaches forgiveness,[72] the first a virtue Samson never displays, and the second one that he mocks in Milton's poem (759–65).

When Grotius concludes his annotations for the Samson story with another citation of his great treatise on international law, it is in part to make the point that the Hebrews are not, *that Samson is not,* sufficiently educated in patience to prac- tice forgiveness; that to live according to the laws of nature is, finally, the condition of nonbelievers. "Hebraei autem non tantas edocti patientiae leges, quantas Christiani" ("However the Hebrews, not having such great laws of patience as the Christians"), Grotius writes, thereupon referring to his own *De Juri Belli Ac Pacis,* where he explains, in language applic- able to both the Philistines and the Hebrews, that the people are the body; that their spirit animates and gives being to their political life. Yet when such union is lost, they act out of hatred, are destroyed by slaughters and, as a people, become utterly extinct. Then the body is destroyed. The spirit is gone.[73] It is no small irony and probably no mere coincidence that Samson quotes a phrase from the subtitle of Grotius's treatise ("jus naturae & gentium" — "the law of nature and nations") as he speaks of Dalila and the Philistines as violating "the law of nature, law of nations" (890) that, in Grotius's accounting, Samson himself seems to violate.

When Scripture is not read by Scripture, we are apt to find competing senses, conflicting interpretations sitting side by side as in Lancelot Andrewes, let us say, or as in the early writings of John Trapp. But when Scripture is read by Scripture, unreconciled senses, contending interpretations, are often swallowed up in interpretive acts of mediation and reconciliation such as we sometimes find in Grotius and later Milton. Once established in alliance with a specific text, each hermeneutic can be transferred to, then tested against, another text through this habit of reading Scriptures by Scriptures, according to the principle enunciated by Milton in *De Doctrina* that "God . . . [is] his own best interpreter" (*YP*, 6.363). What is also telling is the tendency at mid-century and after to impose increasingly negative constructions upon the Samson story as the character of Samson himself comes to seem increasingly ambiguous. Interrogations of Samson, which once seemed to exist only to frustrate such interrogation by exonerating Samson, now are deployed, at least some of the time, in such a way as to foster questioning. The polemic of faith that once subdued questioning in some instances drops away only to be replaced by another kind of polemic that, if often lurking around the Samson story, is now spun around such stories with which Samson's is a piece.

That there are two distinguishable elements in seventeenth century commentary on Hebrews, an interrogation and a polemic, *and* that those elements were being consciously deployed, is suggested by the fact that, in his observations on

Hebrews 11.32, Trapp (1647) wraps a polemic of faith around the interrogation of Thomas Goodwin (1643) from whose observations the polemic has virtually disappeared:

> We find Samson, a godly man, (whom yet we would scarce have thought such, but that we find his name in the list of those worthies, Heb. xi.,) ensnared with a Philistine woman, against the counsel of his parents, Judg. xiv. 3, who clearly laid open his sin to him. And he was in the event reproved for his folly, for his wife deceived him, told his riddle to his enemies; which he in the end perceived. And further to reprove him, in the issue she was given away to another, ver. 16, 17, 20. From all which passages of reproof, a holy man, that had his eyes in his head, could not but see his error. And yet again, a long while after this, (twenty years after, Judg. xv. 20,) when certainly ere that he had repented of this his sin, for which his parents before, and after God, so clearly did rebuke him, he went to Gaza, Judg. xvi. 1, "and saw a harlot, and went in to her," and there escaped narrowly with his life at midnight: and, ver. 4, after that also it came to pass he fell in love with another, as bad as any of the former, Delilah, who was his ruin. But his returning thus to folly cost him dear, for in the end he was taken as a captive to the Philistines, his enemies, and that through her false-hood; deprived of his strength he had spent upon these women; had his eyes, those betraying lights, put out, that had ensnared him; and himself made a fool of, to make his enemies sport. So as no child of God can take any great encouragement thus to return to folly for the future by his example; though comfort they may have therefrom in case they have returned for the time past.[74]

Goodwin is evasive here: does Samson simply backslide into the defeat at the pillars; or is he one from whom we can draw comfort because, after prayer, the spirit again moves him to pull "the pillars of that playhouse of the Philistines"?[75] Goodwin seems to be of two minds; for while he once talks about Samson (with specific reference to Hebrews) in the latter way, he also cites Manoah rather than Samson as an illustration for the proposition that even when prayers are heard one should return to, then perform, one's vows.

Elsewhere Goodwin finds figured in Samson, though a good man, unmortified lusts, and calls him a type of Christ in just those areas where the Samson typology will eventually crumble: as warrior and Nazarite, as judge, magistrate, and deliverer.[76] This is but to say, *yet again*, that various Samsons are available within the works of any given author, often within the same work, and sometimes on opposing pages of a single work; it is but to extend to a range of authors the reminder Jonathan Richardson offered Milton's readers: that St. Jerome, following St. Paul, sanctions any treatment of "the Scripture-History of *Sampson* [as] a Fable."[77] As a fable, the Samson story is not a falsehood but, instead, a fiction from which truth may be distilled; it is one of those "grand Fable[s]" to which Milton alludes in *The History of Britain* and which he there claims is "dignifi'd by our best Poets" (*YP*, 5:16–17). Or as Milton explains in *De Doctrina*, such fables "are not falsehoods, since they are calculated not to deceive but to instruct" (*YP*, 6:761). The chronicle history in which the Samson story figures is not "scripture"; less actual than symbolic history, it exhibits the features of literary romance, as it is described by one of Milton's contemporaries, where "The Heroe . . . [is] at a precipice for ruine, before Miracles are call'd in for his Deliverance,"[78] which in the Samson story is *no* deliverance: not for Samson, not for his people.

Milton's point is fully consistent with the discussion of fabling by Peter Martyr, who, admitting that tragedy is itself a form of fabling, and doing so by referring to the same passage from 1 Corinthians 15.33 that Milton cites in his preface to *Samson Agonistes*, "Euill talke corrupteth good maners," distinguishes between lawful and unlawful feignings, according to those which teach rather than merely delight.[79] One detail in Milton's own fabling — his conversion of the temple of Judges into "a spacious Theatre" (1605) — finds a precedent in Goodwin's reference to "the pillars of that playhouse" and, as we will see later, an analogy perhaps, albeit ironic, in

Thomas Jackson's comments on the "stage and theatre" of the cross on Mount Calvary.[80] Another test of lawful fabling for Milton, apparently, is that it observe distinctions rather than blur them and distinguish between identities instead of confusing them, with *Samson Agonistes* thus being a poem in which we are to read, as Andrew Marvell insists, not Milton's character in Samson's but Samson's character in a tragedy.

No less than the pagans had done with some of their tales apparently, Christian interpreters had distorted the Samson story through apish imitation. One may suppose that others, including the Milton of *Samson Agonistes*, wished to set straight such crooked interpretations. The irony of his own circumstances, focused by the story of Theodates, probably would not have escaped Milton. According to Trapp, Theodates is "a Tragoedian [who] having intermingled some Scripture-matters with his Tragedies, suddenly lost his sight."[81] In analogy with Theodates, the blind Milton presents another version of the Samson story, daringly altering scriptural details, through the light of this new revelation unblinding us to the deeper meanings of the biblical tale, which are embedded within its internal complexities and unavoidable contra-dictions and which, following the lead of commentators like Goodwin, will focus on two interrelated episodes — Samson's downfall in marriages and the falling down of the temple/theater.

These episodes sponsor, as it were, two different and, again, interrelated questions: is Samson's putting his head into the lap of Delilah a temporary or a fatal submission? is Samson exonerated in the temple/theater catastrophe, or does a judg-ment now fall upon him as harshly as it here falls upon the Philistines? Such questioning is sanctioned by the Euripidean precedent cited in the preface to *Samson Agonistes* — a precedent not only for interrogating legend and mythology but for threading Euripidean insight (in the manner of St. Paul) into scriptural texts and tales in much the same way as Milton does in *De Doctrina*. Such questioning is also fueled from unexpected quarters, including women's writings: "What is become of . . . *David* the Victor," asks Rachel Speght, and of "*Sampson* the strong, that was bereft of eyes?"[82]

It should be obvious that fables embedded in various scriptural books have a status different from doctrine, although those fables can be twisted and turned so as to extrapolate from them this or that doctrine or, alternatively, this or that shape of history. As Teiresias explains in *The Bacchae*, "through retelling a story," we "often wander from the truth"[83] with even our histories containing both confused chronologies and obfuscations of purpose, as well as conflicting reports concerning individuals and events. From Milton's point of view, history renders judgments bound up with self-interest and often involves the propagation of errors. If history over time degenerates into fable, the poet may nevertheless purge those fables, wringing from them a higher truth, even as, retelling history, he may elevate it to the key of prophecy. That is especially true when history is reported in its different versions, in "several relations" — to use Milton's own term from *The History of Britain* (*YP*, 5:127–28) — which has the effect of freeing history of both outlandish fable and simple fraud; of offering embellishments to a history that may have existed originally only in skeletal outline.

It may be that "the Lord would have the whole history of *Samson* knowne, from his birth to his death"; but it also appears, from the example of John Mayer (1647), that he never quite revealed enough of that history, leaving it for the commentators to fill in silences and white spaces, as well as the margins of this story. Thus the Book of Judges initially tells us only that "the spirit of the Lord began to move him at times"

(13.25). Then there is a chapter division. When Samson's story commences in Judges 14, we are told simply that Samson's parents "knew not that it *was* of the Lord" (14.4) when their son went to Timnath for a bride. All Samson tells his parents is that this woman "pleaseth" him (14.3); he never says to them that he has a divine commission. Mayer fills in the Judges narrative, differently from Goodwin and in such a way as to exculpate Samson: "*Samson* knew it [the marriage was inspired], and it was revealed unto him, and he made his parents acquainted with it, whereupon they yeelded to his desire, for otherwise both hee and they had sinned herein, which is not to be thought of them, because they are godly and devout persons."[84]

Samson may be used sometimes to emblematize the faithful, the godly, and the devout; but his story is not a matter of faith, Samson is not an article of faith, as is made evident by Andrew Willet, for example, who takes up the Samson story under such headings as "*The diuerse readings,*" "*The explanation of doubtful questions,*" and "*Places of Confutation.*" On the other hand, Willet does not take up the story under topics like "*Places of doctrine*" or "*Places of moral use.*"[85] The implications are important: Samson's story may be interpreted, his character assessed, by the introduction of noncanonical texts. To do so in the circumstances suggested by Willet — with a story that is not a matter of faith and in terms of Samson who is not an article of faith — is perfectly compatible with Milton's interpretive system as outlined in *De Doctrina* (*YP*, 6:574–92). That system, as it happens, is prefigured in Milton's interpretation of other of the Judges stories, sometimes with reference to Rabbinical commentary, which in the seventeenth century had a marked effect on — indeed, through its "varied and often conflicting opinions . . . on numerous subjects,"[86] forced revisionist interpretation of — the Samson story. What Frank McConnell has said, applying the concept of midrashing to *Paradise Lost*, with a few minor adjustments can be transferred to *Samson Agonistes*, which is "Milton's seventeenth-century . . . midrash" on the Book of Judges, with the poet in this tragedy synchronizing the biblical story with "his own radical . . . Christian interpretation" of the Samson legend.[87]

THREE

"Glorious
for a While"

*So what of the ending of the tale? Does that family burial
party . . . look upon the temple rubble and reflect upon
the author of Dagon's discomfiture? Is the institution
of judgeship then a failure? Has the spiral decline been broken
only to become plummeting descent? Where in all this,
for the Israel of the story, lie the beginnings of
Israel's deliverance?*
— *David M. Gunn*[1]

In Pseudo-Philo (first century A.D.), in response to Samson's
taking Delilah as his wife, God speaks:

> Behold now Samson has been led astray through his eyes, and
> he has not remembered the mighty works that I did with him;
> and he has mingled with the daughters of the Philistines. . . .
> And now Samson's lust will be a stumbling block for him, and
> his mingling a ruin. . . . But at the hour of his death I will *re-
> member* him, *and I will avenge* him *upon the Philistines once
> more.*[2]

In the hour of his death, then, Samson is revealed at the pillars praying to die: "Go forth, *my soul*, and do not be sad; die, my body, and do not weep about yourself."[3]

Christianized, such thinking, in the seventeenth century, will give rise to the complementary propositions that temporal punishment reaches no further than the body and that, even if imprisoned on earth, the likes of Samson, keeping their souls, will never be imprisoned in hell.[4] In earlier commentary, though, interpretation takes another turn. Thus, in *The Testament of Dan* (second century, A.D.), Dan speaks out in his last days, explaining that the force of the body accomplishes evil, that anger and falsehood cause the Lord to withdraw from the soul and, when He does withdraw, Beliar rules it: Beliar will rise out of Dan, and from Judah will come the savior and deliverer who will defeat him.[5] But even more liberating than the apocryphal literature for interpreting the Samson story were the traditions of rabbinical literature.

In *The Babylonian Talmud* (400–500), which John Lightfoot was instrumental in bringing into the seventeenth century consciousness, two propositions are set against one another: first, "Samson was a nazirite to a limited extent only"; and second, "partial Naziriteship is impossible."[6] Accordingly, Samson's repeated violations of his vow cause his character to come under review. Of his plea: *Let me die with the Philistines*, it is explained: "This [phrase] was used proverbially to denote readiness to suffer, so that others might suffer too"; and also: the very phrase raises questions about the purity of its speaker, as well as the person's proclivity for being vengeful.[7] Of the same, *Let me die* phrase, it is further said: these words indicate a willingness to lose a right in order that others may lose the same right, and harbored in them is an inclination to be spiteful, "to inflict injury" even if that means "to suffer injury" oneself.[8] Moreover, Samson's words as he tells his parents about the woman of Timnath, *Get her for me*, seemed to refer to his "hankering after idolatry."[9]

Certain details pertaining to the Samson story are filled in by the Talmudists: the name of his mother (Zlelponith), the "ignorant" nature of his father, together with the fact that Samson "WAS THE HUSBAND OF DELILAH."[10] That marriage, together with Manoa's obtuseness, will be assimilated to *Samson Agonistes,* where Samson's mother, as it happens, will be notable only for her absence, perhaps by way of lifting from the Samson story the imprint of the very misogyny that it, as well as Milton's poem, is thought to bear:

> In *Manoah's* wife . . . we may see an example of the womans subjection to her husband. . . . [I]n all these things this marryed couple are to bee imitated by all others in the same estate, by the wives being subject to her owne husband. . . .[11]

But probably the most important consequence of the now ambiguous representation of Samson's character, and a probable cause of subsequent negative valuations of that character, is the association here of Samson with the serpent and adder in Genesis 49.17.

According to one Talmudist, "Samson was lame in both feet . . . *a serpent . . . an adder*"; and it is then explained that Jacob's "was a prophecy of Samson; 'An adder in the path' is taken to mean that he would have to slither along like an adder, being lame in both feet."[12] For some later commentators, Samson's physical deformity would require that he use, in all senses, the methods and devices of the serpent; that he be a trap and a snare. Here we may recall both Origen's words, "some say that Samson too is prophesied of by Jacob," and, much later, a political maxim of Hugo Grotius: such craftiness may cause some people to seem as if they are (like Moses, or like Joseph) true messengers of God, when in fact they are merely "Apes of the true messengers"[13] as Oliver Cromwell was sometimes thought to be. Samson's physical handicap could be construed (and sometimes was) as an outward sign of emotional, psychological, and spiritual deformation. As Jeffrey

Shoulson reports, after reviewing much of the rabbinic literature on Samson:

> Samson's revenge, precisely because it answers the treachery of the Philistines in kind, becomes less distinguishable from the world of pagan violence, whether it is legitimized or not. . . . Samson, the seemingly Hebraic hero, becomes yet another non-Hebraic bully, the emulation of whom raises more difficulties than it solves, if only because it continues the endless cycle of vengeance.[14]

The slow process by which this Samson is brought to full articulation is mirrored in the sixteenth and seventeenth centuries, first, by the creation of an elaborate intertext for the Samson story and, second, by the development of a negative reading of Jacob's prophecy in Genesis through correlation of it with Revelation 7 and by the gradual amplification of annotation for those Revelation verses.

I

Within his annotations for Genesis, Judges, Hebrews, and Revelation, Grotius includes cross references most notably to Numbers, Deuteronomy, Exodus, Acts, Ezekiel, Sirach, Daniel, and Amos and, perhaps most intriguing of all, to his own *De Jure Belli Ac Pacis*, which brings the entire Samson story under the aspect of the law and arraigns its hero at the bar of justice. These are, to use the words of Grotius familiar from a similar situation, "the contexts there adjoyning"[15] and, from the inside, as it were, illuminating the Samson story. Grotius's observations on the Epistle to the Hebrews are unexceptional. "The whole scripture is full of such examples," as we find here in Gideon and Barak, Samson and Jephthah, "all [of whom] were roused by the divine spirit to rule and avenge the people"; and hence, though not named in chronological order, but each "obey[ing] the spirit through faith," "they are called prophets." Moreover, "why neither Samson nor Gideon should be believed to have transgressed the law," or to have sinned, is explained by Grotius in his annotations to the Book of Judges, the annotations (increasingly equivocal) to which he now refers us and in which he makes clear that, though Samson may not sin, he does lots of mischief.[16]

The nature of that mischief is hinted at in the annotation to Judges 14.18 where, once the Philistines resolve the riddle he sets before them, Samson prepares for retaliation. Grotius's instruction is to see those things said in book 3, chapter 21, section 4, of *De Juri Belli Ac Pacis*, where an analogy is drawn between the rights of the Philistines and those of the Hebrews: the Israelites are right to demand in Judges 20 that the Benjamites deliver the offending parties and so, too, "the *Philistins* [to demand] of the *Hebrews* that *Sampson* as a *Malefactor* should be given 'em up, *Judges* xv." Then in his annotation to Judges 15.3, where the Latin vulgate reads, "From this day there will be no blame (guilt) on me against the Philistines: for I shall do you evils," Grotius refers again to *De Juri Belli Ac Pacis*, this time to book 2, chapter 20, section 8, with this comment:

> Neither the law of nature nor the law of peoples prevents one from taking revenge; but because the limit was exceeded, then also so that quarrels (feuds) would not arise from any cause whatsoever, the civil law prevented it, such as is also the law of the Hebrews indeed from God, but it is strongly allowed according to the limit of human laws, by which Law no one is prohibited from avenging himself upon foreigners: upon citizens he is not prohibited, except in the case of minor and daily matters. The reasoning of the sermon sanctified by the cross is different, in which, just as the promise of eternal things is revealed, so there is demanded a contempt for the earthly matters from which vengeance arises. Many people wrongly confuse these things, less harmfully if they attribute it (vengeance) to Hebrew law more than they should, but more (harmfully) if they extend it from those times to (the times of) God's indulgence for us. The heroes in Homer and the other Greek writers, as noted by the Scholiasts, were entirely given over to loves

and to anger. The light of the Evangelist has given other heroes to us, concerning which (light) I shall say with the old man Terentianus, *Now this day brings a different road, demands a different character.*[17]

As Grotius makes clear in *De Juri Belli Ac Pacis*, an eye for an eye philosophy whether practiced by Achilles or Samson, if not a sin, is still "the Justice of the Unjust." If revenge is not evil, patience is still "*much better.*"[18] The Christian Bible supersedes the Hebrew Bible and the new covenant the old one as much so, certainly, as Christus patiens surpasses Samson agonistes. The still nagging questions concerning Milton's thinking on these matters are folded into the juxta-position of poems in the 1671 volume: the order of (and the meaning inferred from) their placement; whether *Paradise Regain'd* and *Samson Agonistes* represent alternative, yet equally acceptable responses to crisis; and whether those re-sponses, weighted with ethical differences, are finally to be weighed differently.

As an avenger, Samson is the perpetrator of enormous cruel-ties and calamities, such as occur in Judges 15 when his former wife and her father are burned alive. Henrici de Cocceii is prompted by Grotius into this assertion:

> This defense of Samson [in the Book of Judges] is frivolous and the entire action is illicit. For it was a private injury inflicted upon him by his father-in-law who gave his wife over to the authority of another: for this private injury he was not permit-ted to take punishment from the whole Philistine people, es-pecially because the Philistine priests took punishment both from the father-in-law and the wife. For this reason, the people of Israel condemned the vengeance of Samson, and handed him over to the Philistines in chains.[19]

When Samson swears he is innocent, Cocceii responds that Samson's people do "not approve this judgment and rightly"; that, indeed, the Philistines committed no injury, nor approved it, and so were not subject to any punishment.[20]

While this episode may be deleted from Milton's account of the Samson story, the larger ethical concerns it raises remain a powerful presence in Milton's poem, which is as much a conversation with biblical exegetes as with key disputants in the arena of international law. Milton's critics have been quick to notice that the poet-polemicist Milton both warns of revenge and defends its use in holy wars in *De Doctrina Christiana*: "But we are not forbidden to take or to wish to take vengeance upon the enemies of the church" (*YP*, 6:755). Yet this passage is also counterweighted by another from earlier in the same work: "it is disgraceful and disgusting that the Christian religion should be supported by violence" (6:123). Ultimately, the question is whether the poet of the last books of *Paradise Lost* and of *Paradise Regain'd* and *Samson Agonistes* means to modify and, in the process, refine the sometimes harsher ethics of the polemicist. Nor can such questions be answered apart from the realization that, read as a political allegory with some of its reference points denoting contemporary England, both during the Civil War years and in the period of the Restoration, its government and church, of which initially critical Milton became eventually hostile, one has got to consider whether Milton would now extend his defense of regicide to killing the king's men and whether even if the enemy (the new Philistines) could be seen within the Church of England, would Milton provoke and promote their destruction.

As Grotius reads Judges 16, Samson is no less given to lies than Delilah and, furthermore, violating an important agreement with God, is himself a betrayer when he confides the secret of his strength to this woman. In the end, while the Hebrews may have devised justifications for taking one's own life, those justifications are suspect and simply serve to emphasize that those who are long on revenge are short on patience. With Grotius in hand, there is no way of not drawing a circle from the temple/theater catastrophe in *Samson Agonistes* to the allusion in its preface to *Christ Suffering* and of not then asserting the enormous difference between the avenging Samson and the patient Christ, the one delivering his enemies and himself unto death and the other dying so that his enemies might be saved.

When it comes to interpreting Genesis 49.16–18 and Revelation 7, Grotius finds, in the former, a prophecy involving the extraction of revenge and fulfilled in Samson and, in the latter, the recognition that "Dan is omitted, because at one time this tribe had sunk to one family . . ., and this family seems to have perished in war before the times of Esdra. . . . . And perhaps this is predicted in Amos 8:14," where it is written: "Those who swear by Ashimah of Samaria, and say, 'As thy god lives, O Dan,' and , 'As the way of Beersheba lives,' they shall fall, and never rise again."[21] In the beginning, Dan, in combination with the other tribes, may have been part of "a great army, like an army of God," Grotius implies as he refers these words in 1 Chronicles 12.22 to Judges 13.15. But in the end Samson is no angel of the Lord; and his tribe, falling into idolatry, is not to be numbered with the elect. Others may still justify Samson, "because in encountering death, he both benefitted his country and took vengeance upon his enemies,"[22] thereby jeopardizing himself in order to liberate his nation; but Grotius seems to think otherwise, and his annotators press us into thinking otherwise as well.

Take, for example, these notes to *De Jure Belli Ac Pacis* added by J. Barbeyrac and intended as elucidations of Grotius's own thinking. Reasoning along with Josephus, Barbeyrac wonders if anyone, "throw[ing] out of his own Body the Divine *Despositum*, . . . will escape the justice of an offended GOD," even as he determines that, because some think it "just to punish Slaves who run away, even from wicked Masters . . . shall we not think ourselves guilty of Impiety if we run away from GOD, the best of Masters?" Thereupon, Barbeyrac complements Grotius's citations of exemplars from Eusebius with this observation: "Those persons ought to have considered that GOD was powerful enough to support them in the midst of the most cruel Torments; and that, even tho' he permitted them to sink under them, he was good enough to have Regard to the Frailty of human Nature, and pardon them a forced Abjuration, on sincere Repentance. So that this Reason did not Privilege them to think themselves exempted from the general Law. They committed a certain Sin, to avoid an uncertain one."[23]

In turn, Grotius parallels Samson's defense of himself to the Philistines with an array of examples:

> *Romulus* in *Plutarch* speaking of *Tacitus*, murder'd by *Laurentes*, [who] says . . . *that Blood must be expiated with Blood.* And the same *Plutarch* of the *Mantinenses* ill-us'd by the *Achaeans;* . . . *such Treatment was* entitl'd *to a Revenge.* . . .[24]

If Grotius adds to these examples ones from St. Ambrose and Livy, Barbeyrac proceeds to supplement the list with citations from Thucydides, Sallust, and Aristides. Yet Grotius, citing Livy, also remembers these warning words from Lucretius:

> *For when each angry Man aveng'd his Cause,*
> *Judge to himself, and unrestrain'd by Laws;*
> *The World grew weary of that brutal Strife,*
> *Where Force the Limits gave to each precarious Life.*[25]

And remembers, too, these words from Euripides:

> . . . *He justly*
> *Look'd on her* [his daughter] *as wicked; by killing her*
> *Himself is yet more wicked far become.*[26]

Grotius responds sagely, arguing that there is no redress when people respond with *"Passion"* or *"Caprice"*: *"If the injur'd Person may take his* Revenge, *the Evil will eternally pass from one t' the other, and one Injustice only shifts and succeeds another. . . .* Good God! *what hast thou done, what Sort of*

Justice is this that must necessarily flow from Injustice? And how far will Evil run, or where will it stop?" In the end, Grotius confronts the paradox that, if a world of barbarity and injustice creates the judges, they themselves, returning evil for evil, sometimes perpetrate the practices they are meant to halt. In their acts of retaliation, because they are now injured parties, they may have the better excuse, although in thus taking revenge, they may be more guilty than the party committing the initial injury, both the injury and its revenge *"in the eye of Right Reason . . . proceed*[ing] *from the same Disease or Weakness of Mind."*[27]

Through a system of cross-referencing, Grotius implicates Samson in this questioning. Where the Book of Judges speaks of Samson's being "a Nazarene unto God," Grotius invokes the Lord's words to Moses in the Book of Numbers:

> [the Nazarite] shall eat nothing . . . produced by the grapevine, . . . no razor shall come upon his head; . . . he shall not go near a dead body. Neither for his father nor mother . . ., if they die, shall he make himself unclean; . . . And if any man dies very suddenly beside him, and he defiles his consecrated head, then he shall shave his head on the day of his cleansing. (6.4–9)

Within this context, it is difficult not to remember the circumstances under which a razor comes upon the head of Samson; or the numbers that have died by his side, their bodies stripped of their belongings; or his father's memorial; or the carcass of the dead lion by which he has been defiled and defiles his parents; or his further defiling in the lap of Delilah. Samson's vow, Grotius reminds us, is not temporary, but "perpetual, from a single command." Then, in yet another cross-referencing for the Samson story (this one to Acts 21.26), we are told of Paul's being dragged from the temple, locked outside its gates, and, arrested and in chains, being carried away from the violent crowd.[28] In Milton's tragedy, Samson, a slave enchained outside the gates of the prison house, is threatened with being dragged to the temple: "come without delay; / Or we shall find such Engines to assail / And hamper thee, as thou shalt come of force, / Though thou went firmlier fast'n'd then a rock" (1395–98). What Samson fears, what partly prompts him to go, is being "trail[ed] ... through thir streets" and humiliated before the crowd (1402–03).

Later on, Grotius links the mentioning of the harlot in Judges 16.1 to the injunction in Deuteronomy 23.17 that there shall be "no cult prostitute." Then he cites the earlier prescription, in the same book, that anyone desiring an enemy captive wife as a wife bring her home, have her shave her head and pare her nails and, "put[ting] off her captives garb, ... bewail her father and mother a full month" only after which time may there be a marriage. Thereupon it is said: "if you have no delight in her, you shall let her go where she will; ... [for] you have humiliated her" (21.11–14). In the face of such an injunction, Samson goes a whoring and, in the matter of his marriages, does not observe such prescriptions. Finally, the "prison house" in Judges 16.21 is likened to the dungeon in Exodus 11.29. As Grotius explains, "It is customary for the eyes of those condemned to the mill to be removed, in order that vertigo might not hinder their labor."[29]

When it comes to the Epistle to the Hebrews, Grotius's cross references may be more interesting than his previously cited annotations. Its catalogue of heroes and description of heroism (11.32–33) are brought under the light of 1 Samuel 12.11 where Barak and Jephthah are singled out as deliverers and, more tellingly, under the light of Ezekiel 18.5 where it is said, "If a man is righteous ... [he] does what is lawful and right." Then the Lord explains that the righteous man "does not ... lift up his eyes to idols ..., ... does not oppress anyone, ... commits no robbery, ... covers the naked with a garment, ... withholds his hand of inequity, executes true justice between man and man, walks in my statutes, and is careful to observe my ordinances." Samuel and Josaphat are cited by Grotius for fitting these precepts "extremely well": "We ought to do the same, but according to the more sublime precepts of the Gospels."[30]

All these scriptural texts in conjunction establish the terms of the enquiry and afford the contexts by which Grotius and his own commentators bring Samson to the bar of justice with the dialectic between their respective annotations holding open the question of whether Samson is sinful even as they lead to the conclusion that he is unjust. This same dialectic plays itself out within *Samson Agonistes*, the tragedy of which, with specific reference to Samson, is epitomized by Daniel 6.22: is he God's "angel"? is he blameless? has he "done . . . wrong."[31] It is the Genesis-Revelation tradition of interpretation that gathers such questions into focus.

In his own interpretation of Genesis 49.5–7, Lancelot Andrewes provides a convenient paradigm for how negative readings, extended to the whole of Jacob's prophecy, over time will develop. In this censuring of Simeon and Levi, says Andrewes, attention is fixed on the fault, then the punishment: they slew men cruelly with the fury of their revenge and with their weapons of violence; there was murder and burglary. Hence their punishment was both civil and spiritual, death and destruction.[32] Such readings were often generalized to the whole prophecy and then extended to — and used to explain — Revelation 7. And such readings of the Samson story crop up in Milton's poem as Harapha chides Samson:

> Fair honour that thou dost thy God, in trusting
> He will accept thee to defend his cause,
> A Murtherer, a Revolter, and a Robber.
>
> (1178–80)

> . . . hadst thou not committed
> Notorious murder on those thirty men
> At *Askalon*, who never did thee harm,

Then like a Robber strip'dst them of thir robes?
The *Philistines*, when thou hadst broke the league,
Went up with armed powers thee only seeking,
To others did no violence nor spoil.

(1185–91)

The judgment Harapha here imposes upon Samson is not just one that a Philistine imposes upon an Israelite, but one that Jewish interpreters, as well as Christian, taking into account Samson's exploits as a judge, used to authorize the harsh judgment they sometimes let fall upon Samson as he hurls down the pillars. It is part of the genius of Milton's poem that he elaborates a character like Manoa and invents one like Harapha so that the interrogation of Samson may proceed from friend and foe alike. Moreover, in the case of Harapha, as the critique of Samson gathers in credibility, both its spokesperson and his people are humanized in the process.

Harapha's language is also reminiscent of those descriptions of the Civil War as years "so long protracted by . . . rapine and bloud"[33] and reminiscent as well of those episodes in the Civil War (his own perhaps unwarranted claims to inspiration, the plundering by his soldiers) on which Cromwell himself would eventually cast a dubious eye, not to mention disillusioned radicals brooding over such corrupting effects as the ravaging of the land, as well as the seizing and amassing of property by both the Army and Parliament. Just these kinds of activities as reported by Christopher Hill are ones in which international law, as it was formulated by Grotius, found justification for private revenge like that taken by the Philistines upon Samson, the activities of Samson himself, murder and theft, according to Grotius, being unlawful and condemned even by Euripides as "hateful to God" himself.[34] Samson would precipitate an apocalypse. The question is whether what he produces is eschatological despair or triumph.

II

It may be that, in 1582, in a Bible published at Rheims, Revelation 7 receives brief, rather spare, annotation. That Dan is excluded from the tribes goes unobserved: there is only the suggestion that the tribes marked for protection constitute "al the elect."[35] In another Bible of the same year, though, we are told further that the preservation of the twelve tribes is an act of mercy preparatory to the execution of justice; and it is noted here that John of Patmos "skipped Dan: & reckoneth Leui."[36] In 1590, Edward Vaughan provides succinct explanation: "Dan . . . is left out, wherby it is thought that Antichrist should come of him: he caused the first Idolatrie"; and three years later, in 1593, John Napier provides elaboration by interleaving Genesis 49 and Revelation 7:

> Among these Tribes *Dan* is left out. . . . Why *Dan* is so left out, the reason appeareth to be, that that Tribe hath bene more accursed than the rest: for by the Spirit of God, it is called (Gen. 49.17) a Serpent, or an Adder, . . . and from their golden Calues and great idolatrie . . . they fel, and neuer rose againe, and so could not be participant of this Christian mark.[37]

Napier surely knows that the serpent and adder in Genesis were often particularized to Samson and, obviously accepting the negative construction placed upon this prophecy, insinuates a double reason for the exclusion of Dan in the Revelation prophecy: this is the tribe of the serpent and eventually of Antichrist, as well as the tribe of idolatry. By 1610, the acknowledgment — "He skipped Dan and reckoneth Leui" — is accompanied by the explication already afforded by Napier: that the tribe of the serpent in Genesis is the tribe of idolatry in Revelation, along with the additional observation that, foreseeing Dan's apostasy, Jacob, in his prophecy, not only anticipates John's exclusion of Dan in Revelation but hints at why there is no mention of Dan in Chronicles.[38]

1 Chronicles 7 becomes one of the hard places in Scriptures for Samson's tribe, reinforcing negative readings in both Genesis and Revelation. Initially, perhaps, commentary is neutral, descriptive, in ways it no longer is today. In the first decade of Milton's century, it was thought that to call Hushim "the sonne of another" meant "he was not the sonne of Beniamin, but of Dan," because Bilhah was mother to both Dan and Naphtali (7.12–13). Now Chronicles is read as "symbolic, not actual history," with emphasis falling upon the grim ordeal of war, young men maimed and killed, fighting as a permanent feature on the landscape of civilization and soldierly morality as sometimes dubious. And in these particular verses, were it not for some clever word play, "Dan would not be included in the tribal list."[39] By the middle of Milton's century, it was being said that while "Some understood under this title, *sons*, the posterity of Dan," Hushim of Dan for his "paucity [is] reckoned in the tribe of Benjamin"[40] and, by the end of the seventeenth century, that even if hinted at "the Genealogy of Dan is quite left out." Indeed, to say that Hushim is of "another" amounts to a slur, which is intended to remind us "that the Tribe of *Dan* had made themselves and their Memory Infamous and Detestable by that gross Idolatry, which began first and continued longest in that Tribe. . . . For which reason many Interpreters conceive this Tribe is omitted in the numbring of the sealed Persons, *Rev. 7.*"[41]

Whatever may happen in the early decades of the seventeenth century, and whether or not Samson is run into (or out of) the Genesis/Revelation equation, it is nevertheless clear that the larger tradition in which Samson sometimes figures — Dan as the tribe of Antichrist — is restored by the end of that century and persists today. Indeed, William Whiston (1706) does no more than re-tangle the threads in a negative reading of Genesis that commentators of the second decade of the seventeenth century had untangled as part of their anti-papist polemic. "[O]ne of the great Instances of Divine Art and Management in the *Apocalypse,"* Revelation 7, says Whiston, seals some for deliverance from that new antichristian idolatry."[42] At the beginning of the eighteenth century, Dan will again be the tribe of Antichrist, as well as of idolatry, as it had been at the end of the sixteenth century, at least for some like Vaughan.

In the late sixteenth and increasingly in the early years of the seventeenth century, Genesis 49 and Revelation 7 get caught up in an antipapist polemic. Elaborating upon previous mystical interpretations (such as one finds in Augustine Marlorat), which regard Ephraim as the tribe of idolatry and Dan as the tribe of Antichrist and the Pope, James Brocard (1582) remarks of Revelation that "the Trybe of Dan is away, but in the place thereof succeedeth Manasses: For Iudas Scariotes was the Trybe of Dan. Whereinto came the Pope."[43] There are always those like William Fulke (1573) who, placing a positive construction on Genesis 49, attached no real interpretive, much less judgmental, significance to Revelation 7; who, like Fulke, complain of those "weake and vaine" interpretations then bringing forth "monstrouse fables concerning Antichrist."[44]

The complaint is clearly leveled against the Papists who, opting for preterist and futurist readings, either located Antichrist in the likes of Dan/Samson or in some unspecified historical figure who would emerge near the end of time, thus freeing the Pope from this odious label. By the end of the sixteenth century, it is commonplace to argue that the omission of Dan from Revelation is "a just vengeance and secret direction of the Spirit of God," owing to the fact, as Franciscus Junius (1596) explains, that members of Dan's tribe "had forsaken and renounced the service of God, and . . . sequestered themselves from the communion of Saintes,"[45] with emphasis falling not faintly as here, but strongly as in George Gifford (1599), on the fact that Dan, if not the tribe of Antichrist, is surely the tribe of idolatry. Gifford acknowledges that "some

of the ancient fathers did take it that Antichrist should come
of the tribe of Dan" but also objects: "This hath been the
cunning of the diuell, to the end that the great Antichrist ought
not to be knowne. . . . But the truth is, the learned Papists,
and euen the Papists of Rhemes, doe see the vanitie of this
collection, that Antichrist should come of the tribe of *Dan*,
and do omit it."[46]

For a brief period, then, there is a Protestant disavowal of
the tradition that Antichrist will come from Dan, which is
a tactic practiced rather notably by Hugh Broughton (1610),
Francis Rollenson (1612), Thomas Brightman (1616), William
Cowper (1619), and Thomas Cartwright (1622) for disallowing
the Catholic evasion of the Protestant interpretation.[47] David
Pareus (1618) gives elaborate articulation to this practice, even
as he moves finally to grant the thesis that Dan is the tribe of
Antichrist, while turning that thesis back upon the Papists:

> *Dan* also is passed by: the reason whereof most of the fathers
> and some also to this day will have to be, because Antichrist
> should come of this tribe: grounding their opinion, on that in
> Gen. 49.17. *Dan is the serpent in the way*: & Iere.8.16 *the snort-*
> *ing of horses was heard from Dan.* And hence arose another
> erroneous opinion. viz. that Antichrist should be a *Jew*: by
> which fiction the devill so deceived the world, as that Anti-
> christ already sitting and reigning in the Church, was not taken
> notice of & avoyded. But this Glosse is frivilous: *Dan shall be*
> *a serpent by the way*, that is, of him Antichrist shall come. . . .
> But the *Ancients* are the lesse to be blamed, not having the
> meanes and knowledge of histories touching Antichrist, which
> we now enjoy, and see with our eyes, & which the Papists them-
> selves cannot but also see, if they would confesse it; & there-
> fore they are the more ridiculous in alleadging such foolish
> things: the vanity whereof *Bellarmin* himself confesseth. For
> where is now the tribe of *Dan*?
>
> Others therefore affirme more probably, that the *Danites*
> are not mentioned, because of old they forsooke the worship of
> God . . . which seems also to be the reason why they are not
> mentioned with the other tribes I *Chro.* 7. But suppose it be

granted, that Antichrist shall come of *Dan*: what doth better suit the Pope then this? For *Dan* signifies to judge. Now who, but the Pope alone, judgeth all men, & himself is judged of none? doe not the Popes parasites make him to be this *Antichristian Dan, or judge?*[48]

Pareus will not finally let go of a thesis, at least in its broad outline, that fits so neatly with his own view of the Book of Revelation as a rehearsal of all the tragedies of human history, especially the tragedy of Antichrist.

When Jacob's prophecy and the Revelation omission are used to interpret one another, when both prophecies (sometimes mythologized in terms of the falling Lucifer) are historicized and then the scrambled history of the Judges text sorted out, certain premises for further interpretation assert themselves. First, Jacob's prophecy and the Judges narrative belong to the same time frame. Second, Dan, a tribe of nearly anonymous membership, produced but one judge — namely Samson. Third, when Samson dies, Dan as a tribe disappears from history (the tribe is not mentioned in Chronicles or later in Revelation). And fourth, Antichrist is, after all, a composite figure, at any time in history gathering into itself numerous personages and throughout history enlisting many more in its membership. "Antichrist," says Perkins, "bee not one particular man, but a state and company of men."[49] The "He-is-Antichrist" formula eventually gives way to "They-are-Antichrist" formulations; and in the process, Samson is swallowed up in Dan, while Dan, though an exterminated and cancelled tribe, still survives in history as a spiritual conception, emblematizing either as a tribe or in the person of Samson all those apostates who, if once of the elect, are now of the reprobate — all those who start life in the spirit but end in the flesh. Indeed, the very conception of Antichrist becomes a vehicle for historicizing Satan and a device for locating, then defining, the evil impulse — its different forms and manifestations — within history, even within England:

"the fall of Babylon . . . shall be accomplished in all, even in this Island of *Great Britain*," says Elizabeth Avery; "Babylon is fallen in some of the Saints, and fallen in the State and National Church of *Great Britain*."[50] Like other biblical figures, Abraham for example, Samson is at once both individual and nation and so figured in *Areopagitica*: "Methinks I see in my mind a noble and puissant Nation rousing herself like a strong man after sleep, and shaking her invincible locks" (*YP*, 2:557–58).

Interpretation is now wrapped in both theology and politics, with the two knotted (as we shall see) in efforts to dismantle the Calvinist/Puritan notion of the perseverance of the saints. Given this line of thought and this particular dispute, it would seem natural enough for Samson, who had achieved the status of patron saint of the revolutionary army, to become implicated in questions concerning the fallibility of the saints and whether, even if anointed, they may not lose their election, falling not just temporarily but fatally. Perhaps more often in perception than in print, the Samson who slaughters and destroys gets aligned with Satan or Antichrist who is himself a slayer of people and who is known by at least one of his names in Revelation as the "destroyer" (so Milton recalls in *De Doctrina Christiana, YP*, 6:350). Samson would be a problematical figure for anyone who counsels, as Milton does, against exchanging evil for evil or repaying evil with evil, arguing instead that evil is to be conquered by good (6:742). Such counsel eventually asks to be read against Samson's own assertion in Milton's poem: "I us'd hostility, and took thir spoil / To pay my underminers in thir coin" (1203–04).

Indeed, it is hard not to imagine Samson involved in the censure that William Whately places on most of the sons of Jacob (including Dan) within the marginal glosses: "The sonnes. Their common faults. / . . . All of them bad except *Joseph* and *Benjamin*. / . . . Deceit is a great sin." Whately thus laments: "O miserable fault, to cover hatred with deceitfull words. . . . To speake one thing and meane the contrary, to pretend a good purpose to cover a bad."[51] Did Whately remember Samson's marriages, his profession of love for Delilah by way of seeking an occasion against the Philistines? He does not say so, but surely knows that the Genesis prophecy was often thought to figure Samson as both serpent and adder, as well as to implicate him in its criticism of Dan. And Whately continues:

> Here was a mixture of impiety, in making religion a cloake to revenge, and of fraud in harbouring and intending, yet disguizing revenge. . . .
> Now I beseech you to take heed of deceit and guile, the deceitfull shall not live out halfe his dayes. To hate and yet dissemble with his lips, laying up deceit within him, is a loathsome thing. . . . It is bad to have used this fraud or covetousnesse or ambition sake . . .; but it is worst of all when it is joyned with revenge and with bloodinesse. . . . It is naught when only good will is pretended, but when religion is made cloake of cruelty and villany, this is to abuse the noblest thing in the world, by making it a drudge to the basest.[52]

What must have been evident to many who fixed a negative reading on Genesis 49.16–18 is that Samson conforms very well to the prototypes and precedents established by the father of his tribe, right down to illustrating Whately's tenet that "one hav[ing] done them wrong, they revenge it upon a whole City . . .: here is injustice and malice both in a very high degree."[53] In this context, it may be no coincidence that Samson's judgeship lasts twenty, not forty, years.

Interrogation of the Samson story owing to an interaction between the Genesis and Revelation texts not only gives impetus to but strengthens challenges to the Hebrews representation of Samson. One way of validating such a practice is, first, to establish that, in comparison with the Old Testament, the New Testament is the more corrupt text, thus especially dependent upon the Old Testament for interpretation, along the way implicating the Pauline texts in this corruption; then to challenge the credentials of the supposedly worthiest of the worthies (David rather than Samson, let us say) in the Hebrews catalogue of heroes and saints. John Goodwin, a republican divine, provides a notable instance, perhaps especially notable inasmuch as he is of Milton's party and on its left extreme, approving the beheading of Charles I and advocating the more excessive practices of Cromwell's army and (as David Loewenstein has reminded me in correspondence), inasmuch as Goodwin's *The Obstructours of Justice* (1649) is heavily influenced by Milton's *The Tenure of Kings and Magistrates*. It is Goodwin who precipitates the sometimes acrimonious debate over the question of the perseverance of the saints and whose writings are the focal point for that debate. Indeed, this debate explains, perhaps better than any other document of the seventeenth century, why Samson sometimes was represented so ambiguously, even why Milton's representation would necessarily be ambiguous.

III

This controversy over the perseverance of the saints, which had profound theological and political implications, raged during the 1650s, when Milton was probably contemplating, if not writing *Samson Agonistes*; and, centering upon the writings of Goodwin, it thus involved one of those few contemporaries with whom Milton is allied by his early biographers. Edward Phillips and John Toland, together with Jonathan Richardson and his son, all allude to the same story: that "together with *John Goodwin* of *Coleman-Street*," Milton escaped death on the condition that he disengage from all political activity; that "spreader[s] of Arminianism" and supporters of the murder of Charles I, comrades in theology as well as politics, their "Books . . . were burnt by the Hangman" as a way of signaling that while their thoughts were censored their lives were spared.[54]

Under the caption, "Saints, not alwayes sin out of infirmity," Goodwin explains that, if some of the saints sin out of ignorance or out of infirmity, others sin out of malice, which is "far greater in demerit, then either of the former." At the same time, claiming the authority of Pareus, Goodwin sets forth the proposition: "certaine it is that true Believers . . . may *sin out of malice*"; indeed, the saddest falls "*of holy Men, as of* Aaron, *making the golden Calf, for which God being* angry *was minded to slay him; and of* David, *committing Adultry and Murther*" show "*that even Regenerate Men may rush [or, fall-headlong] into reigning sin.*"[55] For Goodwin, the real question is whether those who sin not out of infirmity but, worse, malice actually repent.

This is what Goodwin says:

> they that stand in need of Repentance to give them a right and title to the Kingdome of God, are no *Sons of God by Faith*: for were they *Sons*, they would be *heires* also. . . . So that to pretend, that however the Saints may fall into great and grievous Sins, yet they shall certainly be renewed againe by Repentance, before they die, though this be an Assertion without any bottome of Reason, or Truth, yet doth it no ways oppose, but suppose rather, a Possibility of the totall defection of Faith in true Believers.[56]

And Goodwin continues that those anointed by God may be governed by a contrary will, in which case "the flesh . . . prevaileth," with those commencing life in the spirit sometimes ending it in the flesh. Moreover, when the spirit departs from such a sinner, it returns (if in fact it does return) as "a cooler and softer inspiration."[57] This is but a reminder that, as Milton explains in *A Treatise of Civil Power*, "no man can know at all times" if "divine illumination . . . be in himself" (*YP*, 7:242), which, if it is, may justify the use of force but only against apostasy and idolatry and which, if this is the case in *Samson Agonistes*, pits an apostate against the idolaters and eventuates in his own countrymen falling into idolatry.

In *Samson Agonistes*, when the poem is read by celebrants of Samson's regeneration, the cooler forms of inspiration precede the grand moment when, after the spirit of the Lord departs from Samson, Samson claims its return: "I begin to feel / Some rouzing motions in me which dispose / To something extraordinary my thoughts" (1381–83); and the Semichorus thereupon follows suit: "he though blind of sight . . . / With inward eyes illuminated / His fierie vertue rouz'd" (1687, 1689–90).

What concerns Goodwin is the "inward *intanglement*," with Christ warring against Satan within individuals, including saints and heroes, and the possibility of Satan predominating. "[W]hat is Regeneration," Goodwin asks, "but a *renewing again by Repentance?*" But there is not always repentance and regeneration; and when there is not, those implicated are destroyed by God's judgment and their names blotted from the Book of Life. Unlike Perkins and Dickson, then, Goodwin openly entertains the "possibility of the *Saints* final defection," of their falling away, declining, and "becom[ing] a *Reprobate*." From Goodwin's standpoint, to reject predestination in favor of free will necessitates such a conclusion: "To look upon a *Saint*, or a true Believer, as one who may possibly Apostatize, is but to look upon him as being a Creature, and not God."[58]

Revealingly, Goodwin's examples of such apostasy are David, who falls into adultery and murder, and Solomon who declines into idolatry: "a total recidivation from Grace, or true Faith." Reflections such as these are meant to dispel two erroneous theses: that men regenerate cannot fall, and that though fallen they remain righteous. It is easy enough to draw from these reflections the question of whether Samson is likewise to be numbered with those who "*make shipwrack of Faith*"; of whether he is another example of what Goodwin regards as gratuitous election, gratuitous vocation.[59] In Goodwin's comments, as in most of those cited in this chapter, politics and theology are completely intertwined, as they will continue

to be in *Samson Agonistes;* and while Goodwin attaches his
argument for the most part to David and Solomon he allows
both Adam and Samson to sit on the margins of this debate by
referring to both in "The Epistle Dedicatory."

Here Samson illustrates the "misery . . . men brought upon
themselves," causing God "by degrees" to withdraw "that
lively presence of his Spirit from them, by which they had
been formerly raised and enlarged . . .: but now the wonted
presence of this Spirit . . . failing them, the favor and vigor of
their wisdom and understandings proportionably abated and
declined, as *Sampsons* strength upon the cutting of hair, sank
and fell to the line of the weakness of other men." This misery,
Goodwin concludes, exemplifies "a *delivering up . . . to a
reprobate mind.*"[60] When we remember that this debate pits
adherents to predestination (like George Kendall) against
advocates of free will (like Goodwin himself), it becomes clear
with which side in the debate Milton would affiliate, Milton
probably preferring what Kendall calls Goodwin's "*Coleman-
street* rationalnesse"[61] to Kendall's own brand of logic, which
carries the imprimatur of Joseph Hall. In any event, Milton's
Samson is an "example" of such apostasy — of how far the
glorious may fall (166–69) and, because of such folly (822–25),
into what misery (762–65).

An example not to be imitated, Milton's Samson owns up
to being "a foolish Pilot," whose "Vessel trusted . . . from
above" and "Gloriously rigg'd" has now "shipwrack'd" (198–
200) and is thus described by the Chorus: "What Pilot so expert
but needs must wreck / Embarqu'd with such a Stears-mate
at the Helm" (1044–45). "Shipwrack" has always been Milton's
metaphor for calamity in marriage when "a scene of cloud
and tempest," as he writes in *Tetrachordon,* "turns all to shipwrack without havn or shoar" with the marriage itself now
becoming "a ransomles captivity" (*YP,* 2:600–01). It is also
Milton's idiom, deriving from 1 Timothy 1.19, for explaining in *De Doctrina* the crisis of faith accompanying the

abandonment of good conscience (*YP*, 6:509), as well as his metaphor for failed leadership with those aiming at good doing evil, Milton explains in *A Treatise of Civil Power*, thus causing Israel to sin and themselves to shipwreck (*YP*, 7:266). Initially Samson but later Dalila and Harapha — all will appear in this poem as ships that, colliding with one another, wreck. In the words of *Pro Se Defensio*, they are all "shipwrecked of faith" (*YP*, 4:792) and eventually enveloped in "a common ruin" like Milton envisions in *The Readie and Easie Way*: "the shaking and almost subversion of the whole land" (*YP*, 7:426). Indeed, this whole complex of imagery, including storms and shipwreck, is an enduring element in tragedy, indicating the emotional and intellectual chaos within that soon disorders the moral order of the universe; that shakes that universe to its foundation and brings it down in ruin.

This same imagery also participates in the feminization of Samson when we recollect, first, that Dalila herself appears as "a stately Ship / . . . / With all her bravery on, and tackle trim, / Sails fill'd, and streamers waving" (714, 717–18) and, second, that such representations, as Daniel Tuvill reveals, are part of the antifeminist rhetoric of the times with the woman as a ship simile implying that she is "a faire body, but a foule minde" — "like vnto him that hath a good ship, but an ill Pilot."[62] In *Samson Agonistes*, the protagonist is a victim of his own misogyny. This feminization of Samson, as we shall see, crests in the image of him as a phoenix: "*her* ashie womb . . . *her* body . . ., *her fame*" (1703, 1706; my italics).

On the other hand, when we remember with Thomas Pierce that "shipwrack" is a trope for a crisis of faith[63] and remember further that the trope is commonplace in the seventeenth century, producing just such a crisis for the poet of *Lycidas* whose poem initially appears under the title *Justa Edovardo King Naufrago* (or "Funeral Rites for Edward King Shipwrecked"), then the image enveloping both Samson and Dalila, as well as the concept binding all the poems in the King

memorial volume, produces an interrogation of the very
Samson, the Hebrews Samson, in whom Milton's protagonist is thought to find his closest prototype. Even if, unlike
Goodwin, he believes in the perseverance of the saints, Pierce
distinguishes usefully between "a *positive* and a *negative* Re-
probat[i]on" and, having done so here in terms of Aaron, David,
and Solomon, acknowledges that not only "the Best" of them
did "fall *totally*" in the Old Testament, but also the likes of
"*Joseph* and *Sampson* who [similarly] were as *various* in their
Behaviours, as they were *different* in their *Success*."[64] If the
ship imagery, both by feminizing Samson and by implicating
him in a crisis of faith, throws his heroism into question, that
same imagery — now in reference to Harapha as one whose
"pile high-built and proud" is "blown . . . hither" by the wind
rather as earlier "sumptuous *Dalila* [came] floating this way"
(1069–72) — has the effect of eliding Samson with Harapha
(and again with Dalila). Here, Harapha's own haughtiness, as
much as Dalila's supposed villainy, serves as a check upon
our perception of Samson's heroism.

One measure of the fissures in Perkins's arguments is the
fact that he is claimed as an ally by both sides in the debate
concerning the perseverance of the saints — by Goodwin and
Kendall alike.[65] Yet Kendall's own hard-line Calvinism makes
it clear that there are striking differences between his and the
moderated positions of Perkins and irreconcilable differences
between his positions and what we know Milton's to have
been. According to Kendall, people do nothing on their own:
"it is *not we*, but God that *works all our work in us*."[66] As if
in response to Goodwin's preface, he raises as principal examples the figures of Samson and Adam. Speaking of "the . . .
victorious fall of *Sampson*, and the house on the *Philistines*,"
but also keeping his argument distanced from Samson by
attaching it to Samson's lion and Philistine enemies, Kendall
allows that "the *lesse insight* the creatures have into their
actions, the *more* it appears they are directed by the *eye* and

managed by the *hand* of God; and that he stoopes to determine these contemptible motions, to his own glorious ends." No less than Samson apparently, Adam is under God's control, with God himself responsible for the "evil of *punishment*; . . . that evil of punishment is oftentimes an instrument of much good, . . . and alwayes matter of glory to God."[67] Unlike Milton's, Kendall's God stoops to conquer.

God has spoken his mind in Scriptures, Kendall concludes, where it is made clear that Reprobation is not "incompatible with his *honour*" and for which reason it is altogether improper "for men to bring him upon the *theatre of the world*, and put a speech in his mouth of their own penning, such as . . . representing God, or speaking thus according to our doctrine."[68] What Kendall would say of Milton's God in book 3 of *Paradise Lost*, challenging predestination and championing free will (100–128), is clear enough, indeed just as clear as the argument that he would likely make on behalf of Milton's Samson: "though all *Saints* be *Elect*, all the *Elect* are not presently *Saints*, but lie most of them a long time as the rest of the World doth in *wickednes*; only it pleased God to decree to draw them out of it in his own time"[69] as happens with Samson when he hurls down the temple.

A year later Kendall goes on the attack again, this time against Goodwin's examples of "Saints Apostatizing," insisting upon their perseverance, on the fact that God always holds them up. Even if some of those most eminent in the Book of God fall without awareness, Kendall's God always saints the elect; and even if Samson does not make Kendall's list, so long as he is construed as one of the elect, he is clearly comprehended within Kendall's argument, where God never departs from but forever continues to work with the elect. Although "*true Believers* may in some cases become *Apostates*, in part, for a *time*, and *go out* in that sense," they always return again, "they *never become Antichrists*." Those who side with Goodwin, on the other hand, adapting to his Arminianism, challenge the ideas of God's election, as well as St. Paul's faith, and abandon the notion that the saints are never a negative example, intended to keep men from "like fals," but always positive examples meant "to bring . . . [people] to a like repentance."[70]

If Goodwin and his followers are labeled anti-Calvinists in this context, it needs to be remembered that the supposed Calvinists in this debate are often far to the right of their chosen sponsor. They insist, as does Richard Resbery, that God "willed" the Crucifixion, no less than man's Fall, which he both foreknew and foreordained, but, as one supposes the argument would go in the case of Samson, that God never slaughters a saint.[71] Rather, as Christopher Goad maintains, "when we think that God is destroying his Saints, he is [actually] saving them."[72] Or, as does John Pawson, they argue that "Election is of persons, not of kinds; of individuals, not of *Species's*," with God's attention being turned to "his . . . chosen vessel[s]" on the grounds that, not purchasing faith for everyone, "Christ . . . did not lay down his life for all."[73] If Goodwin maintains that the salvation of some saints is doubtful or uncertain, his opponents argue along with Thomas Lamb, one of many dedicating his work to Oliver Cromwell, that their salvation is "without doubt or suspense, certain and absolute," with God's grace being bestowed not generally but on particulars, on the true saints, the best guide to which is St. Paul and his claim that the saints are equal, hence not to be opposed to one another, the weak or foolish being no less justified than the strong and the wise.[74] It is clear that David Dickson has this debate fully in mind when, in 1659, as we noted in the previous chapter, he drops from his commentary on all the Epistles his earlier interrogation of St. Paul's roll call of heroes.

But not all are thus intimidated. Once an ally of Bishop Laud but also a sympathizer with Parliament who thought, finally, that the war would prove disastrous for both sides,

William Twisse was an opponent of Thomas Jackson, as well as of Thomas Goodwin and John Goodwin. Quite orthodox in his Puritanism, Twisse was watchful against doctrinal deviations and heresies, into which the likes of Milton sometimes became netted. A fierce polemicist against Arminianism, yet a major Chiliast and the author of the preface for the English translation of Joseph Mede's commentary on the Book of Revelation, an intellectual ally not only of Mede but Samuel Hartlib, his body eventually dug up by Royalist revengers and thrown promiscuously into a pit, William Twisse, for example, lines up with Kendall and company but is altogether more searching and complicated in his formulations and thus perhaps better than anyone in this group, because of his fine erudition and measured defenses, suggests the bearing of this debate on *Samson Agonistes*.

Twisse's argument is simple enough: to be called is, in effect, to be chosen. There is "no cause," he is convinced, for the predetermined categories either of election or reprobation: "like as good workes are not the cause of Election, so evill workes are not the cause of Reprobation." Very quickly this entire argument gets attached to the character of Samson:

> In the 16 *Judg.* we read a strange story of *Sampson* whose faith is commended *Hebr.* 11. For there we read how he dyes, his heart flaming with desire of revenge, and yet with great devotion prayes unto God to assist him, that he might be avenged of the Philistins for his two eyes. . . . For both the house it selfe was full, and upon the roofe of it there were about 3000 men and women. Here is a strange massacre wrought by *Sampson*, an Israelite. . . . [H]e comes sparkling with zeale to destroy many thousands of them, yea the Princes with the rest, and well pleas'd to destroy himselfe with them, to be avenged of them. . . . And how could this be done by him without some speciall & propheticall instigation & animation received from the spirit of God, we know not. And who doubts, but that God animating him hereunto, all this was lawfull? which without Gods warrant, could be no lesse then abominable & most

damnable sins. Yet undoubtedly God did not animate *Herod*, & *Pontius Pilate* . . .: and why the like is not to be acknowledged of the most barbarous facts committed by *Tiberius*, or any other monster of nature, I know no reason. And as touching shamefull courses, no lesse abominable in the kind of acts flagitious, as these here mentioned of *Tiberius* were, in the kind of acts facinorous; The Apostle professeth both that God gave them up to vile affections, and to the lusts of their own hearts, to the committing of such abominations, and also that herein they received such recompence of their error as was meet; and the errour which God avenged in this manner what was it, but such wherein *Tiberius* was as deep, . . . in changing the glory of the incorruptible God, to the similitude of the image of a corruptible man, and of birds, and of four footed beasts, and of creeping things. God gave them up, that they might receive that recompense of their errour as we meet.[75]

Even for Twisse, Samson is a problematical case; for he raises the question of how we know when instigation and animation come from God and, simultaneously, forces us to address the fact that to accept Samson's actions uncritically involves attributing certain of his cruelties to God himself, thus using what is foul in man to foul God.

Our doctrine, says Twisse, is that God forbids "the ravishing of any, the murthering of any, or any other sin whatsoever," although he does seem to permit the evil spirit to seduce some like Ahab:

> But this is a figurative speech, and signifies not properly any command of God, but rather denotes the secret operation of Gods providence in the hearts of men, even of wicked men; for those as well as Devills, God knows how to make use of, to serve his own turne. . . . Yet neither doth God command any man to doe that which his Law forbids, or to sin against him. . . . As for the power of God in producing sinne, we acknowledge none.[76]

Twisse is insistent that, as Milton's Samson will say, "the contradiction / Of their own deity, Gods cannot be" (898–99). Yet his logic becomes both slippery and clumsy as he tackles the Arminian notion that both God and Satan work *"in* man" as being "as absurd an assertion as ever any man breathed."[77]

This is a perspective on existence belonging to neither of the two Testaments but to "the Tragaedean[s]," especially Seneca, whose lot, says Twisse, was to confuse fate with God and to substitute human will for "divine operation," and then to allow the former to prejudice the latter as if any thing at all could happen, good or evil, without the will of God at once "effecting" good and "permitting" evil. It is not only tragedy *per se* but the Choruses therein that justify the fury of their heroes, with Twisse then wondering:

> Will not such one day, rise up in judgement against many Christians, who unless themselves may be exempted from that providence divine, whereby he moves all things agreeable to their natures, are so apt to condemne God of injustice, and justify themselves, as needing not to have any conscience of sinne.[78]

Too often, from Twisse's perspective, the Chorus is a blunted intelligence in tragedy as is the final Chorus to *Oedipus at Colonus* that, making God and fate one, commend characters like Oedipus and Jocasta who condemn themselves, "becom[ing] selfe executioners of punishment upon themselves for their foule crimes: the one pulling out his own eyes . . .; and the other destroying herselfe."[79] What is noteworthy here is the way in which a disapproving representation of tragedy blurs into a deep reflection on it.

Twisse's overarching argument, that the elect are always of the elect, would seem to compel him to regard Samson as a player in comedy, not tragedy, but the particularity and drift of his reflections, as becomes clear later on, have the effect of bracketing the Samson story in question marks. Twisse, for example, offers an unusually harsh reading of Judges 13: *"Manoahs* Wife had no faith, but only a probability of this," writes Twisse (citing Bertius) as he declares that here both of

Samson's parents are "in temptation, and that a very sore one." Later, in his questioning of Samson — "Did not *Samson* sacrifice himselfe?"[80] — Twisse, even as he protests against such a reading, makes us wonder as readers of Milton if, like Oedipus and Jocasta, Samson does not condemn himself in the catastrophe at the end of his life and if, at the end of *Samson Agonistes*, the commendation of the Chorus does not stand in calculated contrast against its self-condemned protagonist. From such a perspective, as N. H. Keeble remarks, it would seem that, "despite its conclusion," Milton's poem "offers no encouragement to anticipate, still less to trust to, God's blessing on such means."[81] Such a construction on the Samson story, too often identified with our own age, emerges in Milton's time and, if most evident among the Arminians, is also detectable in the writings of those like Pierce and Twisse who, if sometimes mistaken for Arminians, actually were not. To say that David and Solomon fell from grace by resisting it invites such labeling; to say that they resisted grace, but not at the end, not finally, is to slough it off.[82]

The cracks and fissures developing in received interpretation, if not most conspicuous, are often more interesting, not in the conflicting interpretations of opposing camps, but in the divisions and disputes that erupt among thinkers who are members of the same camp; that erupt even within a single treatise. For example, George Downame proclaims that "we deny not, but the spirit may be lost; as the examples of *Saul*, *Sampson*, and *Judas* doe prove":

> howsoever we grant, that the spirit may in regard of them be said to be grieved and dulled; yet we deny, that he is utterly extinguished, or exturbed; though moved and shaken, yet not removed or shaken off.[83]

Other examples are cited later — Adam, David, Peter, and Solomon — to prove that the elect "never wholly fall away," though like Solomon they must repent after their falls or else perish.[84] Oddly, initially *in* the discussion, Samson is dropped from it, Downame thus leaving us to wonder, in this one instance, whether Samson repents and in what sense he is chosen: for salvation or (like Judas) simply to perform some act on earth. David, Peter, and Solomon are also invoked by Richard Baxter, the first two not void of charity but examples of charity decayed, hence not "totally" fallen in contrast with Solomon who concerning his salvation provokes "my own uncertainty."[85] Dropped from consideration, Samson nevertheless remains on its margins — bracketed by question marks.

In another telling example, Nicholas Tyacke reports the following exchange among those who, broadly speaking, adhere to the doctrine of perseverance. When John Preston asks, "Could a truly justified man fall from grace as a result of sin?", Francis White cites David as an example of someone who cannot be in the state of saving grace until he repents. Thomas Morton chimes in with the view that David's election was "unalterable"; for however far he might go, like the Prodigal Son, he can always return. What worries Pemberton and Carlisle about the terms of this debate is "this consequence, the setting up of 'a school of sin'" — a position causing Preston to restate his own case, as summarized by Tyacke, that "although a justified man sinning was subject to God's wrath, there remained in him the 'seed of God' which 'would repair him . . . as in Peter, David, Sampson and others'? God 'did not disinherit them and blot their names out of the Book of Life'. . . . But Dr. White exclaimed against any that should think the prodigall, in acts of drunkeness and whoredom, not to be fallen from grace."[86] If not at the center of this debate, one supposes because he is so awkward an example, Samson now and then appears on its stage, usually not for a solo performance and sometimes only in its wings.

What should be evident from the forgoing discussion is that political allies, indeed major players in the Civil War years, Cromwell and Owen on the one hand, and on the other

Goodwin and Milton, are theologically at odds: not just on questions of election and reprobation as they relate to the debate over the perseverance of the saints, but to issues of providence and grace, dispensations and revelations. Unexpectedly perhaps, these divisions express themselves in *Samson Agonistes* through a protagonist whose views align him with the Calvinist adherents to the idea of the perseverance of the saints — a notion that Milton as both poet and theologian challenges, in *Paradise Lost* and *De Doctrina* advancing positions allying him unmistakably with the Arminians and with Arminian views of the 1660s and 70s given currency by the Quakers. If there are kindred spirits and shared viewpoints here, they are to be found in Samson, Owen, and the early Cromwell with the last of them eventually moving toward the kind of critique of the revolution, including self-critique, folded into *Samson Agonistes*, namely that too much, all too easily, had been credited to divine manifestations, dispensations, and inspiration.

No one would seem to anticipate, or to authorize more clearly, Cromwellian ideology than Robert Sanderson in "Ad Magistratum: The Third Sermon" (1625) as he argues that the magistrates are called upon not to deliberate but to act, never casting scruples, forecasting dangers, or *"expecting commission* from men" because their *"warrant* [is] sealed within them."[87] Samson and Cromwell, by such arguments, are God's workmen and messengers; and their slaughters, evidence of His providence. As reported by Christopher Hill, one Leveller tract of 1649 comments: "You shall scarce speak to Cromwell about anything ... but he will lay his hand on his breast, elevate his eyes and call God to record"; and what Cromwell then puts on record is his belief that following God's providence, even in the most savage of massacres, his victories bear the unmistakable "seals of God's approbation." After storming Drogheda, Cromwell crows: "this is a righteous judgment of God upon these barbarous wretches"; at Dunbar, he marvels:

"the Lord by His good Providence put a cloud over the moon."[88]

As Cromwell represents himself, so he comes to be represented by others. Thus the people of Herefordshire tell Cromwell: God "called you forth and ledd you on . . . , making you a terror to the enemie," as well as "the instrument to translate the nation from oppression to libertie"; and the people of Henly upon Thames insist that he and his officers are "eminent instruments in his great workeings in theis dayes, . . . placeing you in the front of his providences." The people of New England declare that "the Lord . . . made you a glorious instrument of the execution of his just vengeance upon the bloody monsters of mankinde." Correspondingly, Cromwell's officers in Ireland contend that "the Lord broke them and . . ., routed all of them, kill'd many, drowned more," and then "under high and choise dispensations of mercy" led us out of Egypt.[89] Not Cromwell alone, but also such intimates as Henry Ireton and John Owen were obsessed with tracking providence, finding dispensations, believing that history is none other than the story of God's manifestations. Initially, Milton may have praised Cromwell's Puritan religiosity, but as Cromwell himself would come to do, with the failure of the Puritan Revolution, Milton may also have come to question the validity of those claims to providential favor, intervention, and inspiration.[90]

Unlike Milton, Cromwell does not stand and wait, does not comprehend the heroism of inaction, at least not yet, but, as Hill attests, wrestles with God for a blessing, giving history a shove every time God is slow to act, in this way making himself the vehicle for "extraordinary dispensations," and hence God's will the justification for all his actions.[91] If these are the Lord's battles, Cromwell reasons, then his saints should take to the battlefield. If not to the Lord's call, at least they should beckon to Cromwell's: "What is the Lord a-doing? What prophecies are now fulfilling? Who is a God like ours . . .";
and later, with the people themselves having become like the

forming God, Cromwell declares: "I do think something is at the door: we are at the threshold; . . . at the edge of the promises and prophecies."[92] In a later chapter, we will hear Cromwell again speaking for himself in a rhetoric, and with inflections, that are replicated in *Samson Agonistes*, where the tragedy involves not someone on the wrong side but someone on the right side who did some wrong things.

More than a century and a half later, Hegel will stipulate the terms by which this controversy over the perseverance of the saints, and the providential theology implicit in it, will have particular relevance not just to interpreting *Samson Agonistes* but to the very genre in which the poem is cast:

> . . . the spirit of God leads up to God. Taken strictly such a phrase can only imply that the inward life of man is regarded as a purely passive ground, upon which the spirit of God labours. In such a conception the human will disappears as a free will, and at the same time the Divine purpose which motives the 'inworking' . . . can only appear to man as a kind of Fate. . . . God gives a command, and man is obliged to harken.[93]

It is this external opposition between God and mankind with which Sophocles could not dispense, and which the "perseverance" advocates fostered, that Milton's conception of free will resisted and that, resisting, enabled Milton to remain true to the first law of tragedy: people are captains of their fate and rule over their destiny. Not so from Cromwell's perspective. In it, God is the author of all history; and people, essentially powerless, merely God's pawns. Thus Cromwell says to Robert Blake and Edward Montagu: "We have been lately taught that it is not in man to direct his way. Indeed all the dispensations of God . . . do fully read that lesson. We can no more turn away the Evil . . . than attain the Good." Again and again, Cromwell asserts "absolute dependence upon God's providence."[94]

It is precisely within their respective comments on the genres, including tragedy, that, in *Paradise Regain'd*, Jesus proclaims that "man fell / Degraded by himself" (4.311–12) in response to Satan's praise of "the lofty grave Tragoedians" who "treat / Of . . . change in human life" in terms of "fate, and chance" (4.261, 264–65). It is exactly this sort of dispute in which politics colors theology and theology spills back into politics that ambiguates Samson who, if still a figure for celebration sometimes, is more often a character in whom to lodge a critique of oneself and one's culture, of one's own political party or its adversary. Not usually the object of outright repudiation, Samson is nevertheless a character in whom to figure one's own — and one's culture's — desires and defects, a convenient figure through whom to measure the distance between what is and what could be, between the realities of existence and the prospects for a better world.

This is not to say that this controversy had no backlash. John Owen, who had written a scoffing reply to John Goodwin, presents an exact portrait of these supposedly idiot questioners: they are Arminian in creed, Independents in church government and Republicans in politics; and in this context, and with an ironic twist, "republicanism" harkens the likes of Oliver Cromwell to whom Owen addresses his book and who so often justified both himself and his government as being under divine control and rule. No Arminian he. The subversives who wrecked one government were now, it seemed, wrecking another: their only loyalty was to subversion, and their misguided allegiance was given to the rule of charity. For Owen — preacher before Parliament the day after Charles's execution and to the Council of State between 1649 and 1650, Cromwell's chaplain in Ireland, always a proponent of the Presbyterian theory of church government and among the most eminent of the Puritan divines — the doctrine of the perseverance of the saints is one of the "divine truths"[95] of Scripture asserted and showcased in the Epistle to the Hebrews and one essential to maintaining Cromwell's government, which was founded upon it, but which could just as well be critiqued by it. When the Revolution failed, Owen could withdraw from the politics of this doctrine and return to its theology, which needed shoring up as much as did the Epistle to the Hebrews, which was its foundation stone.

In the period between 1668 and 1684, Owen produces *An Exposition of the Epistle to the Hebrews* in four parts, in seven volumes. According to Owen, Hebrews 11.32, beginning with "an interrogation," is followed by a long "confirmation," wherein Owen allows that, if subject to "passions and infirmities," most of those here mentioned "did themselves fall into such sins and miscarriages, as to manifest that they stood in need of pardoning grace and mercy. . . . Samson's taking a wife of the Philistines, then keeping company with a harlot, were sins of a high provocation; not to mention the killing of himself at the close of all, for which he seems to have had a divine warranty."[96] Perhaps the best measure of Samson's current status among the saints, an obvious consequence of the multiple interrogations he underwent from various quarters earlier in the century, is that Owen has a great deal more to say about the others in the Hebrews roll call than he has to say about Samson. It seems clear from another context that, even if Owen is obliged to confirm Samson's saintly status, he is not prepared to number him among "the choicest saints."[97]

The important project is to prop up not Samson but Hebrews in the face of those like Tommaso de Vio Cajetan and Desiderius Erasmus who had denied this epistle to St. Paul and questioned its canonical authority. And that project requires reconfirmation in the face of John Goodwin's and others' "corrupting gloss[es]" of the following propositions: that God's ways are never contrarious, that he neither chooses nor calls wrongly, nor ever abandons even "the weakest, frailest, sinfulest saint," all of whom have "equal certainty" of their election, "a perpetual preservation" of their sainthood and on whose part there is never apostatizing.[98] Milton's Samson, if not Milton himself, will testify to many of these same beliefs.

In turn, the Milton of both *Paradise Lost* and *Samson Agonistes* is one source of the kind of corrupting glosses Owen seeks to eliminate.

Indeed, Milton enters the controversy in *De Doctrina*, chapter 25, "Of Incomplete Glorification . . . and the Perseverance of the Saints," yet enters it warily enough that Maurice Kelley will annotate:

> Thus far, Milton's definition accords with the Reformed view that those whom God initially elects can never fall away, and consequently persevere unto the end. But the reservations "MODO UT IPSI SIBIMET NE DESINT, FIDEMQUE ET CHARITATEM PRO SUA VIRILI PARTE RETINEAT," render Milton's definition an Arminian statement: election is conditional; it requires the cooperation of believers; and believers can and may through their own fault lose faith and fall away completely and finally. (*YP*, 6:506)

The sort of interrogation that John Goodwin promotes and that Owen would silence is at the heart of *Samson Agonistes*.

Interrogation produced controversy, the very terms of which provide Milton's poem with the essence of its drama, the very framework for its tragedy, which is as much private as public, as much theological as political. *Samson* is of a piece with other politicizations of the Samson story, some of which use this story to mount a critique of the dominant culture, its attitudes and their aberrations. If Samuel Cradock is any indication, it seems as if, despite the recuperative efforts of Owen, hereafter Samson will often be cause for suspicion. For in Cradock's commentary, only Samson gets a special and somewhat apologetic note, which explains that, in Samson's case (and Cradock here follows Dr. Gouge), "pulling down the House upon himself . . ., was a lawful act, because he did it [as he did everything else] with a *special warrant*, which was the immediate and extraordinary motion of God's spirit," not *now* failing Samson because of God's earlier commitment to him. Cradock's effort is simply to silence, thereby hiding in theology, a debate that during the 1650s had developed a prominent (and for a long time not to be forgotten) political aspect, were it not that he then equivocates in the manner of Perkins: "The apostle here doth not observe the order of *time*, but of *dignity*; for *Gideon* had a more excellent spirit than *Barak*, and *Sampson* than *Jephtah*."[99]

This sort of blind reasoning is traceable to Peter Damian for whom the "blinded" Samson, "wickedly reveal[ing] his secret," is thereby humbled so that in the end, "fortified" by the spirit, he may become God's partner in destroying the temple and killing the Philistines.[100] Just this sort of assertion, in the instance of Cradock eroded by equivocation, riles George Whitehead and William Penn who, citing Thomas Jenners's argument *"That men are justified imputatively Righteous, and without Spot or Wrinckle in the Sight of God; while yet in themselves Spotted, Wrinckled, Imperfect, Unholy, &c.,"* respond thusly:

> What a monstrous corruption is this! . . . this gross *Antinomian Principle*, of being imputed *Righteous* while actually *Sinful* and *Unholy*, is as corrupt and sinful, as to say, Men are imputedly *Saved*, when actually *Damned*, or imputedly *Saints*, when actually *Devils*.[101]

Jenner is wrong, by their argument, to accuse these "Saints of Sin and Imperfection all their life time" and of thereby accusing God by regarding sin as His device for humbling the saints, who at least in the instances of Job, Noah, David, Peter, and Paul were cleansed of their sins before they died.[102] Not mentioned here, Samson remains a question mark.

Others, still more assertively, will force suspicion of Samson into the foreground of their readings. Let these examples, which cut across class and gender boundaries, which run the political spectrum, serve as a segue into commentary on

Revelation 7, which has implications in need of teasing out for further nuancing reinterpretation of the Samson story. The first is afforded by Katherine Philips's "On the Third of September 1651" — the date marking Cromwell's defeat of Charles and ending the second phase of the Civil War. Philips's husband was a member of Parliament; yet in Wales, surrounded by Cromwell's sympathizers, she revealed her own Royalist leanings in both "Upon the Double Murther of King Charles I" and "In the Fair Weather Just at The Coronation." Nevertheless, although his troops were greatly outnumbered, hence badly routed, while Charles himself escaped, Philips seizes this occasion to upbraid him/them; for even if their cause was right, most were destroyed wantonly, selfishly, predictably but needlessly. Theirs is the mindset of a Samson, his is their tragedy:

> Unhappy Kings, who cannot keep a Throne,
> Nor be so fortunate to fall alone!
> Their weight sinks others: *Pompey* could not fly,
> But half the World must bear him company;
> And captiv'd *Sampson* could not life conclude,
> Unless attended with a multitude.[103]

Greatness is now but air, all ends in despair, Philips writes, with "Heros tumbl[ing] in a common heap . . . / Oh give me Vertue then, which sums up all, / And firmly stands when Crown and Scepters fall."[104] This tragic view of Samson accords with one etched a decade before by Lady Eleanor Douglas whose Samson is a fallen hero, just another man, stripped of his might, with no occupation too base for him and who, in his fallenness, having violated his vows and obligations, now degraded, death paying his ransom, is seen "portraying forth . . . our *British* Union, fast knit and bound, soon dissolved." Great Britain rent in pieces, according to Douglas, is "shadowed out in Samsons exploits."[105] As Douglas implies through the biblical quotation on her title page, Samson is a sign — a sign that the Lord has spoken. Once the revolution had failed, with Samson as its mirror, the same kind of critique would eventually be turned by some revolutionaries against the revolution. Samson's tragedy would become their tragedy — England's tragedy. One need not concede the regeneration of Samson to accede to the conclusion that *Samson Agonistes* "can be seen ... as a political and prophetic work in which the destiny of Samson corresponds to that of England."[106]

One prophetess of the late seventeenth century, Jane Lead, who despite the temporary failure of the Civil War effort sees the millennium in the offing, bids Milton to join his voice to hers in singing in the new Jerusalem. Now, says Lead, in pronouncements that, intentional or not, chafe against the concluding verses of *Samson Agonistes* — now is the time when the "True *Phinix* ... in Heav'nly Flames *Revives*" and a new "Eagle-Bird is a hatching." The phoenix and the eagle, not Samson, are the heralds of apocalypse. Or perhaps Lead means for us to view the eagle and the phoenix as the true Samson and the true Delilah, for she repeatedly analogizes herself with Delilah and seems comfortable doing so given the extent to which Milton, by giving Dalila such prominence, together with some compelling discourse, has begun to neutralize her character in *Samson Agonistes* and given the fact, too, that Milton analogizes his own person with Samson by way, though, of forcing distance and achieving distinction. Moreover, it is as the new, chaste, faithful Delilah that Lead now decodes the mystery of Samson's locks, which answer to the seven seals in Revelation about to be removed by a wise and virtuous woman.[107]

Almost as a paradigm for the later imagings of William Walsh and, simultaneously paving the way for Lead, Milton seems to say (with Walsh):

> ... 'tis possible were she [Delilah] alive, she might tell you in her own defence, that what account you have of her, is from her profest enemies: That however taking the thing as they tell it; if she did commit a piece of treachery, it was against an

Enemy of her Country; and that it is very hard she should be so much run down for the same thing they have so much admired in *Jael* and *Judeth* . . .; she would perhaps push her defence further, and tell you, that tho she delivere'd *Samson* to the *Philistines* to be kept prisoner, yet she never drove a Nail through his head, nor cut it off.[108]

These are the mainlines of Dalila's argument set forth in Milton's tragedy.

Lead believed that the laws for the new paradise would be bestowed upon women and here uses reinterpretations of Judges stories to reflect upon the politics of that new paradise. When all her citations of the Samson legend are heaped together, it becomes evident that, while there is uneasiness with, there is no repudiation of Samson — just the sense that, among Judges, Samson's story, whatever its eventual outcome, is a shimmering reflection of what Richard Crashaw called "the Tragicke Doomes of men," their "flinty Destinyes."[109] And it was, after all, as a tragedy, the high and stately image of which is the Apocalypse, that Milton presented *Samson Agonistes*. For Milton, the theology of election and reprobation swirling around the debate over the perseverance of the saints has its final point of reference in the Book of Revelation and, through this scriptural book, is a forming influence on the tragedy of Milton's poem.

Several
Texts in One

> *. . . Holy Scripture cannot err and the decrees*
> *therein contained are absolutely true and inviolable.*
> *I should only have added that, though Scripture cannot err,*
> *its expounders and interpreters are liable to err in many ways.*
> — *Galileo Galilei*[1]

Robert Bellarmine is the Catholic most frequently cited, among the Protestant commentators, as a sanction for the supposedly Popish interpretation of Revelation 7; and Bellarmine believed, as Francis Rollenson reports disapprovingly, that "the speech of *Iacob* to *Dan* . . . was fulfilled in *Samson.*"[2] After David Pareus, the antipapist polemic begins to drop away from commentary on Revelation 7, as in the example provided by John Mayer: "why art not the tribes set forth in order? and why is the tribe of *Dan* and *Ephraim* left out . . .? . . . *Dan* they say is left out, because Antichrist should come of that tribe." Then Mayer goes on to explain that the order of the tribes is "the order of diuers nations cleauing to the true faith of Christ," which point causes Mayer to speculate further that Dan is left out because it is the tribe of idolatry, "that [it] had rent it selfe from the rest . . ., and dwelt there apart from the rest, setting vp an idoll and priest of their owne, euen till the time of the captiuity."[3] Or witness this additional example afforded by Arthur Dent: "The cause of the omission and skipping of the Tribe of *Dan*, was their continuance in Idolatry from the time of the Judges . . . euen vnto the Captiuity." And Dent concludes: "the reason of this omission, is first their uvworthinesse."[4]

The recognition that Samson is in Dan continues to be preserved (as we have seen, John Diodati is a signal instance) but, again as Diodati illustrates, is often kept under wraps when the commentator switches from Genesis 49 to Revelation 7: "Dan [is] left out in this place for some unknowne cause," writes Diodati as he acknowledges that to be included here is to be numbered with "the elect" and "marked with Gods, and Christs Character."[5] On other occasions, however, the perception that Samson is in Dan, and vice versa, begins to peek out from its cover, owing largely to the recovery of Jewish interpretation, which makes it clear that what once might have seemed like Jesuitical propaganda has a venerable tradition behind it. By the middle of the seventeenth century, even commentators who are inclined to judge Samson favorably will reveal the Samson/Dan connection, sometimes inadvertently and usually awkwardly. Notice the stresses and strains that occur when Samson is seen, then not seen, in the figure of Dan:

> *Sampson of Dan* was an extraordinary Judge. . . . More by cunning, then by force shall they prevaile, so did the *Danites*. . . . And *Samson* used craft as well as strength. . . . *Dan* is omitted in the sealing of the tribes, *Apoc.* 7 . . . *Dan* for his notorious idolatry. . . . Not because Antichrist should come of the tribe of *Dan*.[6]

The latter point remains a matter of dispute, even among Protestant commentators; yet Calvin's inclination to censor Dan/Samson rather than Luther's to celebrate the duo as wily and wise serpents has begun to prevail. Witness this further example provided by John Lightfoot, whose valuation of Samson (as we shall see) changes dramatically between the 1640s and 1660s. By Lightfoot we are reminded that Dan is the tribe of idolatry and of Samson who, once the Judges chronology is sorted out, comes at the end of the narrative and, in his own defeat, figures the defeat of the entire tribe. The chapters of Judges are read as a condemnation of the chaos and violence that those like Samson, perhaps unwittingly, contrived and condoned. His tribe's sign was not, in Jewish tradition, the eagle but "a serpent, or arrow snake"; and the tribe itself became notorious for its laying of "ambushments," thus blocking the way into Jerusalem. By canceling this tribe from the Revelation listing, says Lightfoot, "the Holy Ghost doth point . . . with the finger" and "will not so much as name the names" of those instigators of idolatry, one of whom — and in Lightfoot's chronology the ultimate example of whom — is Samson.[7]

Not naming the names but insinuating a judgment is a delicacy observed by commentators throughout the seventeenth century. Writing in the last decade of this century and thus attesting to the persistence of an interpretation throughout the century, J. W. Peterson is as good an instance as any. Just as Satan seduces by posing as an angel of light, so in all nations (England not excepted), "there are some Crafty, Serpent-like Spirits, having an Appearance of Godliness, that would deceive the very Elect." Later on in this treatise, Peterson invokes this example:

> Now concerning DAN, he is a wicked serpent, a corrupt Generation, that leadeth only into Darkness, for all wickedness shall meet together in him, and from him shall the Man of Sin be revealed. Therefore not any out of him are Sealed, for they

are Vipers; and none of the First-born are found amongst them; but they are all hardened and abominable. . . . As for those of the Tribe of *Dan*, who do stand in the Judaism, they also shall be Converted, but not all of them. For as many as belong to the Beast, will presently turn back to him, and will receive his Mark.[8]

The notion that Dan is the tribe of Antichrist surfaces again and, with it, the imagery of the serpent and viper that had often been attached by Genesis interpreters to both Samson and his tribe. Samson is not specifically named in this censure but seems, nevertheless, to be comprehended by it: who else in this tribe do we know by name? who other than Samson do we know as *the* Danite? The tribe is not sealed for protection, but neither is it extirpated: its (Samson's) legacy will continue on in history, pulling down some with others escaping. Here we find precedent for Milton's revision of the Samson tradition when, in *Samson Agonistes*, not all are destroyed, according to the Messenger's report, but "The vulgar only scap'd who stood without" (1659). Another such precedent will be found in the writings of William Guild,[9] who also helps explain, along with Joseph Mede, why the Revelation connection probably matters to Milton as well as why it impacted so significantly, albeit obliquely, upon the received interpretation of the Samson story.

I

What happens in the intertwining of Judges and Revelation is illustrated by Joseph Mede, who, never mentioning Samson, sets forth a reading of Revelation 7, the implications of which are clear enough. In this "Apocalyptic theatre," the throne of the Elders is circled by four standards, each associated with a tribe and bearing its symbol: Judah's lion, Ephraim's ox, Reuben's man, and Dan's eagle. Its standard situated in the north, its sign that of the eagle (a devouring bird) associated by Mede with "carcases," Dan emblematizes the idolatrous worship that, in John of Patmos's day, was defiling Christianity. Mede formulates what is still the reigning interpretation of Revelation 7 and establishes the principles still governing its interpretation:

> The tribes are in no other part of Scripture enumerated in this order.... [B]esides that Dan does not appear with them at all.... [T]here is a departure here from the rule of all (the enumerations which are made elsewhere, ... so that it can by no means be doubted but that some remarkable mystery ... lies concealed under such a novel and unusual order.... Dan is rejected ..., and Ephraim is passed over, in silence, as the standard bearers of the Israelitish apostasy (Jud. c. xviii and xviiii), and the same as were the patrons of the public idols in Dan and Bethel.... They were therefore, altogether unfit to represent the followers of a purer religion.[10]

First place in John's list ("justly due," says Mede) "is bestowed on Judah, on account of Christ, the King of the faithful, descended from that tribe." On the other hand, Dan seems to be "degraded" by exclusion, and the degradation is rendered emphatic by "the substitution of Levi [who made fellowship with Israelite apostates and idolaters] in the place of Dan." If Levi is elevated into Mede's second quaternion, Dan seems "degraded ... into the fourth quaternion ... *the brethren of [which] ... have no quality in which some excel others*" (my italics).[11] Its standard in the north, recalling that it is to the northern reaches of heaven that Satan goes in rebellion, Dan (and Samson), it appears, have each lost their preeminence. Milton's phrase from *Paradise Lost*, "the *Danite ... Samson*" (9.1059–60), resonates powerfully within this context.

Reading no less than writing Revelation commentary seems to be a very delicate affair; but it also seems impossible to read what Mede wrote without implicating Samson (as the last quotation suggests) in the general demotion and degradation from which no member in the tribe of Dan is exempted.

How could Samson not be implicated in a judgment falling upon a tribe of which he is the chief hero and only judge? When Harapha addresses Samson in Milton's poem as a "League-breaker" and "Robber" who commits "Notorious murder" (1184–88), he seems to do little more than particularize to Samson Mede's general indictment of Dan as he speaks of "the Danish robbers."[12] Mede also makes clear that the contrast in the juxtaposition here of true and false churches becomes explicit when Revelation 7 is set against the chastising epistles to the seven churches or in the contrast inherent in synchronizing this with the prophecy of the beast, thus highlighting the difference between those marked for salvation and those bearing the mark of the beast, the "deserters and revolters."[13]

It should be clear from much of the forgoing discussion that Revelation 7.7 is typically glossed by Genesis 49.16–18, with the eighteenth verse of Jacob's prophecy sometimes cited as the prayer that Samson delivers at the pillars; and both the Genesis and Revelation passages are often coordinated with this or that episode in the Book of Judges. There is nothing improbable or implausible, strained or eccentric, about this collocation of texts. On the other hand, Genesis 49 and Revelation 7 are also fraught with interpretive problems. Is Jacob's prophecy general, particular — or both? Is it to be construed positively or negatively, and how did Milton construe it theologically and use it poetically? When the prophecies from Genesis and Revelation are interconnected, does the "Samson in Dan" reading still pertain, or is the particularity of Jacob's prophecy blotted out in the generalized prophecy of Revelation 7? That is, do good or bad angels preside over the judgment and holocaust that are to follow? Is Dan, by implication, included in the Revelation listing of the twelve protected tribes? Or is Dan's name thus omitted from the list by scribal error or omitted, instead, by intention and, if the latter, because of the idolatry rising up in that tribe or because Dan is the tribe of Antichrist, Beliar, and Satan?

What are the implications here for the Samson story, and do they have any bearing on Milton's version of the same story? It has been said elsewhere that "Samson is by no means a centerpiece of Revelation commentary."[14] That is true, but it is true too that only in Revelation 7 does his story achieve focalization — and only sometimes and then only in fleeting moments. Otherwise, the Samson story is an allusion, explicit sometimes and other times quite hidden. The story is a parenthesis or a marginal gloss, providing interpretive similes and analogies, which, in turn, produce now positive, now negative formulations about Samson. Here he is heroic — a Christian warrior or one of the elect and one of the faithful, a member of the true church. There he is of the false church, not one of the elect at all, his character tarnished, his status diminished, by his association with the tribe of Dan and by its associations with idolatry and Antichrist. Samson is now one of the elect, now one of the reprobate. If interpreting the Book of Revelation is a very delicate affair, interpreting Samson within the Revelation tradition is a more difficult matter still, with confusions arising from misreadings, or from truncations of evidence where too much gets omitted, or from hints of interrogations that are themselves unhelpful without elaborate contextualizations and explanations.

What is important, first of all, is that we acknowledge the long tradition of viewing the Book of Judges as part of an interleaved history belonging to a period when "there was no open Vision":

> The Book of *Judges* has an essential Relation to the Books of *Moses* and *Joshua*, the most part of the Captivities of the People of *Israel*, being a Consequence of the Quarrels with the Nations which they had subdued, and with their Neighbours. . . .[15]

What is of further importance is that we mark the points at which the Book of Judges, and especially its Samson story, intersect with the New Testament, particularly the Book of

Revelation. For example, the place called Dan, where idolatry is first set up, is, according to John Lightfoot, the site for the transfiguration of Jesus. Armageddon is supposed to take place, as Patrick Forbes remembers, on the same ground where Jael murdered Sisera. John Bale in a marginal gloss crossreferences Revelation 7 and Judges. John Trapp uses Judges 5 to gloss the spiritual kingdom of Revelation 1; Joseph Mede links Revelation 17 and Judges 12 to explain their common rhetorical features; James Durham associates the idolatry in Judges 17 with that in Revelation and the fire in Judges 9 with that in Revelation 8, and William Hicks parallels the same fire with the final coming of Christ. Sampson Price and William Perkins both invoke Samson in their explications of the epistles to the seven churches, the one suggesting that Samson is the antithesis of the true church and the other formulating a contrast between Samson and Christ. By Guild the Samson story is intruded upon the scene of judgment in Revelation 8, by Hezekial Holland upon the scene of the celestial battle in Revelation 12; ånd Thomas Cartwright uses the same story to expiate on the importance of awaiting the call before avenging and of then avenging (as he thinks Samson does) only "publiquely."[16] Still, once these encroachments of the Samson story have been marked, it is important to scrutinize their implications. What is at issue? What does the Samson story illuminate?

In *De Doctrina Christiana*, Milton offers instruction concerning the sacred dialect of the Book of Revelation and how to read it: here there is a special kind of troping ("*ten horns are ten kings*") "to denote the close relationship between the symbol and the thing symbolized" (*YP*, 6:555; cf. 296). First, physical or natural images signify heavenly or human beings, often both. The star falling from heaven, trailing light like a comet, is an angel or human or both; it is the falling Lucifer, as well as various historical personages differently identified by different commentators but by virtually all of them associated with apostasy — with falling away from the divine vision. That star may be mythologized as Lucifer/Satan or historicized as any number of figures, sacred or secular, individually or collectively — this or that personage of the church, this or that king or magistrate, or all of them wound up together in a single image: "not one onlie individuall person," says William Guild, but "a sucession of manie."[17] The star is called wormwood by way of emphasizing that, whatever identity it may be given, the being the star refers to is known by his effects.

Second, the sealing of the tribes in Revelation is an interruption between the sixth and seventh seals but pertains chiefly to the opening of the seventh seal. Thus, chapters 7–9 of Revelation are of a piece; they are continuous with one another and interdependent upon one another for interpretation. As one commentator states: the apostasy of the four angels in Revelation 7 "is gradually set forth" in Revelation 8, "all these expressions setting forth the gradations of the Apostasie."[18] Revelation 7, in its marking and sealing of the tribes, in its placing of those tribes under God's protection, simply prepares the stage for the scenes of judgment — of wrath and vengeance — that will follow. The issues focused here are those of war and peace, justice and mercy. Who is responsible for each? The chief interpretive dispute involves the nature of the angels assembling at the beginning of Revelation 7, whether they are good or bad angels and then whether the avenging angels in subsequent judgment scenes are God's emissaries or Satan's. Some thought no determination was necessary inasmuch as God uses both kinds of angels in executing his judgments. Others like Guild thought this question mattered very much indeed, and then proceeded to hang their prophetic theology upon it. In any event, it is less the Samson allusion than the theology containing it that matters here; for that theology has an important bearing on Milton's poem and perhaps on one of its chief cruxes.

Confusion has been fostered, in part by my previously talking too loosely about a Revelation tradition involving the third angel of the Apocalypse when that angel, more exactly, is but an aspect of a tradition of interpretation centered in Revelation 7. Others risk confusion by insisting upon a naive literalism: Revelation, they say, speaks of a star called wormwood, not an angel. Coincidentally, only with reference to Guild can such literalism be turned to interpretive advantage. It is not these agents of destruction that matter to Guild so much as the commissioner and executioners of that destruction and their roles in the cosmic, cataclysmic drama. The ultimate commissioner is God; but he is careful in the assignment of certain tasks like destruction. He commissions his executioners from among Satan's brood and then restricts Satan's power to promote destruction through those he uses as his agents. As evidence of God's mercy, some are always saved, but that is God's doing, not the impulse of Satan or the satanically inspired instruments of his justice. What we witness in Revelation 7–9, then, is God's judgments, Satan's plagues, and finally God's mercy. Those judgments are published by the trumpets; that mercy is evident in those who survive the devastation they announce. Guild's theology, in part, would seem to fit nicely with Milton's, and even to explain Milton's notable departure from scriptural tradition in saving some from Samson's slaughter. With reference to the slain Philistines and the dead Samson, no less than with reference to the vulgar who escape the slaughter, the biblical adage holds: the beam of balance, the scales, the weights in the box — all are *God's* work. Permissive providence comes into play and with it, distributive, proportionate justice.

As this new phase in the apocalyptic drama commences, four angels assemble. They are known by their signs, one of which is Dan's eagle, "the *Carnivorous Eagle*," Henry More explains (and he is following Mede), "that feeds upon dead carkasses."[19] The angel of Dan, so to speak, occupies the northern region, the region of darkness and of Satan. Though not all commentators rushed to judgment on these four angels, most did (William Guild among them). John Bale, for example, identifies these four angels as "antichrists with their pestilent decrees and traditions" — as "the ungodly magistrates with their ignorance and blindness."[20] Pareus refers to this assemblage as "evill Angels . . . Satan & his Angels, . . . all Antichrists agents" from which no part of the world is free; and Guild, in line with this tradition, speaks of this cluster as "Angels of darknesse and . . . hurting Angels . . ., or Satans emissaries"; for they hinder the wind or the ministry of the Word. Then comes another angel who is Christ and who, coming from the East, would save, not destroy; who thus marks and seals God's servants so that "the destroying Angel" will not hurt them. This angel marks the twelve tribes and seals them under God's protection.[21]

If these twelve tribes provide "the Analogy of new Jerusalem,"[22] as Mede thought, the omitted tribe of Dan is its opposite, an analogy for Babylon, the city of Antichrist. Or if Samson is then remembered as the chief magistrate produced by the Danites, he may very well be remembered also as an Antichrist or as an associate. Or if Samson is remembered as Dan, a serpent in the way and an adder in the path, he may be seen (as sometimes he was) as the fulfillment of Jacob's prophecy and as one blocking the way into the spiritual city. Still, the indictment of Samson is seldom in the form of bald assertion but registers itself in hints that, if Samson is not Satan or Antichrist, nevertheless both he and his people are implicated in idolatry and thus pave the way for the dragon to reign.

It may also be useful here to recall the various representations of Samson as a backslider often accompanied both by the hope that this is a temporary aberration and by the worry that it may constitute a fatal submission. Perhaps Milton once embraced the notion that Samson was the prototypical soldier, even the patron saint of the New Model Army; and if so, he must eventually have comprehended the irony of such mythologizing as when he worries, in "A Letter to a Friend" (20 October 1659), that there may be "some inward flaw" in the now dangerously ruptured commonwealth and worries even more over the army's "backsliding from the good old cause," then "relapsing & so soon again backsliding" from the "great deliverance" that seemed at hand (*YP*, 7:324, 325). Thomas Goodwin's early critique of the Samson story cited in chapter 2, if Milton knew it, must have seemed oddly prophetic — and pointedly relevant to 1659 when Milton's hopes, at least for a time, collapsed into despair as, in the two versions of *The Readie and Easie Way*, he worries over "this general defection of the misguided and abus'd multitude" (*YP*, 7:388) before reaching an understanding of his misplaced trust in having "spoken perswasiom . . . to som . . . whom God may raise . . . to become children of reviving libertie; and may reclaim, though they seem now chusing them a captain back for *Egypt*" (7:463; cf. 388).

Samson's tragedy, as Goodwin defined it and Milton would later represent it, is the tragedy of God's Englishmen. J. H. Hexter describes the situation exactly:

> This is . . . heroic tragedy. . . . It is tragedy because circumstance and event provide only the setting in which Puritanism, through its own inner flaws and failings, thrusts itself down the path to disaster. It is heroic because Puritanism itself in the days of its triumph and its catastrophe was no trifling, hole-in-the-corner affair — because Puritanism was indeed heroic, magnificent in its virtues and force, magnificent even in its failings: Samson Agonistes but Samson still.[23]

Judgments were now falling, sometimes silently, on Samson — not on Samson as Dan but on Samson as England.

The Samson story undergoes a curious sea-change when brought into contact with not only the Book of Revelation but also Rabbinical interpretive traditions and noncanonical literature, as well as the controversy over the perseverance of the saints, especially when it is remembered that the Book of Judges was thought to have a scrambled narrative; that, for purposes of interpretation, its crooked narrative had to be made straight. When that happens, the Samson story becomes a coda for one phase of history: Samson dies and then the Danites disappear, the idolatrous tribe of Dan is never mentioned again — not in Chronicles, not in Revelation. Samson could thus be aligned with Beliar or Satan, he could be construed as the Beliar or Satan or Antichrist rising out of the tribe of Dan; or he could be imagined as under the rule (hence as one of the limbs) of such demonic agents. And I say *could* because, even if the consequences of interpreting the Genesis and Revelation prophecies according to one another must have been obvious to most commentators, they were often reluctant to give to the obvious bold, precise formulation. Silence was more convenient and had the effect of casting suspicion on Samson, even censure, minus outright repudiation or condemnation. In certain moods or postures or actions, Samson was like Satan or Antichrist; yet he found his ultimate identity in neither. He was, as Milton might say, a tragic hero, not part of Satan's damned crew.

II

What stands behind the various interrogations of the Samson story, both in the sixteenth and seventeenth centuries, are "questions" and "disputations," often attached to the Judges narrative and certainly fueled by the suspicion cast upon Samson by glosses surrounding Genesis 49 and Revelation 7. As in some of this commentary, like the annotations supplementary to those of Matthew Poole, those interrogations can be muted, or silenced, by environing glosses: "*Quest.* Did not *Sampson* transgress . . .? *Answ.* It was in it self a legal Pollution"; "*Qu.* How could so great a Building, containing so many thousands of People, rest upon two Pillars so near placed together? . . . *Answ.* Instances are not wanting. . . ."[24] Other times, though, these interrogations are segregated, now to illustrate that God has given "his weake seruants power aboundantlie to ouercome" and now to illustrate that in the example of Samson, or "of Israel, in *Sampson*," we learn "not to tempt the Lord: neither is it wisedome for men to make such daungerous experience."[25] And once segregated, such interrogations become more rigorous; they are intensified, on the one hand, by factoring into interpretation noncanonical material and, on the other, by the practice, signally important to Milton, of correlating scriptural texts. This meant reading the Judges story and Jacob's prophecy in Genesis together and, in turn, that prophecy in concert with the cancelling of Dan from the list of protected tribes in Revelation, and all these texts in terms of Hebrews 11.32.

Initially, perhaps, interpretation of the Samson story had been ruled by the Hebrews text and made to conform to its positive representation. What we can say, provisionally, is that the early modern period inherits three interpretive traditions concerning Samson, each of them allied with a different (or different set) of scriptural texts: the Epistle to the Hebrews sponsors the most positive evaluation, a hermeneutic of exoneration, celebration, and recuperation; the Book of Judges, on the other hand, full of hesitations and reticences, generates a hermeneutic of interrogation; and finally from Genesis and Revelation in concert comes a hermeneutic of downright suspicion. Each hermeneutic can thus be transferred to, then tested against, another text through the habit of reading Scriptures by Scriptures, according to the principle enunciated by Milton in *De Doctrina* that "God . . . [is] his own best interpreter" (*YP*, 6:363). At the same time, this habit combines with another of reading oneself and one's own times out of scriptural history. This Milton does frequently. It is just that, as the Puritan Revolution seems more and more doomed to failure, Milton subordinates the Apocalypse, through which he had viewed the intermixture of tragedy and comedy in history, to Genesis and Judges through which he now glimpses — especially in the story of Samson — tragedy in its pure, unsaturated form. The full horror of Milton's tragedy is encapsulated in the lines, "Blood, death, and deathful deeds are in that noise, / Ruin, destruction at the utmost point" (1513–14).

The tragedy Milton glimpses may be new; but there is nothing new in his using the Book of Judges as a lens on the tragedy of the Civil War years when, if I may use the language of Thomas D'urfey, the "former Tragick Scene" of Judges seems to be "design'd again," refiguring history; and nothing new either in Milton's, along with many others, casting the Civil War as "this horrid Tragedy" — "*Englands Tragedy.*"[26] It is just that, unlike the anonymous writer here, Milton sees the Restoration not as converting tragedy into comedy but as deepening the nation's tragedy — "this so horrid spectacle" (1542) — in which the dissenters are "Actors" to be sure: participants in but by no means the principal cause of the tragedy. Like John Goodwin's, Milton's initial equations may have been crude ones. The Philistines may have comprehended Jesuits, Papists, Atheists within "that bloody and butcherly Generation, commonly knowne by the name of Cavalieres" and at once "mak[ing] rapine and spoile of all goods and possessions," while sharing with one another "a posture of hatred, and malice, and revenge."[27] The Army itself may seem to be undertaking, Samson-like, the glorious work of casting out these devils under a call, or warrant, or commission from God, its actions according with what Goodwin thinks are proper and clear principles of righteousness and honor. Goodwin writes his treatise, after all, within the context of the coda to the Book of Judges, "that inhumane butchering and quartering out into pieces of the *Levites* wife," a "bloody horrid" retaliation now being acted out again on an entire nation.[28] And not just Goodwin but Edmund Staunton marks the parallels between the Judges story of the Israelites and Benjamites and England's current history, its "Idolized Festivals, *with Playes and Interludes,*" its need

for men of zeal who, waiting upon God, act by *"special instinct,*
and by *motion extraordinary,"* in ways that, saving some of
the enemies, will reassert the principle of God's proportionate
justice.[29] With a very different politics, Robert South draws
similar parallels between the villainous period of Israelite history when people claimed to live as the spirit moved them —
"without check or control"; when they acted, sometimes
perilously, "with eyes lift up to heaven, and expostulations
with God, pleas of providence and inward instigations," taking
the Book of Judges and its supposed "providential dispensations"
as a warrant for whatever they might do. With South and
others, despite their different politics, Milton would probably
acknowledge a "great . . . resemblance . . . [what South will call
an "accomodation"] between this [the Book of Judges] and the
late civil war"; would find their "tragical scene[s]" and "horrid"
acts corresponding, especially in their respective pretensions
to divine illumination and impulse. But whereas South would
use the last chapters of Judges — the time when there was no
king and when the people were doing as they pleased — to
describe "the late civil war [as] . . . the Devil's works in a second
edition, . . . a foul and odious copy,"[30] Milton shifts stories and,
in a turn of the lens, affords an altogether more complicated
critique of the Civil War as England's tragedy, juxtaposing the
defeat of an individual and the demise of a nation.

The real problem (for South and Milton alike) is not what
blow this or that side strikes to the other but, rather, the fact
that the nation is torn asunder and the people paralyzed, unable
to act. Whom they name as heroes is less important than the
terms by which they define heroism as a "greater fortitude
of mind" and by "the justness of . . . [their] cause."[31] Unlike
Staunton, on the other hand, Milton would not be as ready,
even in 1645, to celebrate the people (and certainly not in his
later experience of defeat) as "the strength of a Nation,"
compelled by others to move backward instead of forward.[32]
Rather, from Milton's (and Samson's) point of view, as he led

forward his people pulled backward. By choosing "Bondage with ease" over "strenuous liberty" (271), they are thus at the very center — deeply implicated, if not the chief culprits in — this historical tragedy. But held in the captivity of his blindness even at the end, still enchained by his resentments and past ways, Samson bears enormous responsibility too and thus, with the Philistines, is caught in a common ruin. What C. F. Burney would say of the Judges history comes very close to describing Milton's tragic emplotment of the same story:

> In the history of Samson, in particular, the conception of the hero as a divinely appointed deliverer of his people seems little suited to the narrative; since his actions, so far as his personal volition is concerned, are wholly dictated by his own wayward inclinations, and he does not in any way effect deliverance or even respite from the foreign yoke.[33]

Gerhard von Rad reads the Judges story as if his text were *Samson Agonistes*: "the stories about Samson . . . show the failure of a charismatic leader, and divine powers wasted. . . . Samson himself perishes in the chaos which he spreads out around himself."[34]

If Robert South sees the Church broken and mangled like the Levite's daughter, King Charles as a sainted hero whose death completes this historical tragedy in which the rebels (including Milton) are the villains and in which God and his providence are chief actors, Milton sees the Church as one of the nation's betrayers, chief of whom was its tyrannical king, and perhaps even Samson/Cromwell as a flawed leader, the revolutionaries themselves as sometimes culpable, and a back-sliding people choosing themselves a captain back to Egypt. Most of all, he sees God fouled by those who themselves are foul and providence maligned in the process. He finds not glory but horror in God's supposed revenge, thus giving to his version of history a deepened tragic sense.[35] Interestingly, intriguingly, as we shall see, Milton's implied critique resembles Cromwell's critique of himself, enough so that it seems to borrow from it, deploying Cromwell's rhetoric in the same way that on occasion that rhetoric curls back upon Cromwell himself. *Samson Agonistes* is the moment when the critiques of the Revolution afforded by enemies like South and allies like Cromwell converge within a shocking moment of recognition.

As a neotype of Samson, Milton himself takes on the mantle of heroism, freeing himself of South's charge that as "a blind adder . . . [he] spit[s] so much poison on the kings person and cause," in this way eclipsing his prototype as much as, from South's vantage point, Charles I eclipses David.[36] Perhaps the very notion that, with the restoration of kingship, what commences as tragedy completes itself as comedy — the symbolic significance thus attached to tragicomedy, as well as to rhyme — leads Milton, who had already associated rhyme with bondage, not liberty, now in the preface to his tragedy, to belittle the "error of intermixing Comic stuff with Tragic sadness and gravity; or introducing trivial and vulgar persons." Another of the many ironies of this preface, another of its asymmetries, is that in *Samson Agonistes* itself, in the characters of Dalila and Harapha and intermixture in them of comic elements, Milton will do exactly what his preface protests against, albeit in a politically charged, ideologically pertinent way.

Within this context, as we remember Samson as Dan, or Samson as Israel, we should recall the impulse to use the Book of Judges as a way of glimpsing contemporary history (Israel then, England now), and for the same purpose the Book of Revelation. Likewise, we should remember that Samson was the adopted saint of the Puritan revolutionaries; that in the seventeenth century he had become anglicized; that not just Rome but England was regarded as the seat of Antichrist; that Antichrist just as often enthroned himself within individuals as nations; that there was a developing sense that Antichrist might occasionally install himself within those who appeared to be saints. When all this is remembered, then the relevance of Samson to God's Englishmen (and to their spokesperson John Milton) becomes increasingly evident.

One need not read Samson as Dan but still can draw from Jacob's prophecy, and then from the Judges story, the apt inference and make the appropriate application: "this very selfhood is the serpent and venomous adder on the way, for it walketh very dangerous steps upon the paths of righteousness; it turneth righteousness into selfhood, to do what it will. . . . And so sucketh poison out of God's office of a judge, and thereby afflicteth the miserable, and stingeth with this poison round about in the way of the office, as an adder and serpent."[37] A story that had been a window for looking upon others could just as easily be a mirror for glimpsing the self as well as the tragedy of self modulating into the tragedy of civilization in its full apocalyptic dimensions.

The suspicion surrounding Samson in the Genesis/Revelation representation initially had been subdued by the Hebrews Samson; but as the seventeenth century wore on, that suspicion, being roused again, forced an adjustment upon representations of Samson in connection with the Hebrews text. Indeed, as the century progresses, the Old Testament Samson, and the Samson implicit in Revelation 7, begin to prevail. Although unqualified adulation for the heroes of Hebrews is still to be found, as in William Hickes,[38] it is no longer the order of the day, not by 1659 anyway when Milton is lamenting the backsliding of the Puritan saints. How the pressure from other biblical texts, and from other interpretive traditions, was felt upon the Hebrews text — how these various pressures modified received interpretation — is strikingly evident in the writings of Lightfoot and Broughton, the latter of whose works Lightfoot edited.

Both these scholars, each with a firm grasp of Hebraic traditions and Rabbinical writings, are fully aware of the competing traditions of interpretation that had accrued to the Judges narrative and its Samson story. Indeed, Broughton is so aware of the implications of contending interpretations and of their consequences for reading Scriptures by Scriptures that, wishing to sustain the heroic Samson of Hebrews, he argues for the integrity of the Hebrews text (it is not corrupt, the New Testament is not corrupt), shoring up St. Paul's authority and confirming his authorship. Correspondingly, Broughton must strengthen positive readings of Genesis 49 by way of defusing negative readings of Revelation 7. When he notes that Deborah, Gideon, and Jephthah all come from Joseph, he seems aware that such an observation opens the way to remembering Samson in Dan and thus to implicating Samson in the Revelation censuring of that tribe. Hidden in but eventually emerging from such observations is what will become a sharp contrast between Joseph and Samson as saviors of their people and deliverers of their nation.

Alone among the commentators I have read, Broughton mounts an elaborate argument against negative readings of Revelation 7: first, by espousing a wholly favorable reading of Genesis 49; second, by allying Samson with Judah rather than with Dan ("God chose the Judges . . . *Samson*, of *Dan* with *Judah*: for *Dan* . . . being a frontier Town, ougt to have none"); third, by restoring Dan to Revelation's tabulation of the twelve protected tribes ("Dan is in force named; though . . . in name he is not expressed"); and fourth, by insisting that Dan is emblematically among the tribes in Revelation 21. Having thus sanitized readings of Genesis 49 and Revelation 7, and then sanitized the whole of the New Testament (if the New Testament be corrupt, it cannot be from God), Broughton is able to keep in tact the received reading of Hebrews 11.32, which regards Samson as an unqualified hero of faith who, in death, conquers his own — and God's — enemies.[39] This argument in behalf of Samson thus entails one in behalf of St. Paul: if Paul's endorsement of Samson's heroism is to be sustained, Broughton must free him from the charge, levied by some, that he is implicated in a corruption of the Judges text — must establish, that is, metaphysical validity for Paul's supposed claim that Samson judged for forty years. Broughton's initiatives pave the way for others like Leonard Hoar to offer this sort of explanation:

> In the beginning of Sampsons being judge, must Samuel be born and dedicated, and all that corruption in worship practised by Elies sons, and judgment denounced and executed: as is recorded in 1 Sam. the six first Chapters, viz While Sampson with Eli governed 20 years, and after that Eli alone 20 more, and that compleats that 40 years ascribed to Eli in 1. Sam. 4, 18.[40]

As for Milton and Lightfoot, Rabbi Levi Ben Gerson is a principal authority for Broughton but, as an authority, is used here to uphold received readings and not, as he will be used by Lightfoot and Milton, to qualify and revise them. Broughton would concur with those who believe that the first sin, in the countertype, is idolatry; and he prefers to see Dagon, and not Dan, in that countertype. In contrast, Lightfoot and Milton regard the New Testament differently and, in the crucial instance of Revelation 7, interpret John's prophecy differently. Here there may be a biographical connection to be explored, as well as intellectual indebtedness yet to be documented.

Admittedly, if Milton might appeal to the Erastians but side with the Independents, Lightfoot, adopting certain Erastian positions, belonged to the Presbyterian majority; and he is known to have thought that Charles I was murdered. This is David Masson on Lightfoot: "This eminent theologian, deemed the most learned Orientalist or Rabbinical scholar of his age, had been educated at Christ's College, Cambridge, with Chappell for his tutor, and had completed his studies there just when Milton was beginning his."[41] Milton and Lightfoot attended the same college. They had the same tutor, William Chappell. Both of them must have known Joseph Mede, fellow at Christ's and of his innovative work on the Book of Revelation. Later, both men would apparently have some association with Theodore Haak, and both would come to be sorted (along with Thomas Goodwin and Andrew Marvell) among Cromwell's "Adherents More Or Less Cordial."[42] As Milton defended Cromwell, Lightfoot dedicated a book to him: one volume of *The Harmony, Chronicle, and Order of the New Testament* (1655) and, in the same year, upon assuming the Vice-Chancellorship of St. Catharine's College, Cambridge, delivered a panegyric on Cromwell. What would probably have drawn Milton's attention to Lightfoot is that he was regarded as the foremost Rabbinical scholar of the age and is usually credited with opening to the modern world the fountains of Talmudical learning. His influence on biblical exegesis was particularly notable in the last decade of Milton's life, with Lightfoot overseeing and revising the work of both Brian Walton and Matthew Poole.

Lightfoot's conception of the two testaments parallels Milton's own. The Old Testament is the better maintained text and yet, because "suspect" in "the chronological accuracy" of its narratives, is, as Milton argues in *De Doctrina*, subject to adjustments specifically in matters of chronology (*YP*, 6:588). The New Testament, though more authoritative than the Old, is a damaged text from which higher truths must be drawn by carefully reading Scriptures, which, in the words of *The Readie and Easie Way*, is "to be interpreted by the scriptures themselves" (*YP*, 7:379, 456). The same dislocation, disorder, and transposition of passages that Milton, in *De Doctrina*, finds in the New Testament book of God's judgments (see *YP*, 6:587–88) Lightfoot finds in Revelation's Old Testament counterpart. The fragmentation and disruption of narrative sequence, evident "more signally" in Judges "than in any other place," is a device of this same text for achieving meaningful juxtapositions, illuminating connections:

> I shall not trouble you with large discourses, to show, why these stories are displaced, and laid in this place . . .; I shall only commend this to your conception. Samson, their last judge,

after whose death their state declined, was of Dan: and their first public idolatry was in Dan. Samson's life was sold for eleven hundred shekels of silver of every Philistine prince. And then look at the eleven hundred shekels of silver consecrated for making Micah's idol, which was set up in the tribe of Dan; and you may easily perceive, that the Holy Ghost hath laid these stories thus together, that their sin in Dan, and shame in the fall of Samson of Dan, might be cast up together. Their last judge, Samson of Dan, came to so fatal and unhappy an end; and no wonder, for their first idolatry was in Dan.[43]

In the aforementioned sermon (dated 1663), Lightfoot explicates Judges by reference to Revelation: idolatry first broke out among the Danites; and "thereupon, Dan is omitted to be named among the sealed of the twelve tribes, Rev. VII."[44] In another sermon, also expounding Judges and presumably belonging to about the same time, Lightfoot turns attention to Hebrews:

> The apostle, in the Epistle to the Hebrews, chap. xi, reckoning up that noble catalogue of men, famous for faith and great actions under the law, — at ver. 32, mentions three, that may seem to be something questionable: and those are Gideon, and Samson, and Jephthah: men, indeed, that had done great acts, but that, in the close, came off with some foul blot. Gideon "made an ephod. . . ." Samson pulled down the house upon his own head, and so became "felo-de-se," or guilty of his own death. And was not Jephthah guilty of the death of his own daughter?[45]

As we have already observed, Milton moderates the blame that Lightfoot and others place upon Samson for his own death, having the Chorus explain that the Samson who "Pull'd down . . . destruction on himself" was "self-killed, / Not willingly, but tangl'd in the fold" (1658, 1664–65). Still, importantly for one reading of *Samson Agonistes*, during the 1660s, Lightfoot also invites paralleling Israel then with England now.

Lightfoot is a pivotal figure here for two reasons. First, his

writings reflect the shifting understanding of, as well as the
new inflections given to, the Samson story. It is easy to infer
from him that, in the instance of Samson's mother, not Samson, God takes away any reproach for defilement and that when
Samson goes to the rock of Etam he is, like others of his kind,
going to what this commentator seems to have understood as
one of the "lurking-places for wild beasts and robbers."[46] What
Lightfoot is now saying about the Samson story, in 1662, differs
markedly from what he was saying about the same story
in the 1640s, when his reading of this tale was inlaid with
clichés of an earlier interpretive tradition. In his earlier reading,
Samson was "a type of Christ" who "died by his own hand
gloriously"; his death marks not his own failings but rather
the failure of Israel's state policy which was Danite. The dis-
located narrative in the Book of Judges here allows for the
juxtaposition of Micah, "the first destroyer of religion," and
Samuel, "the first reformer of religion." Jacob's prophecy foresees "the great deliverance of Israel from the Philistines, by
Samson, of the tribe of Dan." This prophecy, moreover, envisions Dan as Samson biting the heels of Philistine horses, overthrowing their riders, and, like Christ, destroying by dying.[47]

One signal effect of emergent interpretation of the Samson
story, witnessed to by Lightfoot certainly, is to challenge and
force revision of the usual Samson/Christ typology. It is not
simply a typology of difference that comes to prevail but a
typology of *such* difference that it either gets virtually silenced
(as in the instances of Werner Rolewinck and Hugo Grotius)
or (as in examples afforded by both Thomas Taylor and
Rembrandt) is subjected to startling reversals. In Rolewinck's
chronology for Scripture, the Samson analogy includes only
Hercules, the basis of the analogy being their miracles of
strength for which Judges 13 provides the proof text. Hercules,
not Samson, participates majorly in the typology of Grotius's
poem, where Samson is mentioned but once and then by way
of differentiating Christ "the Nazarite" from him: "Not as

Sampson by vow, nor of that Sect but so called of that City."
To read *Samson Agonistes* within the context of Grotius's play
is to stumble repeatedly into difference: Grotius's Jesus who
shuns no misery, refuses no shame in contrast with Milton's
Samson who decides to go to the temple/theater in order to
avoid their "trail[ing him] through the streets," thus shaming
him as if he were "a wild Beast" (1402–03).

Thomas Playfere comments interestingly — and pointedly
— as he argues that "No griefe doth so cut the very heart of a
generous and magnanimous man, as shame and reproach":

> In Scripture we haue a plaine proofe. Mighty *Sampson*, being
> about to pull the whole house vpon his owne head, said this: *O
> Lord I pray thee strengthen me . . . that* I may be at *once avenged
> of the Philistines. . . .* He desired rather once to dye valiantly,
> then long he liue wretchedly. For as Saint *Ambrose* writing of
> *Sampson*, saith, For a man to liue, or dye, is naturall: but for a
> man to liue in shame and contempt, and to bee made a laughing-
> stocke of his Enemies, is such a matter, as no well bred and
> noble minded man . . . can ever digest it. Yet the Lord God pro-
> miseth . . . that shame shall be the reward of all his enemies.[48]

Shame, it seems, is even worse than death for Milton's Samson — a position perhaps sanctioned by Playfere but also the
basis of a typology that, once invoking Christ, asserts enormous difference. Marking discrepancies may bruise the Sam-
son/Christ typology, but formulating those differences as
oppositions eventually breaks its head. Typology, which had
the effect of cancelling out the Old Testament stories as stories,
once eroded through the subversive force of disparities and
differences, becomes the prelude to a restoration of the
integrity of those stories. Their sharp, yet intricately woven,
narrative lines become evident again.

III

Lightfoot's writings are important both to the immediate
and larger arguments of this book: they reveal both the shift

in and drift of interpretation for the Samson story during the early modern period whether we think in terms of the demise of the Samson typology or modifications to interpretations of the story under the pressure of the Genesis-Revelation connection. In the first instance, we may start with the simplest of formulations: Perkins's remark that Samson "slue more by his death, then by his life: so Christ . . . saved more by death then by life."[49] The first part of the formulation, echoing Judges 16.30 *is* clichéd and often is attached to another cliché: that Christ destroys more effectively than Samson by defeating death and by taking away its sting from the world. The cliché is nicely encapsulated by Thomas Taylor: Samson was a notable type of Christ, killing more at his death than in all his life, and Christ at *his* death overcame his enemies all at once.[50] This is conventional typology: Samson's act of destruction is inconclusive, partial: Christ's, definitive and complete. By revising the cliché in order to contrast Samson who takes life and Christ who saves life, Perkins opens the way for those formulations emphasizing discrepancies and eventually opposition between Samson and Christ. Hidden in Perkins's formulation is the awareness that there are creative and redemptive acts and also acts, like Samson's, which are parodic of such; that to be overthrown by one's enemies and to overthrow them mark a radical difference, not a vague similitude. To juxtapose Samson the destroyer and Christ the creator, as Perkins does, is, in fine, to anticipate the later demise of this common typological pattern.

As another example, see Richard Bernard's invocation of Samson and Delilah in a seemingly conventional fashion. The convention (as exemplified by Roger Williams, let us say) is to show "Christian" Samson fast asleep in "Antichristian" Delilah's lap. This is the passage from Bernard:

> Wee see that a man addicted to whoredome, and led with such an inticing whore, and made drunke by her; can hee in that state forsake her? Yea though he sometime awake and con-

sider with himselfe of his estate, yet as long as she is with him, he still yeeldeth, as *Samson* to a *Dalilah*, till he come to destruction. Such is the state of the great pompous Clergie and Clerkes of Rome; and therefore no marueile they returne not, being drunk with the pleasures, profits and honors of that state. . . .[51]

What Bernard says is not, in context, conventional at all. Samson is not here God's Englishman hoodwinked into momentary submission: he is, in the analogy, the Roman clergy enticed into a fatal submission. Within this allegorical system, the Pope as the fallen star "is Antichrist. . . . Rome is Babylon, that very Church the Whore, and all thereof Antichristians." That is, the Pope is the Great Beast of Revelation, Delilah the "inticing whore," and Samson (as the "pompous Clergie and Clerkes of Rome") the two-horned dragon who mutilates and falsifies the word. Like that clergy, Samson might easily be regarded, in one mood and from one perspective, as one of the "walking spirits of Antichrist." Bernard is emphatic: Antichrist is a conglomerate — *all thereof Antichristians*, or his limbs. Bernard also makes clear, early on, that whereas Christ "winneth . . . and subdueth . . . by the sword, which cometh out of his mouth," Antichrist scores by miracles, "by force and feare of death, if they will not submit themselves to his will."[52] One cannot review the Samson story according to such criteria, either in its biblical or Miltonic versions, without implicating Samson in the myth of Antichrist. This does not mean that Samson *is* Antichrist, only that in fleeting moments, in certain postures, he may strike a resemblance to Antichrist.

We can now draw a line from Perkins's typology of difference and the unconventional typology of Bernard to the pronouncements of Lancelot Andrewes, Thomas Jackson, and Henry Thorndike on the Samson story — in the first instance to the contrast forged between Elias and Samson, and in the latter to the insistence that, *"No type at all, not so much as a shadow of Christs humilitie and patience in all his sufferings"*

(Jackson),[53] Samson parodies the very notion of typology (Thorndike). It is a small step from these assertions to those representations by Marvell and Milton in which now Milton and now Christ are depicted as countertypes of Samson, the latter point left to the inference of readers of the 1671 poetic volume with the preface to *Samson Agonistes* providing important promptings.

"Elias must do, as his commission was to do it, from Heaven," Andrewes writes; "he might not interline his commission":

> And again, who sees not that Elias's fire and Sampson's foxes are not all one? God's "arrows" as lightning from Heaven, and these *tela ignata Satanae*, Satan's trains and fireworks from under the ground. In one, the hand of God must needs be; in the other, the paw of the devil, the malice of man, the fury or treachery of forlorn creatures.[54]

There is no "Righteousness," as Andrewes suggests elsewhere, in the "indirect means" employed here. If Satan seems to come upon Samson as Samson himself comes upon the foxes, Satan will come upon him again in the form of Delilah, then his strength will go out, "marr[ing] the fashion of the birth quite" — a birth promising deliverance to a people "never delivered."[55]

On other occasions, and in favorable assessments, Andrewes acknowledges Samson's place in "the Calendar of Saints" where he is numbered not with "men of peace" but "men of war"; allows a typological connection between Samson and Christ in the announcements of their respective births (two angels versus a host of them); and admits that "God has sent many saviours [including Samson] to free people from the yoke of enemies." But Samson's life, it seems, brings into question his end, "whether pain or shame had the upper hand," as well as the nature of that pain and shame, and whether a judgment does not in fact fall upon Samson as it falls upon the Philistines:

the end was the destroying of sin by destroying this Temple. It went hard, . . . for the dissolving whereof neither the Priest might be suffered to live, nor the Temple to stand; but the Priest be slain, and the Temple be pulled down, Priest and Temple and all be destroyed. *But sin was so riveted into our nature; and again, our nature so incorporate into His, as no dissolving the one without the dissolution of the other.* No way to overwhelm sin quite, but by the fall of this Temple. *The ruin of it like that of Samson's.* That the destruction of the Philistines, this "the dissolving of all the works of the devil."[56]

A sinner and a sinful nation — Samson and the Philistine in Samson — perish together.

When in a 1635 sermon Jackson declares that, "while *Sampson* in his strength and weaknesse and dejected state" has been in his death regarded as "a lively type of Jesus . . ., whilest he lived here on earth," Samson is *no type at all, not even a shadow*, he probably anticipates why Samson is not arrayed among Milton's "shadowie Types" in *Paradise Lost* (12.303) and, in any event, makes clear that if the terms of comparison are Christ's humility and patience, no comparison is possible; for Samson is "rather a foile by his impatience to set a lustre upon the unparalleld meekness of this true Nazarite of God by an *Antiperistasis*":

> *Sampsons* last prayers unto the God of his strength were, that he would give him power at the houre of his death, to be revenged on his Enemies, for the losse of his eyes. Jesus of Nazareth, the true Nazarite of God, when he came unto the crosse on mount *Calvarie*, the stage and theatre for his enemies sport and triumph over him in this solemne feast, prayes heartily, even for those that hoodwinkt him . . . And for the Roman Souldiers . . .: he prays for both in such a sweet and heavenly manner, as no Prophet had ever done for his Persecutors — *Father, forgive them, for they know not what they doe.* He did not so much as either lift up hand or voice, or conceive any secret prayer against one or other of his persecutors, during the time of his lingring, but deadly paines; as knowing, this was the time wherein his body was to be made as an anvile, that he

might doe the will of his Father by the Sacrifice of himself, and sufferance of all other indignities more bitter to a meere man, than twenty deaths, though of the crosse.[57]

The allusion to *Christos Paschon* in Milton's preface to *Samson Agonistes* forces just this kind of contrast and drives home just this point, which had been implied by Hugo Grotius and which then would be, as we have already seen, reinforced by George Sandys.

John Guillory remarks upon Milton's choosing "so regressive a biblical text" as he draws attention to the lines describing Samson at the pillars as "perhaps Milton's greatest revision" of a biblical story.[58] Guillory's observation should be enlarged to include Milton's revision of not only the scene at the pillars but the circumstances surrounding it, with all these revisions conspiring to fracture the usual typology. Whether Samson prays is called in doubt and, in lieu of the prayer recorded in Judges, are Samson's taunting words to the Philistines. Even if he prays, Samson must be judged finally by his actions as we remember with James Nalton that "some may pray like Saints, but in the mean time live like Devils."[59] The temple of Judges, in analogy with Jackson's account of the Cross on Calvary, becomes the theater of *Samson Agonistes*, the stage for Samson's sports of cruelty and blood performed at a "solemn Feast" (1311; cf. 983). Samson is not only reluctant to forgive (954) but scornful of those who practice forgiveness (759–62) and, rather than displaying patience and humility by submitting to indignities, is "content to go" (1403) to the temple/theater (however questionable his going may be) only because he wishes to avoid such indignities.

In 1659, Herbert Thorndike comments in a way that continues the fracturing of the usual typology:

And, truly, when Samson cast away his own life to do mischief to God's enemies and the enemies of his people, out of this express consideration, of being revenged upon them for putting out his eyes; can any man's heart be so hardened by misunderstanding the Scriptures, as to say that this can be reconciled with the principles of Christianity, which forbid all revenge?.... It is said indeed [by St. Augustine; see also Grotius] that Samson did this as a figure of Christ; Who killed His enemies, the powers of darkness, by His Death. And it is certainly true. But that will not answer the reason formerly alleged. Whether we say, that Samson's death was a figure of Christ's by the intent of Samson, or by the intent of God, Whose providence so ordered things to come to pass, that his death might figure Christ's death; it cannot be said, that the intent of figuring Christ's death could make that agreeable to God's law, which otherwise was not. Rather we are to advise, whether sinful actions, and not according to God's own law, were fit to figure Christ. Nor will it serve the turn to say, that he did it by the motion of God's spirit; which we are indeed to allow, that the judges being prophets were endowed with. For it is not to be said, that the Spirit of God moveth any man to do that, which the will of God declared by His law forbiddeth.[60]

Responding to the notion that the Apocryphal books are to be excised because they do not agree with the New Testament in doctrine and spirit, Thorndike remarks, "but . . . the like are found in the Old [Testament]," especially in the stories of Razias, Judith and Tobit's angel, who are "the greatest blocks of offence; not considering the fact of Jael, or that of Samson. . . . If offence be taken at them, why not these," Thorndike asks, having observed earlier that Razias and Samson share "the same motive."[61] Thorndike and Milton are Arminians with different coats, the Anglican Arminianism of the former, the sectarian Arminianism of the latter, representing less different opinions than differences in tone and emphasis.[62]

When Milton himself thinks of God's messages "not rightly understood" he thinks, interestingly enough, of the Book of Judges, the story of Jephthah, as he argues in *The Doctrine and Discipline of Divorce*, "*That Man is the occasion of his owne miseries, in most of those evills which hee imputes to Gods inflicting*" (*YP*, 2.234). Milton holds steadfastly to the belief that the spirit never leads mankind into sinful actions, nor moves people to do what God's law forbids. In *De Doctrina*, he declares that "GOOD WORKS are those which WE DO WHEN THE SPIRIT OF GOD WORKS WITHIN US, THROUGH TRUE FAITH," that "*whatever is not in accordance with faith, is sin*" and, most important of all, that "the works of the faithful are the works of the Holy Spirit itself. These never run contrary to the love of God and of our neighbor" — or to the law of "charity" (6:638, 639, 640). The overwhelming question for interpretation of *Samson Agonistes* is whether, as Samson and the Chorus claim, the work at the temple is the work of the Holy Spirit; whether that work accords with faith, love of God and neighbor, and conforms to the law of charity; and finally whether by the "imitation of . . . [an] example" (let's say, of Samson) Milton will "*stir*" his people "*to emulation, and save some of them*" (6:641). Counsel offered in "The Response of John Phillips [to John Rowland]," where Milton's hand is sometimes seen, is relevant here. Those who introduce violence to history must await "Christ the avenger": "He is not Christ's, but the devil's, deputy who does not imitate Christ's example" (*YP*, 4:943).

Christopher Hill becomes an especially important voice within this context because, by providing the terms for contrasting Roger Williams's rather conventional allusion to Samson and Delilah with Bernard's more curious one, he creates a larger perspective within which to view this crumbling typology.[63] Hill allows for the rhetoric that Milton himself sometimes deploys: Antichrist is the devil's vicar; the Pope is Antichrist and his church at Rome, the temple of Antichrist. Or as Milton observes in *De Doctrina*: "The great enemy of the church is called *Antichrist*. He is to arise from the church itself" (*YP*, 6:604). But also like Hill, Milton is able to separate reductionist rhetoric from conceptual complexity. There is not one Antichrist; there are many. They are Antichrists who, like Bishop Hall in the 1640s, follow the ways of Rome, one of whose ways is the conducting of inquisitions; they are Antichrists who, like the civil magistrates of the late 1650s, were becoming enforcers of conscience by "legislating" scriptural interpretation, which is finally to seize rule over the spirit of God within us.

Milton well understood that Antichrist had invaded England and had enthroned himself not only among but within the Royalists. *But not just within the Royalists.* He could be found within the Puritan revolutionaries, even within John Milton, just as easily as he is found within Jesus as Milton's protagonist *into himself descends* in *Paradise Regain'd* (2.111). Antichrist, both for Milton and his century, is among us and within us, as likely to be found among the saints as in obvious sinners, and chiefly evident in those who observe the forms and not the spirit of religion — in those, let us say, who pray in order to destroy, who traffic with the reprobate only to be seduced by them, who are idolaters making idols of themselves (or being turned into idols by others), such as will happen to Samson at the end of Milton's version of his tragedy. When the Samson story intersects with Revelation commentary, it is often as part of a larger reflection upon private and public roles, upon spiritual and carnal warfare, upon the uses and abuses of power and force, upon marrying outside one's religion (and marrying infidels), upon such fornication as a form of idolatry (both political and spiritual), upon the priority of God's law and the possibility of ever transgressing it (on whether God ever gives such permission and whether, and in what circumstances, he rescinds his own decrees), upon whether Antichrist is a foreign invader or an inward traitor — issues that, often attached to the Samson story, become irrevocably involved with it in *Samson Agonistes.*

It is as if the entire discourse that engaged the Samson story is caught within the huge embrace of Milton's poem more often to discredit than to credit Samson. For example, within the context of Grotius's poem where Jesus, all that he hates, will "with patience beare," think of Milton's Samson driven by that spirit of "Revenge," which, once it "doth . . . the Minde ingage," says Grotius, in its ravings dispels "all sense but rage."[64] And think, too, of Milton's Samson who "slaughter'd foes in number more / Then all . . . [his] life had slain before" (1667–68) in contrast with the "much more glorious . . . victories of *Christ*; who by suffering for Sinne, subdued it; led Captivity captive, was the death of Death; triumphing over Hell, and those Spirits of Darknesse."[65] Like his tribe, Samson is a figure of promise until the whole tribe falls into idolatry.

As the old typologies fracture and crumble, secular rather than sacred analogies achieve prominence: Samson and David become Samson and Hercules, Samson and Christ become Hercules and Christ and, within Milton's writings, Samson and Christ are eventually viewed in analogy with Milton as neotype. At the same time, we witness some bizarre reversals. Take for one example Thomas Taylor who, giving Samson no place among the special types of Christ, formulates a surprising set of analogies wherein Samson is likened to Satan and Delilah to Christ in order to suggest that Jesus learns in the desert of Satan's strength and there "as *Dalilah*, when she knew wherein *Sampsons* great strength lay, did soone disarme him, so Christ spoyled Satan of his lockes."[66] Similarly, James Nalton brings Delilah and Christ together through analogy: "And the Lord Christ may say to them, just as *Dalilah* said to *Sampson, How canst thou say thou lovest me, when thy heart is not with me?*"[67]

Take for yet another example Rembrandt's depiction of the Timnath wedding scene, modeled (as Mieke Bal reports) on Leonardo Da Vinci's *Last Supper*:

> Isolated from the men around her, who are involved in their own deals, the woman sits in the middle, with a crowned head, in the position of Christ. This is not an ordinary typological interpretation. It is not Kallah [the name Bal gives to the woman of Timnath] who prefigures Christ, it is Christ who reminds us of Kallah, of her sacrifice, the desacralizing sacrifice of pure

revenge. At the moment of her execution we see her neither act nor speak. How will *she* be revenged?[68]

In the topsy-turveydom of the Book of Judges and Milton's poem, the sacrificers are eventually sacrificed, the victims victimized, and the avengers avenged, in the case of Samson by his very own hand.

An important effect of Lightfoot's writings is that they point to what eventually enables a new interpretation of the Samson story to emerge: the practice of reading Scriptures by Scriptures, the emergent understanding that scriptural texts are interpretable once their literary strategies are deciphered and only after considerable mental exertion, the scholarly weighing of Hebraic readings with Christian exegesis and the factoring of both into interpretation. It was Lightfoot's vast knowledge of the Rabbinical writings that probably most affected his own understanding of the Samson story and that, upon dissemination, effected a new interpretation of that tale. Rabbinical literature is the primary source and sanction for Dan as the tribe of Satan and Antichrist and, once this literature had impinged on Genesis 49.16–18 and Revelation 7.7, for involving Samson with such figures and implicating him in such concepts.

From Lightfoot's vantage, in the initial chapter of its Samson story, the Book of Judges enfolds an allegory about reading: "But his wife said unto him, If the Lord were pleased to kill us, he would not have received a burnt offering and a meat offering at our hands, neither would he have showed us all these *things*, nor would he at this time have told us *such things* as these" (13.23). The lesson to be learned through "inference," says Lightfoot is this:

> If the Lord were pleased, that the Scriptures should not be understood, — he would never have written them, he would never have charged all to study them. God never writ the difficulties of the Scripture only to be gazed upon and never understood: never gave them as a book sealed, and that could never be

unsealed . . ., — but that they might be more seriously read, more carefully studied. . . .[69]

Milton makes the identical point, albeit without specific reference to Judges, first in *De Doctrina* (*YP*, 6:578–80), then in *Paradise Lost* (12.511–14).

With regard to the Samson story, the pressing questions always were: first, how, if the interpreter is reading according to the spirit, this story should be interpreted? and second, what happens to traditional readings when they are set under the light of Christian ethics and revelation? This was a common enough tactic for Milton whether he was reading sacred or secular history, whether he was scrutinizing the lives of biblical heroes or historical personages. When the poet functions as an historian (and this presumably is the role he must assume in recording the Samson story from the Book of Judges, one of the major historical books of the Bible), he should avoid "injecting . . . maxims or judgments on historical exploits"; and as Milton implies in another letter to Henry de Brass, his role is to narrate, not to prove — is to comprehend history, not codify it (*YP*, 7:501, 506). Milton is writing tragedy that, because it suspends explicit judgment, is not produced beyond the fifth act.

One of the many ironies of Milton criticism is that the portrait drawn of Charles, and the standard by which Charles is then judged harshly — "He was seldome in the times of War, seen to be sorrowfull for the slaughter of his People or Soldiers, or indeed any thing else, whether by nature or custome his heart was hardened I leave for others to judge"[70] — is the portrait (minus the judgment) some of Milton's critics would accept as "standard" for Cromwell and Samson, as well as for the poet himself, with the very qualities others abhorred in Charles, once transferred to Cromwell/Milton/Samson, becoming, as it were, a badge of their honor. One early effect of the Reformation questioning of Samson was to create a neo-typology as an alternative to the Christ typology that over the

centuries had accrued to the Hebrews text. The point of comparison in such instances is not now the biblical Jesus but
modern-day counterparts of, let us say, the biblical Samson:
"They had not such clear light as we: for they look for what
we haue therefore it were shame for vs, if at least we have not
so great constancie as they."[71] Such comparisons just as often
have the effect of exalting the neotype over the type, Milton
over Samson for example, as they emphatically do in Andrew
Marvell's dedicatory poem to *Paradise Lost*:

> the argument
> Held me a while, misdoubting his intent
> That he would ruin . . .
> The sacred truths to fable and old song,
> (So Sampson grop'd the temple's posts in spite)
> The world o'erwhelming to revenge his sight.[72]

If both figures are blind, Milton, casting off spite, is providen-
tially spared the life that Samson loses; he displays the patience
and charity that in Samson are found wanting.

But before returning to Milton and then examining impinge-
ments of these traditions upon his last poems, we need to
notice that the various tensions and divisions within the
Samson hermeneutic of the seventeenth century are seeded
in the Reformation theologians. Let us look first at Luther
and Calvin, then at Hooker in England. Luther may have used
Samson's fall "into huger sins" as an occasion for counseling
that "No man has ever fallen so grievously that he cannot
stand up again" and, conversely, that "no one has such sure
footing that he cannot fall"; he may even celebrate Samson as
a hero of faith and associate him with the serpent in the way
from Genesis 49, and do so in positive, complimentary formulations.[73] It was common enough to regard the Epistle to
the Hebrews as "a little Book of Martyrs"[74] and, if its author
had no time "to tell" of all those enrolled in this catalogue,
Luther has not "time enough to explain all these stories and to
see how Samson, David, Solomon, Aaron, and others literally

and accurately signify Christ."[75] The author of Hebrews may not himself mention Jesus here, but he does provide later commentators with a text on which to hang their typologizing. Even so, Luther is insistent: Samson, however much admired, is *never to be imitated*; indeed, he "would be useless and dangerous to imitate," even as Luther avers that "Abraham's victory is more glorious." Luther also, and very pointedly, registers hesitations concerning all the bloodshedding in the Samson story and Samson's vengeful spirit: "I often wonder about the example of Samson. There must have been a strong forgiveness of sins in his case."[76]

With Calvin, such hesitations deepen into a critique of Samson. This figure in Hebrews may be invoked as an illustration that "In every saint there is always to be found something reprehensible. Nevertheless although faith may be imperfect and incomplete it does not cease to be approved by God." On the positive side, Samson is not one of those who press for signs of his election, and Judges does seem to sanction the annihilation of the wicked, "provided that honest zeal and the wisdom of the Spirit direct us to do so."[77] It is just that, as Calvin scans the Samson story, he comes to recognize that it is Samson's parents (apparently not Samson) who exemplify the proposition that the saints are frightened and fearful when the spirit of the Lord visits them: Samson's parents fear they will die but do not; by inference, Samson, never frightened or fearful, not even at the end, does die. And Samson's end is a genuine problem for Calvin because, "though there was some mixture of honest zeal, yet it was a violent, and therefore sinful, avidity of revenge that predominated."[78]

Implicit in Calvin's assessment of Samson — an assessment achieved apparently by letting the Samson of Judges play against, and qualify, the Samson of Hebrews — is what will be a later tendency to exchange for the Hebrews Samson as a model of faith the example of Manoah who, because he does not see the visiting angel or hear the angel's promise, because he does not cross-examine the circumstances and does not ask if the promise will really be fulfilled but is concerned, instead, with how to accomplish its fulfillment — just because of these responses Manoah emerges, at least for some, as a truer model of faith than Samson. Moreover, the strategies for valuation hinted at in Calvin's assessment suggest, as John Todd will later claim, that in biblical narrative "character is shown by actions and results, rather than by description."[79] And so it is in Aristotelian tragedy as well, as it is, too, in the Revelation tragedy as comprehended and explained by Pareus, whose own understanding Milton admits to sharing.

Small wonder, then, that Hooker should go to such great lengths in disallowing Samson as a model; for this biblical figure is too easily lionized by those who abuse divine authority — by those, in fine, who are self-proclaimed extirpators. With reference to the Samson story, Hooker explains that his "purpose . . . is to show that when the minds of men are once erroniously perswaded that it is the will of God to have things done which they phancie, their opinions are as thornes in their sides never suffering them to take rest till they have brought their speculations into practice."[80] Such men mask their errors in divine authority: they become what they behold, instilling in themselves the very attitudes they would annihilate in the world. The critique that Hooker here formulates is the same one that, less than a century later, Lightfoot and apparently Milton formulate in terms of the Samson story. That critique, in analogy with the ones formulated in Genesis 49 and Revelation 7, becomes "double-fac't" and "double-mouth'd" (971), to use Dalila's words from *Samson Agonistes*. It is a critique of Dan in Samson and of Samson in Dan; of *both* self and society and, as played out in *this tragedy*, of Milton in the Revolution and of the revolution in Milton.

It seems odd in literary discussions to regard any text as sacrosanct, even a text like the Epistle to the Hebrews (in Milton's day still usually attributed to St. Paul) — and odder still to use such a strategy in literary discussions of Milton. To treat the Bible as dogma, not "literature," is an obstacle to literary criticism — is to erect a barrier against interpretation. Surely Milton knew that the Bible is a structure out of which beliefs emerge, not a structure for imposing them. From the very beginning, Milton was accused of "trifling and abusing the Scripture," specifically the Pauline texts; and historically much feminist (or feminist-oriented) criticism has posited that Milton was not beyond such trifling.[81] Such language Milton himself would use to describe the practices of others, but never in relation to his own. Where Milton finds "notorious abuse of Scripture," as in Matthew Griffin, it derives, as Milton explains in *Brief Notes upon a Late Sermon*, from the habit of confirming "one wrested Scripture with another," from misapplication of one text to another and, in a "jugle with Scripture," from citing as proofs for an interpretation what are, in fact, refutations of it (*YP*, 7:476, 477). Milton's own methods of interpretation may produce misinterpretations; yet he nevertheless holds steadfastly to the method, elucidated in *De Doctrina*, of interpreting the New Testament, and of proving every interpretation of it, "by reference to the Old" (*YP*, 6.576).

Within the confines of the present discussion, Milton's concern in *De Doctrina* for "comparison of one text with another" (*YP*, 6:582) — let us imagine it as a concern for putting the right (or as Milton would probably say, a new) interpretation on Hebrews 11.32 — would involve the collocation of the relevant verses from Genesis (and perhaps 1 Chronicles and Amos) with the Samson story in Judges, then the collocation of all these texts with the pertinent verses from Ecclesiasticus, Hebrews and Revelation. Milton would probably further argue for the independence of his interpretation (otherwise, why hazard one?):

> Every believer is entitled to interpret scriptures . . . for himself.
> He has the spirit, who guides truth, and he has the mind of

Christ. Indeed, no one else can usefully interpret them for him, unless that person's interpretation coincides with the one he makes for himself and his own conscience. (6:583–84)

There is this crux, however: even as Milton would assert the freshness of his own interpretation, with which precursors would he align his reading of the Samson story — with Luther, William Gouge, and the regenerationists? or with Hooker, Lightfoot, and the generationists? Calvin, as we have seen, is more complex in his thinking than the two sides in the debate have usually allowed. Insofar as this debate — and alignments within it — are also political gestures, with whom would Milton have sided — the hard-line Calvinists like Kendall and his cohorts, or the Arminians for whom Grotius, John Goodwin, and the Quakers were major spokespersons?

And there is this further crux. The two Testaments are beset with very different problems of interpretation. First, "the external scripture, particularly the New Testament, has often been liable to corruption and is, in fact, corrupt. This has come about," Milton explains, again in *De Doctrina*, because the New Testament "has been committed to the care of various untrustworthy authorities, has been collected together from an assortment of divergent manuscripts, and has survived in a medley of transcripts and editions" (*YP*, 6:587–88). With reference to the Old Testament, and especially the historical books, among which we may number Judges, "the chronological accuracy of their narrative often seems suspect" (6:588). It is the New Testament texts (including Hebrews 11.32, one presumes) that pose the real interpretive problems for Milton, and he knows not "why God's providence should have committed the contents of the New Testament to such wayward and uncertain guardians, unless it is so that this very fact might convince us that the Spirit which is given to us is a more certain guide than scripture, and that we ought to follow it" (6:589).

Milton, that is, writes what Scriptures tell; he writes especially of what is hidden deep in the scriptural texts — and out of an awareness that there is no easily defined relationship between these texts (as they relate to the Samson saga, for example), and hence there can be no easy relationship between these texts, the interpretive traditions they generate, the competing ideologies of those traditions, and Milton's poems. Milton comprehends that there will be interpretive disputes or "disagreements"; and in the face of such knowledge, Milton urges that those disagreements be tolerated until a new revelation allows for their resolution. It is fully in keeping with everything we know about Milton (*Tetrachordon* is as good an example as any) that, for him, coherence involves, and perhaps necessarily contains, systematic contradictions. This is doubtless what made the Samson saga such a good story for the poets. The story had been approached by the Reformation theologians, and was being approached increasingly during the seventeenth century, with a hermeneutic of suspicion.

We have just scanned backward. Let us now scan forward: from the tensions evident in the writings of Luther, Calvin, and Hooker; to the cautious inquiries by Perkins, Dickson and Trapp; to the more rigorous interrogations of Grotius, Jackson, Thorndike, the Goodwins, Lightfoot, and Milton, which are obviously caught up in the seventeenth century dispute over the perseverance of the saints; to the new Samson hermeneutic of the eighteenth century; to that same hermeneutic which reigns today. With Hugo Grotius, John Goodwin and John Lightfoot paving the way, Milton is the central figure in the formation of a new Samson hermeneutic and *Samson Agonistes* the crucial text. It is a poem that, following no one and corresponding point by point with no existing interpretation, nevertheless has points of intersection and exhibits moments of overlap with the various interpretations here brought under review.

If the early modern period began by appropriating the Samson of Christian tradition, it proceeded, under the influence of the Reformation theologians, by practicing various forms of subversion. Stephen Greenblatt outlines two stages in the process of cultural subversion, but not the whole process, not even the crucial stage in the process we have here described. First comes a cautious *"testing* of the subversive interpretation" by the Reformation theologians. By the time we reach the seventeenth century, however, there is a *"recording* of alien voices," a registering of "alien interpretations,"[82] with orthodoxy (Perkins and Dickson are notable examples) tolerating the subversive inquiries that might prove the undoing of orthodox interpretation of the Samson story through their practice of containment — that is, by enveloping interrogation within a polemic of faith, thus implying that the new interpretation confirms, is even subordinate to, the old. Orthodoxy sometimes wins out through this procedure — and sometimes not: the process may continue, as it seems to do here, with a subversion of the containment such as is achieved by the efforts of Thomas Jackson and Henry Thorndike, Hugo Grotius, John Goodwin and John Lightfoot.

The success of the subversion of the orthodox interpretation can be measured, on the one hand, by the gesture of Dickson who, as we have seen, is forced to abandon the interrogation altogether in an act of open defiance and denial of it and, on the other hand, by Trapp who can now, as he had not done before, analogize Samson with the reprobate in his reflections on Revelation 7. The consequences of these various interrogations for orthodox interpretation, which had come to center on the Hebrews text, are most dramatically evident in Owen's four-part commentary on the Epistle to the Hebrews which, remarkable for its length (seven volumes in William Goold's nineteenth century edition), shores up the walls of orthodox interpretation by disregarding altogether interrogations by alien voices. Owen's rehabilitation of the Hebrews text, begun in the 1650s, was not ready for publication until 1668 and 1674 respectively.

Nevertheless, this effort, so stridently anti-Arminian and

anti-Goodwinian, raises tantalizing questions about Milton's undertaking in a poem that, even if begun before the Reformation, was not published until after it. Where does Milton align himself in this debate? Where — and how — does *Samson Agonistes* intersect with it? Joan S. Bennett is immensely helpful here:

> Milton . . . did not accept the doctrine of predestination or 'perseverance.' Nevertheless, his politics and poetry express and explore the belief . . . in a dynamic, antinomian ethic. . . . This is the central theme of *Samson Agonistes*, which embodies legalistic mentality in the Chorus and dramatizes antinomian liberalism in Samson.[83]

Yet Bennett's statement requires further extension and refinement. Milton regarded the idea of absolute reprobation, repugnant to right reason, as a moral outrage but also resisted the idea that election precluded total apostasy: to be damned by another is different from being damned by oneself. Much of the polemic driven by the concept of the saints persevering is assimilated to *Samson Agonistes* — as Bennett allows, to its Chorus as well as its protagonist, both of whom often assert beliefs Milton rejects and articulate arguments stemming from the very side in the debate that Milton resists. Yet, however we answer the aforementioned questions, does it not seem obvious that, syncretist that he was, Milton would array these different Samsons, these different Samson hermeneutics in his poem, and allow them to participate in its jostling perspectives, as well as sponsor its competing representations of the legendary Samson? Does it not seem evident, too, that he might admonish readers of the Samson story, both as it is related in the Book of Judges and in his poem, with John Goodwin's wisdom: "Be . . . admonished . . . that importunity of an inward solicitation is no argument that the perswasion, unto which you are solicited, cometh from God."[84]

After all, by 1659, as we have already noted, Milton came

to believe that "divine illumination" is something "no man can know at all times to be in himself, much less to be at any time for certain in any other" (*YP*, 7:242).

Edward Phillips is emphatic: "It cannot certainly be concluded when . . . [Milton] wrote . . . *Samson Agonistes*"; the anonymous biographer, probably Cyriak Skinner, affords the only reliable clue: Milton began *Paradise Lost* and "*a Body of Divinity*" before and "finish't [them] after the Restoration. As also . . . *Paradise regaind, Samson Agonistes*, a Tragedy."[85] On the basis of the historical record we can say the following: whenever *Samson* was written, it was published in 1671; but probably as Skinner proposes, it was begun *before* the Restoration and finished *after*. Even if we disallow the full parallelism — begun before, finished after — if not substantially revised during the 1660s, *Samson* is written then. The timing is important; for in the words of Dewey D. Wallace, Jr., "a new spirit of critical inquiry" now reigns in scriptural commentary and religious thinking.[86] And it is this *new* spirit marked by searching inquiry that animates *Samson Agonistes*.

Obviously, Milton knew what had been the dominant interpretation of the Samson story and knew, too, that such an interpretation contained the seeds of its own destruction. The Samson story, probably born as a folktale, survives in Scriptures and in their interpretive traditions, all of which differ according to the text in which they are centered. The story is an appropriation from culture and affords a critique of that culture. As a fable, moreover, this story was peculiarly susceptible to diverse readings. One commentator remarks that "in popular folklore all is white on one side and black on the other. Samson is the hero and the Philistines the villains."[87] In Milton's poem, Dalila, as we have already noted, complains differently and more complexly: "Fame . . . / . . . with contrary

blast proclaims most deeds, / On both his wings, one black,
the other white, / Bears greatest names in his wild aerie flight"
(971–74).

Early on, the Hebrews text had been used to reinforce, indeed
to sharpen, antitheses. Yet, the same text would be used, during
the sixteenth century and increasingly during the seventeenth
century, to blur antitheses, especially as attention reverted to
the Judges narrative, to the complexity of its literary strategies,
and to the possibility that, in the very act of appropriating
this story and in the very placement he gave to it, the Judges
redactor was submitting it to reinterpretation. According to
the commentator cited above,

> One should not think that the attitude of the Israelite story-
> tellers toward Samson is entirely neutral. However no moral is
> expressed. . . . As a popular hero Samson needs no explanation;
> as a charismatic hero he is hard to swallow.[88]

It is the latter realization apparently that prompted the New
Testament reinterpretations of the Samson story, both in
Hebrews and Revelation, as well as their seemingly contrary
judgments.

The Judges narrative, aligned with Hebrews, nudged interpretation in one direction. Even if the Book of Judges, as a
"Historie," was "a faithfull Recorder, as well of the Vices as
Vertues of the Sancts" — "a perfect mirrour wherin every one
may behold both the deformity & beauty of his own person";
those deformities were seemingly thrown into the distance
by "the catalogue of the faithfull captains of *Israel*, who by
faith wroght righteousnesse, and ouercame Kingdomes" and,
in the case of Samson, brought down "Satans Kingdome."[89]
The Genesis prophecy, aligned with that in Revelation, pulled
interpretation oppositely, laying emphasis on Dan's, or Samson's, apostasy and idolatry; on their demonic features and
antichristian behavior; on the fact that after Samson's death
no righteousness is wrought, only wickedness, and no

deliverance is accomplished by him. Jacob's prophecy in the first book of the Bible was a constant reminder that, in the last book of Scriptures, Dan seems to be cancelled from the Book of Life and, by implication, Samson denied his status among the elect. The collocation of Judges and Hebrews may have sponsored the regenerate Samson of critical orthodoxy; yet the collocation of the Genesis and Revelation texts sanctions an alternative Samson. As the Samson story moves through history, these opposing interpretations play against one another until, in the seventeenth century, they become inextricably involved.

FIVE

Thought
Colliding
with Thought

*[it is] the coherence of deliberate and systematic
incoherencies; . . . or . . . the difficult coherence regulated
by the maneuvering between the truth and the whole truth.*
— *Meir Sternberg*[1]

By the seventeenth century, certain counter tendencies had
already obtruded upon orthodox interpretation of the Samson
story; and ubiquitous reference to this story was prompting
new interpretation. That Samson was so often present in
parentheses, or on the margins of a text, is not evidence of
subordination or marginalization but of the fact that, part of
the mental furniture of the age, the Samson story was a
repeated point of reference and concern — a token, as it were,
of early modern culture. Here it inspires a piece of sculpture
and there a fine painting. Now it is a subject for da Vinci, now
for Rembrandt. Here it is a story woven into the de'Medici

tapestries; and there the same story appears on one of two paired panels hanging in the treasury of Santa Maria della Salute in Venice. It even occasions an oratorio and is the subject of many biblical dramas, as well as numerous book illustrations, eventually including some for Milton's poem, the most recent and unusual of which are by the British artist, Robert Medley.[2]

The Samson story had been part of a long, oppressive process of cultural indoctrination; it had been used (was part of a continuing effort) to tell people how and what to think, especially as regards a vengeful deity crushing his enemies in retaliatory gestures. But if this story had been deployed to defend certain beliefs and to uphold certain forms of authority, in another act of appropriation it could be used to probe those same beliefs and to question some of those authorities. If allowed to express the viewpoint of an alien culture, as well as certain alienated voices within Milton's own culture, the Samson story could be turned against itself. If presented in such a way that it gave form not to one but to a variety of perceptions of Samson, his story could be liberating, especially if it were cast not in a set of declarative sentences but in a series of interrogatives through which Samson engages in repeated self-questioning and through which Milton lets the emphasis fall on the temple/theater catastrophe: whether to go to the temple in the first place, news of what goes on there, and of what happens to whom.[3]

Through this systematic interrogation, the Samson story is summoned not to sanction but to subvert cultural authority in the guise of institutionalized readings, orthodox interpretations, the *one* authentic and authorized tradition. The story is used by Milton to frustrate, not foster, platitudinous Christianity. A story that had subtended so many tragedies in human history, so many national disasters, now issues forth as a warning and thus becomes a way of averting the disaster it had so often courted. Orthodoxy had accomplished one appropriation, had achieved one kind of containment; but through the Samson story, orthodoxy could also be challenged on its own terms: by an appropriation of this story in which the previously subordinate and dissident elements in the tale achieved focalization and emphasis and through which, in turn, earlier containments could then be subverted. *Samson Agonistes* brilliantly exemplifies "the close connection of history-painting and the drama":[4] it contains the poetry of history, the politics of poetry, within a mental theater replete with visionary forms.

It is also of a piece with Milton's last poems, as Christopher Hill explains, all of them "wrestling with the problem of the failure of the Revolution, trying to apportion blame and look forward from defeat."[5] But this perspective is also enlarged, as well as particularized, by Nancy Armstrong and Leonard Tennenhouse in their contention that "Tradition has it that the older man succeeded as a poet because he failed in politics":

> But it is just as plausible to say that the later poetry mounted a critique, however inadvertently, of the entire universe of meaning that a humanist education had prepared Milton to reproduce. We will go so far as to suggest that in . . . *Samson Agonistes* . . . Milton entered into a struggle through which the ideals he held as a Protestant reformer and political activist eventually triumphed. This was a struggle for the signs and symbols of political reality itself, a struggle, therefore, to say what that reality was.[6]

A story that had been used to glimpse others' failings, to register a critique of alien culture, might continue to be that: it could still be used to expose the Philistines and, especially in the 1660s, to castigate the Royalists.

But the critique could now be turned back upon itself in such a way that it mirrored not just others' failings, but one's own. It could expose the failings of the revolutionaries without repudiating the Revolution; it might be used to annihilate the errors of selfhood without destroying the self. If Cromwell is implicated in such criticism, it is less as the leader of the Revolution than as a representative of the forces behind as well as of those unleashed by it. The critique of culture here, which Cromwell does not escape, is, nonetheless, one that, however tardily, he himself begins to prosecute. Thus, Cromwell and Milton aim at the same targets, often deploy similar rhetoric, with *Samson Agonistes* sometimes containing haunting reminders of what Cromwell had said, or of what had been said about him (by way of apologia, criticism, and defense) in letters, reports, and speeches.

"Warr wearied hath perform'd what Warr could do," in the famous words from *Paradise Lost* (6.695). The cause was too good to have been fought for; or as Hugo Grotius had remarked, to enter combat "purely as the Tryal of a good Cause, or as an Instrument of Divine Judgment, is vain, and far from true Piety."[7] In his time and after, Milton's own story would be aligned with Samson's story; and by others, Milton himself would be measured in terms of Samson. But in *Samson Agonistes* Milton allows for our measuring not only himself but Cromwell against Samson, his Englishmen against the Israelites, and those other Englishmen against the Philistines. In doing so, he discovers that distinctions blur, that there is too much of Samson on both sides — and too much of the Philistine; that there is not enough of the spiritual Israel on his own side to win the Revolution, let alone sustain its ideals.

The Samson story had previously been used to fix blame on one party and to exonerate another, even to heroicize certain of its members. In one seventeenth century allegorization of his story, Samson is of the elect, the Philistines are the reprobate, with the "Tragoedie of *Samsons* life" bursting into comedy when, in his end, God turning "his sinne . . . vnto his owne glorie," Samson delivers the Church from her enemies, thus illustrating that God "forgetteth the sinnes of the elect, and crowneth them with compassions."[8] This is decidedly not the message of Milton's poem, which greatly problematizes the standard identification of Delilah with Satan by developing a provocative intertextuality through which Samson is aligned with Satan, and Dalila is allowed to make a compelling case for herself, even as sometimes she acts as a mouthpiece for Milton.

Indeed, the very sort of message embedded within the typical seventeenth century allegorization of the Samson story wherein Samson belongs to the elect and Delilah, together with the Philistines, is among the reprobate — such a message is at odds with Milton's Arminian theology. Instead, for Milton, although Samson's story had been used to shadow, even to aggrandize, Milton and others,[9] now that same story would become a vehicle for implicating both sides — as well as both an individual and his allies — in one another's falls. The experience of defeat may be, as it was for Adam, an exercise in blame-shifting; it may be too, as it seems to have been for Milton, an occasion for discovering the enemy not only outside but within — within one's own faction and as much within Cromwell as within one's own self. As was the case with England's leader, a man of "ideological schizophrenia," "the conflict between radical Puritanism and conservative constitutionalism [played itself out] within the breast of Cromwell,"[10] as well as within some of his cohorts with whom Milton's chief affinity was often no more than a broad republicanism.

Such affinities themselves become frayed as Milton experienced disappointment in some of Cromwell's actions and with those of some of Cromwell's followers as they oversaw a government less of "experiments" than of "expedients," initiating and approving massacres in which all opponents of the English republic were, from Cromwell's point of view, criminals to be extirpated by people, the likes of himself, who were driven by necessity and directed by providence but also who, in the end, Samson-like, "failed to transform England into the New Jerusalem he hoped to achieve."[11] In the famous "Sonnet 18" (*CP*, 241), Milton himself had cried out for vengeance in the face of slaughtered saints and mourning martyrs, their scattered bones, the bloody fields they covered, not only of the dead but the hurt, including women and children. It is just that, now, like Cromwell, Milton would find some of that brutalizing enemy in his own nation and among his own people; and here we may need the reminder that the tragedy glimpsed through the Book of Judges was not so much that of the Philistines as of the Israelites.

As we move to situate Milton's understanding of the Samson story within its scriptural intertext, we should remember that the commentators on Hebrews tend to exculpate Christ-like Samson by excoriating the antichristian Philistines. Commentators on Judges, though often persisting in the practice of castigating the Philistines, also extend their critique to Samson and his people, but with differing inflections. Commentators on 1 Chronicles as well as Amos emphasize the culpability of the Israelites themselves for perpetuating a culture of violence and for un-Nazariting their Nazarites, for de-propheting their prophets. Commentators on Genesis and Revelation deepen this critique of the Israelites, focusing it (as 1 Chronicles had done) on the tribe of Dan and extending it to Samson himself, thus opening the way for Milton to situate his own historical critique within the character of this legendary hero, implicating in that critique both sides in the Revolution and not only the Hebrew religion but organized Christianity as well.

Samson as Dan, Samson as Israel, Samson as Christ, Samson as Cromwell/Milton, Samson as England is the perfect figure in whom to center such a critique and through whom to project not just a history but, more precisely, a political history — one with both a tangled and a tragic emplotment. The demise of a nation is figured in the defeat of its leader. Culpability is shared, the people usually bearing the brunt of it by not taking advantage of the Lord's favors, by "forgetting God," as Henry Ireton and others like Sir Henry Vane complained, "and after all these shakeings and awakenings . . . growing cold and dead to him and his wayes"; or as Cromwell thought, by becoming a nation now in "a bleeding, nay almost dying, condition."[12] Milton simply shifts attention from people to their leaders or, better, fuses both the leader and his people in the character of Samson, with the question then emerging: "Whether *England* be *Sampson . . . because it is strong;* or because 'tis imprison'd, shaven close, and hath lost its *two eyes.*"[13]

Richard Garnett understood something of this strategy when he claimed *Samson Agonistes* as "a national poem, pregnant with a deeper allusiveness than has always been recognized. . . . Particular references to the circumstances of . . . [Milton's] life are not wanting. . . . But, as in the Hebrew prophets Israel sometimes denotes a person, sometimes a nation." Samson, if here the representative of John Milton, is there "the representative of the English people in the age of Charles the Second. . . . 'Samson Agonistes' is thus a prophetic drama, the English counterpart of the world-drama of 'Prometheus Bound.'"[14] Yet *Samson Agonistes* affords an ironic contrast, first, of Prometheus who suffers because he will not reveal his secret and Samson who suffers as a consequence of publishing his; and second, of death scenes and burial grounds — of fame (secular and sacred, earthly and spiritual) — with *Samson Agonistes*, in this contrast, falling short of Christian ideals more admirably figured (and surely more nearly met) by Oedipus at Colonus than Samson in Gaza. As Thomas Newton once remarked of this now favorite yoking of plays (and playwrights): "there is scarcely a single thought the same in the two pieces."[15]

As I have argued in the first chapter of this book, *Samson Agonistes* conforms more nearly to the Euripidean examples of heroism revalued and of cultural values reviewed, then redefined, as in the Heracles plays and *The Bacchae*. That is, in accordance with tragedy as conceptualized by Euripides and John of Patmos, *Samson Agonistes* is a cosmic drama, at once mind-shattering and mind-transforming: classical blurs into

Christian tragedy here as certainly and as magisterially (and with the same ironic interplay) as in *Christos Paschon*, the play Milton's preface invokes as *Christ Suffering*, as well as the title of a tragedy Milton contemplated but never wrote. If in our own time, a whole school of critics thinks that tragedy is antithetical to Christianity, that Christianity is beyond tragedy,[16] during the early modern period many thought differently — indeed so differently that both the Samson plays and the Christ plays already mentioned, together with their source books of Judges and Revelation, were presented as models of Christian tragedy. Milton outlines plans for "Biblical Tragedies" and "British Tragedies" (*YP*, 8:539–96), in the very juxtaposition — or interleaving — of them, suggesting that in one we glimpse the other.

Moreover, the different forms of the Samson hermeneutic wound around different biblical texts find correlatives in the different forms of interpretation sponsored by *Samson Agonistes*. There have been two lines of approach to Milton's tragedy represented, respectively, by the "regenerationists" (like William Riley Parker, A. S. P. Woodhouse, and Mary Ann Radzinowicz) whose hermeneutic is one of celebration and by the "generationists" (like John Carey, Irene Samuel, and myself) whose hermeneutic has been one of suspicion and interrogation. Stanley Fish occupies a pivotal position — that of mediation. One of the questions now on the table of literary criticism is whether Milton's interrogation of Samson yields a regenerate Samson or, instead, dropping such a polemic, delivers the highly ambiguous and culpable Samson of the generationists. A separate question is whether Samson, in all his ambiguity and paradox, is to be seen as a negative example, especially within the context of *Paradise Regain'd*, or more positively in the context of radical Puritan politics or of God's people defeated but still enduring through the Restoration years. In which direction does Milton's mediatorial poem — or should mediatorial criticism of it — move: toward

the Samson of religious and critical orthodoxy, or toward
the Samson of the dissenting tradition of interpretation?
Milton criticism needs to occupy the mediatorial space Fish
stands in but also needs to mediate in such a way as not to
allow the questions of *Samson Agonistes* to be swallowed up
too easily in the answer of faith and in such a way as to argue,
with Thomas N. Corns, that "the ideological implications
of the Miltonic *oeuvre* are convoluted, ambivalent, and in-
ternally contradictory to an extent that has not hitherto been
appreciated."[17]

What is so striking about Milton's last poems — *Samson
Agonistes* no less than *Paradise Lost* — is not only their various
interrogations, their free-standing contradictions, but the
amount of irresolution they contain. In his tragedy, as we
observed earlier, Samson first numbers himself with what will
become the worthies of Hebrews, then withdraws his name
from that list. The Hebrews Samson thus seems both to belong
and not to belong to Milton's poem. Moreover, the canceling
of Samson's name from this list may be no less freighted with
significance than the canceling of Dan's name from the list of
the twelve protected tribes in Revelation. In *De Doctrina*,
where Milton's Arminianism is most conspicuous, as he reflects on those names not written into the Book of Life in
Revelation 13.8, he asks: "Who are these but the unbelievers,
whom God deserted because they followed the beast"; and in
the Yale edition of Milton's prose writings, this observation
is glossed editorially by *Samson Agonistes*, lines 631–32:
"Thence faintings, swounings of despair, / And sense of
Heav'ns desertion" (see also *YP*, 6:190). On the other hand,
Milton also says, in *De Doctrina*, that the "decree of reprobation . . . [is] of temporal punishment, and at any rate not an
absolute decree" (6:190). On these matters, as we have seen,
Milton is very much an anti-Calvinist, though he also seems

to think we should not be too quick, nor too rash, in our judgments of those we think are to be counted with the reprobate. His thinking accords with the sectarian Arminians who, envisioning people cooperating with grace, resist all schemes that underplay, and thus undermine, freedom of choice, human effort and moral striving.

What appears to problematize any judgment that might fall on Dan/Samson, from Milton's point of view, is that there is no absolute reprobation in God's scheme, no absolute decree against Dan — or against Samson in Dan: "there is no reprobation *except* for those who do not believe *or do not persist* [in their belief] . . . no reprobation from eternity of particular men" (*YP*, 6:190; my italics); nor are people "predestined to destruction except through their own fault and . . . *per accidens*" (6:190). Or as Milton explains in *Artis Logicae*, it can be "truly said that every effect of a *per accidens* cause can be reduced to a *per se* cause" (*YP*, 8:227). The fault, that is, lies not in the stars but in ourselves. Absolute decrees are inventions, contrivances, through which, with no need of redemption, the saints who, becoming engulfed by sin and committing horrific crimes, can remain saints. Milton, on the other hand, would pierce their cover, exposing the possibility that they are otherwise. And Milton does so in a poem without an authoritative narrative voice, thus reminding us of his repeated declaration, going back to *An Apology Against a Pamphlet*, that "the author is ever distinguisht from the person he introduces" (*YP*, 1:880).

Outside the boundaries of all contestation concerning Milton's judgment of Samson are two facts: Milton never singles out Samson as the greatest of the Judges, let alone mentions him when he names or lists the judges; and he defends tyrannicide and regicide but never genocide. He could not make the point more clearly than when he complicates the Judges story by inching toward a more sympathetic portrait of *some* of the Philistines — "a third / More generous far and

civil, who confess'd / They had anough reveng'd" (1466–68) —
and then alters the Judges text to allow for the survival of
"The vulgar only" (1659). Samson claims to be of the elect —
by God's "special favour rais'd" (273), thus acting with "command from Heav'n" (1212) — a perception the Chorus shares
with Milton's protagonist whom they describe as "solemnly
elected" (678) above the rest of men. Moreover, even if fallen,
Samson is confident of readmission to the elect, of his perseverance as a saint: "Justly" afflicted, Samson invests his faith
in a God "Gracious to re-admit the suppliant" (1171, 1173).
Manoa typically puts the brakes on such assertions, in the
"Omissa" lines (see fig. 5) doubting Samson's calling (1531,
1534–35) as earlier he had questioned whether Samson's
marriages were divinely sanctioned (420–24). In the end,
though, he shares his son's confidence, declaring that, "best
and happiest yet," all this has happened "With God not parted
from him, as was feard, / But favouring and assisting to the
end" (1718–20). What was once, according to Manoa, "pre-
sumptuous to be thought" (1531) is now a certainty. What
Manoa, the Chorus, and Samson each accept as fact Milton
brackets in question marks: whether the God who has withdrawn from Samson really returns to him; whether Samson is
"a person rais'd," his "part from Heav'n assign'd" (1211, 1217),
or merely chosen to perform some earthly acts; whether faith
and repentance (in his case) are attendant upon his supposed
election or hard-won fruits of it? Is Samson anointed by God,
this poem asks; or is he just another self-styled emissary? The
"Omissa" — the very lines we are asked to insert into Milton's
poem immediately before its reported catastrophe — are the
bearers of such questioning within a poem shot through with
question marks.

In *Paradise Lost*, the angels as a category are "Elect above
the rest" (3.184), "blessed Spirits elect" (3.136; cf. 360, and
6.374–75), but may also fall irrevocably and, by their own
"doom / Canceld from Heav'n" (6.378–79), become "Spirits

reprobate" (1.697) just as the human "Race elect," making its way "back to *Egypt*," can choose an "Inglorious life" of servitude and reprobation (12.214, 219–20). As Stephen M. Fallon observes, in *Paradise Lost* "Calvinist and Arminian perspectives coexist," but not "peacefully."[18] In *Samson Agonistes*, Fallon might have gone on to say, the situation is more like the one in *De Doctrina*. Tensions subside as the characters in the poem pull in one direction, while the drama as a whole, pulling oppositely, implies that the tragedy is in part that of Calvinist-centered religion. Here, words of the Semichorus, describing the Philistines, redound upon Samson as we remember him as a character who, finding in "deaths benumming Opium . . . [his] only cure" (630), thereupon prays for "speedy death, / The close of all my miseries, and the balm" (650–51).

These moments in Milton's poem anticipate the Semichorus's description of those who call for "Thir own destruction to come speedy upon them":

> So fond are mortal men
> Fall'n into wrath divine,
> As thir own ruin on themselves t' invite
> Insensate left, or to sense *reprobate*,
> And with blindness internal struck.
>
> (1681–86; my italics)

Is Samson, even if originally of the elect, redeemed from — or mired in — his chosen reprobation? Does the episode at the temple/theater mark a recovery for Samson or his persistence in error — yet another fall? In addressing these questions, it needs to be remembered that Milton might have linked Samson to the line of David in either *De Doctrina* or *Paradise Regain'd*, but chooses not to do so. In *De Doctrina*, he might have catalogued Samson among the heroes of faith in his citation of Hebrews 11.32, but he names only Gideon; he might have listed Samson among the judges of Israel in the same work but mentions only Gideon and Jephthah (*YP*, 6:625, cf. 738; also 366).

Indeed, it might be said of the example just cited from *De Doctrina* that, even if not spoken, the name of Samson is nonetheless heard when Milton explains that *judgment* refers to a reign, not a judicial session, and thereupon illustrates with reference to "Gideon, Jephthah and the other *judges* who are said to have *judged* Israel for many years" (*YP*, 6:625). But it should also be said, perhaps even more loudly, that the naming of Samson before Jephthah in Hebrews, the favorable judgment on Samson that seems harbored in this very procedure, were Milton sensitive (as he seems to have been) to such rhetorical strategies as precise ordering and derogatory omission, would require that this poet actually name Samson here, and perhaps even omit the name of Jephthah by whom, according to *The Doctrine and Discipline of Divorce*, God's revelations were "not rightly understood" (*YP*, 2:235).

Yet it is Gideon and Jephthah through whom the Milton of *Paradise Regain'd* exemplifies those who from lowliest plight "attain'd / . . . to highest deeds" (2.437–38). It is Gideon about whom, as a breaker of images, Milton, in the Trinity College manuscript, contemplates writing the tragedy, *Gideon Idoloclastes* (*YP*, 8:556). It is Gideon who, anointed for judgeship by spiritual command, in *Brief Notes upon a Late Sermon*, is called "this worthy heroic deliverer" (*YP*, 7:473) and who, in *De Doctrina*, is presented as a signal example of a person "outstanding for his faith, and piety" and, "behav[ing] in accordance with the same principle" as Joseph, refuses a kingdom (*YP*, 6, 366; 735). On the other hand, Jephthah, despite the fact that, in *The Doctrine and Discipline of Divorce*, he does not understand revelation and thus does not know how God would, or should, be worshipped (*YP*, 2:235), still figures as an exemplary judge who, albeit in contrast to Gideon, when visited by an angel, knows the angel is God and so addresses him (*YP*, 6:237, 252) and who, in *Samson Agonistes*, is remembered for defending Israel "by argument / Not worse then by . . . shield and spear" (283–84). Samson is nowhere in Milton's writings the recipient of such unequivocal praise except from himself. Within *Samson Agonistes* itself, as James Holstun remarks, Milton lets Samson be drawn into error by examples such as Gideon and Jephthah, supposedly great and virtuous according to the opinions of the wisest and gravest, rather as Milton's contemporaries would be drawn into similar error by so readily and uncritically invoking, and accepting, the example of Samson himself. As Holstun goes on to say, Samson is quick to add his name to this roll call of heroes, unaware apparently of the tragic dimensions or faults of either of them.[19]

It is of some importance, then, that Samson is never acknowledged as a judge, not even in the poem to which he lends his name; nor, however strong, is he ever distinguished in polemic, lacking by his own admission the requisite "double share / Of Wisdom" (53–54). Moreover, it is Samson's parents, not Samson, who in *De Doctrina* are cast in the Gideon-like role of being visited by an angel and of knowing this visitor is God (*YP*, 6:234) — a point not lost on Milton's Samson who immediately recalls that his birth was foretold "Twice by an Angel, who at last in sight / Of both my Parents all in flames ascended" (24–25). Samson's parents, not Samson, are exemplary knowers and interpreters of revelation, perhaps Samson's mother more so than his father; for she is, according to George Fox, a hero of faith "who believed more in God then her husband did, & declared her confidence."[20] Indeed, tradition, if sometimes representing Manoa as "a person of . . . great virtue" with "few men his equals" — "an excellent man" and "the onely esteemed Prince" among the Danites, indeed "one of the greatest men of his generation"[21] — more often would have it that Manoa, "almost spent with iealousie and suspition," was also intellectually obtuse, even "an 'ignorant man'."[22] It is an oddity of Milton's poem that Samson's mother does not appear among the *dramatis personae*, but at the same time these caveats concerning Manoa are very much at play in *Samson Agonistes*.

"A good example," Milton explains (again in *De Doctrina*), "leads in good men, to an imitation of that example" and on to "emulation" (*YP*, 6:641). While others from Judges (a scriptural book from which Milton takes comparatively few proof texts) afford such examples, Samson (with one exception that proves the rule) never does, and even in the exception Samson is never named inasmuch as Milton's interest is in a biblical idiom, not a human exemplar. Judges shows the rewards awaiting the nations obedient to God and the punishments befalling those that go astray (*YP*, 6:756, 804). According to Milton, it offers testimony "that angels often take upon them as their own the name, the person and very words of God and Jehovah" (6:256); and that oaths should be kept so long as they are not unlawful (6:685). Judges also legitimizes the cursing of God's enemies (6:675). That is, Judges is a source book for good *and bad* examples: Eglon shows that "certain temporary virtues (or . . . what look like vertues) are found in the wicked," for example "liberality, gratitude and justice" (6:646); Gideon and Deborah, both exemplifying "the distinctions of public life" (6:733), display respectively high-mindedness and humility (6:733, 734–35). And, as a hero of faith, indeed no less "outstanding for his faith" than his "piety" (6:366), Gideon also displays fortitude; and Jael figures honorable deception. (In *Samson Agonistes*, Dalila compares herself favorably to Jael [989–90]). On the other hand, as a usurper as well as one of Milton's subjects for a biblical tragedy, Abimelech, in seizing a kingship, reveals ambition; and those gathering around Jephthah illustrate false friendship.

Only once in *De Doctrina* does Milton actually refer to Samson through scriptural citation (Judges 15.19: *his spirit returned and he lived*), and then by way of explaining the phrase as a biblical idiom (cf. 1 Samuuel 30.12), with Samson awakening into consciousness, from which state he might be judged kindly, or harshly (*YP*, 6:408). It is also a moment of recovery located in Samson's thirsting subsequent to a great act of deliverance, not in his preparation for deliverance by hurling down the pillars. Within this context, the recovery, the awakening, is a prelude to judgment, "Dan. xii. 2: . . . *some to eternal life, some to shame and eternal contempt*"; and the "return" is to be understood in the broadest sense since "the wicked do not go to God at death, but far away from him" (6:406, 407). It bears repeating that as in the preface to *Samson Agonistes*, so here in *De Doctrina*, book 1, chapter 13: references to 1 Corinthians 15, to Euripides as an astute interpreter of Scripture, and to the Samson story are all knotted together.

If we remember that Samson had been used to illustrate the proposition that some begin their life in the spirit but end it in the flesh, and also recall that Grotius cross-references 1 Corinthians 15.32–33 with Isaiah 22.13 and Galatians 6.7–8 — where, in the first instance, oxen and sheep are slain, and there is eating of flesh and drinking of wine because "to morrow we die" and, in the second instance read, "Be not deceived; God is not mocked: for whatsoever a man soweth, that shall he also reap. For he that seweth to his flesh shall of the Spirit reap corruption" — when we recall this conjunction of passages, then 1 Corinthians reads like an oblique commentary on the Samson story. This possibility is reinforced by other of Grotius's scriptural correlations, this time for 1 Corinthians 15.34, especially his citation of 1 Samuel 25.37, the story of Nabal, his becoming stony of heart before he dies, with death here being the Lord's way of holding back evil even as he turns it upon the head of its doers. Thus, the Lord makes victims of those who victimize. But along with this citation of 1 Samuel in conjunction with 1 Corinthians, Grotius cites the judgment scene in Genesis 9.24 where Noah blesses some sons as he curses one of them, together with the call for an awakening in Joel 1.5: "Awake, ye drunkards, and weep."[23]

So often when it comes to illustrating Samson's "spiritual strength," the adventure chosen, instead of Samson at the pillars, is "*Sampson . . .* cloathed with the spirit, then . . .

grappl[ing] with a Lion" — or some other episode from among his early adventures — by way of emphasizing that even if initially "Full of divine instinct" (526), when his locks are lopped off, "the spirit of God is withdrawn" and then by way of asking whether that spirit ever returns; whether, even if Samson prays for vengeance at the end, the catastrophe at the pillars is God's work — or the Devil's.[24] The passage previously cited from *De Doctrina* concerning the return of Samson's spirit, if it does not resolve interpretive issues, certainly makes clear that Milton is sensitive to the *idioms* of inspiration and to the language by which people lay claim to it. A complementary passage from *Paradise Lost*, moreover, shows Milton brooding over the validity of such claims as he speaks of those "feigning . . . to act / By spiritual [power], to themselves appropriating / The Spirit of God" (12.517–19).

Samson is a particularly apt figure around whom to circle such concerns inasmuch as "all men make not the mater very sure, whether he be savid or not." Those confident of his salvation are likely to argue along the lines of St. Thomas More's Vincent:

> god may dispence wher he will & whan he will, & may commaund [of his emissaries] . . . to do the contrary, . . . as sampson had by inspiracion of god, commaundment to kill him selfe, . . . pulling down the howse vppon his own hed at the fest of the phelisties.[25]

Just as likely, those who think Samson is saved will also argue, as does More's Antonye, that "Sampson . . . be savid . . . For the philisties being enimies to god, & vsing Sampson for their mokkyng," it is altogether "likely that god gaue hym the mind . . . to bestow his own life vppon the revengyng of thos blasphemous philisties." In such times, Antonye concludes, "it pleasid god" to be with Samson as "aperith by these words":

> *Irruit virtus domini in samsonem* . . . the power or might of god russhed into Sampson . . . this thing that he did in the

pullying down of the house, was done by the speciall gifte of strength . . . gevyn hym by god.[26]

This is not, however, the way Milton's Arminian ally, John Goodwin, argues; nor is it the direction in which the argument in *Samson Agonistes* will move. And it is noteworthy, too, that More's editors allow, "It is not clear in Judges 16" that God really commands Samson to do what in prayer he hopes to accomplish: revenge himself upon his enemies even if he must die himself in the process.[27] Nor, as Holstun remarks, is the issue clarified in *Samson Agonistes* where "the source of Samson's final inspiration (from within? from above?) is notoriously ambiguous."[28]

John Goodwin, whose *Obstructours of Justice* (1649) was both influenced by *The Tenure of Kings and Magistrates* and then burned along with Milton's *Eikonoklastes* and *Pro Populo Anglicano Defensio* in 1660, addresses precisely these questions, raises exactly these issues, with reference to Samson who, "when his hair was cut , . . . [became] then *but like other men*, . . . step[ing] out of the ways of grace, into the ways of the pride, . . . the injustice, . . . the rashnesse . . . and baseness of the world. In fact, he engaged these questions and issues within a treatise where devils are numbered with Dan.[29] Or as he explains elsewhere, again with specific reference to Samson, men bring misery upon themselves: "God . . . insensibly, and by degrees withdrew that lively presence of his Spirit from them, by which they had been formerly raised and enlarged."[30]

As "the wonted presence of this Spirit of God," having departed, fails them, "their wisdom and understandings [are] proportionably abated and declined, as *Sampsons* strength upon the cutting of his hair, sank and fell to the line of the weakness of other men." The weakness such men fall into, says Goodwin, is *"a delivering up* [or, giving over] *to a reprobate minde"*:

So that this Judiciary Act of God, in giving men *over to a Reprobate Minde*, imports nothing but the total withdrawing of

all communion and converse by his Spirit with them, hereby
leaving them in the hand, and under the inspection, of such a
minde, or understanding, which is naturally, properly, and entirely their own.[31]

Thus what they do, they do of their own accord. Furthermore,
not all saints partake of God's glory in the same degree just
as not all stars shine with the same intensity. Indeed, as Samson may be thought to illustrate, no less than the Philistines,
"Mens ingagements and actings are never like to rise higher
than the level of that good which is desired and hoped to be
obtained by them" with Samson's spirit, it would seem never
as fully disciplined (as was that of Jesus) by repentance, mor-
tification, and self-denial nor "raised and heightened" by a
willingness to confront "the bloudy hatred and malice of the
World for righteousness sake."[32]

Goodwin's *The Divine Authority of Scriptures Asserted*,
The Obstructours of Justice, and *Redemption Redeemed* afford
principles for wrestling with the thorny issues raised by the
Samson story:

(1) as when Goodwin deplores all forms of dissembling when
seeking an occasion for revenge (which would include, presumably, Samson's feigning love for two women by way of exter-
minating their people), and acknowledges that some like David
"deserved death for the hand which . . . [they] had in the shed-
ding of it"
(2) or when Goodwin resists the notion of God as a spirit rushing upon and compelling people to actions requiring dispensations only because the actions are so horrific (like the temple
catastrophe?) that men, fearful of taking responsibility for such
actions, ascribe them to God,
(3) or as when Goodwin describes "this Judiciary Act of God,
in *giving* men *over to a Reprobate Minde*" in terms of "the
persons mentioned" who, when God was with them, neither
glorifed him nor gave him thanks (Samson is one of the few
named).[33]

As with Goodwin, so with Milton: permissive providence is a
principal evidence of God's justice in the world; honor and

charity are standards by which to judge all actions; and violence, according to the value system formulated in *De Doctrina*, is "disgraceful and disgusting . . . [to] the Christian religion" (*YP*, 6:123).

Unquestionably Milton inhabited what Michael Lieb calls a "culture of violence." The question is whether Lieb's reading of the Samson story is Milton's:

> There is no equivocation on Milton's part in his depiction of Samson's [final] act. . . . The act is conceived not just with approval but with applause: Milton celebrates it. The energy of the act, indeed its uncompromising barbarity, is held up as a model of heroism and courage on the part of one who refuses to be subjected by tyrants of whatever stamp. . . . Milton emphasizes at this pivotal juncture that the individual responsible for the enactment of the slaughter carries it out alone, single-handedly. His actions are the true mark of a hero indeed.[34]

The issue is whether Milton condones or criticizes that culture; whether he underwrites or undermines practitioners of violence; whether, legitimating, he is complicit in those practices or, evading them, rejects the cultural barbarism subtended by the Samson story.

These are issues on which *The History of Britain* sheds some light. The land of Albion becomes Britain when "a remnant of *Giants*" known for their "excessive Force and Tyranie" is destroyed by Brutus (*YP*, 5:16). It is not the heroism of Corineus, wrestling with a Giant, "heaving him up by main force, and on his Shoulders bearing him to the next high Rock," then throwing him "headlong all shatter'd into the Sea" (5:17) — it is not the "heroism" of Peter Du Moulin bestrewing the rocks with Milton's "shattered brain" or, for that matter, of Samson in the Bible "beat[ing] to pieces his enemies"[35] or, finally, of Samson dashing the brain and shattering the sides of Harapha in *Samson Agonistes* (1240–41), these are not deeds that Milton emulates. Instead, he exalts the exemplary heroism of Gorbonian (no "Juster man liv'd . . . in his Age"), who builds temples rather than tears them down at a time when "Violence and Wrong seldom was heard of" (5:33).

When, in this same work, Milton moralizes the story of Elidure and Archigello, thus supplementing Geoffrey of Monmouth, he eliminates the feature of violence from the tale, thus magnifying the "deed . . . Heroic" and through that deed emblazoning the lesson of brotherly love, which, as French Fogle argues, "shines more clearly without this touch of violence" in which Elidure threatens the nobles with loss of their heads if they do not crown his brother (*YP*, 5:34). If there are eruptions of violence in history, their first cause is often a punishing God, both in The Book of Judges and in *The History of Britain*, where, in the first instance, a nation's enemies act at God's pleasure — "they shall be *as thorns* in your sides, and their gods shall be a snare unto you" (2.3). Then an angry God declares that he "will not henceforth drive out . . . any of the nations" so that "through them" he "may prove Israel" (2.21–22). Or as Milton himself explains in his *History*, which repeatedly parallels past and present, "when God hath decreed servitude on a sinful Nation, fitted by thir own vices for no condition but servile, all Estates of Government are alike unable to avoid it. God had purpos'd to punish our instrumental punishers, though now Christians, by other Heathen, according to his Divine retaliation; invasion for invasion, spoil for spoil, destruction for destruction" (*YP*, 5:259). Vengeance belongs to the Lord whose agents are more often the wicked, not the good men of history.

As Irene Samuel reminds us, "Milton himself had lived through a long civil war during which God's will was all-too-seriously called upon as sanction" by both sides.[36] In *Samson Agonistes*, he brackets from the Book of Judges a tragedy, which reflects upon that history, as if to acknowledge with Francis Barker that "tragedy is likely to be more historical than much history":

Where histories tend toward either the replication of some dominant story which seeks to justify and legitimate whatever is in actuality dominant, or protest against the dominant *on its ground*, tragedy, on the other hand, discloses the problematicity — the unforeclosed character, and thus the critical and diacritical value — of the historical.[37]

Milton knows, certainly, that stories like Samson's are invented by the victors as justification and legitimization; that this story was used not just to communicate but to condone barbaric cultural practices; and that this story tells us more about what a culture would forget than about what it would remember. It tells us an enormous amount, as we will see in the next chapter, about Cromwell's own providential theology as distinct from Milton's.

What we see in plays like *The Bacchae* in conjunction with *Christos Paschon* is that powerful men, with their vision blurred, are public dangers, a marked contrast with those who, as lovers of peace, cherish human lives and humane values. What we see in *Samson Agonistes*, foregrounded in the line (an icon of barbarism), "A thousand fore-skins fell, the flower of *Palestin*" (144), is Samson, by insinuation, persisting in the sports of cruelty, akin to the butchering of corpses and counting of the dead by numbering foreskins, then heaping them in a pile and creating with them a trophy — a primitive practice associated with alien cultures upon which the Israelites supposedly represented an improvement. As Richard Trexler documents, "striking visual evidence . . . comes from the military life of ancient Egypt, where some friezes "show heaps of penises as part of the booty displayed before the pharoah" and where also "Egyptian written records include inventories of Libyan penises gathered to the same end." "In Midrashic lore," moreover, "the Amalekites cut off the circumcised members of the Israelites (both from prisoners and corpses)," tossing them in the air as they shouted obscene curses.[38] Early on, this form of military humiliation even had currency among the Israelites, although in the instance of *Samson Agonistes*, the resulting effeminization is an attribute not of his enemies but of Samson himself.

Indeed, this culture of mutilation and violence is no less a repugnant feature of Jewish civilization than, in the form of the Crucifixion story, it is of Christian culture. In *Christus Paschon*, for instance, its author makes clear that Christ himself, a victim of cultural violence, but never an exponent for it, is both a Jew and a Rabbi (179–80), in this way saving his play from the anti-Semitism of some later such plays, by indicting not an entire culture but the mob mentality, the violent component, within any culture whether it be some Jews in the time of Jesus or some Christian theologians in his own day or some avid Christians in Milton's time. It might even be said that Milton follows suit, in the poetry of the 1671 volume, never speaking of Christ, and in his tragedy displacing the passion story onto Samson, in the process underplaying the network of typology that figured so prominently in both his epic poems, indeed the very ideas of typological triumph and fulfillment folded into those poems. In *Samson Agonistes*, Milton develops an unflattering typology, its inflections falling not on similitude but difference.

That is, what we see in *Samson Agonistes* is a tragedy, which, as *Christos Paschon*[39] claims to be, is written "along the lines of Euripides" (3), in which the barbarism of Hebrew culture, an aspect of all cultures still too much with us, now internalized by Samson and defeating him, is likewise the culprit that slays Jesus, indeed that continues to slay his spirit, often in the name of Christianity, in Milton's own day. This "land of the Hebrews" (1595), a place of slaughter, this "land of the barbarians" (1708), ruled by brutality and rife with destructive impulses, exhibits both a "savage" character and a "barbarous mind," along with "hateful judgement" (485–88), its "raging . . . hateful mob" (483, 485) conspiring toward "an even worse catastrophie" (490). The mob is an element within culture — hostile, hateful, lawless, vengeful and murderous, killing from envy — and, in its slaughtering of others, displays the "bloodthirst and evil heedlessness" (1177) of a violent people. It is, most explicitly, this element of culture, represented by "The vengeful mob" (660; cf. 786), "the murderous, evil-doing mob" (679), "the lawless mob" (1318), a "mob [that] is savage, especially now when it rules" (2035); that, if it defined an aspect of Jewish culture in the time of Jesus, now defines an aspect of Christian culture, no less so in Milton's day than in the time when *Christos Paschon* was written.

The spirit of *Christos Paschon* carries over into Grotius's *Christus Patiens* and then Sandys's translation of it, *Christ's Passion*, where again the attack is leveled against a people as "Rebellious Vassals" with "savage manners," an "impious Race," full of malice, engaged in sports of cruelty and blood.[40] Only after the horror do these people flee the scene, thus "too late . . . warm[ing] their savage brests" and, hence, for their crimes deserving "calamities," says Sandys, "more horrid, then ever befell any other Nation."[41] If the Jewish people seem to embody the primitive ethical system Jesus would transcend, it is an ethical system in which Peter and Mary — in which Christianity itself — is implicated. Moreover, just as in *Samson Agonistes* there are different types of Philistines, so here there are different classes of people among the Hebrews: "Some, with transfixed hearts, and wounded eyes, / Astonisht stand" and "some [who] . . . to the last extend their Barbarous hate," some who mock Jesus, some who laugh and others who cry, some with faces of "perfect woe," others who tear their garments and some their hair, and still others filled with terror.[42] In the Book of Judges, no less than in these passion plays, and certainly no less than in *Samson Agonistes*, the tragedy is not of an alien culture but of Samson's own people, as well as the people of Jesus, with Samson in both the Book of Judges and Milton's poem serving as their representative and Jesus as their foil. The tragedy is shared by Samson and his people.

If the church liturgy as practiced in the sixteenth century yoked the Samson and Jesus stories in such a way as to suggest that the surest bond between them is their passions and deaths, the liturgy as modified in the seventeenth century brackets in question marks whether there are any significant bonds at all between Samson and the Son of God.[43] With the relevant liturgy assigned to late March, the comparison — or contrast — between Samson and Jesus, made during the Lenten season or Easter time, sounds less like a song of joy than an aria of violence where, in the case of Samson, sex and violence are linked in a perversion of *imitatio Christi* and where, in their turn, the forms of violence threatened or practiced by Samson, the dismemberment and destruction of the human body, are a literal enactment of the Eucharist no less so, indeed no less repugnantly so, than the stories of Christ's passion and crucifixion. In sum, what we see in *Samson Agonistes* is how religion, Jewish or Christian, erupting in violence, desolates the world with wars.

In his own juxtaposition of Samson's story with that of the Son, Milton forces a distinction between those who slay and those who save, between the destroyers and the preservers, in the process marking not resemblance but difference between Jesus and his own Christian self on the one hand, and Samson on the other, even as he uses both figures to reinforce, yet once more, the proclamation of *Paradise Lost* that "to create / Is greater then created to destroy" (7.606–07). This triangulation within *Samson Agonistes* finds its counterpart in 1 Corinthians 15 where countertype (Satan) and type (Adam) both front Christ (their antitype), their fulfillment. In the parlance of the biblical commentators of his century, Milton simply subordinates the "Parallel" to the "Disparity," the type (Samson) not just to the antitype (Christ) but to the neotype (Milton) in the hope that, unlike Samson, Milton himself will break through the cycles of history where the order of the day has been to meet spite with spite or, in words from *Samson Agonistes*, "To pay my underminers in thir coin" (1204), "dealing dole" among one's foes (1529).

Milton, it seems, tells the Samson story anew, writing against its grain, looking at the underside of the tale as it is usually told, thus exposing its occlusions. Milton seems to be saying that the truth of the Samson story, the truth of history, like Truth itself, is the victim of violence, not its promoter. In challenging (as will one of his finest recent critics)[44] the practice of getting rid of tensions and contradictions in biblical narratives in the interests of presenting straightforward lessons, Milton (as Regina M. Schwartz would want for him to do) is reopening and rewriting biblical narratives in a new key, even as he enunciates conflict as their key, in a meditation on violence that modulates into a critique of it, that critique including prophecy, which during the Civil War years had become one of that war's chief legitimators.

Again, John Goodwin is a valuable point of reference. If for Goodwin, the spirit of the Lord never *rushes*, it is interesting that Milton, who uses the term once before in vague connection with "inspiration," in *Paradise Regain'd* should describe the *rushing* winds of the Son's "ugly dreams" (4.408, 413–15). In *Samson Agonistes*, the word is virtually a framing device, its being used in Samson's opening soliloquy to describe his "restless thoughts, that like a deadly swarm / Of hornets arm'd, . . . / . . . *rush* upon me thronging" (19–21; my italics). Milton invokes the word again in the choral ode where Samson is told, "Go, and the Holy One / Of *Israel* be thy guide": "that Spirit that first *rusht* on thee / In the Camp of *Dan* / Be efficacious in thee now at need" (1427–28, 1435 [my italics]–1437). Moments later Manoa asks: "What noise or shout was that? it tore the Skie" (1472) to which the Chorus responds, in language reminiscent of the Fall in *Paradise Lost*: "Noise call you it or universal groan" (1511; cf. 9.1000–02).

The catastrophe in *Samson Agonistes* has the same rhetorical markers as the tragedy of both *Paradise Lost* and *Christos Paschon*. In *Christos Paschon*, earth, indeed all of Creation, is "trembling" (873, 1061; cf. 1106, 1210) and eventually "shaking . . . with unstoppable turmoil" (2252). It has the same markings as the tragedy of *Christus Patiens* in the Sandys translation: an "earthquake," the center in "sudden throwes," all of nature disturbed, with "trembling Earth [showing] a sad distemper," then "groaning" and "with a horrid motion sh[aking]."[45] In both *Christos Paschon* and *Samson Agonistes*, sons are returned to their fathers for burial, with, in the latter poem, the son's returning to his father's house finding its counterpart in *Paradise Regain'd* where the Son returns in triumph to the home of his mother — a moment, for those who have read the poem, bound to resonate with two others in *Christos Paschon*: the first, when after the death of Christ, his Mother seeks solitude, goes "where there is rest . . . / To the son's house" (1631–32) and later, returning to her own home, to "the house of Mary / Where . . . the dear disciples," along with the Chorus will then come, finds "the Lord stand[ing] within the doors" "when the doors were locked" (2480–81, 2498). When this context is invoked, it would appear as if the resurrection is encrypted within the last lines of *Paradise Regain'd* where Jesus is described as "unobserved / Home to his mother's house private return[ing]" (4.638–39).[46] None of the Gospel writers mentions Mary's house. Only Mark reports no apparition after the death of Jesus, which scene, when otherwise reported by the Gospel writers, depicts Mary and Mary Magdalen at the tomb of Jesus or the unwitting disciples not recognizing Jesus on the road to Emmaus with Jesus otherwise appearing to them at their hideaway and later by the sea of Tiberias. John says that Jesus appears to Mary when, upon leaving his tomb, he is journeying to his father's house in heaven (Matthew 28, Luke 24.13–35, John 20–21). These apparitions, moreover, are stories of emerging understanding, of dawning vision.

The idiom of vision and inspiration in Milton's brief epic, it should also be clear, is everywhere more muted than in *Samson Agonistes*: "Thou Spirit who ledst" (1.8); "the Spirit leading" (1.189); "by some strong motion I am led" (1.290). The catastrophe in *Samson Agonistes*, in the context of a *rushing* inspiration, not to mention the examples from *Paradise Regain'd* nor early in *Samson*, is bound to recall the dictum that the motions from God working within the prophet "are gradual and progressive; not violent and instantaneous."[47] Even the most innocuous of phrases takes on layers of meaning and special import when read as biblical idiom and then contextualized accordingly. Such is true of "Yet once more" (1) in *Lycidas* and of "Now of my own accord" (1643) in *Samson Agonistes*. In Milton's as well as scriptural usage, the idiom stresses the independency of an action as it also does, for example, in Joost van den Vondel's *Samson, of Heilige Wraeck, Treurspel* (1660) where Samson's people, not in cahoots with the Philistines but "of their own accord, to justice moved, / Bound him and brought him to his enemies."[48] In Milton's poem, Samson, who, had been acting by "commands" from the Philistines, now acts of his own accord as the human race, when falling, in *De Doctrina*, acts "OF ITS OWN ACCORD" (*YP*, 6:168, 173, 174). It is crucial to Milton's argument in *De Doctrina*, and again in *Paradise Lost* (3.111–34), that humankind thus acts independent of any command or commission; for the Fall is foreseen, not foreordained. Similarly, in *Mansus*, Apollo "dwelled" in the house of Manso "of his own accord" (*CP*, 177), independent of any petition from the poet; and in *The Judgement of Martin Bucer*, Fabliola, "not enjoyn'd" by any other, "of her own accord" does public penance for her second marriage (*YP*, 2:450), with a later citation from *Tetrachordon* urging a peaceful "turn[ing] away . . . from that which afflicts and hazards our destruction; especially when our staying can doe no good, and is expos'd to all evil" (*YP*, II, 623).

The phrase seems always to imply *without prompting from anyone, or provocation by any external authority* as it had in Euripidean tragedy:

> I hereby put
> Myself on record that *of my own free will*
> I volunteer to die for these and for
> Myself.
>
> (530–33)

> I offer up my life
> For them *of my own accord*, but won't be forced.
>
> (550–51)

> It was brute force that brought him in, and not
> *his own accord* . . .
>
> (885–86)

> I did not start
> This feud *of my accord*.
>
> (985–86)[49]

Milton follows suit. Thus, in *The History of Britain*, the Caledonians "of thir own accord" start a war (*YM*, 5:87; cf. 357, 359, 389); and in the same work, making the distinction explicit, Milton speaks of mischief done by the Saxons "whether by constraint or of thir own accord" (5:154) and, later, of Harold going into Normandy "of his own accord" or "by the Kings permission or connivence" (5:390). In *A Treatise of Civil Power*, St. Paul becomes a servant "of his own accord, . . . not made so by outward force" (*YP*, 7:267), while profane and licentious men may be considered to have "departed" the Church of their "own accord" or to be "excommunicate," with Milton's mind becoming increasingly "alienate[d] . . . from a violent religion expelling out and compelling in" (7:269). Then, in *The Present Means*, Milton looks to the people, without compulsion or even nudging, but "of thir own accord," becoming "partakers of so happy a Government" (*YP*, 7:395). A phrase that, in Milton's usage, means without commission or coercion, command, constraint, or connivance; without petitioning, prompting, or provocation, much less enjoining, nudging, or warranting; without so much as a hint that an action may be foreordained — such a phrase is an unhappy choice if the poet means to suggest that Samson receives a divine commission with which he chooses to cooperate; that the destruction of the temple/theater is cooperatively the work of God and Samson, a miracle or simply an example of God working through his earthly emissaries.

In his prose works, no less than in the final books of *Paradise Lost*, as John R. Knott, Jr., remarks, "The real thrust of Milton's attack . . . is directed against those who appropriate to themselves 'the Spirit of God'"[50] — a gesture that binds liberty, both one's own and that of others, and privileges compulsive acts over patient waiting for promptings from the spirit. In the Book of Judges, the spirit of the Lord that initially "began to move" Samson, in the end and unbeknownst to him, "was departed from him" (13.25, 16.20). In *Samson Agonistes*, Samson claims otherwise, that "Some rouzing motions" compel that he "with this Messenger will go along" (1382, 1384). The word *spirit*, in this poem, is used just three times: once by Samson who asserts its absence not in himself but in Harapha "bulk without spirit vast" (1238); and later by the Chorus who hope first that the "Spirit that first rusht on Thee / In the Camp of *Dan* / Be efficacious in thee now at need" (1435–37) and who then declare that upon those Philistines, "Drunk with Idolatry, drunk with Wine," God "a spirit of phrenzie sent, / Who hurt thir minds, / And urg'd them on" to "Thir own destruction" and "Insensate left, or to sense *reprobate*, / And with blindness internal struck" (1670, 1675–77, 1681, 1685–86; my italics).

De Doctrina, in a passage already cited, provides the apt gloss: "there is no reprobation from eternity of particular men. For God has predestined to salvation all who use their free will, on one condition, which applies to all. None are predestined to destruction except through their own fault and, in a sense, *per accidens*" (*YP*, 6:190). As it speaks of the Messenger who, "relating the Catastrophe, what *Samson* had done to the *Philistins*, and **by accident** to himself," the Argument to *Samson Agonistes* (*CP*, 575; my bold), as it addresses the old chestnut of Samson as a suicide, invokes the same principle, as do Manoa's words in the poem proper: "The accident was loud" (1552). It is not fate but inner character that finally determines Samson's lot. The final catastrophe is not God's but Samson's doing. Strength comes to Samson as a gift from God, but how that gift will be used — or abused — is determined by Samson himself. The choice is his own. He oversees his destiny and rules his fate. God intervenes, to be sure, but less as a "living dread," setting "a spirit of frenzy" loose upon the drunken Philistines, than as the permissive providence, administering distributive justice, proportionate justice and exemplifying mercy by sparing some of those Philistines from the slaughter.

The New Testament site for the scriptural idiom — *of his own accord* — is John 11.49–52, where the high priest Caiaphas **NOT** *of his own accord* speaks truth, "Ye know nothing at all" — the same truth that the Son in *Paradise Regain'd* attributes to Plato, "The first and wisest of them all [who] profess'd / To know this only, that he nothing knew" (4.293–94). At the climactic moment in Milton's poem, the implicit question is: does Samson really know what he and the Chorus claim to know, that he is actually propelled to the temple / theater by "rouzing motions" (1382), that yet once more the spirit has "rusht" upon him (1435)? In the Book of Judges, at the beginning of his story, Samson knows but tells no one (14.4); in Milton's poem, on the other hand, in the end, Samson thinks he knows and tells everyone (1381–83). And, as climax nears, having hitherto performed by "commands impos'd" (1640), Samson claims to act of his own accord (1643). If we do not know what caused Samson to come hither, neither do we know what brings the Messenger hence — "providence or instinct of nature" (1545), divine warrant or natural impulse. We do know, however, that in its largest context John 11, through its representation of a temple destroyed, figures both the destruction of the human body and the devastation of the material temple of the Jews.

In John 11.52, Caiaphas acts *not* of his own accord; that is, he acts after divine intervention, under the influence of divine inspiration, and with divine warrant. Origen may have engaged in some double-talk concerning Caiaphas, implying that while he prophesies the real question is whether he prophesies by the Holy Spirit; and thereupon concludes: "It is clear that it was not the Holy Spirit which inspired these words."[51] The point is that not all who prophesy are prophets, and not all who speak the truth know what they say, Origen argues in a counter statement to those who think false prophets are gifted with prophecy, even in their acts of deception, and think this way right into the seventeenth century when it is still said that God "caused this wicked man [Caiaphas] euen as hee did Balaam, to be an instrument of the holy Ghost";[52] that "God so guided his tongue, that he unwittingly prophecyed of the fruit of Christs death."[53] In the twilight years of Milton's century, it is still argued that "The *Spirit of Prophecy* sometimes fell upon wicked men" and even upon people like Saul who, for awhile "rejected of God . . . did also Prophecy."[54]

At least in the early modern period, on the matter of interpreting these verses, there is consensus, from Erasmus and Calvin on: **NOT** *of his own accord* — "not of myself," says Erasmus, means that "the spirite of prophecie dyd bryng foorthe a godly prophecie by the mouth of a wicked man . . ., that Jesus should by his death redeme and save the Jewes"; or as Calvin contends, Caiaphas, plotting the death of Christ, utters a prediction not of his own making but with "a higher impulse guid[ing] his tongue."[55] Augustine Marlorate explains similarly that, whether of the elect or the reprobate, "Wee are al the instruments of God." Thus *NOT of his own accord* — or the alternate translation, "not of hym selfe," or "myself" —

means, as John Pawson explains, "he spoke by the instinct of God": "the Evangelist geveth us to understand that his tongue was guided by God";[56] that the gift of prophecy, though not in the same degrees, is available to all God's people, saints as well as sinners; that, in the words of Joseph Hall, "God over-ruled his tongue . . . to utter unawares an oracle-like prophesie concerning Christ," for which interpretations and for which prophecy Grotius invokes the authority of Euripides.[57] Or as George Hutcheson remarks, God, in such instances, foils the intentions of sinners by "over-ruling" them, "enlarg[ing] this prophecy, which *Caiaphas* uttered unawares," letting some thus gifted to fall into "grosse errours," in the process modifying their agenda[58] as, in *Samson Agonistes*, God apparently revises Samson's intention of revenging himself on *all* the Philistines. For, contrary to the Judges text, some of the Philistines survive the catastrophe. On the other hand, God may let an already fallen hero fall again.

If the scriptural idiom, "not of his own accord," points to divine commission, inspiration, and warrant, the phrase "of my own accord" (1643), pulls oppositely, implying that Samson acts without divine authority, although not without divine intervention evident in God's sparing some of the Philistines: apparently those people "More generous," and charitable, who had their fill of revenge (1467). At every crucial juncture in *Samson Agonistes* Milton puts the brakes on Calvinistic notions of election and reprobation of which Samson, Manoa, and the Chorus are harbingers; and he does so not only by employing the rhetoric of the Bible but of biblical commentary with specific reference to the Samson story. St. Augustine says, according to Peter Martyr, that Samson "did these things, *not of his own accord*; but by the gift and counsell of the holie Ghost," for those like Samson "be the ministers of God; and that which they doo, God himselfe dooth it by them."[59]

Of his own accord denies the agency to God which *NOT of his own accord* credits to him. When free will comes into play, we need to concede with Martyr that, while not all men are given the "efficacie and vehemencie of spirit," those who are, even if in possession of gentler forms of inspiration, may be known by the way in which their minds incline toward God's laws, never tending toward "things euill and forbidden, being repugnant to the word of God."[60] Perhaps we should notice as well that when Grotius annotates Judges 16.30, "And Samson said, 'Let me die . . .,' " with a citation of his own *De Jure Belli Ac Paces*, the passage is rendered in translation as "The frame or manner of being a Body [i.e., a whole people] is taken away, when the Citizens do either *of their own accord* dissipate themselves, by reason of some general contagion or sedition. . . ."[61] The starting point — and end point — for criticism are still, as they were for Richard C. Jebb, "The catastrophe, [which] . . . consists in Samson deliberately pulling down the temple of Dagon on his own head and those of the spectators. Samson's will is the agent of the catastrophe."[62]

The editors of the Yale Milton are less reluctant than Milton in using Samson as an example; indeed, they very tellingly slide the Samson story under Milton's text at precisely those moments when that story might seem an obvious point of reference and is made one *by them*, but not always by Milton: (1) Samson's rejection of Dalila as a sanction for divorce, (2) fornication as a kind of idolatry, and (3) the exclusion of unbelievers from the Book of Life (*YP*, 6:170, 190 372, 694). Though he does not rush to judgments, nor is he rash in his judgments, Milton does affirm the Arminian (and Quaker) principle that the saints do not always persevere; that "they were and are *Reprobated* from the *Life*, who go from the *Command of God*, and they have lost his *Image*."[63] If Milton does not declare Samson to be of the reprobate, he nevertheless forces the question. Sometimes there is good reason why Milton himself (his editors notwithstanding) might avoid reference to Samson; other times the editorial annotation is provocative.

In the first instance, there is no dispensing with God's laws when it comes to marriage — or divorce; and, in any event, if Samson's second marriage, by implication, is probably not divinely sanctioned (*YP*, 6:372; cf. 650), then the pertinent issue, as outlined in *The Doctrine and Discipline of Divorce*, is that what God "never joyn'd" no one should "hinder . . . from unjoyning" (*YP*, 2:328). Milton does not here let go of the point either: such marriages "God himself dis-joyns" (2:265); He forbids such "mis-yoking mariages," such "mis-matching with an Infidell," this "mixture of minds that cannot unite" (2:270); or in *Tetrachordon*: He "joynes not unmachable things but hates to joyne them, as an abominable confusion" (*YP*, 2:651; cf. 650), "it being all one in matter of ill consequence, to marry, or to continue maried with an Infidel" (2:683). Samson engages in pernicious casuistry, both when he argues for the lawfulness of his marriages and when he goes to the temple, depraving the letter of the law with sophistical justifications that, if they tell us anything at all, argue for Samson (to appropriate and adapt Milton's own language) as "an improvident and careles deliverer" (2:692). He is no savior of the world.

The second example — Samson's going to the temple — is more complicated. Permissible dispensations — permissible forms of idolatry occurring when God suspends his own decrees — are best illustrated (in *The Doctrine and Discipline of Divorce*) by David entering the house of God and eating the shew bread (cf. Matthew 12.3–4, Mark 2.25–26, Luke 6.3–4), which was "ceremonially *unlawfull*" (*YM*, II, 300) and (in *De Doctrina*) by "Naaman the Syrian" (2 Kings 5.17–19) bowing down in the house of Rimmon (*YP*, 6:694). In the Divorce tract, Milton cites this episode involving David to illustrate both the common practice of "the Pope . . . dispenc[ing] with any thing" and the rarity of such dispensations, which are always "left to the decision of charity, ev'n under the bondage of Jewish rites" and "much more under the liberty of the Gospel" (*YP*, 2:300, 299). The rule of charity applies, *even* under the Jewish law: "to do well" (Matthew 12.12), and "to do good . . . to save life," not "to do evil" and "destroy *it*" (Luke 6.9). Moreover, even if (as Milton argues in *De Doctrina Christiana*) a work of faith is not always of the law (*YP*, 6:491), dispensations are so extraordinarily rare that they are left unspecified by the law.

In the case of Naaman the Syrian, Milton writes with remarkable caution, observing in *De Doctrina*, that, while going to the temple may be "allowable," it might also have been "safer, and more consistent with reverence for God, to decline" going to a place of idol-worship and to "relinquish . . . altogether" any civil duties that might take one to such places (*YP*, 6:694). There should finally be checks on one's public duties. The example of Naaman is also cited by Martyr as an illustration of "that . . . which was not in his power; namelie, that he should dispense with the lawe or commandment, which concerneth the flieng from idolatrie. Undoubtedlie, all mortall men are bound, without anie exception, unto that precept," which stipulates: do not do evil for the sake of good.[64]

What is so striking about Samson, within the context of the law and in view of his judgeship, is that so often he is lawless, neither abiding by the rules of others' societies nor by those of his own, regularly relying upon dispensations from the law even as in *The Doctrine and Discipline of Divorce* Milton is emphatic in his insistence that "the Jew was bound as strictly to the performance of every duty as was possible, and . . . [hence] could not be dispenc't with more then the Christian, perhaps not so much" (*YP*, 2:302). What Milton says here, he repeats still more emphatically in *Tetrachordon*: "A dispensation is for no long time, is particular to som persons rather then generall to a whole people; alwaies hath charity the end, is granted to necessities and infirmities, not to obstinat lust" (*YP*, 2:658). Given the terms of Milton's argument here, the question is unavoidable: is the lustful Samson who seeks an occasion against the Philistines (namely their destruction) a candidate for a dispensation? Furthermore (and Milton's point needs underscoring) when granted, such dispensations belong "more . . . to the christian under grace and liberty, then to the Jew under law and bondage":

> To Jewish ignorance it could not be dispenc't without a horrid imputation laid upon the law, to dispence fouly, in stead of teaching fairly; like that dispensation that first polluted Christendom with idolatry. (2:658–59)

Put simply and Miltonicly, in words taken from *The Doctrine and Discipline of Divorce*, the ways of God preclude "pit falling dispenses" (*YP*, 2:230).

In *The Doctrine and Discipline of Divorce*, Milton devotes three chapters to dispensation of the law, especially to what he calls "the fancie of dispencing" (*YP*, 2:302), where he is emphatic:

> . . . dispensation . . . can never be giv'n to the allowance of sin, God cannot give it neither in respect of himselfe, nor in respect of man: not in respect of himselfe, being a most pure essence, the just avenger of sin; neither can he make that cease to be a sinne, which is in it selfe injust and impure. (2:296).

As for man, if a dispensation cannot be provided for his good, neither can it be given for his evil:

> Nor to the evill of man can a dispence be given . . . how can the same God publish dispences against that Law, which must needs be unto death? Absurd and monstrous would that dispence be, if any Judge or Law should give it to a man to cut his own throat, or to damne himselfe. (2:297).

To abrogate the law, Milton argues, is to impugn both the law and the one who made it: "is to embroile our selves against the righteous and all wise judgements and statutes of God; which are not variable and contrarious," now "permitting" and now "forbidding" (2:320–21; cf. 317).

Samson's initial response to the Public Officer is: "Thou knowst I am an *Ebrew*, therefore tell them, / Our Law forbids at thir Religious Rites / My presence" (1319–21). And later:

> Shall I abuse this Consecrated gift . . .
> . . . and add a greater sin
> By prostituting holy things to Idols;
> A *Nazarite* in place abominable
> Vaunting my strength in honour to thir *Dagon*?
> Besides, how vile, contemptible, ridiculous,
> What act more execrably unclean, prophane?
>
> (1354, 1357–62)

Samson is appalled by the thought of once again abusing his strength, of going to the temple and there "prostituting holy things to Idols" (1358). Samson knows his Naziriteship forbids his going, that to go is to put man above God. He goes anyway, prompted by a God of "jealousie" who dispenses with his laws in order to make face-saving gestures, in order to release his rage and salvage his pride (1375–79). The *IF* Samson flaunts here is a very big *if* indeed:

> I with this Messenger will go along,
> Nothing to do, be sure, that may dishonour
> Our Law, or stain my vow of *Nazarite*.
> *IF* there be aught of presage in the mind. . . .
>
> (1384–87; last line, my emphasis)

The questions now tumbling forth are ones we have heard before: is Samson's going to the temple an instance of God's dispensing with the law or, instead, a shameful abrogation of it? is there — or is there not — "presage in the mind"? And, if so, does it come from above or below, from God or from Satan?

Milton's own thinking outside *Samson Agonistes*, these examples supplementary to those we have already reviewed, makes such questioning both more riddling and more pressing. Here we need to take into account *Animadversions* where Nazarites, "faithfull" to doctrine and God's laws, not only are heralds of God's truths but make "a kind of creation like to Gods" by replicating his spirit and likeness in a springtime of "good workes" (*YP*, 1:721); *The Reason of Church-Government* where a distinction is drawn between political and moral aspects of God's law, the latter "perpetually true" (*YP*, 1:764), a set of moral absolutes corresponding with the will of God and not to be rescinded by Him; and *The Tenure of Kings and Magistrates* where Milton complains about those who transform "the sacred verity of God" into "an Idol with two Faces" (*YP*, 3:195) as Samson seems to do in his conversation with the Public Officer and Chorus concerning why he will not go to the temple/theater he then visits. Additionally, we need to think about how Samson's going to the temple resonates with a play like Vondel's *Samson* where it is understood by all parties, first, that Jewish law forbids Samson from "set[ting] his foot in Dagon's temple" and, second, that even "The priests of Dagon will not allow it so that if there is to be play-acting (as it were), if this temple is to become a theater, it will happen in a court outside the temple.[65]

The encounter with the Public Officer is Milton's invention, though as an invention, presented in conformity with what becomes for Milton a type-scene in which the Samson of Judges (16.15, 17) is tempted — or "mocked" — by Delilah "three times" before, relenting, he acquiesces in her request as now he succumbs to the command of the Public Officer. Three times Samson is assailed, and three times says *no*: "I cannot come" (1321), "I will not come" (1332), "I will not come" (1342) until finally he says, "Because they shall not trail me through thir streets / Like a wild Beast, *I am content to go*" (1402–03; my italics). With the Chorus providing a segue to his revised response — "Where the heart joins not, outward acts defile not" (1368) — Samson, as he moves to accommodate what earlier he called "such absurd commands" (1337), argues, on the contrary, that God "may dispense with me or thee / Present in Temples at Idolatrous Rites / For some important cause, thou needst not doubt" (1377–79); that he will "comply" with the Officer's request because, entailing nothing "Scandalous or forbidden in our Law" (1408–09), it defies neither God nor his edicts. Such are Samson's obfuscations; and they have the effect of recalling the proposition that laws are to command what is good, and restrain what is evil, with the implication that to dispense with the law, especially divine law, is to turn the moral universe upside down and inside out.

Samson's arguments exhibit none of the subtlety or reticence of Milton's own and ultimately require that he contradict his own (and Milton's) premise that God's laws are immutable, inviolable; that "the contradiction / Of their own deity, Gods cannot be" (898–99). As the headnote to *The Doctrine and Discipline of Divorce* declares: "*that God dispenc't by some unknown way, ought not to satisfie a Christian mind*" (*YP*, 2:296). In *Samson Agonistes*, the protagonist aligns himself with the capricious God of the Chorus — a God "with hand so various," indeed "contrarious," that he is always changing his "countenance" (668–69, 684); a God, not bound by "his own prescript" (308), who can "with his own Laws . . . best dispence" (314). At the same time, the Chorus worries that to "give the rains to [such] wandring thought," to "edicts, found contradicting" (301–02), leads into perplexities without "self-satisfying solution" (306), in its turn casting doubt on the justice of God's ways. The Chorus might have gone on to say that, complying with the Philistines, going to their temple, captures the moment described in *Pro Populo Anglicano Defensio* when the law, no longer ruling over a man, comes to be ruled by him; when people themselves become "tyrants over the law" (*YP*, 4:383) in order to ascribe to God horrors for which they themselves do not wish to take credit. What Manoa hopes for — that God will return Samson to his "sacred house" with Samson averting God's "further ire, with praiers and vows renew'd" (518, 520) — looks ahead with irony to Samson at the pillars, perhaps praying, perhaps not.

The beginning and end of the 1671 poetic volume, yoked together imagistically, are at odds conceptually. In *Paradise Regain'd*, Jesus goes to the temple to hear and learn, eventually standing atop the temple in triumph. What he learns enables

him to begin the deliverance of his people: "victorious deeds /
Flam'd in my heart, heroic acts . . . / To rescue *Israel* from the
Roman yoke, / Then to subdue and quell o're all the earth /
Brute violence and proud Tyrannick pow'r" (1.215–19).
Alternatively, "His fierie vertue rouz'd . . . / . . . into sudden
flame" (1690–91), Samson assails his enemies whom he kills,
in this same act killing himself. His going to the temple, within
the interpreting context of *Paradise Regain'd*, must inevitably
be read in terms of the Son's counsel that, when God's "purpose is / . . . to declare his Providence," His "Angels . . . /
. . . themselves disdaining / T'approach thy [Satan's] Temples"
(1.444–45, 447–49). Israel's God thus puts Dagon to the test.
By combat "decid[ing] whose god is God" (1176; cf. 1150–55)
is Samson's way but, most emphatically, not the way of
Milton's God. If Samson's way is to tear Dalila limb from limb,
to cut to pieces the bodies of his enemies, and finally to destroy
Dagon's temple, it is worth remembering that "Dagon was
represented like a woman, with the lower parts of a fish";[66]
that the mutilation of women and demolition of temples are
of a piece with one another.

   More complicated still, perhaps, is Milton's exclusion of
Samson's name from his discussion of unbelievers, deserted
by God and thus excluded from the Book of Life. This is a
speaking silence. The omission of Samson's name from
Milton's various listings and citations of the biblical judges
may have once seemed innocent, but would scarcely have
seemed so in the latter part of the seventeenth century: not
after Milton's demonstrated knowledge and deft deployment
of biblical poetics; not after the precision of such biblical listings had been established both in terms of logic and sequence;
not after so much had been made of the graduated lists and
demotional tactics in such catalogues — of their significant
silences; and certainly not after the context afforded by *Paradise Lost* where Samson is remembered as "the *Danite*"
(9.1059) and by *Paradise Regain'd* where Dan is represented

(with Bethel) as the tribe of idolatry whose members, "Un-humbl'd, unrepentant, unreform'd," "wrought their own captivity" (3.415, 429–32). Silence concerning Samson here seems calculated as when, for example, Hugh Broughton places David among "the noble warriors" (without mention of Samson) and then presents Deborah, Gideon, Ambimelech, and Jephthah as "defendours of the people" (again, without mentioning Samson).[67] Jacob Boehme's comments are representative, especially his conclusion that by the tribes two figures are usually represented, Christ and Adam, a good and an evil man, and thereupon his conclusion that Dan is the spirit of selfishness in the world and the determiner of strife.[68] To name Samson by his tribe, and then to elide Adam and Eve with him, as Milton does in *Paradise Lost*, is an act loaded with meaning.

Henry Ainsworth reminds us that Dan in Genesis 49.16 is Samson: "This prophesie was fulfylled in *Samson*. . . . So the Chaldee paraphrast explayneth it" and "the Ierusalemy Thargum nameth him, saying, *this is Samson son of Manoah*." What is paraphrased here as a prophecy of "suddayn and unexpected victory," and understood as a history of a tribe dealing "chiefly" with "the history of this Danite judge," is given a very different spin when it is remembered, with Louis Ginzberg, that the Haggadah considers Samson to be one of "the three least worthy of the judges"; that "the Danite descent of the anti-Christ is obvious"; that "Samson and Solomon were never recognized by God as . . . 'servants of the Lord'." When it is allowed, again with Ginzberg, that "There was a weak side to his character, too" and that "severe punishment produced no change of heart. He continued to lead his old life of profligacy in prison," then Ainsworth's conclusion follows:

> Samson went from bad to worse: He started by marrying a heathen woman, and finished by becoming a captive of a heathen harlot at Gaza. It was therefore at this place that he met his fate at the hands of Delilah, who deserves this name, "she who

makes poor," as it was through her that Samson became poor: he lost his strength, his wisdom, his piety.[69]

Dan and Samson, each is seen in the other; the image is here positive, there negative.

Milton's lifelong association of Samson's tribe with idolatry is abundantly evident in *Of Reformation* (*YP*, 1:573–74), *Eikonoklastes* (*YP*, 3:549–50), *Paradise Lost* (1.485) and, as we have seen, *Paradise Regain'd*. In *Samson Agonistes*, in a striking departure from the letter (if not the spirit) of the Judges text, Milton transforms Samson himself into an idol — a secular bird — with Samson now achieving in his own death what Dalila had hoped for in hers: "A Monument" surrounded by laurel and palms and visited on festal days — and his acts enrolled in legend and sweet lyric song (1733–37). In a touch worthy of Dante, the idolaters have themselves become idols, both now remembered in the terms by which they sinned. Milton's secular hero, with "branching Palm" over his tomb (1735), is a marked contrast to the saintly heroes, with "branching palm" as they are described in Revelation 7.9 and remembered in *Paradise Lost* (6.885). The contrast, in turn, contains the reminder that, unlike most, Samson's Nazariteship is not temporary and involves the provision that Nazarites "should not violate themselves with funerall moornings,"[70] not at the death of their parents and not at the time of their own deaths either. Yet the best gloss on this passage in *Samson Agonistes* may be the notation of Sandys concerning the fact that Moses, who saw the land of promise from Dan, was deliberately buried in an unknown sepulcher in order to diminish the possibility for Israelite idolatry,[71] which Samson's monument in Milton's tragedy both forecasts and encourages.

Here is a haunting reminder that only those from the marked tribes are among the palm-bearing multitudes, a group from which Dan (and some thought Samson within Dan) had been excluded. Thomas Fuller's succinct remark best catches the fine nuances described within this moment of *Samson*

Agonistes: "As *Samsons* lustre did rise, so it did set in this tribe."[72] A life beginning in marvel ends in tragedy. If Milton provides a capstone to such an argument, it is to be found in *De Doctrina* where he explains that names recorded in the Book of Life do not signify predestination but rather a status earned by certain people "on account of their works"; and correspondingly "those people not marked down" are eliminated not by divine decree but by their own choices and actions when, at the time of their apostasy, "they became inveterate and hardened sinners," with "*destruction wait[ing] for them with unsleeping eyes*" (*YP*, 6:170). Even the saints do not always persevere, and that they do not is the mark of a theology predicated upon freedom of choice, acting of one's own accord, freely asserting one's will; and then taking responsibility for one's actions and their consequences.

Critics have scanned and rescanned allusions to Samson in Milton's writings as a clue to reading *Samson Agonistes*. What needs to be emphasized is that such allusions, so carefully woven into Milton's polemic and lending force to it, cannot be understood apart from their context; and what needs to be asked is whether another question may not yield as many — and different — interpretive clues for reading Milton's poem. That is, we may ask about Milton's other representations of Samson *or*, just as profitably perhaps, inquire into his handling of the Book of Judges where the Samson story is inscribed. These two concerns intersect, as it happens, in *Pro Populo Anglicano Defensio*, which contains the most elaborate — and revealing — of these allusions and where the allusion to Samson, moreover, is injected into a discussion of another episode in the Book of Judges.

Milton is as emphatic here as he had been in *The Tenure of Kings and Magistrates*: Ehud has a "special warrant from God" when, in Judges, he is "raysed to deliver Israel from *Eglon*" (*YP*, 3:213); "it was right for Ehud to slay [Eglon]," Milton says in *Pro Populo*, just as it was right for David, "being a private citizen," to refrain from killing Saul: "He would not kill his foe by treachery" (*YP*, 4:402). It is within this context that Milton, altogether more guardedly, invokes "the heroic Samson," who, "whether prompted by God *or* by his own valor, slew at one stroke not one but a host of his country's tyrants, having first made prayer to God for his aid" (4:402; my italics). Milton thereupon concludes that at least "Samson . . . thought it not impious but pious to kill those masters who were tyrants over his country, even though most of her citizens did not balk at slavery" (4:402). Milton equivocates not when judging Ehud or David, only when judging Samson whose plan is to thwart God's own plot for testing his people: "ye have not obeyed my voice: why have ye done this? Wherefore I also said, I will not drive them out from before you: but they shall be *as thorns* in your sides, and their gods shall be a snare unto you" (Judges 2.2–3). Thus, in *De Doctrina*, Milton speaks confidently of Ehud who "acted upon divine prompting"; of Deborah who "*arose*"; and of Gideon, "outstanding for his faith and piety," who "*through faith subdued kingdoms*," while Samson, though presumably meriting an allusion, is never mentioned by name (*YP*, 6:764, 366, 734, 738, 625).

If in *Pro Populo Anglicano Defensio* Milton equivocates on the issue of whether Samson acts as a private or public person,[73] in *Samson Agonistes*, confronting the issue again — "But I a private person," "I was no private but a person rais'd" (1208, 1211) — Milton hesitates yet another time, on this occasion over the matter of Samson's prayer, his protagonist standing at the pillars "as one who pray'd / *Or* some great matter in his mind revolv'd" (1637–38; my italics). Nor does Samson here speak the prayer ascribed to him either in Genesis (49.18) or Judges (16.28) but instead, with head erect, taunts the crowd (1640–45). In this moment of "vision at the pillars," Joan Bennett pleads with us to hear Samson "calling defiance to Satan," both of which propositions are subject to questioning and neither of which is easily confirmed.[74]

What we hear instead in Samson's slide from "a private person" to "a person rais'd" is something more like what Cromwell himself deplores, "private interests, for the public good":[75] Samson's marriages as a pleasurable means of achieving his political goal, the destruction of a nation. If his private revenge had led earlier to Samson's being given over to the enemy, is the revenge about to be exacted at the temple suspect or honorable? Is this eye for an eye retaliation more of the same: the justice of the unjust? And does it not invoke as a standard for judgment the Grotian exclamation: "how dangerous it is . . . to punish any Man" to exercise revenge, "especially with *Death*, either for his *own* or the *publick* good."[76] With the law invoked as arbiter in so many of Milton's earlier prose tracts, and repeatedly in his epic poetry, now Milton brings the tragedy of *Samson Agonistes* under the aspect of international law.

The questioning is part of the historical record and, more so than Madlyn Millner Kahr reports,[77] is there in the early years of the Reformation, some thinking Samson is inspired and others doubting it. It is of some import here that the temptations of the Son and Samson had been correlated, first, to suggest that neither temptation involves a visionary experience and, second, to illustrate specifically through the scenes atop the pinnacle and at the pillars that not everyone who begins life with the spirit has it in the end. A poem continually posing alternatives, rather than confirming through Samson's last words his defiance of Satan, seems to ask instead whether the figure of Samson, in his defiance, does not at once invoke Satan and display a marked resemblance to him, especially in their respective mockeries of Jesus. In *Paradise Regain'd*, Satan mocks the Son's lowly birth (2.412–21) just as in its companion poem, in mocking those "principl'd not to reject / The penitent, but ever to forgive," Samson mocks both Socrates and the Son, each of whom, *"Divinely Brave,"* injured and dying, forgives.[78]

In this regard, the sentiments of Milton's poem contrast strikingly with those in Vondel's, where the Chorus urges, "Mingle then, / . . . yet a drop / Of mercy with your justice. Let revenge / Be now abated. There will follow you / The honour of forgiveness to a foe."[79]

In *Samson Agonistes*, Milton brings all these issues into focus: does Samson act as a private or public person? is he divinely compelled, or does he act of his own accord? at the pillars, is he at prayer or not? in his final posture and climactic act, does he evoke the Son or Satan? And once gathered into focus, Milton interthreads these issues (ethical, political, and religious), asking questions of Samson such as he never asks of Samson's classical prototype Hercules — a figure whose "glorious and Heroic deed" as recounted in Seneca's *Hercules Furens* is, according to Milton in *The Tenure of Kings and Magistrates*, the suppression of tyranny (*YP*, 3:212–13). In contrast, the Samson of Milton's tragedy is lodged in paradox: the deliverer himself needs deliverance and, in the end, instead of delivering his people, delivers himself (along with some of the Philistines) unto death.

Those characteristics of Seneca's Hercules, which might be construed as compromising his heroism, are, by Milton, either transferred to Samson or, if already part of the Samson story, made points of emphasis: his haughty pride, his dreadful deeds, his revenging hand, the bloody slaughters, and, most haunting of all, the prophetic ending in which Hercules, burnt up in a holocaust, imagines the Theban temples falling down and crushing him. The propriety of using the word "Holocaust" in criticism of *Samson Agonistes* has been questioned, despite Milton's usage of the word in this poem (1702) and despite the fact that *The Oxford English Dictionary* credits Milton with the first such usage of the word. So, too, the propriety of Milton's displacing Samson's prayer with a taunt has been questioned as "not true to the [Judges] text, nor worthy of the occasion" and as a diminishment of Samson in relation to his Herculean counterpart.[80] Such interrogations, in Euripidean fashion, go to the very heart of *Samson Agonistes*: is this a poem that confirms or challenges Samson's heroism?

As with the Hercules story in Seneca and especially in Euripides, so with the Samson story in Milton's tragedy: a dubious eye is cast upon traditional heroism; as Erich Segal says of Euripides' *Heracles*, the investment is in "people, not paragons." Indeed, with Euripides, traditional notions of heroism fracture and fragment into pairs like Jason and Medea or, in the case of Milton, Samson and Dalila, with the pairs themselves mirroring not just clashing cultures but divisions within a culture and with heroism itself diminishing, if not disappearing, in the realization, sharply etched by Segal, that "The case of Heracles himself . . . [to which we may wish to add that of Samson] . . . is darkened by Euripides' [Milton's?] insistence that we observe . . . that even the culture-hero has murder in his heart."[81] Yet, there also remains this difference between the plays by Euripides and Milton. In *Heracles*, as Hegel observed long ago, its protagonist, "not strictly a moral hero," championing what is right, battles the monstrosities in men even as he rises above the prevailing — and baser — characteristics of his age.[82] In Euripides' final play, *The Bacchae*, the palace may fall, the king himself may be torn to pieces, but the theater itself is not, as in *Samson Agonistes*, destroyed.

Milton's Samson story not only derives from the Book of Judges but constitutes a pointed allusion to it as a book of tragedies, Samson's chief among them. Northrop Frye comes near, but also misses, the mark as he explains that Judges contains "a series of stories of traditional tribal heroes . . . set within a repeating *mythos* of the apostasy and restoration of Israel":

> This gives us a narrative structure that is roughly U-shaped. . . .
> This U-shaped pattern . . . recurs in literature as the standard
> shape of comedy. . . . The entire Bible, viewed as a "divine com-
> edy," is contained within a U-shaped story of this sort.[83]

It is just this sort of pattern — tragedy giving way to comedy — that Milton ridicules in his preface to *Samson Agonistes* as "the Poets error . . . which by all judicious hath bin counted absurd" (*CP*, 574) and that the Samson story subverts in the Book of Judges, where this U-shaped pattern is broken as an individual's defeat becomes a looking glass on national disaster. The Samson story, defying the pattern of tragicomedy, which in Milton's day some saw replicated in the Restoration, emerges from Milton's pen as pure tragedy, Milton here underscoring the lesson of his age (and of the Samson story) that many are killed, and few spiritually enlivened, by the sword.

Given Samson's repeated transgressions of the law and, through them, the subversion of his own judgeship, together with his reversion to revenge at the pillars, his tragedy is thrown into relief when viewed against the backdrop of Grotian precepts, chief among them the declaration that "the *Law-Maker* ought not to take away the Law, without a *Reasonable* Cause for it, which if he does, he transgresses the Rules of *Political* Justice." To this declaration, add another: that "*God* alone is sufficient to Revenge the Crimes committed against himself . . . [and] certainly the same may be said of *other* Offences."[84] Nor is it ever right to go to war when the people are not so inclined, or when the likely outcome will be the ruination of a nation.

Indeed, when we remember the consequences of Samson's actions, short and long term — the destruction of the Philistines and eventual ruination of the Danites, his entire tribe falling into idolatry — then we may begin to contemplate Milton's tragedy as an affirmation of Grotian precepts: the first cited at the beginning of this chapter, that to engage in combat merely as "the Tryal of a good Cause . . . is vain, and far from true piety"; and second, that "to trample upon all temptations whatsoever, rather than dissolve Humane Society, this truly is the proper work of Justice" — and of the true Judge.[85] *Paradise Regain'd*, in conjunction with *Samson Agonistes*, makes the point powerfully, with this poetic volume resonating with two other declarations belonging to the year of its publication. One comes from the Puritan divine Nicholas Lockyer, exiled the year before, lamenting this period of *"long wandering in the Wilderness,"* of *"double punishments and troops of calamities"* to be alleviated only by *"look*[ing] *more into our selves"*; the other from the nonconformist John Tillotson who, while railing against *"this howling Wilderness . . .* a wicked and ill-natur'd World," revels in anticipation of "that happy hour . . . when we shall pass . . . into *the promised Land."*[86] The yearning, now, is for the recovery of the lost paradise — for *paradise regained.*

From Political Allegory
to an Allegory
of Readings

*The tension, subversive or creative, between the establishment
icon and the defiant dissenter is not unknown to previous readers
of Milton. . . . Because of the radically different agendas it
supports, the contrast continues to agitate Milton criticism.*
— Balachandra Rajan[1]

Milton's last poems are of a piece. In each of them, the poet
makes interpretive choices in the full realization that to reject
a representation, or an interpretation, on theological or political grounds does not preclude its use in poetry. For example,
is such power actually given Satan that he takes Jesus to the
top of the highest mountain, and then to the top of the pinnacle? Or are these kingdoms seen by Jesus in spirit — in a
vision? If, in *De Doctrina Christiana* and *Paradise Regain'd*,
Milton seems to reject this notion that the temptations of
Jesus in the wilderness occur in vision and are no more than a

243

mental event, he seems, alternatively, to credit the same tradition, first in Adam's dream in *Paradise Lost* (8.300–11) and then again, in the same poem, in its penultimate book: ". . . in Spirit perhaps he also saw . . ." (11.406–11). Again in *Paradise Lost,* Milton submits to the orthodox interpretation of the Fall (Adam and Eve are sinless until they eat the fruit) even as he capitalizes on the drama inherent in the dissenting interpretation of the same event that regards the Creation and Fall as coextensive with one another. As Milton retells the old story, its climactic center shifts from the moments in which Eve and Adam eat from the apple (9.780–84, 997–1004) to the moment in which Adam achieves consciousness of his fallen state (10.720ff.). If *Paradise Lost* is a poem with a double plot, its drama proceeds from the moment (in the underplot) when Satan, "stretcht out huge in length" (1.209), comes to an awareness of his fallenness and moves unremittingly to the parallel moment (in the main plot) when, "On the ground outstretcht he lay" (10.472), Adam achieves consciousness of his own fallen state. Or, yet again in the same poem, Milton will have Adam proclaim the doctrine of the *felix culpa* (12.469–78) which God has just disclaimed (11.84–89). In Milton's last poems, traditions converge and often compete with one another in ways which force the recognition that, in each of these poems, we encounter not one but many texts, here complementing and there contradicting one another.

Much in *Samson Agonistes* depends upon our recognition that Milton accepted the negative judgment placed on Dan, sixth son of Jacob, as a consequence of this tribe of 62,700 men, of Samson's tribe, being excluded from the Revelation listing. (The very name signifies "judgment, or the judge."[2]) This negative judgment was effected, as we have seen, by interpretation of Jacob's prophecy in Genesis, wherein Samson himself is implicated in the judgment to the extent that, if not everyone, certainly some thought that Jacob's prediction concerning the tribe was "accomplished in Samson, who was descended from Dan."[3] If Dan is the tribe of idolatry and, for some, the tribe from which Antichrist will arise, Samson, no less than Dan, was thought to be the serpent in the way, the adder in the path, blocking the way into Jerusalem and representing a false form of salvation through destruction that would be swallowed up in the creative salvation represented by Christ. This is by no means a novel position to hold in the early modern period. When Lancelot Andrewes distinguishes between Elias's inspiration from God and Samson's from Satan, it is by way of suggesting that the impulse to slay, common to both Samson and Satan, is nullified by Christ who comes into the world to save. Andrewes is emphatic: Samson had "No such authority" as Elias had; and Andrewes continues that Christ contrasts with both precursors and "forbids" even "the act or spirit of Elias."[4] It is noteworthy, therefore, that, if in *Paradise Lost* Samson is a fixed presence at the moment paradise is lost, in *Paradise Regain'd*, Jesus, while in the wilderness, shows the way for recovering the lost paradise. Moreover, if the Revelation listing is remarkable for its exclusion of Dan, it is notable too, not simply for including the tribe of Judah, but for moving this tribe to the head of the list. The tribe of Judah, from which Samson's mother comes and from which Jesus is born, thus stands against the excluded tribe of Dan, Samson's tribe, from which Antichrist is sometimes said to arise and from which idolatry is born.

If the juxtaposition of the Son and Samson is a defining feature of the 1671 poetic volume, so too is the combination of the two sides of the Genesis-Revelation tradition. Dan as the tribe of Antichrist, Dan as the tribe of idolatry — both jostle within each poem and within the volume as a whole. The sharpening antitheses within the dialogue of the first poem make for a natural association of Satan and his cohorts with Dan and of Jesus with the tribe of Judah. Samson's presence in this volume would seem to force out of hiding his associations with Dan as its only judge — with the tribe that, according to

Genesis, would become a serpent in the way and that in Revelation, therefore, is cancelled from the Book of Life. Milton's
last poems, rather than scuttling such interpretations as
"dubious," rather than bespeaking the loss of "one of the most
picturesque of medieval fables,"[5] evidence the recovery and
reconstitution of this much disputed tradition, as well as a
delicate and deft application of it. These poems testify to, and
demonstrate, the availability and efficacy of this tradition for
poetic appropriations.

In the words of Jacob Boehme, God did not create the judges;
rather it was "the murmuring, stubborn, and opposite self-
will . . ., which will not be obedient to God . . ., nor endure to
be judged and led by his spirit, that hath caused . . . Dan . . . [to
be] born." Dan is the "determiner of strife" in history, "a
divider" — Dan is the adder and serpent, whom Christ, riding
over, will defeat; he emblematizes the spirit of enmity in the
world and, as such, is a negative image, not a positive one.[6]
Indeed, the bite of the serpent, the sting of the adder, tramp-
ling down honor and charity, led some to object early on
that "the Lords battels" were being fought "with the Devils
weapons"[7] — a view that some of Cromwell's allies would
adopt from their critics and, in the process, a view that could
be used to mount a critique not just of Samson/Cromwell but
of their people, Israelite or English, and not just the Philistines
among them.

In analogy, surely the primary target of the critique in Judges
is not the Philistines but the Israelites according to the principle so sharply articulated by George Sandys when, in his
annotations to Hugo Grotius's *Christus Patiens*, he refers to
God's punishment of his own people, to "those . . . calamities
which the Divine Vengeance inflicted on the *Iews*: more, and
more horrid, then ever befell any other Nation."[8] The Samson
story in the Book of Judges affords an obvious perspective on
the tragedy of the Civil War years, a means of glimpsing the
failures of the Revolution and of anatomizing the experience

of defeat. In biblical history, two tragedies — the death of Samson and the defeat of the Philistines — have their fifth act together and, in yet another later act, the tribe of Dan disappears from history. In *Samson Agonistes*, through its protagonist, Milton allows us to glimpse Cromwell and in him the forces of violence unleashed by the revolution. Yet Milton also hopes to avert a repetition of the tragedy in which, beyond the fifth act, his own nation, already bowed down, is eventually defeated. In what others would call "the triumph and the tragedy of Oliver Cromwell"[9] Milton perceives the tragedy but also foresees the *eventual* triumph of English history.

I

In *Paradise Regain'd*, once Jesus is in the desert and as the first temptation is about to commence, "The fiery Serpent" flees his path, as well as the "noxious Worm" (1.312). Are we to remember the serpent in the way, the adder or viper in the path from Genesis? And if we happen to be retrospective readers of the 1671 poetic volume, are we to notice that, if Jesus's temptations are inaugurated with the image of the fiery serpent, Samson's conclude (his life ends) in the image of a blazing "ev'ning Dragon" (1692)? And more: are we to notice that Jesus's removing of obstacles from his path (in the form of the fiery serpent) parallels Samson's rejection of Dalila, both "a manifest Serpent" (997) in his way and "a viper" (1001) in his path? Does the tragedy sometimes assume a parodic relationship with the brief epic? These questions, once we turn to Milton's poems, seem self-answering.

Earlier variorum editors like Thomas Newton and Henry John Todd are virtually silent on the fiery serpent and noxious worm, both fleeing the path of Jesus in *Paradise Regain'd*; but Walter MacKellar cites the "fiery flying serpent" from Isaiah 14.29, along with a correlative passage from the same prophet, "the viper and fiery flying serpent" who come from "the land of trouble and anguish" (30.6),[10] then reminding us that this serpent comes from cockatrice eggs, which, once crushed, produce the adder/viper, along with its works of bloodshed and violence, "wasting and destruction" (59.5–7; cf. Job 20.16 and Jeremiah 8.17). MacKellar's citations, including Numbers 21.6–7 and Deuteronomy 8.15, have the advantage of interconnecting, through scriptural imagery, the "fiery" serpent in *Paradise Regain'd* and the "flying" dragon of *Samson Agonistes*, even if they miss the primary referent, which seems to be Genesis 49.17 in conjunction with Revelation 7.7.

The worm or "the snake, trodden under foot," causes Ad de Vries eventually to remember Dan and then to recall that, in Jewish tradition, "the symbol of the tribe was the snake; this may be related to the legend, that from his tribe would come the Antichrist; but also in Rabbinical literature the tribe has always been associated with idolatry."[11] In Christian tradition, on the other hand, with the precedent provided by the Book of Revelation, the symbol of the tribe of Dan is the eagle of which, as Alexander Ross reminds us, there are two types: those that "delight . . . in rapine," feasting upon "mans flesh," and those that are his protectors; those that in their role as destroyers are associated with the ruins of empire, and those that are deliverers, identified with "the Temple of Peace."[12] Milton's poem seems to invoke the former type: "as an Eagle / His cloudless thunder bolted on thir heads" (1695–96). Indeed, the eagle seems as much a predator, and its mission as menacing, as the "ev'ning Dragon . . . / Assailant on the perched roosts, / And nests in order rang'd / Of tame villatic Fowl" (1692–95). By some accounts, moreover, the eagle is the natural enemy of the viper; and the viper, killing the male during insemination and then being killed by its young during the birthing process, is taken as an icon of revenge.[13]

It is only fitting that poems, directly or obliquely, about regaining paradise should participate in the recovery and rebirth of images. While he is in the wilderness, Jesus confronts

Satan in the images of the fiery serpent and noxious worm in anticipation of their encounters at the end of his life when, from the cross, he will bruise the head of the serpent and when at the end of time the serpent, now in dragon form, will be forever bound. Moreover, if Jesus here fronts Dan in the image of a fiery serpent fleeing his path, in the 1671 poetic volume, through the juxtaposition of poems and through their intertextuality, Jesus also is made to front Samson — even through their names. Jesus is never Christ in *Paradise Regain'd* but sometimes the Messiah and more often the Son. Samson is similarly referred to as my/his/thy "son" ten times in *Samson Agonistes*. What is in a name? The *sun* is in both their names, either by pun or supposed etymology, as if to suggest through this juxtaposition of "heroes" that each may "boast" his "light," in words from *Areopagitica*, "but if we look not wisely on the Sun it self, it smites us into darknes" (*YP*, 2:550). The sun is also there in the emblematizing images of the eagle and phoenix, the one bird represented as flying into the sun and the other often depicted with a sun disk on its head or with rays of light emanating from it.

The initial encounter between Jesus and Satan in the wilderness is no more than a dress rehearsal for the many confrontations between Christ and Antichrist in history and at the end of time. The point, made so well by Luca Signorelli in his frescoes — "The Stories of Antichrist," "The Coronation of the Chosen," "The End of the World," and "The Calling of the Chosen and Ante-Hell," is now made with equal force and brilliance by Milton. The polarization of Jesus and Satan is as much a function of their dialogue as of poetic imagery, and that polarization is accentuated by Milton's establishing a fierce contrast between the tribes of Dan and of Judah — of Satan/Samson and Christ/Jesus. The tribe of Samson, Dan is associated with "all th' Idolatries" and "heathenish crimes" as Jesus wonders:

Should I of these the liberty regard,
Who freed, as to their ancient Patrimony,
Unhumbl'd, unrepentant, unreform'd
Headlong would follow; and to thir Gods perhaps
Of *Bethel* and of *Dan*? no, let them serve
Thir enemies, who serve Idols with God.

                                      (3.418–19, 427–32)

On the other hand, when Satan and Jesus encounter one
another, his adversary reminds the Son that *"Juda's* Throne"
is "Thy Throne" (2.424–25), the throne on which sat the "offspring" of Gideon and Jephtha "So many Ages" — a seat about
to be regained by Jesus and from which he will "reign in *Israel*
without end" (2.439–42). This is the throne of David (3.357),
with Jesus "his true Successour" about to be installed in
"David's royal seat" (3.373). Jesus, in turn, tells Satan: "I mean
to raign / *David's* true heir, and his full Scepter sway / . . . over
all *Israel's* Sons" (3.404–06).

Within this context, Jesus invokes the tribe of Dan — the
tribe of idolatry and, by implication, as much Satan's tribe as
it is the tribe of Samson and Antichrist (3.431). Here, we are
not allowed to forget Jesus's lineage with Judah and David
(4.108, 147, 379, 471) nor, in *Samson Agonistes*, that its protagonist is of "the Camp of *Dan"* (1436) or that he is delivered
to the Philistines by the men of Judah (251–56). It was
sometimes said that Samson's going to Etam, where there was
a temple, is but a harbinger of his going to the temple of Dagon,
where the poem's catastrophe occurs. This redundancy con-
cealed in the plot of the Samson story is yet another reminder
of the once supposed meaning of Samson's name: "there the
second time."[14]

Each temple, of course, has its associations with the idolatry
Samson has come to figure in himself (451–56; cf. 1733–42)
and would finally pull down by *not* going to the temple (1354–
62) — that Jesus does pull down by resisting Satan, then
defeating him, atop a temple. However, Milton does more than

merely associate Samson as a Danite with idolatry; for through his representation of an extraordinary act of displacement, he also brings into play the Genesis tradition that makes of Dan/ Samson a serpent in the way, an adder (or sometimes a viper) in the path. With other commentators, Milton may have felt that as theology certain constructions placed upon Jacob's prophecy were trivial. But what within the realm of theology may have seemed inconsequential, insignificant could also, once appropriated for poetry, be given a psychic accent and significance.[15] Certain images in Jacob's prophecy — the serpent/ adder/viper (the key elements in an alternative Samson tradition) — could, within a mental theater, be turned to poetic advantage, with Milton here playing with both the positive and negative interpretations of Jacob's prophecy and playing with its real and apparent meanings as well.

The serpent/dragon and then eagle, both of which, if they are Old and New Testament emblems of Dan (Samson), have their political as well as personal associations for both Cromwell and Milton. On the one hand, in his Fifth Monarchist attack upon Cromwell and the Protectorate, John Rogers figures his adversaries as "an Oyled Pillar," in appearance like a "Serpent . . . looking so like a lamb" and in voice sounding "like a Dragon."[16] As much so as with Milton, this imagery is part of an effort to demonize Cromwell, who is now a mock-saint, now a legendary serpent, and now an old dragon; here a fiend, a three-headed monster, and there the Antichrist or one of his limbs.[17] Indeed, Milton himself is often represented as an adder/serpent, and his family insignia include the spread-eagle.[18] The serpent/dragon and eagle, moreover, constitute the first two items in the triple simile of *Samson Agonistes*; the words are spoken by the Semichorus, which fact does not diminish the magnificence of the poetry but does suggest a limitation of consciousness not shared by all readers and which images participate in a venerable tradition as old as Aeschylean drama — the whole complex of images (viper,

snake and eagle) all appear in *The Libation Bearers* and "a
flying snake" in *The Eumenides*:[19]

> His fiery vertue rouz'd [he]
> From under ashes into sudden flame
> And as an ev'ning Dragon came,
> Assailant on the perched roosts,
> And nests in order rang'd
> Of tame villatic Fowl; but as an Eagle
> His cloudless thunder bolted on thir heads.
> So vertue giv'n for lost,
> Deprest, and overthrown, as seem'd,
> Like that self-begotten bird
> In th' *Arabian* woods embost,
> That no second knows nor third,
> And lay e're while a Holocaust,
> From out her ashie womb now teem'd,
> Revives, reflourishes, then vigorous most
> When most unactive deem'd,
> And though her body die, her fame survives,
> A secular bird ages of lives.

(1690–1707)

To grasp (as John Carey does) the contrastive force of "but"
in line 1695 is to situate Samson very precisely within the
Genesis tradition as Milton focuses the paradox that "Samson
came along the ground [as a serpent] *but* attacked [as an eagle]
from above."[20] When we remember from Genesis that the
serpent in the way is Dan and/or Samson, the image achieves
its full resonance; when we remember from Revelation that
Dan's/Samson's image is the eagle, then two similes at the
end of *Samson Agonistes* make sense less as poetic fancy than
as borrowings from the Samson traditions.

II

Indeed, the traditions accruing to the Samson story afford
both the "scholarly learning" and the "imaginative rectitude"
that Edward Tayler expects from readings of the triple simile

concluding Milton's poem.[21] Samson is here emblematized in his different attitudes, and in terms of the different hermeneutics, that by now attend his story and impart to it an interpretation more layered and complicated than the one Kester Svendsen offers:

> In the lines from *Samson Agonistes*, the analogies with Samson are carefully thought out. Even "dragon," commonly pejorative, fits the context and harmonizes with "eagle" as dynamic energy exploded in righteous violence upon the enemies of God. Samson, like the phoenix, achieves a new life through self-sacrifice and death. The legendary bird is not destructive. . . . The rapid change here from dragon to eagle to phoenix typifies Milton's way of capitalizing upon accepted associations, then altering their image to make a new point; for the shift expresses Samson as a force expending itself, like his passion, and leaving the mind purged as fire but renewed.[22]

Through transference and displacement, distortion and censorship, Milton imparts psychic significance to an unpleasant prophecy faintly recalled in one of Samson's moments of rage. What had, by tradition, been used to indict Samson is, by Samson, transferred to Dalila and thus becomes his device for indicting her (936, 1001; cf. 997). These aspects of self and revelations of self are displaced onto Dalila; the reproach of Samson is translated into his (and the Chorus's) reproach of her — and in such a way that disallows all positive interpretations of the prophecy, that insists upon the negative constructions and that finally implicates Samson in them. It remains an oddity of Milton studies that mostly positive readings of Jacob's prophecy survive within the historical record.[23]

Samson has little regard for the "Adders wisdom"; and what he knows of it he claims to have learned from Dalila and then just enough of it to "fence" himself off from her "sorceries" (936–37), to deafen him to her charms. Ad de Vries, once again, provides a pertinent gloss. In the Bible and throughout the

Middle Ages, he reports, the "adder" is the name sometimes used for the "flying serpent" or "Dragon";[24] and in Milton's century, devils/dragons/temples/idolatry, in conjunction, are associated with acts of treachery and destruction. What makes such a gloss seem impertinent and, for some imaginatively feeble, is the fact that the dragon image, because of its association with Satan, is, according to Edward Tayler, "scarcely applicable to Samson at this point in the tragedy," and so Tayler opts for the meteorological dragon/comet rather than the mythological dragon/serpent.[25]

Yet, as William Fulke makes clear, even in its meteoric manifestations, some see in these *"fire-Drakes . . .* the Devil himself" and, in "this Devill . . . a flying Dragin," who signifies the unstoppable force of evil in the world. Even if only impressions, such natural phenomena are portents of civil and political upheaval, omens of "notable Calamities": "wars, seditions, changes of Commonwealth."[26] No less than the comet in book 2 of *Paradise Lost,* the evening dragon here in *Samson Agonistes* sounds an alarm and, simultaneously, signals a political point. No less than the fire-drake, according to Edward Topsel, the flying dragons or serpents are "the natural presage of evil," as well as "Prophets of their own destruction." They symbolize enmity and discord: "The greatest discord is betwixt the Eagle and the Dragon," says Topsel; "Dragons . . . do principally fight with Eagles." But also in their "swim[ming] . . . over to seek better food in *Arabia,*" they harmonize imagistically with the phoenix of *Samson Agonistes,* "that self-begott'n bird / In th' *Arabian* woods embost" (1699–1700).[27]

The flying dragon or serpent, the eagle, the phoenix — they are a natural constellation of images, in their conjunction unleashing meanings too often obscured, or simply ignored by Milton's critics. And the first of those images makes abundantly clear that there is as much typological difference between Samson and Hercules as there is between Samson and the Son, in slaying the dragon Hercules and Jesus not only conquer their own passions but quell the dragon who is a killer of men. Dragons and temples, idolatry and mass slaughter, emanating from the same serpent image converge on a shared point of reference and meaning. It is no small irony that Cromwell who eventually would be figured as the Great Beast and Antichrist of the Book of Revelation should have been represented to Charles I by Archbishop John Williams as "the most dangerous Enemy that his Majesty had": "every Beast hath some evil Properties; but Cromwel hath the Properties of all evil Beasts."[28] Nor should that satiric work be forgotten in which Cromwell is no god, though perhaps a "super-excelling" hero, moreso than "*Hercules*, who by an invincible fortitude, endur'd a Confinement which might intitle to a quotidian incountring of Monsters, and not less frequent triumphs o'er wild Beasts in Passions."[29] Elsewhere, in the same sort of distinction Milton implies between Hercules and Samson, it is said of Cromwell that, no Hercules, he is a person with the beast within.[30] Samson and the Son, Cromwell and Milton — all are netted within not only the Hercules myth but the whole complex of images knotted together in the triple simile at the end of *Samson Agonistes*. We should note now what we will elaborate later: both the deeply embedded typological patterning in Milton's tragedy and the potentiality for its triple simile, an invitation to read analogically and allegorically, simultaneously to evoke current history and to encode political allegory.

In view of Milton's lately published writings, together with their remarkable intertextuality and symmetry of images, the fiery comet at the end of *Samson Agonistes* recalls "in the night a meteor shooting flames from the East," in *The History of Britain* lighting the way of Britain's enemies, "directing thir course" (*YP*, 5:65) and, later in this same work, portending not "Famin only, . . . but the troubl'd State of the whole Realm" even as the image of "a blazing Star . . . seen to stream terribly, not only over *England* but other parts of the World," eventually marks the fall of an aspiring hero "for soaring too high" (5:329, 394). In Milton's *History*, "fiery Dragons . . . foresignifie" violence and bloodshed, a reign of terror, scorching the land, pillaging monasteries, "sparing neither Priest nor Lay," and capturing those not slain (5:244). The dragon/comet of *Samson Agonistes* does not erase, much less evade, association of the shorn Samson with Satan (as a new risen sun shorn of its beams) in the initial book of *Paradise Lost* (1.594–96) or (as the burning comet) of the next book (2.708). That association is later underscored by their minds "revolving" at crucial moments in their respective poems (4.31; 1638) but, even more, by what appears to be a deliberate symmetry in which both the end of *Samson Agonistes* and Samson's opening soliloquy in the poem echo Satan in *Paradise Lost*, especially his casuistical rhetoric. Not only are the characters of Samson and Satan elided in this way but also the persons of Samson and Milton, the former exclaiming "How many evils have enclos'd me round" (194) and the latter allowing how he has "fall'n on evil dayes" and is now "with dangers compast round" (7.25, 27).

In the words of Ann Baynes Coiro, "When Samson cries [out]" in his opening soliloquy (18–22), "we hear the narrator of *Paradise Lost*," together with "the autobiographical poet" but, more, "we hear Satan"; and, again, "When Samson laments his enslavement . . . we hear Satan's fury."[31] Previously, John Hollander made the same telling point: the consequences of thus eliding the characters of Samson and Satan through a shared rhetoric are "as profound as they are within the earlier epic itself — as when Satan echoes the narration or Adam, Satan."[32] Samson and Satan bleed into one another as each character repeatedly misreads and misrepresents his predicament even as Samson and Milton are gradually decoupled by virtue of their destructive and creative impulses, respectively, as well as their contrasting status as false and true prophets.[33]

It is not easy to read *Samson Agonistes* without cross-referencing characters and speeches with counterparts in *Paradise Lost* and *Paradise Regain'd*, where, in the latter poem, once baptiz'd, the Son begins "Musing and much revolving in his brest, / How best the mighty work he might begin / Of Saviour to mankind" (1.185–87). Distinct from the revolving mind of Jesus bent upon mankind's deliverance are the previously noted parallels in *Paradise Lost* and *Samson Agonistes*, where revolving minds produce recollections of Satan's fall as a prelude to Samson's defeat; where Satan's fall is an analogue to the fall of Adam and Eve and where Samson's defeat is implicated in the demise of his people. Nor is it easy to read Jesus on Satan in *Paradise Regain'd* (a passage Edward S. Le Comte describes as "virtually a blurb for *Samson Agonistes*"[34]) and not think of Samson:

> thou com'st indeed,
> As a poor miserable captive thrall
> Comes to the place where he before had sat
> Among the Prime in Splendour, now depos'd,
> Ejected, emptied, gaz'd, unpitied, shun'd,
> A spectacle of ruin . . .
>
> (1.410–15)

Nor, for that matter, is it easy to read in other commentators that *"Great Whales . . .* signifieth a serpent, a dragon"[35] and not think of Satan in *Paradise Lost* "extended long and huge" as "that Sea-beast / *Leviathan*" (2.195, 200–01). Or, when we read in the poets of Samson as a Promethean hero, "His private Wrongs . . . excite[d]," bursting his bonds and breaking the chains of the Israelites — "He rouz'd his gen'rous Might, pursu'd the Stroak, / Till *Israels* Chains like his own Bands were broke"[36] — it is hard not to think of an "heroic" Satan, again in *Paradise Lost*, breaking his adamantine chains as he rears from the burning lake (1.221).

As early as "On the Morning of Christs Nativity" where the dragon is an image of "Horrour" (*CP*, 70) and as late as *The History of Britain* where "fiery dragons" in the heavens signal invasion (*YP*, 5:243–44; cf. 332), these flying serpents/dragons are, for Milton, portents of bloodshed, violence, destruction, and of altogether primitive acts of atonement. The point here is not to establish through coded images, allusions, or echo that Samson *is* Satan but to bring into awareness fleeting resemblances and through them to press the question: is Samson acting demonically or not when he hurls down the pillars? is Satan's paw or God's hand more evident here? Even if these questions are unanswered — and unanswerable — in *Samson Agonistes*, they are nevertheless the questions that really matter. Further, they are the questions at the very heart of the Puritan dilemma–and its surest markers. "The saint, as God's instrument on earth, was both specially equipped and specially obliged to discern providences," writes Blair Worden. He then goes on to explain that the best evidence of sainthood is that God keeps his chosen ones alive in the most trying and seemingly impossible circumstances and, more, that the chief mark of their sainthood is that they are customarily shown at prayer. That Milton equivocates on whether Samson is in fact at prayer, that Samson thereupon dies in the temple/theater catastrophe — these details complicate Samson's heroism, as do the facts that misunderstandings of one's election, and of one's claims to providence, are most strikingly evident, Worden explains, when God's supposed deliverers deliver no one and, instead of serving Christ, seem to stand in opposition to him.[37]

The gloss de Vries provides on the serpent as flying dragon reinforces these points by gesturing toward a tradition prominent in the seventeenth century and sanctioned by some of its most notable scriptural commentators. Annotating Genesis 3.1, Henry Ainsworth remarks, "The greater serpents, are called *dragons.* . . . And in the new Testament, the same thing is called both *a dragon* and *a serpent,*" thus aligning Satan with the speaking serpent in Genesis and the great dragon in Revelation.[38] The "flying Serpents are called Dragons," according to the annotators of the 1645 Bible issued in association with the Westminster Assembly;[39] and the winged dragons are not just any serpent but the devil and his limbs. Once again, the association (mentioned above) of dragon/devil/temple/ idolatry is relevant here. More than a dreary feature in academic discourse, the image of the fiery serpent is a staple in seventeenth century poetry, and a staple of Christian art as well, where the serpent often appears in conjunction with the eagle and sometimes with the phoenix.[40]

Samson was often identified with the adder in Genesis and, in the positive formulation of Luther and later Rollenson, with the adder's wiliness and wisdom — an identification that in Milton's poem Samson transfers to Dalila but of which he also retains traces as when, by the Chorus, he is figured as "an ev'ning Dragon" (1692). In transferring his own emblem to Dalila, Samson also transforms the positive construction once placed upon Jacob's prophecy into the more usual negative one — and in such a way that this snarer of others becomes his own snare. In *Paradise Lost*, as he tempts Eve, Satan is referred to as "the wilie Adder" (9.625). Samson clearly has little regard for the serpent's wisdom often attributed to him, sometimes with the intention of exonerating him from folly. Yet, the later figuring of Samson as the fiery, flying dragon of the night has the effect of turning the adder/serpent/dragon imagery back upon Samson himself. Try as he may, Samson cannot escape his association with this complex of imagery. The Chorus sees to that.

The adder comes forth in all his wiliness as Samson does in his encounter with Dalila and, in his wiliness, represents her (and so too the Chorus will represent her) as both "serpent" and "viper" (763, 997, 1001). Dalila, early on called a "specious Monster" (230), in virtually the same breath Samson addresses her as a *"Hyaena"* (748), is referred to as "a poysnous bosom snake" (763); she is the serpent in Samson's way, the viper now being driven from his path. We may recall that the image appears earlier in Milton's writing, in *Pro Se Defensio*, where

Milton says that no "other beast [is] so noxious and infamous" and where the image itself is associated not only with "loathsome fraud" but, in an annotation, with "wanton destructiveness and deception" (*YP*, 4:751). If in its first characteristic it is appropriate for Dalila, in its second feature it seems altogether more apt for Samson. It might be said that Samson's act of displacement is actually Milton's displacement, his way of peeling negative associations away from Samson and then fixing them on Dalila; and this could be said more credibly, perhaps, were it not for the fact that what Samson displaces onto Dalila is by the Chorus shifted back to Samson himself. Dalila may have stood in Samson's way, but Samson has himself stood in the way of others and, more, now stands in his own way.

The point is simply this: the Samson tradition sponsored by the Genesis/Revelation connection is operative in *Samson Agonistes*; yet it is just one of several interpretive traditions that cross within the poem. The Genesis/Revelation tradition no more contains the poem than do the Judges or Hebrews traditions, all of which are nevertheless contained by the poem. There is an impressive economy to *Samson Agonistes* where we find these various scriptural texts and their different hermeneutic traditions all circulating at once. What *is* special, however, about the operation of the Genesis/Revelation tradition in Milton's poem is its incorporation of a hermeneutic of suspicion that, in concert with the hermeneutic of interrogation sponsored by the Book of Judges, forces questions to be asked and problems to be addressed. Milton's way as a poet is to raise questions about Samson with discretion and tact, through oblique allusion, coded language and imagery. Thus the various Samsons of the various Samson traditions are arrayed in the magnificent, and magnificently compacted, speech of the Semichorus. Jewish and Christian traditions of interpretation, Old and New Testament hermeneutics, Genesis and Revelation, are synchronized in the images of the fiery dragon/serpent and the devouring/avenging eagle. Here in *Samson Agonistes* Dan's insignia become Samson's emblems.

III

This is but to say that, arrayed in this passage, within its deftly devised system of images, are the various Samsons of scriptural traditions: first, Samson is figured as "an ev'ning Dragon"/fiery serpent, which is how Samson is imaged in Genesis and how his tribe is subsequently remembered in Revelation commentary; then he appears as the avenging, devouring eagle with its thunder-bolting wrath and vengeance, which is how, arguably, Samson is imagined in Judges and how his tribe is actually imaged in Revelation; finally he is imagined as a phoenix — the bird dying into new life, Christ's one time emblem, and the now disputed symbol of regeneration and resurrection, all of which Samson himself figures, if not in the Hebrews text, certainly in the commentary that accrued to it and in the typology spun around it. All these images — dragon, eagle, phoenix — frequently discussed, and sometimes visualized together, are here compacted almost into one.[41] In this allusive scheme, as John Hollander remarks, interpretive authorities, who may have hovered until now around the poem, are suddenly transported from "the margin into the text," not as "specific quotation, or direct allusion, . . . [but] rather like a trope." Such images, in Hollander's formulation, perform "the role of minor scholia."[42]

The phoenix image is at once curious and complicated, remarkable in its "complexities," "contradictions," and "multiplicity of variants," hence a particularly apt image in *Samson Agonistes*, especially when we remember with Guy R. Mermier that its "appearance . . . is linked . . . to important political events," like the founding of temples.[43] In this (and other) unexpected ways, the phoenix, pinpointing ironies, is also compromising of Samson's heroism. Nahum Tate and

Richard Bentley identify the curiosity: "We had never any other Tradition of the Compassionate *Phoenix* than as a Female Bird," says Tate; and according to Bentley, the phoenix is "a fictitious Nothing" with "no Being but in Tale and Fable."[44] It is in this latter sense that Milton refers the image to Alexander More in *Pro Se Defensio* where More, "deplumbed," the deception stripped away, the fiction exposed, is seen for what he really is: not a phoenix but a "foul hoopoe" (*YP*, 4:784). The tradition of the *Physiologus*, on the other hand, identifies the complexity of the phoenix image in its association with both the renewal and the dissolution of life.

A prominent image in seventeenth century poetry (in the poems of John Donne and Richard Crashaw, for example), the phoenix is only *sometimes* a symbol of resurrection (it is so in *Epitaphium Damonis* perhaps but not in *Pro Se Defensio* or, later, in *Paradise Lost* and not simply — or easily — so in *Samson Agonistes*). Take as an additional, highly positive example (this one veering toward secularism) William Turner's declaration that "Phoenixes *should rise again, and flourish in their Ashes*"; that these heroes of "English Liberties," these heroes of the present age (the 1670s), "*who fell in Defence of the* Protestant Religion," will rise and receive their crowns.[45] But in another instance, Samson and the phoenix come together within a single constellation, as this time the commentator explains that even godly men — those like Ezekiel who are "a Phoenix amongst men" — display infirmities and fall, Elias and Samson (in his "effeminate folly") cited here among the examples.[46] Samson's "foul effeminacy" (410) remains an issue in *Samson Agonistes* where Milton's protagonist is also described as "effeminatly vanquish't" (562). Every person may be potentially a phoenix. Yet not all become one. The still unanswered — and perhaps forever unanswerable — question of Milton's poem is whether the potentiality to which Samson aspires and the expectations the Chorus has for him are actually achieved. Furthermore, which of these images, and these images in which of their valences, have the fullest bearing on *Samson Agonistes*?

Both in its association with the palm and in other of its associations, the phoenix participates in, even underscores, the multiplying ironies in Milton's poem: in its connection with the palm tree, the phoenix, along with the "branching Palm" (1735), emblematizes Samson's earthly fame; and in its association with political events — with the founding of temples, for instance — the phoenix underlines not only the political content of Milton's poem but the irony attendant upon the transference of an image of temple-founding to a scene in which a temple is demolished. This irony deepens in a poem where God's people seem to be choosing a captain back to Egypt, especially when we recall the association of the phoenix with the exodus of God's children from Egypt; and in a story that marks the end of judgeship, this time when we remember that the phoenix had often been used to represent the bond of unity between a king and his successor. Indeed, when Turner uses the phoenix to signify heroic figures in the 1670s, it is as a foil to those who, acting out revenge like Hercules, mock virtue, including justice, thus ensuring that a rebounding justice will destroy them in vindication of those they have ruined.

When Samson dies, no new judges arise in his place. Rather, the tribe of Dan dies out of history. This bird of paradise is here not to mark the recovery of paradise but yet another loss of it; not to elide Samson and Christ but, instead, to sort the slayer of men and their savior into two very different traditions of heroism (1268–96), either of which, says the Chorus, "is in thy lot, / *Samson*" (1292–93): the warrior-heroes who conquer by "invincible might" (1271) and the saintly heroes who exhibit "patience" in "the trial of thir fortitude" (1287–88). Owing to his blindness, the Chorus thinks that Samson is more likely to be numbered "with those / Whom Patience finally must crown" (1295–1296). The Chorus, that is, forces upon readers of Milton's poem the comparison — and contrast — of Samson patiens and Christus patiens. It also makes clear that *Samson Agonistes* is no *Samson Triumphans*.

The outcome of Samson's tragedy places a check on the Chorus's speculation that, crowned by Patience, his life will conform to the heroic pattern of the saints' lives. But more, the catastrophe also situates Samson within the tradition of conquering heroes even as it asks how well his life conforms to theirs. Is Samson with "celestial vigour arm'd" (1280)? Is he (as the Chorus proclaims earlier) God's "glorious Champion, / The Image of thy strength, and mighty minister" (705–06)? If the Chorus's imagined defeat of the Philistines who, "surpris'd / Lose thir defence, distracted and *amaz'd*" (1285–86; my italics), is meant to recall the corresponding moment in *Paradise Regain'd* when Satan "smitten with *amazement*" (4.562) falls, the polar figures in the comparison, the Son and Samson, themselves polarize in the recognition that a temple still standing in the one poem is paired with a temple demolished in the other. Ironies then tumble forth from the concluding lines in one of the Chorus's speeches: "This Idols day hath bin to thee no day of rest" (1297). On this "Idols day," as it happens, Samson goes to his final rest in the aftermath of which this idolater himself becomes an idol. If Samson is no Christus patiens, neither is he a Gideon idoloclastes.

John Guillory suspects (as I have been arguing) that the phoenix, this "secular bird" in *Samson Agonistes* (1707), often invoked to confirm Samson's heroism, is in process of being dislodged from a theological context: "it is really becoming a 'secular' image. . . . The existence of the phoenix, after all, is a fable, and not a wholly acceptable emblem for Christ (neither is Samson)."[47] "The Translator's Prologue" to Grotius's *Sophompaneas* makes the point that the tragedian's borrowings better come from "*the sacred Oracles of Truth*" than from Greek "*Fable*" and then, in a later annotation, that when drawing from Scripture, tragedians should avoid its errors and fablings as in the instance where David mistakenly invokes the phoenix in Psalm 92: "The just shall flourish as a *Phoenix*; whereas hee should have said, as a Palme tree." That is, except where there is textual corruption, the fable of the phoenix "is no where," although even scriptural writers may sometimes seek through such figures to illustrate "those things, which belong to heavenly truth." Doing so, however, as 1 Corinthians testifies, they "saw in part, and Prophesied in part."[48]

What has no place in the Bible should have, if not none, certainly restricted space in biblical poetry so that when — and if — the phoenix appears within a scriptural poem, then its traditions and connotations are secular, not sacred, and civil rather than religious. The same point had been made by William Burton in an annotation to the first epistle of Clement I to the Corinthians, where the phoenix is invoked as a symbol of the resurrected Jesus and, in this connection, with resurrection as a perpetually recurring event. In the words of Patrick Young, "this passage of the *Phenix*, the Emblem of the Resurrection," raises doubts on the part of some "that the Author *should use this instance as an example of absolute truth*," such commentators at once questioning the efficacy of using rhetorical ornaments to convey matters of doctrine, of deploying an image of something which does not exist, which has no reality to figure forth, to substantiate the resurrection as the ultimate reality.[49]

In the flickering analogies of book 5 of *Paradise Lost*, Raphael now an eagle, now a phoenix, is more like the latter, "that sole Bird" (5.272) enshrining his relics in the sun, Milton here relying quite explicitly on a secular iconography.[50] Indeed, what blurs three similes into one — Alexander More, Raphael, and Samson, each a phoenix — is their only *seeming* to be one. Wrapped in the phoenix simile of *Samson Agonistes*, however, is this further suggestion. Milton probably knew as well that the time period figured in Revelation 7 was sometimes associated with Constantine, the symbol of whose era was the phoenix, itself "all radiant with the rising sun-beams" of "happy restoration" and, as E. B. Elliott explains, a symbol "represent[ing] the empire as now risen into new life and hope" as it forgets "all former prognostications of Antichrist and fearful coming evils." Into this apocalyptic setting come the threatening, destroying "*tempest-angels*," those "desolating invaders, . . . burst[ing] in fury," underscoring the irony inherent in the phoenix symbol: that this "image of the very kingdom of Christ . . . was altogether more like a dream than a reality,"[51] a fable, a fiction, not an embodiment of reality or truth, neither an oracle of personal redemption nor of cultural renewal.

The citation of 1 Corinthians by St. Paul in the preface to *Samson Agonistes*, as well as the previously cited reference to 1 Corinthians by Clement I in an annotation to Grotius's tragedy, reinforces the Pauline point that our knowledge is imperfect and our prophecy imperfect (13.9), as, therefore, is our understanding, hence interpretation, of scriptural stories like that of Samson. Thus as with the phoenix, so with the Samson story it seems to emblematize: Milton's objective is to see both figure and story not *in part* but whole again. Moreover, the effect in the annotations to Grotius's *Sophompaneas* of using scriptural practices to challenge those in the noncanonical books, of distinguishing in the process between the phoenix as rhetorical ornament and doctrinal sanction, and of then juxtaposing the two epistles to the Corinthians, one by St. Paul and the other by Clement, is to challenge the whole notion of using nonexisting images, figures with no bearing on reality, as examples or illustrations of enduring truths.

Different representations of Samson and his era are thus coded into a sequence of images, which by virtue of its implied progression (from Satan/Samson to Christ) asks that a choice be made but which also, by virtue of its linguistic and syntactical procedures — "as an ev'ning Dragon . . . but as an

Eagle . . . Like that self-begott'n bird . . . A secular bird" (1692, 1695, 1699, 1707) — forestalls choosing. Like many earlier editors and critics of Milton, Tayler and Kerrigan emphasize progression within this image sequence: Samson enters the theater as a dragon, swoops down with the vengeance of an eagle, and arises again as a phoenix. In their respective readings, each image is superseded by what follows it.[52]

Alternatively, Thomas Newton advances another possibility nearer to the one proposed here:

> It is common enough among the ancient poets to meet with several similes brought in to illustrate one action, when one cannot be found that will hold in every circumstance. Milton does the same here.[53]

Rather than being arranged in an ascending order, the three images, part of a triple simile, achieve parity, thus lodging the temple catastrophe in the ambiguity of multiperspectivism. Or as D. H. Lawrence might say, what we witness here is less "the modern process of progressive thought" than "the old pagan process of rotary image-thought" where each "image fulfills its own little cycle of action and meaning, then is superseded by another image."[54] The sequence of images is an active complication of reading, a challenge to interpretation and, if from one perspective it figures progression and transcendence, from another it implies circularity and regression: from serpent to phoenix and from phoenix back again to worm-serpent with wings. That is, the image curls back upon the first item in the sequence or, when the entire volume is taken into account, upon the noxious worm in the path of Jesus when his temptations commence.

Thus, as van den Broek documents with the example of Hesiod, the phoenix is sometimes "the symbol of a cyclical event." It may also be a portent of some "important turn in world history" — the rebuilding of Rome, the beginning of a new era in Egypt, the founding of Constantinople, or the emergence of "a completely new phase of the Jewish religion." But when the promise is measured against the outcome, as in the Samson story, the image may be of history rolling back into its former self. When we remember, again with van den Broek, that the phoenix "acts as the inaugurator of the three eras *ante legem, sub lege* or *sub gratia,* starting with Abel, Moses, and Christ, respectively"[55] and, within this context, that with Samson the law of vengeance should be giving way to the law of laws, then the cyclical nature of history inscribed within the Samson story emerges. If in *Paradise Regain'd* history passes from the rule of law to the rule of love, in *Samson Agonistes* history reverses itself, then stalls, in an era of vengeance. The old view — that *Samson Agonistes* is "totally unconnected" with Milton's epics[56] — no longer pertains, given the elaborate system of intertextuality that this chapter has identified.

IV

Like Samson himself, each of the images within the triple simile is inlaid with ambiguity and paradox as both the eagle and phoenix further attest. In the peroration to *Areopagitica,* Milton may have wished to identify Samson with Christ as the true strong man rising up as a nation from sleep. He may have wished to associate Samson and Christ alike with the eagle on whose wings the nation would be lifted into the promised city of Jerusalem. Or he may have been thinking of the Christ of Revelation as he had so recently been described by William Twisse in the preface to Joseph Mede's now translated *Clavis Apocalypticae:*

> God awakening as it were out of sleep, and like a gyant refreshed . . .: and the Lord Christ awakening, and stirring up his strength for the raising up of *Jacob,* and the restoring of the desolations of *Israel,* and blessing us with a resurrection of his Gospel, and discovering the man of sin, and blasting him with the breath of his mouth.[57]

He may even have wished to recall the popular prophecy of "Master Truswell" (dating from 1588 but often repeated during the seventeenth century, very notably in 1642): "Then shall there come an *Eagle* out of the East, and his Wings spread with the Beams of the *Son of Man*. . . . And the *Son of Man* with the *Eagle* shall be exalted. And there shall be an Universal Peace over all the World."[58] Yet in the experience of defeat, which probably came upon Milton sooner than other of his Englishmen, the poet may also be rejecting any alliance between this prophecy and that in Revelation 7, where Christ is the angel coming from the East to put the twelve tribes under his protection, and emphasizing instead that this is also the moment in which the tribe of Dan, the camp of Samson, whose emblem is the eagle, is cancelled from the Book of Life.

Though in 1644 Samson may have been the prophet of the New Jerusalem, the patron saint of the Revolution, as well as the heroic model for soldiers in the New Model Army, when all this seemed lost, it must have dawned on Milton and others that "According to tradition, . . . [Samson] exemplifies the lowest category of prophetic experience,"[59] although even within that tradition Samson is not always acknowledged to be a prophet. While Josephus designates Samson "a prophet," Louis Ginzberg reports that "The Rabbis speak of Samson as one upon whom God's spirit rested, but do not consider him a prophet."[60] Within the drama of *Samson Agonistes*, where there is no narrator as in the Book of Judges to proclaim that Samson's acts are divinely inspired or commissioned, Manoa can credit his son with prophetic powers, Samson can claim prophetic status for himself, while the force of the poetry submits Samson's claims, as well as Manoa's crediting of them, to intense scrutiny.

The criticism focused on Cromwell, both with the impending failure of the Revolution and in its aftermath, is easily and deftly registered through the Samson story:

> *Impulses Extracted from the Miscellanies of* John Aubrey,
> *Esq . . . Oliver Cromwell* had certainly this Afflatus. One that
> I knew, that was at the Battle of *Dunbar,* told me, that *Oliver*
> was carried on with a Divine Impulse; he did laugh so exces-
> sively, as if he had been drunk; his Eyes sparkled with Spirits.
> He obtain'd a great Victory; but the Action was said to be con-
> trary to Humane Prudence. The same fit of Laughter seiz'd
> *Oliver Cromwell,* just before the Battle of *Naseby;* as a Kins-
> man of mine, and a great Favourite of his, Collonel *J. P.* then
> present, testified.[61]

Historical recollection by allies matches perfectly with the
historical record compiled by an adversary like Sir Harbottle
Grimston talking to Bishop Gilbert Burnet: "Cromwell . . . fell
down upon his knees and made a solemn prayer to God,
attesting his innocence and his zeal . . .; he submitted himself
to the providence of God." Or as Clement Walker reports:

> at last the Spirit of the Lord called up Oliver Cromwell, who
> standing a good while with lifted up eyes, as it were in a trance,
> and his neck a little inclining to one side, as if he expected
> Mahomet's dove to descend and murmur in his ear; and sending
> forth abundantly the groans of the Spirit, spent an hour in prayer.
> In his prayer he desired God to take off from him the govern-
> ment of this mighty People of England, as being too heavy for
> his shoulders to bear: An audacious, ambitious and hypocritical
> imitation of Moses. It is now reported of him, that he pretendeth
> to Inspirations; or that when any great or weighty matter is
> propounded, he usually retireth for a quarter or half an hour
> and then returneth and delivereth out the Oracles of the Spirit.[62]

Historical recollection and contemporary report, in their turn,
are in accord with Cromwell's own revelations, in which we
glimpse remarkable correspondence with the Samson ethos.

The Samson tradition is there as part of the historical record;
so too the Cromwell lore. The interconnections are there for
Milton to discern and draw upon, uniquely, and if not fully
assert, then insinuate. As others had developed analogies
between Cromwell and Moses, Gideon, Phineas, Elijah, David,
and Samson's foxes (biblical analogies that, for the most part,

Cromwell himself encouraged), Milton, throwing another biblical analogy into the mix, allows for the Samson story to enfold a critique, as well as an exoneration, of Cromwell who mended his ways whereas Samson did not. And the Samson analogy, among all the others which include Romulus, Augustus Caesar and Sejanus, is particularly apt in that, as with Samson so with Cromwell, the image is "varied, shifting, contested,"[63] full of contradiction, paradox, and ambivalence. It is an analogy into which Milton can situate himself and, simultaneously, maintain a distance, as if to challenge the other term in the comparison to live up to expectations and meet professed ideals. It is an analogy, whether or not Milton is fully conscious of it, in which biblical and British tragedy both intersect and harmonize.

Indeed, many of these analogies are set in relief within a dramatic poem whose historical focus is less on "the fate of Oliver Cromwell's remains," tossing his carcass "To dogs and fowls a prey" (694),[64] than on the remains of a myth in which Cromwell, Milton, and God's Englishmen were all for awhile entrapped. The "hero" of the New Model Army gradually enlarges into "the hero of the Puritans," indeed into "the hero of Puritanism and of Nonconformity":

> he led in the death of the King and the overthrow of the old monarchy. . . . What he did was to lead Puritanism to a victory over the old order. . . . He led Puritanism to a military victory and glory, overthrew Anglicanism — if only for a time — broke through the divinity that hedged in a King, . . . and set up a brief personal dictatorship.[65]

However, the very qualities exalting Cromwell as a war hero diminished him as a statesman. As Antonia Fraser remarks, "qualities so natural to his character, decision, speed and dash in a critical situation, the ability to strike and strike hard, could in the far more ambiguous sphere of politics turn to something else."[66] They could turn into tragedy as Cromwell's triumphs turned into troubles.

Initially, all of Cromwell's doings were perceived by him
(and sometimes represented by others) as God's doings. In the
words of Laura Lunger Knoppers, as a chief evidence of God's
providence in the world, repeatedly it seems, "Cromwell loses
his own will in the will . . . of God."[67] In possession of extraordinary dispensations, he was (like his prototype Samson)
executing God's will, implementing God's design for history.
"God would by things that are not, bring to naught things
that are," Cromwell writes to "a worthy member of the House
of Commons."[68] Moreover, the minister of God's justice,
Cromwell was the protagonist in a drama, a dumb-show
scripted from above, in which all that we see are "the shakings,
changes, and extraordinary out-goings of the Lord himself"
and in which all victories, including routings and executions,
are, in Cromwell's words, "a great favour from the Lord . . . an
absolute victory obtained by the Lord's blessing upon the godly
party." Putting weapons into one's hand "for the terror of evil-
doers," God makes the enemy, as Cromwell reported to
Colonel Valentince Walton and as his biographers are wont to
report, "as stubble to our swords."[69]

In the beginning, Cromwell was unwavering in such
convictions, even to the point of apologizing to Lord Philip
Wharton for outward appearances:

> It's easy to object to the glorious actings of God, if we look
> too much upon instruments . . .: Good kept out, most bad re-
> maining.
>   Be not offended at the manner; perhaps no other way was
> left. What if God accepted the zeal, as He did that of Phineas,
> whose reason might have called for a jury?[70]

Those displeased with God's instruments are finally displeased
with God and are left by him, Cromwell says elsewhere, "to
the blindness of their minds."[71] Apparently, Cromwell was
for a time as confident as Samson that an extraordinary spirit
rushed upon him, that rousing motions propelled him onward,
and that his actions, sanctioned by divine dispensations, bore

the seal of divine approval. He also appears to have been as inimical as Samson to the proposition that God should do his own avenging. Whatever the appearance of things, Cromwell, again like Samson, was confident that God was never the contradiction of His own deity, at least not in the end: "God is not the author of contradictions. The contradictions are not so much in the end as in the way."[72] The hope is for justice. The goal is deliverance. Yet to his critics, Cromwell was not only an instrument for violence but a dispenser with both his own oaths and the law. He exemplified contradiction, if not in the end, certainly in God's means to it.

Hence, Cromwell was notorious, as "notorious" as Samson (1186), for his methods: for tearing up the Book of Common Prayer and for tearing down monasteries and castles, activities, "the Lord's doing," he and his cohorts performed (they thought) as the "Lord's workmen."[73] Indeed, he was so notorious for tearing up and tearing down that the Quaker Thomas Aldam, in an interview with Cromwell, tore to pieces his own cap in order to dramatize what he would do to Cromwell's government. As we have seen, Cromwell admonished Lord Wharton, "Be not offended at the manner; perhaps no other way was left," with these words shifting responsibility from man to God, "Him alone." "[N]one other but the hand of God" is responsible, "none are to share with Him." "We have been lately taught," says Cromwell, "that it is not in man to direct his way." And he goes on: "Thus you see what the Lord hath wrought for us. Can any creature ascribe anything to itself?" God defeats his enemies, bringing them "to their utter ruin." This is God's way: "wherever anything in this world is exalted, or exalts itself, God will pull it down." He deals hard blows, even to the point of leading people into "dark paths through . . . providence and dispensations," although Cromwell then begins to hesitate when it comes "to set[ting] up . . . that providence hath destroyed and laid in the dust."[74] A hero in his own eyes, Cromwell was often in the eyes of his critics a hero run amok, an iconoclast not in a positive but a negative sense, a puller down — a demolisher of churches and a destroyer of governments.

If Samson practices what in his own time was preached, Cromwell preaches differently than he practices. Whatever his ways with the King's army, Cromwell complains of his own troops being "spoiled and robbed, but also sometimes barbarously and inhumanly butchered and slain."[75] When it comes to justifying his status as a messenger of God's wishes and an executer of His will, Cromwell asks, as Samson never does, how we know "whether it be of God or no" and answers in a way that sounds more like the Milton of *De Doctrina Christiana* than any of the characters in *Samson Agonistes*:

> our best way is to judge the conformity or disformity of [it with] the law written within us, which is the law of the spirit of God, the mind of God, the mind of Christ. . . . I do not know any outward evidence of what proceeds from the spirit of God more clear than this, the appearance of meekness and gentleness and mercy and patience and forbearance and love and a desire to do good to all and to destroy none that can be saved. . . .[76]

There is a huge discrepancy between what Cromwell says and does and a rupture, too, between what he says at different times about his own calling. Here he exudes confidence: "I have not sought these things," he tells his brother Richard; "truly I have been called unto them by the Lord."[77] His attitude seems to be, *follow whatever light you think you have*:

> If, when we want particular and extraordinary impressions, we shall either altogether sit still because we have them not, and not follow that light that we have; or shall go against or short of that light that we have, upon the imaginary apprehension of such divine impressions . . . — which are not so divine as to carry their evidence with them, to the conviction of those that have the spirit of God within them — I think we shall be justly under a condemnation. . . . I cannot but think that in many of those things, God hath spoke to us.[78]

But then Cromwell's confidence wanes: although he believes he is acting out God's will, at a prayer meeting (as Charles Firth reports) he refuses to claim divine revelation: "I cannot say that I have received anything that I can speak as in the name of the Lord. . . . We are very apt, all of us, to call that Faith, that perhaps may be but carnal imagination." While Cromwell still believed, probably, that mankind could be spoken to by the Spirit, he also came to believe, says Firth, that when "'divine impressions and divine discoveries' were made arguments for political action, they must be received with the greatest caution." It is worth noting, too, that, as Milton does with Samson, Firth compares Cromwell in defeat to the newly fallen Satan.[79]

Initially, Cromwell sounds like Samson; later like Gideon — with whom as a leader betrayed by his people he had been compared — and then less like someone victorious over than someone conquered and defeated by temptation. A man obsessed with his divine dispensations, who once said they were neither "vain imaginations, nor things fictitious";[80] a man led and driven by necessities, manifestations of providence, and eternal laws, finally owns up, as Firth astutely observes, to having made "too much of outward dispensations," worrying that "all . . . these dispensations . . . should end in so corrupt reasonings of good men; and should so hit the designings of bad." If supposed dispensations are no more than self-deceptions, God's grace turns into wantonness in which case the spirit of God becomes "a cloak for villainy and spurious apprehensions."[81]

Eventually, Cromwell seems to have come around to thinking (as did Grotius) that to determine heroism, or lack thereof, justice or criminality, "it is requisite to be acquainted with the Degrees of Men's *Illumination*, or other inward Dispositions of Mind, the Knowledge of which no Man is indulged."[82] If Cromwell's earlier attitude was *follow whatever light you have*, he seems to have eventually acquired what his Elders in

New England called a "Heroicall magnificence" and through which, then, he could avoid acting in certain ways so that even if his thinking here intersects, and there overlaps, with that of Samson, it is thinking that is not only in advance of but runs deeper than Samson's: the end is "our deliverance from slavery, and the accomplishment of our just rights and libertyes," as Cromwell was reminded by his petitioners from Bury St. Edmunds; it is the removal of all "grievances . . . stumbling-blocks and obstacles" so as to become "eminently instrumental in laying the foundation of our peace and liberty."[83] This noble cause, as both Marvell and Milton came to think, was too good to have fought for. Cromwell occasionally voiced misgivings. It is almost as if what Firth describes as Cromwell's own "imperfect, undiscriminating, . . . justice," finally "too much alloyed with revenge,"[84] provides the bare bones of a critique that Milton will embed at the very heart of *Samson Agonistes*. But with this proviso.

Whatever his practices, and despite his occasional insistence that people pay for their "cruelties" with their "bloods," Cromwell can worry over the people returning evil for good (Samson's fault, according to some) and can say that he is "more willing to that way, for the prevention of blood and ruin, than to the other of force," though necessity, or "overruling providence," may finally prevail. He allows, moreover, that he would "rather miscarry . . . [that is, "do wrong to"] a believer than to an unbeliever . . . — but let's take heed of doing that which is evil to either!" At times he sounds like Grotius, laying emphasis as previously noted on justice and righteousness: "how dangerous a thing is it to wage an unjust war; much more, to appeal to God the Righteous Judge therein." Other times, he says he cannot let "inhuman barbarities . . . escape unpunished and unrevenged" and also objects, as we noted in an earlier chapter and despite his own practices, "to violence and ransac" as "villanous act[s]" and "dangerous example[s]." At still other times he sounds just like Milton: "Would all the Lord's people were prophets. I would all were fit to be called, and fit to call" in this period of "changes and turnings," "turnings and tossings," in these winding and wandering ways of providence.[85]

The great battles/miracles of Cromwell's lifetime, *God's* controversies and battles, belonging to the third of September, were retrospectively qualified by the date of Cromwell's death, 3 September 1658, in the same way that, for many, the miracles of Samson's life seemed qualified, if not nullified, by the temple catastrophe. Previous victories culminated in spectacular defeats for these leaders — and for their nations; and those defeats, in turn, raised questions about the extent to which either figure evidenced prophecy breaking into history or providence governing it. The issue, for Milton, is not one of focusing criticism on a leader like Cromwell but, instead, on the overwhelming force of the Revolution that he represents, that he himself attributes to God ("God hath made these revolutions"), and "the only parallel" for which he can find (and that Milton in his turn will accentuate in *Samson Agonistes*) is "Israel's bringing out of Egypt through a wilderness."[86] Samson's rhetoric in Milton's poem sounds like that of Cromwell, with Cromwell's own self-critique furnishing an outline of the one Milton will fix on Samson. It is no small irony, therefore, that the language used within the context of the disinterring and mutilation of Charles I's enemies to describe Charles's own death and "similar horrid spectacles" is identical to that deployed by Grotius in *Christus Patiens* to describe the "horrid day," "horrid'st Act," and "horrid motion" of the Crucifixion and by Milton in *Samson Agonistes* to describe the temple/theater catastrophe: "this so *horrid spectacle*" (1542; my italics).[87] There is a point at which the excesses on both sides — these supposed horrific acts of injustice — meet. That point is the temple catastrophes in each poem with "*Calvary* . . . rent from the top to the bottome, seeming to threaten dissolution of the world, its complete annihilation, and return to original chaos," and it is on such points that Milton fixes his critique. As Sandys explains, when the veils are torn, separating the priest from the people, a dove supposedly was seen flying away from the temple, angels were heard (according to St. Jerome) saying they would leave this place forever in anticipation, as Josephus reports, of its destruction.[88] In this destruction of a temple is the remembrance of another temple demolition, this one undertaken by Samson, who in *Samson Agonistes* brings ruin and destruction to their utmost point.

V

The phoenix, rising and falling in cycles, indeed enclosed within cycles of history from which the Son breaks free and an image therefore of entrapment in time and history, is finally bound to earth and, as such, is a potent reminder that hidden within this climactic image, with its implied personal and historical progression, is the Derridean "possibility of a catastrophic regression and the annulment of progress."[89] The phoenix determines when it will die, builds a funeral pyre, and, turning towards the sun, burns itself up. It revives, first in the noxious form of a worm that, growing toward maturity, eventually assumes wings again.[90] The image is appropriate to Samson (more perhaps to him than Christ) in its association with those who are self-killed, even if not willingly; with those who choose the time and place of their death only to rise again in baser, not more perfect, form; with those for whom fire itself is a destructive element; and with those, finally, who, instead of breaking through the cycles of history and their own errors, are bound down and eventually crushed by both.

Yet the phoenix image as deployed in *Samson Agonistes*, enveloping Samson, also embraces Dalila, "prompt[ing] a sinister memory" of her, both because this "secular (and feminine) phoenix" here embodies fame, black and white and double-mouthed, and because, again like her (not to mention the first two items in the triple simile), the phoenix image is highly, "disturbingly ambiguous" as is everything else in this complex poem.[91] Like both the flying dragon and eagle, the image of the phoenix seems to encapsulate simply, neatly, positively. Yet each image, when placed under scrutiny, also shatters under the pressure of its own contradictions — and in such a way as to pose alternatives for interpretation rather than close down interpretation in a definitive formulation.

The flying dragon and eagle are not annihilated in the phoenix image; rather, this image reverts to the worm/serpent that later will assume wings. As the phoenix reverts to the form of a winged worm, thus recalling the image of the flying serpent/dragon, we may simultaneously remember the apocalyptic promise and calculate the distance, if any distance at all, that through Samson we have traveled toward it. In the words of William Bryan:

> . . . the Lord shall reign with his saints upon the earth, when Paradise shall be again revealed unto man, and evil shall disappear. — The serpent and dragon, being chained in the abyss, shall have no longer a manifestation in man, but every man shall become a real manifestation of God, as he was in the Paradise before the fall.[92]

Are we thus to remember that Samson, a would-be reformer, did not reform the life of his people, indeed did not even reform his own life? The phoenix may represent the promise of Samson's life, but it is a life in which the serpent and dragon still are manifestations, startlingly so.

If, as Lightfoot thought, the Samson story in Judges begins with an allegory about reading, that same story as unfolded in *Samson Agonistes*, moving from a personal to a political allegory, produces, in the poem's conclusion, not only the climax in a political allegory but also an allegory of *readings*. Within a biblical frame of reference, the various scriptural representations and interpretations of the Samson story may be regarded as interventions — or supplements, in the Derridean sense.

That is, each of the Old Testament representations (in Genesis, 1 Chronicles, Amos, and Judges), credibly a response to a story circulating in tradition, attempts to freeze the story within some interpretive perspective. As such, each is a fixing — a coagulation — of what had been a fluid narrative and shifting story. New Testament representations (in Hebrews and Revelation) are, in their turn, reinterpretations of Old Testament readings — efforts at sorting the story into frameworks of positive and negative readings. *Samson Agonistes* is yet another representation and reinterpretation — another supplement, as it were, to these supplements and, in its coda, manages a marvelous distillation of each Samson (from each interpretive tradition) into a pictorial image, with the evening dragon/serpent, the eagle, and the phoenix all rendering a distinctively different portrait of Samson; with the whole sequence of images forming a kind of picture puzzle in which the images are both insignia of Samson and portents of the poem's tragedy. If *Paradise Lost*, as Don Cameron Allen once remarked, "could be called an allegory about allegory,"[93] if as John Lightfoot thought the Book of Judges contains an allegory about reading, now with shifting inflections Milton's tragedy, initially a personal and political allegory, becomes an allegory of *readings*.

Brought in contact with one another, the representative Samsons of each biblical text modify one another in Milton's new representation, the ambiguity of which is an essential aspect of Milton's evaluation. That evaluation, rife with analytical power, implies that any notion of a representative Samson attached to this or that scriptural text is menacing to Milton's own representation. To cast *Samson Agonistes* as a drama "never . . . intended" for the stage, nor ever intended to be "produc'd beyond the fift Act" (*CP*, 574) is tantamount to saying that this poem, like the Samson story itself, can only be "contaminated by supplementary re-presentation"[94] of the sort that reflects by way of deambiguating the character of Samson.

In his annotations to Grotius, Francis Goldsmith, in a comment already alluded to in chapter 1, offers the most telling gloss on Milton's hope that *Samson Agonistes* will never be produced beyond its fifth act. If among the Greeks, fabling in tragedy often begins with the Chorus, which "after the fifth Act . . . as a Judge gave sentence of those things which had bin acted," that practice, in an exemplary way, "is for the most part omitted by *Seneca*" and, from Grotius's point of view, should be discouraged in current biblical tragedy. Now urged to relinquish its role as judge of characters, the Chorus itself, Goldsmith implies, quoting Ben Jonson's translation of Horace, should be summoned to judgment according to its commitment to *"wholesome justice, laws / Peace, and the open ports that peace doth cause."*[95] In the end, we are not allowed to forget that in this theater of judgments, both of God's and of our own, Milton presents a tragedy of and about justice — "that justice which exalts a nation . . ., which," in the words of Thomas Weld, "not only builds but repaires a land. And if justice may run down like water, it may meet . . . with the stream of blood which hath already been spilt, and stop it."[96]

One by one, each picture image of Samson (evening dragon/serpent/eagle/phoenix) is effaced in the presence of a character who, while subsuming, is still greater than the sum of these emblematic parts. *Samson Agonistes* is a story of reawakening and renovation, not of Samson but of his story, through a supplement that, as Derrida might say, is "a rebirth or a reactivation of the origin"[97] — a companion piece to the Judges narrative in its mirroring of the complicated consciousness embedded within its stories. It is a consciousness that perceives contending cultures within conflicting characters, within heroes and heroines pitted against their enemies (Samson against Dalila, Jael against Sisera, Dalila against Jael); it is a consciousness that comprehends the extremes of experience, as well as of emotion, and that, containing contrary perspectives, colliding systems of value, in the words of Meir

Sternberg, "give[s] a sense of a full world along with a full registration of the world, a plurality of viewpoints on existence, in coexistence."[98] What Sternberg here claims for the biblical narrative Thomas Corns claims for *Samson Agonistes* — a poem in which we behold "the coexistence of contradictions" — and explains as "originating in the complexities of registral and political situations Milton negotiated and in the complexities of political psychology."[99]

In its elicitation of contending interpretations, the Samson story has often seemed a summons for choosing between interpretations as they are represented by the different Samson hermeneutics in the Bible and arrayed within the triple simile with which *Samson Agonistes* ends. The choice of many has been to privilege the last item in this pictorial puzzle (the phoenix) and, doing so, to choose a regenerate and triumphant Samson, a Samson who is a type of Christ. Others have opted for Samson in another of his manifestations. Doubtless, some will choose not to choose, arguing that Milton's text militates against choice. This is a valid, even necessary stage in interpretation, if not the ultimate interpretive maneuver, especially when choice or lack thereof is construed, with Donald F. Bouchard, as symbolic action: when "fail[ing] to choose is to be bound to the past, to be overcome by past mistakes: it is to be a captive of history."[100] It is to be Samson and to recapitulate his mistakes. If Milton's Samson is, finally, an oracle, Bouchard's words encapsulate the warning it speaks.

When we choose not to choose, we must abandon (if in fact we hold to them) ideas of definitive context and definitive interpretation; of a Milton with an unchanging mind; of a *Samson Agonistes* that is, in any sense, a redundant repetition of the epics; and of a Milton angling in this text of darkness for a pious interpretation, or producing through this text pious scholia for its scriptural counterparts. We must open our eyes to new contexts without, in the process, blinding ourselves to old cruxes. New contextualizations are a way of discouraging, but obviously do not safeguard against, reductionist interpretations. Old cruxes are not exits from but entrances to the interpretive problems of a text like *Samson Agonistes*: cruxes such as Samson's appeal to divine commission for his marriages and Manoa's denial of those appeals, or such as the ethical inconvenience of Milton's presenting Samson and Dalila as married while evading the customary justification for their marriage, or Samson's claiming divine warrant for his actions even as Milton equivocates on whether Samson prays and then, as if to remove equivocation, altogether eliminates the words of that prayer usually accepted as authorizing Samson's claim of divine inspiration. We must stop explaining every transgression from scriptural or interpretive traditions in terms of Milton's supposed desire to aggrandize Samson and give him the buckles of a hero. Instead, we should see in Samson "a strange compound — an embodied paradox."[101]

We must be infinitely more judicious in allying tradition — any tradition — with Milton's poetry; for the risk is always in showing Milton ruled by what, in actuality, his poetry rules over. There may be a tighter fit between the criticism we write and the various Samson traditions of the seventeenth century than there is between *Samson Agonistes* and those same traditions. Great poems, it seems, have a knack for exposing the limits, and limitations, of our criticism even as they probe the theoretical foundations on which our interpretations rest. In the resistance it offers to all existing schools of interpretation, *Samson Agonistes* stands as a reminder to its critics that we should correct not only others' mistakes, but also our own, and we can do that only after acknowledging a capacity for making mistakes. After all, those who never alter their opinions are like standing water and breed reptiles of the mind; but, then, those who know this also know the difference between altering opinions and surrendering principles.

Milton's *is* a poetry of choice. Criticism thrives on choices. As critics of *Samson Agonistes*, we can choose this Samson over that one or, alternatively, we can choose resolution — *or irresolution*. We can choose not to choose in which case we will hold in our hands, and will have taught in our classrooms, and will regale the readers of our criticism, with a very Derridean text indeed. Whereas some will want only one Samson, and then usually the regenerate Samson of a modern critical tradition and of an older religious orthodoxy, Milton may have aspired to something else. He may have wished to attach not one but a range of senses to the Samson story, an obvious enough procedure for a poet (both outsider and dissenter) of the Protestant tradition, which, as Frank Kermode describes it, "abhor[s] the claim of the institution to an historically validated traditional interpretation."[102] Milton may have been resisting both absolute adherence to a tradition and absolute break from it: he may have wished to inscribe within the poem he published last in the 1671 volume several Samsons and several texts at once. Milton restores to *Samson Agonistes* what had been atrophying since the passing of Greek drama, the Chorus — the interrogative element.[103] From one perspective, certainly, he may be seen as achieving, through his own interrogation of the Samson story, a perfect juxtaposition of contending interpretations, of conflicting images, with his meaning inhering in irresolution itself. From another perspective, of course, he may have meant for the irresolution of one poem to resolve itself in the resolution of the poem with which it is paired and which affords it an interpreting perspective. In this sense, *Samson Agonistes* is not so much a poem that completes as one that is completed by Milton's epic vision.

Drama is centered in conflicts that do not easily resolve themselves, in contradictions that may defy resolution. The nagging question is what did Milton, and hence what are we to privilege: the deconstructionist uncertainties of *Samson*

Agonistes or the Christian revelations of *Paradise Regain'd*? Does context, in this instance, interpret text? Does narrative reign over drama, supplying for it an interpretive voice? *Paradise Regain'd* and *Samson Agonistes* are supplements to scriptural texts, but what is the relationship between the poems themselves? "PARADISE REGAIN'D . . . To which is added *Samson Agonistes*" — does the title page for the 1671 poetic volume imply subordination or indicate supplementation? Rather than answering themselves, these questions seem only to breed new ones: should we privilege the Miltonic voice (presuming we can find it) and its proclamations (presuming we can trust them to be Milton's) — at all? does the poetry exist for, and take its energy from, answers it gives or from questions it asks? *Paradise Regain'd* and *Samson Agonistes*, then, are less about promoting individual interpretations than proffering a range of possibilities for interpretation.

The 1671 poetic volume formulates alternatives and frustrates choice. But how frustrating are its frustrations? Has Milton built a mental theater with no exits — a theater we can leave only by tearing it down? Or is the Milton of *Samson Agonistes* one about whom it should be said: "the *Poets Heart does not go along with their Pen*,"[104] at least the words of a pen for so long misinterpreted. As Grotius (citing Homer) once remarked in a way that drives this point home: it is like hell, people are hell, "Whose Heart and Tongue do ever disagree."[105] No division here between the heart and the head, the poet and the theologian, unconscious and conscious meanings. If there are divisions in *Samson Agonistes*, they are calculated, not a barrier to but an aspect of the poem's meaning. Indeed, this poem, always available to contradictory interpretations, reveals at its very heart that, "for the late Milton," tragedy, instead of deriving from indecision, is, in the eloquent formulation of Victoria Kahn, having to decide; is "what our decisions look like."[106] And, too, what those decisions might have looked like.

NOTES

Notes to Preface

1. The worry over the relation of poetry and theory, though it may seem peculiar to our own time, goes back at least two centuries to a critic for whom Milton's reconstitution of tragedy is an issue; see, e.g., John Penn, *Letters on the Drama* (London, 1796), 30.

2. See, respectively, Stanley Fish, *How Milton Works* (Cambridge, Mass. and London: Belknap Press of Harvard University Press, 2001); Barbara Lewalski, *The Life of John Milton* (Malden, Mass. and Oxford: Blackwell, 2000); John T. Shawcross, *The Uncertain World of "Samson Agonistes"* (Cambridge: D. S. Brewer, 2001); and Derek N. C. Wood, *"Exiled from Light": Divine Law, Morality, and Violence in Milton's "Samson Agonistes"* (Buffalo, Toronto, and London: University of Toronto Press, 2001).

3. See F. Michael Krouse, *Milton's Samson and the Christian Tradition* (Princeton: Princeton University Press for the University of Cincinnati Press, 1949).

4. See Robert Sanderson, *XXXIV Sermons . . . Whereunto, Is Now Added a Sermon [Ad Clerum], Printed by a Correct Copy under the Authors Own Hand*, 5th ed. rev. (London, 1671), where the point, once made on the title page, is underscored in some copies on its verso, "Now published in his own copy." See also James Ussher, *A Body of Divinity, or the Summe and Substance of Christian Religion*, 3rd ed. (London, 1640), title-page notation; and cf. James Ussher, *A Body of Divinity, Of the Summe and Substance of Christs Religion*, 6th ed. (London, 1670), title-page notation.

5. See the trilogy of children's science fiction, *His Dark Materials*, by Philip Pullman, especially the third book of the series, *The Amber Spyglass* (New York: Alfred A. Knopf, 2000).

6. John Carey, *Milton* (London: Evans Brothers, 1969), [7].

7. See both William Riley Parker, *Milton's Debt to Greek Tragedy in "Samson Agonistes"* (Baltimore: Johns Hopkins Press, 1937), and Samuel S. Stollman, "Milton's Samson and the Jewish Tradition," *Milton Studies* 3 (1971): 185–200.

8. Jeffrey Shoulson, *Milton and the Rabbis: Hebraism, Hellenism, and Christianity* (New York and London: Columbia University Press, 2001), 244–45.

9. Lewalski, *The Life of John Milton*, 523–24.

10. See John Trapp, *Theologica Theologiae, The True Treasure; or a Treasury of Holy Truths* (London, 1641), 115; John Weemes, *The Christian Synagogue* (London, 1623), 30–37, 49; Richard Simon, *A Critical History of the Old Testament*, tr. Richard Hampden (London, 1682), pt. 2, 31; and Simon Patrick, *A Discourse about Tradition Shewing What Is Meant by It* (London, 1683), 36.

11. See George Whitehead and William Penn, "Concerning the Scriptures," in *A Serious Apology for the Principles and Practices of the People Call'd Quakers* (London, 1671), 50.

12. Archibald Lovell, "The Translatour to the Reader," in Richard Simon, *The Critical History of the Religions and Customs of the Eastern Nations* (London, 1685), A2.

13. See John Owen, *Certain Treatises* (London, 1649), A3.

14. See Simon Patrick, *A Discourse about Tradition*, 10 (also 11), 32, 33.

15. See Dayton Haskin, *Milton's Burden of Interpretation* (Philadelphia: University of Pennsylvania Press, 1994), xv; see also xvi; and both J. B. Sanson de Pongerville and Louis Raymond de Véricour in Harry Redman Jr., *Major French Milton Critics of the Nineteenth Century* (Pittsburgh: Duquesne University Press, 1994), 185, 107.

16. Thomas M. Gorman, "The Reach of Human Sense: Surplus and Absence in *Samson Agonistes*," *Milton Studies*, 39 (2000): 193, 200, 194.

17. See James Holstun, *Ehud's Dagger: Class Struggle in the English Revolution* (London and New York: Verso, 2000), 345.

18. See Toni Morrison, *Paradise* (New York and Toronto: Alfred A. Knopf, 1997), 18, 87.

19. See Walter Raleigh, *Milton* (1900; reprint, New York: Benjamin Blom, 1967), 85.

20. See Shawcross, *The Uncertain World of "Samson Agonistes,"* 100, 93, 95; see also 85.

21. See J. Martin Evans, *The Miltonic Moment* (Lexington: University Press of Kentucky, 1998), 117–32; Phillip J. Gallagher, *Milton, the Bible, and Misogyny*, ed. Eugene R. Cunnar and Gail L. Mortimer (Columbia and London: University of Missouri Press, 1990), 131–70; Anthony Low, "*Samson Agonistes* and the 'Pioneers of Aphasia'," *Milton Quarterly* 25 (December 1991): 143–48; and Alan Rudrum, "Discerning the Spirit in *Samson Agonistes*," in *"All in All": Unity, Diversity, and the Miltonic*

Perspective, ed. Charles W. Durham and Kristin A. Pruitt (Selinsgrove, Pa.: Susquehanna University Press, and London: Associated University Presses, 1999), 245–46, 249, 254.

22. I borrow this apt phase from the recent essay by Dennis Kezar, "Samson's Death by Theater and Milton's Art of Dying," *English Literary History* 66 (Summer 1999): 296.

23. Henry McDonald, "A Long Day's Dying: Tragic Ambiguity in *Samson Agonistes*," *Milton Studies* 27 (1991): 282.

24. William B. Hunter, *"De Doctrina Christiana: Nunc Quo Vadis,"* *Milton Quarterly* 34 (October 2000): 101.

25. I quote from David Loewenstein, *Milton and the Drama of History: Historical Vision, Iconoclasm, and the Literary Imagination* (Cambridge and New York: Cambridge University Press, 1990), 126, 129, 131, 151, 148, 147; but another essay by Loewenstein is equally illuminating, "The Revenge of the Saint: Radical Religion and Politics in *Samson Agonistes*," *Milton Studies* 33 (1996): 159–203.

26. See Michael Lieb, *Milton and the Culture of Violence* (Ithaca, N.Y. and London: Cornell University Press, 1994), 235–36; and also by Lieb, "The God of *Samson Agonistes*," *Milton Studies* 23 (1997): 4, 19, 20 (a special issue of *Milton Studies* under the title *The Miltonic Samson*), and "'A Thousand Fore-skins': Circumcision, Violence, and Selfhood in Milton," *Milton Studies* 38 (2000): 209 (another special issue of *Milton Studies* entitled *John Milton: The Writer in His Works*). See, again, "The God of *Samson Agonistes*," 15.

27. Francis Barker, *The Culture of Violence: Essays on Tragedy and History* (Chicago: University of Chicago Press, 1993), viii, 205.

28. See Laura Lunger Knoppers, *Historicizing Milton: Spectacle, Power, and Poetry in Restoration England* (Athens and London: University of Georgia Press, 1994), 4; and Kezar, "Samson's Death by Theater," 327. Blair Wordon makes clear that the Samson story afforded numerous political analogies, especially for Milton's allies, and the Book of Judges numerous parallels to contemporary experience; see "Milton, *Samson Agonistes*, and the Restoration," in *Culture and Society in the Stuart Restoration: Literature, Drama, History,* ed. Gerald MacLean (Cambridge and New York: Cambridge University Press, 1995), 111–36.

29. I take this distinction from Janel Mueller, "Contextualizing Milton's Nascent Republicanism," in *Of Poetry and Politics: New Essays on Milton and His World*, ed. P. G. Stanwood (Binghamton, N. Y.: Medieval and Renaissance Texts and Studies, 1995), 264.

30. See *Altering Eyes: New Perspectives on "Samson Agonistes,"* ed. Mark R. Kelley and Joseph Wittreich (Newark: University of Delaware Press, and London: Associated University Presses, 2002).

31. David Quint, *Epic and Empire: Politics and Generic Form from Virgil to Milton* (Princeton: Princeton University Press, 1993), 280, 281, 278–80.

32. David Norbrook, *Writing the English Republic: Poetry, Rhetoric and Politics, 1627–1660* (Cambridge and London: Cambridge University Press, 1999), 490, 435, 7, 190.

33. Harold Skulsky, *Justice in the Dock: Milton's Experimental Tragedy* (Newark: University of Delaware Press, and London: Associated University Presses, 1995), 11, 96.

34. See Richard S. Ide, "The Renaissance Heritage of *Samson Agonistes*," in *Soundings of Things Done: Essays in Early Modern Literature in Honor of S. K. Heninger Jr.*, ed. Peter E. Medine and Joseph Wittreich (Newark: University of Delaware Press, and London: Associated University Presses, 1997), 152–77; and Mark R. Kelley, "Milton's Euripidean Poetics of Lament," in *Altering Eyes*, ed. Kelley and Wittreich, 132–67, as well as Kelley's dissertation of the same title, The Graduate Center of The City University of New York, 2002.

35. See Norbrook, *Writing the English Republic*; Frank Kermode, *The Genesis of Secrecy: On the Interpretation of Narrative* (1979; reprint, Cambridge, Mass. and London: Harvard University Press, 1982); and Haskin, *Milton's Burden of Interpretation*.

36. Skulsky, *Justice in the Dock*, 16, 24.

37. Kermode, *The Genesis of Secrecy*, 40.

38. Shoulson, *Milton and the Rabbis*, 240–61. Shoulson's book is a wonderful elaboration of an argument initially advanced by Jason P. Rosenblatt, *Torah and the Law in "Paradise Lost"* (Princeton: Princeton University Press, 1994), with an extension of both their conclusions to *Samson Agonistes*.

39. See Noam Flinker, "Typological Parody: Samson in Confrontation with Harapha," *Milton Quarterly* 24 (December 1990): 138, 136; and by the same author, "Pagan Holiday and National Conflict: A Philistine Reading of *Samson Agonistes*," *Milton Quarterly* 25 (December 1991): 160.

40. See, respectively, Keith N. Hull, "Rhyme and Disorder in *Samson Agonistes*" and Peggy Samuels, "*Samson Agonistes* and the English Renaissance Closet Drama"; both these conference papers are summarized in *Milton Quarterly* 25 (December 1991): 164, 170. See also Derek N. C. Wood, "Catharsis and 'Passion Spent': *Samson Agonistes* and the Problem of Aristotle," *Milton Quarterly* 36 (March 1992): [1]–9; Stanley Fish, "Spectacle and Evidence in *Samson Agonistes*," *Critical Inquiry* 15 (Spring 1988): 556–86; Ashraf H. A. Rushdy, "According to Samson's Command: Some Contexts of Milton's Tragedy," *Milton Quarterly* 36 (October 1992): 69–80; Jane Melbourne, "Biblical Intertexuality in *Samson Agonistes*," *Studies in English Literature 1500–1900* 36 (Winter 1996): 111–27; and Skulsky, *Justice in the Dock*, 12. Ashraf H. A. Rushdy's often brilliant observations are finely elaborated in *The Empty Garden: The Subject of Late Milton* (Pittsburgh and London: University of Pittsburgh Press, 1992).

41. Fish, *How Milton Works,* 599.

42. Laura Lunger Knoppers, "'Sung and Proverb'd for a Fool': *Samson Agonistes* and Solomon's Harlot," *Milton Studies* 26 (1990): 249.

43. Knoppers, *Historicizing Milton,* 10, 43, 61, 11–12.

44. Lana Cable, *Carnal Rhetoric: Milton's Iconoclasm and the Poetics of Desire* (Durham, N. C. and London: Duke University Press, 1995), 42, 223, 170, 189.

45. Victoria Kahn, "Political Theology and Reason of State in *Samson Agonistes,*" *South Atlantic Quarterly* 95 (Fall 1996): 1066, 1069, 1067, 1086–87.

46. William Blake, "The Mental Traveller," in *The Complete Poetry and Prose of William Blake,* rev. ed., ed. David V. Erdman (Garden City, N. Y.: Doubleday, 1982), 485.

Notes to Chapter 1

1. Balachandra Rajan, "Milton Encompassed," *Milton Quarterly* 32 (October 1998): 87.

2. I am quoting from Francis Barham, *The Adamus Exul of Grotius; Or the Prototype of "Paradise Lost,"* tr. Barham (London, 1839), 4. Barham refers to Jerome Ziegler, portions of whose Samson play are translated and reproduced by Watson Kirkconnell, *That Invincible Samson: The Theme of "Samson Agonistes" in World Literature* (Toronto: University of Toronto Press, 1964), 3–11, under a corrected title and date: *Samson, Tragoedia Nova* (1547) / *Samson, A New Tragedy.* Kirkconnell remarks that this play contains "no hint of Samson prefiguring Christ" (156), which is not the case in so many of the other analogues he cites.

For the sequence of plays on the subject of Christ suffering, see, first, the anonymous Greek play of the eleventh or twelfth century, *Christos Paschon,* sometimes attributed to Gregory Nazianzen (329?–390?) as on the title page to the Antwerp edition of 1550 (*Diui gregorii Nazianzeni Theologi, Tragoedia Christus patiens, latino*) and as in Milton's preface to *Samson Agonistes.* The play, published in the early modern period as *Tragoedia Christus patiens,* was then reprinted as *Christus Patiens. Tragoedia Christiana,* ed. J. G. Brambs (Leipzig, 1885) and as *La passion du Christ: tragedie,* tr. and ed. Andre Tuilier (Paris: Editions du Cerf, 1969). See also Hugo Grotius, *Tragoedia Sophompaneas Accesserunt, tragoedia ejusdem Christus patiens. et sacia argumenti alia* (Amsterdam, 1627, 1635), and then *Christs Passion. A Tragedy. With Annotations,* tr. George Sandys (London, 1640). The British Library identifies two separate editions of 1640 (see Shelf Nos. 643.a.42 and 11409.b.31) and then gives these dates for subsequent editions of the Sandys translation: 1682, 1687, 1748, and 1845. After Milton, see René Rapin, *Christus patiens: carmes heroicum* (London, 1674, 1713), which was then translated by C. Beckingham under the title *Christus Patiens: Or, The Sufferings of Christ An*

Heroic Poem. In Two Books (London, 1720); cf. Francis Bragge, *The Passion of Our Saviour [To which is added a Pindarick Ode on the Suffering God. In Imitation of Rapins Christus Patiens]* (London, [1730?]). For discussion of the early *Christos Paschon*, see Thomas Kranidas, "Milton and the Author of Christ Suffering," *Notes and Queries*, N. S. 15 (1968), 99, as well as Venetia Cottas, *L'influence du drame "Christos paschon" sur l'art cretien d'Orient* (Paris: Librarie orientaliste Paul Geuthner, 1931). And see, too, Johann Friedrich Duebner, *Christus Patiens et Christianorum poetarum reliquiae dramaticae. Ex codicibus emendavit et annotatione critica instruxit*, in Euripides, *Fragmenta* (2 vols.; Paris, 1846–47), 2:[1]–78 (both Greek and Latin texts, plus annotations).

See, finally, the exemplary plays by George Buchanan, *Jephtha* and *The Baptist*, in *Tragedies*, ed. P. Sharratt and P. G. Walsh (Edinburgh: Scottish Academic Press, 1983). The latter play was published separately in 1577, 1578, 1579, 1618, 1642, 1740, and 1823; the two plays appeared together in 1590, 1593, 1600, 1601, 1609, 1611, 1621, and 1732. Two seventeenth century publications of Buchanan's works are relevant here: the first, a translation once attributed to Milton, *Tyrannicall-Government Anatomized: Or, A Discourse Concerning Evil-Councellors. Being the Life and Death of John the Baptist* (London, 1642; new style 1643); and the second, an edition of *Baptistes* appearing in Amsterdam (1656). Both these titles underscore the political valences given to biblical stories, the latter the way in which such stories become political allegories — or covers — under which to place the history of the poet's own times.

3. Joost van den Vondel, *Samson, or the Holy Revenge*, in *That Invincible Samson: The Theme of "Samson Agonistes" in World Literature*, tr. and ed. Watson Kirkconnell (Toronto: University of Toronto Press, 1964), 127, 131.

4. See Hugo Grotius, *His Sophompaneas, or Joseph. A Tragedy. With Annotations. By Francis Goldsmith* (London, 1652), [B2v]. I quote from the headnote to the play itself (the front matter to the play has separate signatures). On the meaning of the title, see Goldsmith's annotations, which he says are "gleaned out of . . . *Vossius* and *Grotius* themselves" ([44], 61).

5. Vasily Rozanov, "My Prediction," in *The Apocalypse of Our Time and Other Writings*, ed. Robert Payne (New York: Praeger, 1976), 237.

6. Nigel Smith, *Literature and Revolution in England 1640–1660* (1994; reprint, New Haven and London: Yale University Press, 1997), 15; cf. 76–77.

7. I am grateful to Stephen Goldsmith for sharing material from his book-in-progress, *Blake's Agitation: Criticism, Politics, and Affect.*

8. Anon., *The Cloud Opened; Or, The English Heroe* (London, 1670), 17, 47. Later editions appeared in 1809 and 1810.

9. The titles are all probably published in London, except for the Graziani play published in Bologna. Tragicomedy is the dominant mode of theatrical publication in 1671. See Aphra Behn, *The Forc'd Marriage . . . A Tragi-Comedy*; Pierre Corneille, *Nicomede. A Tragi-Comedy*, tr. John Dancer; John Crowe, *Juliana or the Princess of Poland. A Tragicomedy*; Edward Howard, *The Womens Conquest: A Tragi-Comedy*; and Samuel Tate, *Adventures of Five Houres: A Tragi-Comedy*. Corneille's play is published in Dublin, the others in London. See also Francis Kirkman who, while cataloguing comedies and tragedies as well, publishes *A True, Perfect, and Exact Catalogue of All . . . Tragi-Comedies . . . Ever Yet Printed and Published* (1661; reprint, London, 1671).

10. See Hugo Grotius, *Christs Passion. A Tragedy. With Annotations*, tr. George Sandys (London, 1640), 62–63.

11. See H. B. Charlton, *The Senecan Tradition: Renaissance Tragedy* (1946; reprint, Folcroft, Pa.: Folcroft Press, 1969), xxii.

12. See E. H. Gombrich, *Norm and Form: Studies in the Art of the Renaissance*, 2nd ed. (London and New York: Phaidon, 1971), 48.

13. See Erin Henriksen, "Sacred Reader, Sacred Writer: Scriptural Models for Early Modern Books," unpublished diss., The Graduate Center of The City University of New York, 2002; and Jeffrey Shoulson, *Milton and the Rabbis: Hebraism, Hellenism, and Christianity* (New York and London: Columbia University Press, 2001), 250, 249. I do not mean to suggest that Samson is never depicted triumphant, only that Milton's poem sabotages the tradition represented, let us say, by Guido Reni's *Samsone Vittorioso*, a painting from the Palazzo Publico on exhibit at the Pinacotecca Nazionale in Bologna.

14. Hill, *Milton and the English Revolution* (New York: Viking Press, 1978), 3.

15. Barker, *The Culture of Violence: Tragedy and History* (Chicago: University of Chicago Press, 1993), 104.

16. As in Thomas Newton's annotations to *Samson Agonistes*, in *The Poetical Works of John Milton*, ed. Henry John Todd (7 vols.; London, 1801), 7:427.

17. Hill, *Milton and the English Revolution*, 9.

18. Nigel Smith, *Literature and Revolution*, 86.

19. William Empson, *Milton's God*, rev. ed. (London: Chatto and Windus, 1965), 238, 241.

20. George Sandys, tr., "To the Kings Most Excellent Majestie," *Christs Passion* by Grotius [A4v].

21. See David Norbrook, "Euripides, Milton, and *Christian Doctrine*," *Milton Quarterly* 29 (May 1995): 37–41.

22. See esp. Richard Cumberland, "Preliminary Observations on *Samson Agonistes*," in *The Poetical Works*, ed. Todd, 4:357.

23. For discussion of this point, see T. B. L. Webster, *The Tragedies*

of Euripides (London: Methuen, 1967), 190, and Anne Pippin Burnett, *Catastrophe Survived: Euripides' Plays of Mixed Reversal* (Oxford: Clarendon Press, 1971), 172–73. Carole S. Kessner was the first to recognize Milton's indebtedness in *Samson Agonistes* to "the much more humanized hero of Euripides' *Heracles*"; see "Milton's Hebraic Herculean Hero," *Milton Studies* 6 (1975): 243–58.

24. See Euripides, *Heracles*, in *The Complete Greek Tragedies: Euripides II*, tr. William Arrowsmith, ed. David Grene and Richmond Lattimore (1956; reprint, Chicago and London: University of Chicago Press, 1969), 98–99,100: his father fearing that "If he awakes and breaks his bonds, / he will destroy us all," "pil[ing] murder on murder," Herakles "sits" there, "like a ship . . . / moored to a piece of broken masonry; / and . . . close beside me, corpses lie."

25. See Richard Paul Jodrell, *Illustrations of Euripides, On The Ion and The Bacchae* (2 vols.; London, 1781), 2:33, as well as *Illustrations of Euripides, On The Alcestis* (London, 1789).

26. See John K. Hale, "Milton's Euripides Marginalia: Their Significance for Milton Studies," *Milton Studies* 27 (1993): 24, 28.

27. David Quint, "Expectation and Prematurity in Milton's *Nativity Ode*," *Modern Philology* 97 (November 1999): 195.

28. See Giles Firmin, *The Real Christian, or a Treatise of Effectual Calling* (London, 1670), whose work was responded to by Richard Baxter in 1671 and Andrew Croswell in 1745; as well as John Tillotson, *Sermons Preach'd upon Several Occasions* (London, 1671). Sometimes, an "Imprimatur" appears on the verso of a title page: see the Puritan divine Thomas Gataker, *An Antidote Against Errour, Concerning Justification* (London, 1670); the staunch Royalist Robert Sanderson, *Ad Clerum. A Sermon Preached at a Visitation Holden at Grantham*, 5th ed. (London, 1671); and the nonconformist and anti-Catholic polemicist Daniel Whitbie, *The Certainty of Christian Faith in Generall, and of the Resurrection of Christ in Particular* (Oxford, 1671). No imprimatur appears in Stephen Crisp, *An Alarum Sounded in the Borders of Spiritual Egypt* (London, 1671), or in the 1672 edition either — a point worth mentioning only because of the ostentatious announcement that one is missing, NO "Approbation of the Learned Doctors of this Age" (Aa). Milton's 1671 poetic volume affords the only example I know of where "Licens'd" is so boldly featured. It is as if the "imprimaturs" are commendations of their respective publications, whereas the example from Milton seems to announce scrutiny of the work followed by a warrant to publish it without commendation.

29. John Spurr, *England in the 1670s: "This Masquerading Age"* (Oxford and Malden, Mass.: Blackwell Publishers, 2000), 15, 215, 220, with Spurr here quoting from *Calendar of State Papers Domestic 1670*, 322.

30. Spurr, *England in the 1670s*, 229, xii, 85.

31. Ibid., 94.

32. See Daniel Heinsius, *De Tragoediae Constitutione* (1611; reprint, Lugduni Batavorum, 1643), 170, 197–98, and the translation, *On Plot in Tragedy*, by Paul R. Sellin and John J. McManmon (Northridge, Ca.: San Fernando Valley State College, 1971), 116, 130.

33. Euripides' plays, as well as many by Aeschylus and Sophocles, have "Hypotheses" in the place of arguments, most of which are added to early manuscripts as part of the scholia. It is the tradition of Euripides, however, that contains the richest materials for the study of such hypotheses. Byzantine scholars of the thirteenth and fourteenth centuries elaborated what were largely descriptive hypotheses into "much more extensive prefaces" with exegetical hints and guides. See Rudolf Pfeiffer, *History of Classical Scholarship: From the Beginning to the End of the Hellenistic Age* (1968; reprint, Oxford: Clarendon Press, 1998), 196; see also 193–95.

34. See Francis Goldsmith's annotation in Grotius, *Sophompaneas*, tr. Goldsmith, 54. Goldsmith admits to following Vossius here, as well as Grotius's preface to Sophocles' *Electra*, 55.

35. Stephen B. Dobranski, "Samson and the Omissa," *Studies in English Literature 1500–1900* 36 (Winter 1996): 162, 163, and more recently, *Milton, Authorship, and the Book Trade* (Cambridge and New York: Cambridge University Press, 1999), 41–61.

36. Dobranski, *Milton, Authorship, and the Book Trade*, 56; see also 55.

37. See Erin Henriksen, "Sacred Reader, Sacred Writer," unpublished dissertation.

38. Anne Ferry, *The Title to the Poem* (Stanford, Ca.: Stanford University Press, 1996), [279].

39. Dobranski, "Samson and the Omissa," 152.

40. St. Ambrose also remarks of Lehi, "even today, the place is called Agon, because there Samson won a great victory by his overwhelming strength," although Ambrose also may be cited as one who argues that eventually "the Spirit of God departed from him"; see *Letters*, tr. Sister Mary Melchior Beyenka (New York: Fathers of the Church, 1954), 184, and then "The Holy Spirit," in *Theological and Dogmatic Works*, tr. Roy J. Deferrari (Washington, D. C.: Catholic University of America Press, 1963), 101. In the same work, Ambrose opines, now with reference to the Epistle to the Hebrews: "Would that he had been as careful to preserve grace as he was strong to overcome the beast!" (99).

41. See, e.g., Augustin Calmet (1672–1757), *Taylor's Edition of Calmet's Great Dictionary of the Holy Bible* (4 vols.; Charleston, Mass., 1812–14), 2 (no pagination): "Samson" and 4:76.

42. See John Lilburne, *The Iuglers Discovered* (London, 1647), 6. Robert Sanderson, *XXXIV Sermons*, 5th ed., rev. (London, 1671), 124: Sanderson has no doubt about the divine warrant of the judges but is

equally certain that it was "never intended by *God* that inspired them, or by those *Worthies* that did them, for *ordinary* or *general* examples." Joseph Hall follows Martin Luther when he argues: "All the acts of *Samson* are for wonder, not for imitation"; see Hall, *Contemplations on the Historical Passages of the Old and New Testaments* (3 vols.; Edinburgh, 1770), 1:361. These views are persistent. Thus Daniel Smith remarks that, "while charity may hope this was the case [that Samson repented and found pardon], the sacred history is far from holding him up as a model for our imitation"; and, similarly, William Anderson Scott, thinking Milton's interpretation less subtle than his own and Milton's representation of Samson inadequate to the occasion, says that "Samson's acts are more for our wonder than for our imitation." See Daniel Smith, *The Life of Samson* (New York, 1840), 94; and William Anderson Scott, *The Giant Judge: Or the Story of Samson, the Hebrew Hercules* (San Francisco, Ca., 1858), 309.

43. Peter Damian, *Letters 1–30*, tr. Owen J. Blum (Washington, D. C.: Catholic University of America Press, 1989), 253.

44. Peter Martyr (Pietro Martire Vermigli), *The Common Places of the Most Famous and Renowmed Divine Doctor*, tr. Anthonie Marten (London, 1583), pt. 2, 418.

45. Thomas Wood, *A Dialogue Between Mr. Prejudice . . . and Mr. Reason* (London, 1682), 21–22.

46. Martyr, *Common Places*, pt. 3, 182.

47. Paul Sellin, "The Last of the Renaissance Monsters: The *Poetical Institutions* of Gerardus Joannis Vossius and Some Observations on English Criticism," in *Anglo-Dutch Cross Currents in the Seventeenth and Eighteenth Centuries*, ed. Andrew Lossky (Los Angeles, Ca.: William Andrews Clark Memorial Library, 1976), 16.

48. Cf. Vondel, *Samson*, in *That Invincible Samson*, tr. and ed. Kirkconnell, 135.

49. Despite the title-page attribution to John Phillips, Robert W. Ayers proposes collaboration, concluding that this work "certainly issued from Milton's own household and . . . is probably in good part by Milton"; see "The Response of John Phillips [to John Rowland]," tr. James I. Armstrong, in *YP*, 4:876, 912.

50. Ben Jonson, *Seianus His Fall. A Tragoedie*, in *Ben Jonson*, ed. C. H. Herford and Percy Simpson (11 vols.; Oxford: Clarendon Press, 1932), 4:350.

51. Cf. *Electra*, in *The Plays of Euripides*, tr. Moses Hadas and John Harvey McLean (New York: Dial Press, 1936), 329: "Evil deeds afford precept and example to the good." St. Paul's reliance upon the Greek poets, "one of them a Tragedian," is remembered in *Areopagitica* as well (see *YP*, 2:508).

52. See Gerard Vossius, "Addend. *1. 2* Institut. Poetic.," as reprinted

by Grotius, *His Sophompaneas,* [B1], and also Vossius, *Poeticarum Institutionum* (Amsterdam, 1647), book 2 (separate pagination), 34, 72, and Index *d3.

53. John Carey, *The Complete Shorter Poems,* 2nd ed., ed. Carey (London and New York: Longmans, 1997), 356.

54. See E. R. Dodds's comment in Euripides, *Bacchae,* ed. Dodds, 2nd ed. (Oxford: Clarendon Press, 1960), lvi. On attribution, see John Edwin Sandys, *A History of Classical Scholarship: From the Sixth Century B.C. to the End of the Middle Ages,* 3rd ed. (3 vols.; 1920, reprint, New York: Hafter Publishing Co., 1958), 1:50, 417.

55. The practice is acknowledged but repudiated by Michael Cacoyannis, "Introduction," *The Bacchae,* tr. Cacoyannis (1982; reprint, New York: Meridian, 1987), xxiii–xxiv.

56. See William Riley Parker, *Milton's Debt to Greek Tragedy in "Samson Agonistes"* (Baltimore: Johns Hopkins Press, 1937), 247 (my italics), who seeks to replace the critical commonplace that Milton's debt was chiefly to Euripides — an argument made most notably by Sir Richard C. Jebb, *"Samson Agonistes* and the Hellenic Drama," *Proceedings of the British Academy* 3 (1907–08): 341–48.

57. Parker, *Milton's Debt to Greek Tragedy,* 247 (my italics), 6, 248, 123, 115, 205–06, 248.

58. Moses Hadas and John Harvey McLean, "Introduction," in *The Plays of Euripides,* tr. Hadas and McLean, xiii.

59. See Roger Ascham, *The Scholemaster,* in *Elizabethan Critical Essays,* ed. G. Gregory Smith (2 vols.; London: Oxford University Press, 1904), 1:24; and Charlton, *The Senecan Tradition,* l.

60. See George Buchanan, *Jephtha,* in *Tragedies,* ed. P. Sharratt and P. G. Walsh (Edinburgh: Scottish Academic Press, 1983), 94, 16, 78, 82–83.

61. See Buchanan, *The Baptist,* ibid., 149, [21], [95].

62. See Ann Norris Michelini, *Euripides and the Tragic Tradition* (Madison: University of Wisconsin Press, 1987), 233.

63. Burnett, *Catastrophe Survived,* 172–73, 180.

64. Norma T. Pratt, *Seneca's Drama* (Chapel Hill and London: University of North Carolina Press, 1983), 25.

65. For these quotations from *Hercules Furens,* see *Seneca His Tenne Tragedies,* tr. Jasper Heywood, ed. Thomas Newton (1581; reprint, Bloomington and London: Indiana University Press, 1964), 24, 41.

66. Ibid., 50.

67. Ibid., 32–33.

68. See Pratt, *Seneca's Drama,* 116–17; see also 121.

69. Thomas Fuller, *A Pisgah-sight of Palestine and the Confines Thereon* (London, 1650), 214.

70. For these quotations from Euripides' *Heracles,* see *The Complete*

Greek Tragedies: Euripides II, tr. William Arrowsmith, ed. David Grene and Richard Lattimore (1956; reprint, Chicago and London: University of Chicago Press, 1969), 62.

71. Ibid., 63, 88, 111.

72. Ibid., 113, 114, 115.

73. Pratt, *Seneca's Drama*, 28.

74. For these quotations, see Euripides, *"Alcestis" and Other Plays*, tr. John Davie, ed. Richard Rutherford (London and New York: Penguin Books, 1996), 119, 104, 106, 107.

75. For these references to and quotations from Euripides, see *The Bacchae*, tr. Cacoyannis, 28, 82, 48.

76. Ibid., 6, 49, 69.

77. Milton's own revulsion at blood sacrifice is clearly evident in his marginal note to *The Heraclidae* where he remarks on the "extreme horror" with which "the oracle commanding Macaria's sacrifice to the gods is heard"; see *The Works of John Milton*, ed. Frank Allen Patterson et al. (18 vols.; New York: Columbia University Press, 1931–38), 18:316.

78. Desiderius Erasmus remarks: "beware lesse with theyr tales they deceyve you, and bryng you into a previouse erroure, always remembring, what was truly sayd of a certaine poete of yours: euyll woordes corrupte good maners." See *The Paraphrase of Erasmus upon the Newe Testament* (2 vols.; London, 1548–49), 2 (second pagination): xli.

79. Hugo Grotius, *The Rights of War and Peace: Including the Law of Nature and of Nations*, tr. A. C. Campbell (New York and London: M. Walter Dunne, 1901), 225.

80. Merritt Y. Hughes, ed., *"Paradise Regained" . . . and "Samson Agonistes"* (New York: Odyssey Press, 1937), 539.

81. See Jean Le Clerc, *The Lives of Clemens Alexandrinus, . . . Gregory Nazianzen, and Prudentius the Christian Poet* (London, 1696), 276; and also the headpiece to the annotations by Sandys, in Grotius, *Christs Passion*, [74].

82. William Stanley MacBean Knight, *The Life and Works of Hugo Grotius*, Grotius Society Publications, No. 4 (London: Sweet and Maxwell, 1925), 117–19.

83. See the annotation by Sandys to *Christs Passion* by Grotius, [74].

84. See Robert Cooke, *Censvra Qvorvndam Scriptorvm* (London, 1614), 118–19. In addition to Vossius, Cooke cites Roberto Bellarmino, *De Scriptoribvs Ecclesiasticis* (Coloniae Agrippinae, 1613), 50–51, 130, 134–36 and Baronius, *Annali Ecclesiastici Tratti da quelli del Cardinal Baronio per Odorico Rinaldi Trivigiano* (Rome, 1583), 1:444, no. 135–36; plus Antonii Possevini, *Apparatus Ad Omnium Gentivm Historiam* (Venice, 1597), the last of whom is supposed to have said: "The tragedy of Christ under the name of Gregory Nazianzenus is not by him . . .: That tragedy which is entitled Christus Patiens, is rightfully judged

by learned men to be the work of Apollinaris Laodicenus rather than Gregory" (see Cooke, 118–19). In this summary by Cooke, Vossius is said to draw attention to the corresponding plays by Gregory and Grotius, yet complains about Gregory being overly "comic in the tragedy"; and Bellarmino thinks the play is lacking Gregory's usual "seriousness," especially in its descriptions of Mary "mourning."

85. See Sandys, tr.; the dedication to King Charles, in *Christs Passion* by Grotius, [a4v].

86. See Grotius, *Christs Passion*, tr. Sandys, 73, 68.

87. Knight, *The Life and Works of Hugo Grotius*, 117–18.

88. See Grotius, *Christs Passion*, tr. Sandys, 5–6, 55, 107.

89. See ibid. While "English scholars of the Reformed Faith appear to have begun the attack upon St. Gregory," it was the so-called Leyden group, which, rather than asserting Gregory's authorship, allowed the question of the play's authorship to remain open (ibid., 118–19). What finally caused so many, both Protestant and Catholic, to surrender on the question of Gregory's authorship was the discrepancy between his own theological conservatism and the radically unorthodox theology of the play. What perplexes Daniel Heinsius, who is inclined to credit the play to Gregory, "if, in fact, this is his writing," is his knowledge that Suidas, in supposedly attributing the play to Gregory, "does not mention it by name," together with his sense that, stylistically, there is something rash in the play; see Heinsius, *De Tragoediae Constitutione*, 198, and also the translation by Sellin and McManmon, *Of Plot in Tragedy*, 130, as well as Justus Lipsius, *De Cruce* (1593; Antwerp, 1594), 47–48, 119, where Gregory's authorship is assumed as it had been in volume 38 of *Patrologia Graeca*, ed. Jacques Paul Migne (Paris, 1862), devoted to Gregory Nazianzen and in cols. 131–338 devoted to *Christus Patiens, Tragoedia*. Vossius, as earlier observed, allows for the possibility that either Gregory or Apollinaris is the author of *Christos Paschon*; see *Poeticarum Institutionum*, book 2 (separate pagination), 34, 72, and Index *d3.

90. Cf.: Grotius, *Sophompameas*, tr. Goldsmith, 23, and *Samson Agonistes* (667).

91. I adapt this phrase from the prose translation of George Buchanan's *Baptistes* (at one time attributed to Milton): *Tyrannicall-Government Anatomized*, 28.

92. See the epigraph to Primo Levy's *The Awakening*, tr. Stuart Woolf (1965; reprint, New York and London: Simon and Schuster, 1995).

93. See Lord Falkland's "To the Author," in Grotius, *Christs Passion*, tr. Sandys, [a7].

94. This and all subsequent translations of *Christos Paschon*, based on the Bramb edition cited in fn. 2 above, are by Alan Fishbone of The Greek and Latin Institute, The Graduate Center, The City University of New York. Hereafter, citations, given by line number, appear parenthetically in the text.

95. See Grotius, *Christs Passion* tr. Sandys, 13, 15, 70, 36.

96. Kirkconnell, *That Invincible Samson*, esp. "Descriptive Catalogue," 143–215.

97. Euripides, *The Bacchae*, tr. Cacoyannis, 50–51, 58.

98. Debora Kuller Shuger, *The Renaissance Bible: Scholarship, Sacrifice, and Subjectivity* (Berkeley, Los Angeles, and London: University of California Press, 1994), esp. 89–127.

99. See Thomas Pierce, *A Decad of Caveats to the People of England, Of General Use in All Times* (London, 1679), 364; *Christos Paschon* (747, 1646–47); and Grotius, *Christs Passion*, tr. Sandys, 73.

100. See Henry Smith, *Twelve Sermons Preached by Mr. Henry Smith* (London, 1629), Dv; and Edmund Staunton, *Rupes Israelis: The Rock of Israel. A Little Part of Its Glory* (London, 1644), 12.

101. See Thomas Pierce, *A Correct Copy of Some Notes Concerning Gods Decrees, Especially of Reprobation* (London, 1655), 11; and the annotation by Sandys to *Christs Passion* by Grotius, tr. Sandys, 78.

102. Richard Baxter, *The Grotian Religion Discovered, At the Invitation of Mr. Thomas Pierce in His Vindication* (London, 1658), B3.

103. George Sandys, *The Poetical Works of George Sandys*, ed. Richard Hooper (2 vols.; London, 1872), 2:[481].

104. See James Shapiro, *Oberammergau: The Troubling Story of the World's Most Famous Passion Play* (New York: Pantheon Books, 2000), 97, and also "Fragments from the Lost Writings of Irenaeus," in *The Anti-Nicene Fathers*, ed. Alexander Roberts and James Donaldson (10 vols.; New York, 1899), 8:572.

105. Hugo Grotius, *Of the Rights of War and Peace . . . in Which Are Explained the Laws and Claims of Nature and Nations*, tr. John Morrice (3 vols.; London, 1715), 1:122.

106. See Sandys, tr., *Christs Passion* by Grotius, 45, 58, 113–14.

107. George Sandys, *A Relation of a Journey Begun An: Dom: 1610* (London, 1637), 149.

108. Fuller, *Pisgah-sight*, 214.

109. See both Davis P. Harding, *The Club of Hercules: Studies in the Classical Background of "Paradise Lost,"* Illinois Studies in Language and Literature: Vol. 50 (Urbana: University of Illinois Press, 1962), 99, and G. Karl Galensky, *The Herakles Theme: The Adaptations of the Hero in Literature from Homer to the Twelfth Century* (Totowa, N. J.: Rowman and Littlefield, 1972), 205–06. For a discussion of Samson as "a Herculean hero," see Carol S. Kessner, "Milton's Hebraic Herculean Samson," *Milton Studies* 6 (1975): 243–58; Anthony Low, *The Blaze of Noon: A Reading of "Samson Agonistes"* (New York and London: Columbia University Press, 1974), 176–79; and John Mulryan, "Through a Glass Darkly": Milton's Reinvention of the Mythological Tradition (Pittsburgh: Duquesne University Press, 1996), 132–36; also Sir Richard C. Jebb, "*Samson Agonistes* and the Hellenic Drama," 341–48, and J. C.

Maxwell, "Milton's Samson and Sophocles' Heracles," *Philological Quarterly* 33 (January 1954): 90–91. Maxwell, like Low, pursues similitudes, whereas Jebb commences the enquiry to which my own book returns. Hercules and Samson — "how far is the parallel just? what are the points of analogy?" (345).

110. William Massey, *Remarks upon Milton's "Paradise Lost"* (London, 1761), 70.

111. Sandys, *A Relation of a Journey*, 149.

112. Grotius, *Christs Passion*, tr. Sandys, 45, 113–14, 15, 6.

113. See Grotius, *Of the Rights of War and Peace*, tr. Morrice, 2:606: cf. 1:118, 121–22; and *Opera Omnia Theologica* (3 vols.; Amsterdam, 1679), 3:114.

114. See Jean Levesque de Burigny, *The Life of the Truly Eminent and Learned Hugo Grotius* (London, 1754), 19.

115. See Vossius in *Sophompaneas* by Grotius, tr. Goldsmith, [B1–B1v] (first pagination).

116. See Goldsmith in ibid., [A3v] (second pagination).

117. Thomas Pierce, *A Decad of Caveats*, 290–91.

118. See Grotius's dedicatory epistle, *Sophompaneas*, tr. Goldsmith, [A6].

119. See Goldmsith, in ibid., B3.

120. For Grotius on Hercules, see *Of the Rights of War and Peace*, ed. Morrice, 2:507.

121. See Grotius, *Sophompaneas*, tr. Goldsmith, 15, 24, 23.

122. Ibid., 41, and *Samson Agonistes*, line 10.

123. Lancelot Andrewes, *Ninety-Six Sermons by . . . Lancelot Andrewes*, ed. J. P. Wilson (5 vols.; Oxford, 1840–43), 4:[241]; see also 248–49.

124. Matthew Poole et al., *Annotations upon the Holy Bible* (2 vols.; London, 1683, 1685), 1: annotations to Judges 13.25 and 18.19.

125. Shuger, *The Renaissance Bible*, 91, 90.

126. Ibid., 5.

127. In this paragraph, I have consolidated various perspectives, each valuable in its own right, into a context for reading *Samson Agonistes*; see Shuger, 7, 9, 32, 137.

128. See Jerome Ziegler, *Samson, A New Tragedy*, in *That Invincible Samson: The Theme of "Samson Agonistes" in World Literature*, tr. and ed. Watson Kirkconnell (Toronto: University of Toronto Press, 1964), 4.

129. Grotius, *Sophompaneas*, tr. Goldsmith, [A5].

130. See John Penn, *Letters on the Drama* (London, 1796), 53–57, 33, 36–37, and *Critical, Poetical, and Dramatic Works* (2 vols.; London, 1798), 2:222. In *Letters*, Penn is particularly struck by "the effect of apt allusions . . . and political remarks" in *Samson Agonistes* (74). See also William Mickle, "A Critique on the *Samson Agonistes* of Milton in Refutation of the Censures of Dr. Johnson," *European Magazine* 13 (June

1788): 401–06. And for Gotthold Ephraim Lessing's view of tragedy, see *The Laocoon, and Other Prose Writings of Lessing*, tr. and ed. W. B. Rönnfeldt (London: Walter Scott, n.d.), 214.

131. Gotthold Ephraim Lessing, *Lessing's Theological Writings*, tr. Henry Chadwick (London: Adam and Charles Black, 1956), 16–17.

132. Clement of Alexandria, "The Second Epistle," in *The Ante-Nicene Fathers*, ed. Roberts and Donaldson, 8:6.

133. David Pareus, *A Commentary upon the Divine Revelation of the Apostle and Evangelist John*, tr. Elias Arnold (Amsterdam, 1644), 26 (first pagination).

134. See Sandys's annotation in *Christs Passion* by Grotius, 119.

135. See, e.g., Ziegler, *Samson, A New Tragedy*, in *That Invincible Samson*, tr. and ed. Kirkconnell, 9, 10.

136. Shoulson, *Milton and the Rabbis*, 241.

137. C. A. Patrides, *Milton and the Christian Tradition* (Oxford: Clarendon Press, 1966), 130.

138. Grotius, *Christs Passion*, tr. Sandys, 59, 23.

139. As quoted by Patrides, *Milton and the Christian Tradition*, 134. John Rogers reports and reviews the larger context in which Gregory's phrase appears. See Rogers's essay, "Delivering Redemption in *Samson Agonistes*," in *Altering Eyes: New Perspectives on "Samson Agonistes*," ed. Mark R. Kelley and Joseph Wittreich (Newark: University of Delaware Press, and London: Associated University Presses, 2002), 83; as well as his source, *Nicene and Post-Nicene Fathers*, ed. Philip Schaff and Henry Wace, 2nd series (14 vols.; Grand Rapids, Mich.: Eerdmans, 1983), 7:431.

140. See Shapiro, *Oberammergau*, 65; cf. 14–15, 60.

141. Ibid., 82, from which I borrow the phrase, not the application of it. Shapiro's book reports two important facts of literary/cultural history relevant to the present discussion: first, "Plays about the Crucifixion didn't exist before the twelfth or thirteenth centuries"; and second, the period between the twelfth and fifteenth centuries experienced a "proliferation of Passion treatises" (48, 49).

142. John Weemes, *The Christian Synagogue* (London, 1623), 49.

143. Rebecca W. Bushnell, *Prophesying Tragedy: Sign and Voice in Sophocles' Theban Plays* (Ithaca, N. Y. and London: Cornell University Press, 1988), 109.

144. See Vossius, *Poeticarum Institutionum* (Amsterdam, 1647), book 2 (separate pagination), 34. Later, Buchanan's plays are added to the mix; ibid., 72.

145. Euripides, *Heracles*, in *The Complete Greek Tragedies*, tr. Arrowsmith, ed. Grene and Lattimore, 111.

146. Michelini, *Euripides and the Tragic Tradition*, 262.

147. Eve Kosofsky Sedgwick, *Epistemology of the Closet* (Berkeley and Los Angeles: University of California Press, 1990), 48.

148. See Peggy Anne Samuels, "*Samson Agonistes* and Renaissance Drama," unpublished diss., The Graduate Center of The City University of New York, 1993, 44; and Richard S. Ide, "The Renaissance Dramatic Heritage of *Samson Agonistes*," *Soundings of Things Done: Essays in Early Modern Literature in Honor of S. K. Heninger Jr.*, ed. Peter E. Medine and Joseph Wittreich (Newark: University of Delaware Press; London: Associated University Presses, 1997), esp. 152–57 and 173–74, on the contradictory implications of the triple simile with which *Samson Agonistes* concludes.

149. I am improvising upon Weemes's theory of "double reading"; see *The Christian Synagogue*, 32.

Notes to Chapter 2

1. J. Alberto Soggin, *Judges: A Commentary* (London: SCM Press, 1981), 258. Negative criticism of Samson, says Soggin, is "a line begun by Martin Luther," while the line of positive representation is exemplified by Milton (259). The history, as well as Milton's place therein, is vastly more complicated than Soggin acknowledges.

2. See Gladys J. Willis, *The Penalty of Eve: John Milton and Divorce* (New York, Berne, and Frankfurt am Maim: Peter Lang, 1984), 110; and Leland Ryken, "Introduction," in *Milton and Scriptural Tradition: The Bible into Poetry*, ed. James H. Sims and Leland Ryken (Columbia: University of Missouri Press, 1984), 15. See also F. Michael Krouse, *Milton's Samson and the Christian Tradition* (Princeton: Princeton University Press for the University of Cincinnati, 1949), who accepts Samson's sainthood as incontrovertible both in the tradition and in Milton's poem: "The Samson whom we meet in Milton's play is a saint" (104). "Rupert of St. Heribert," is, says Krouse, "the only commentator who ever called Samson's sainthood in question" (130). Murray Roston also thinks that if *Samson Agonistes* has a biblical counterpart, it is Job not Judges. But more important, "the sensitive, soul-searching hero" of Milton's poem, once brutish but now tragic, exhibits "a profound moral consciousness," thus finding his counterparts not only in Job but in Hercules; see "Milton's Herculean Samson," *Milton Quarterly* 16 (December 1982): 85.

3. Desiderius Erasmus on the Epistle to the Hebrews, *Paraphrases on the Epistles*, in *Collected Works of Erasmus*, tr. John J. Bateman (86 vols.; Toronto and London: University of Toronto Press, 1993), 44:250, 252.

4. Here I follow Mieke Bal, *Death and Dissymmetry: The Politics of Coherence in the Book of Judges* (Chicago and London: University of Chicago Press, 1988), 9 (epigraph), in quoting from Robert G. Boling,

Judges: Introduction, Translation, and Commentary (New York: Doubleday, 1975), 3 (epigraph). The translation in *The Geneva Bible,* ed. Lloyd E. Berry (Madison, Milwaukee, and London: University of Wisconsin Press, 1969), reads: "Concerning the Iudges, euerie one by name, whose heart went out a whoring, not departed from the God, their memory be blessed. Let their bones flourish out of their place, and their names by succession remaine to them that are moste famous of their children."

5. Alexander A. DiLella, *The Anchor Bible: The Wisdom of Ben Sira,* tr. Patrick W. Skehan (New York: Doubleday, 1987), 520.

6. See, e.g., Joan S. Bennett, "Dalila, Eve, and the 'Concept of Woman' in Milton's Radical Christian Humanism," in *Arenas of Conflict: Milton and the Unfettered Mind,* ed. Kristin Pruitt McColgan and Charles W. Durham (Selinsgrove: Susquehanna University Press; London: Associated University Presses, 1997), 252.

7. See Harold Fisch, *Poetry with a Purpose: Biblical Poetics and Interpretation* (Bloomington: Indiana University Press, 1988).

8. James H. Sims, "Preface," in *Milton and Scriptural Tradition: The Bible into Poetry,* ed. James H. Sims and Leland Ryken (Columbia: University of Missouri, 1984), vii (my italics).

9. Ibid., viii.

10. See Regina M. Schwartz, *The Curse of Cain: The Violent Legacy of Monotheism* (Chicago and London: University of Chicago Press, 1997), esp. 128–32.

11. Fisch, *Poetry with a Purpose,* 5.

12. Frank Kermode, *The Art of Telling: Essays on Fiction* (Cambridge, Mass.: Harvard University Press, 1983), 191; cf. 199.

13. See Franz Joseph Schierse, *The Epistle to the Hebrews,* tr. Bene Fahy, ed. John L. McKenzie (London: Burns and Oates,1969), 97; Alexander C. Purdy and J. Harry Cotton, *The Interpreter's Bible,* ed. George Arthur Buttrick et al. (12 vols.; Nashville: Abingdon Press, 1952–57), 11:734; and Theodore H. Robinson, *The Epistle to the Hebrews,* ed. James Moffatt (New York: Harper and Brothers, 1933), 172.

14. See, e.g., Bernhard W. Anderson, *Understanding the Old Testament,* 4th ed. (Englewood Cliffs, N. J.: Prentice Hall, 1986), 201; W. Lee Humphreys, *Crisis and Story: Introduction to the Old Testament* (Palo Alto, Ca.: Mayfield, 1979), 32; Claus Schedl, *History of the Old Testament* (5 vols.; Staten Island, N. Y.: Alba House, 1972–73), 2:277; and Charles F. Pfeiffer, *Old Testament History* (Grand Rapids, Mich.: Baker Book House, 1973), 230.

15. John M'Clintock and James Strong, *Cyclopaedia of Biblical, Theological, and Ecclesiastical Literature* (12 vols.; New York, 1887–89), 9:314.

16. Ibid., 9:314.

17. Ibid., 9:316. Hermann Samuel Reimarus spent twenty years completing a work left unpublished until after his death, when Gotthold Ephraim Lessing, obtaining some fragments of the study, published them under the title, *Woffenbutteler Fragmente* in 1774 and 1777, with other fragments brought forth by different writers in 1787 and 1862. The fragments posed a radical challenge to Christian orthodoxy.

18. F. Michael Krouse, *Milton's Samson and the Christian Tradition* (Princeton: Princeton University Press for the University of Cincinnati, 1949), 47; see also 48–49.

19. Louis Ginzberg, *The Legends of the Jews*, tr. Henrietta Szold (7 vols.; Philadelphia: Jewish Publications of America, 1909–38), 4:47.

20. James Peirce, *A Paraphrase and Notes on the Epistle of St. Paul*, 2nd ed. (4 vols.; London, 1733), 4:45, 46.

21. Peirce, *A Dictionary of the Holy Bible*, (3 vols.; London, 1759), 1:381, 3:1116–17, 1:382.

22. For the quotation, see John Dunton, *The Athenian Gazette: or Casuistical Mercury* (5 vols.; London, 1691), 1: no. 25. Dunton here provides the first explicit criticism of *Samson Agonistes* (see ibid., 5: no. 14), within the same piece in which he appraises Buchanan and Grotius as poets. But see also Mary Astell, *The Christian Religion, As Profess'd by a Daughter of the Church of England* (London, 1705), 213, cf. 354; and William Walsh, *A Dialogue Concerning Women, Being a Defence of the Sex. Written to Eugenia* (London, 1691), 80–81. Lines 7–10 are the relevant verses in Marvell's dedicatory poem.

23. See Simon Wastell, *Microbiblion or the Bibles Epitome* (London, 1629), 467–68; Joseph Exon (Joseph Hall), *A Plaine and Familiar Explication (by Way of Paraphrase) of All the Hard Texts of the Whole Divine Scripture* (London, 1632–33), 342 (second pagination); Thomas Taylor (1576–1633), *Christ Revealed: Or the Old Testament Explained* (London, 1635), 57–62; Thomas Lushington, *The Expiation of a Sinner. In a Commentary Vpon the Epistle to the Hebrewes* (London, 1646), 280–81; Paul Knell, *Israel and England Paralelled* (London, 1648), 5; and Henry Hammond, *A Paraphrase, and Annotations upon All the Books of the New Testament: Briefly Explaining All the Difficult Places Thereof*, 5th ed. (London, 1675), 756, 895. The quotation is from Thomas Wilson (1563–1622), *A Complete Christian Dictionary*, 8th ed. (London, 1678), n.p.

24. David Pareus (1548–1622), *Theological Miscellanies*, tr. A. R., in Zacharias Ursinus, *The Theologicall Summe of Christian Religion* (London, 1645), 843. The interrogation, if still overruled by polemic, is more forcefully represented by Joseph Wybarne who, though he may not approve of the fact, makes clear that to many (especially poets) the interrogation is what really matters: "The deedes of *Sampson* are scoft at by many, not knowing with what spirit he did them"; at the same

time, at least in Judges, Samson's sins "are registred with the point of a Diamond in the glasse of true history"; see *The New Age of Old Names* (London, 1609), 72, 73. Wybarne arrives at his own estimate apparently by privileging the Hebrews over the Judges Samson and thinks others should do the same.

25. Hugo Grotius (1583–1645), *Of the Rights of War and Peace . . . in Which Are Explained the Laws and Claims of Nature and Nations*, tr. John Morrice et al. (3 vols.; London, 1715), 2:452.

26. William Gouge, *A Commentary on the Whole Epistle to the Hebrews* (2 vols.; London, 1655), 2:173–74, 176–77, 178–79. Gouge died in 1653; this commentary was first published in 1655.

27. Samuel Bird, *The Lectures of Samuel Bird of Ipswidge vpon the 11. Chapter of the Epistle vnto the Hebrewes, and vpon the 38. Psalme.* (London, 1598), esp. 95–103.

28. William Perkins (1558–1602), *A Clovd of Faithfvll Witnesses, Leading to the Heavenly Canaan* (1607; rpt. London, 1622), 464. Other editions: 1608, 1609, 1618. 1631.

29. Ibid., and see also *The Souldiers Pocket Bible* (London, 1643), 2–4.

30. Grotius, *Of the Rights of War and Peace*, tr. Morrice et al., 2:463.

31. Perkins, *A Cloude of Faithfull Witnesses*, 172–73, 460.

32. William Perkins, "A Treatise of Vocations, Or, Callings of Men" and "A Direction for the Government of the Tongve According to Gods Word," in *The Works of That Famovs and Worthie Minister of Christ . . . W. Perkins* (Cambridge, 1605), 905, 536.

33. See William Perkins, *A Godly and Learned Exposition or Commentarie vpon the Three First Chapters of the Reuelation* (London, 1607), 172; plus also by Perkins, "A Declaration of the Trve Manner of Knowing Christ Crucified" and "A Warning against the Idolatrie of the Last Times," in *Works*, 716, 838. Perkins knows that in Revelation some "have their names blotted out" because, in sinning, they renege upon their faith but also seems reluctant to identify Samson with Dan in this respect; see his *A Godly and Learned Exposition or Commentary upon the First Three Chapters of the Revelation* (London, 1606), 174, and "A Table . . . Booke of Life," sig. 3v.

34. Perkins, *A Godly and Learned Exposition* (1607), 94, 131–32.

35. David Dickson (1583?–1663), *A Short Explanation, of the Epistle of Pavl to the Hebrewes* (Aberdene, 1635), 275. Other editions appeared in 1637, 1649 and 1839.

36. See *Select Practical Writings of David Dickson* (Edinburgh, 1845), 12.

37. Dickson, *A Short Explanation*, 276.

38. John Bramhall, "Discourse II: Sermon Before the Marquis of Newcastle" (January 28, 1643–44), in *The Works of . . . John Bramhall* (5 vols.; Oxford, 1842–45), 5:100.

39. Dickson, *A Short Explanation*, 275–76; cf. also by David Dickson, *An Exposition of All Pauls Epistles*, tr. William Retchford (London, 1659), 211; see also 207–08.

40. See Dickson, *An Exposition*, tr. Retchford 207; and cf. also by David Dickson, *The Epistle of Paul to the Hebrews* (London, 1659), 262, 267. The two volumes are bound together with the British Library Shelf No. 1602/51[.] Other editions: 1684, 1764.

41. David Dickson, *Truth's Victory over Error* (Edinburgh, 1634), 66, 68.

42. Ibid., 125–36.

43. Thomas Ager, *A Paraphrase on the Canticles, Or, Song of Solomon* (London, 1680), 144.

44. John Trapp (1601–1669), *A Commentary or Exposition upon All the Epistles and the Revelation of John the Divine* (London, 1647), 394; cf. Trapp, *A Commentary or Exposition upon All the Books of the New Testament* (London, 1646), 890; and *Annotations upon the Old and New Testament* (5 vols.; London, 1654–62), 5:890. For Trapp's reading of the Samson story in Judges, see ibid., 1:81–93 (second pagination).

45. Trapp, *A Commentary . . . upon All the Epistles and the Revelation*, in the section called *Mellisicum Theologcum* and under the headings, "Apostasie," 682–83 (my italics).

46. Trapp, "Anger," in ibid., 668, and "Apostasie," in ibid., 682.

47. John Trapp, *Theologia Theologiae, The True Treasure; or a Treasury of Holy Truths* (London, 1641), 115, 154–55; and *A Commentary . . . upon All the Epistles and the Revelation*, 64.

48. Trapp, *A Commentary . . . upon All the Epistles and the Revelation*, 518; cf. Hugh Broughton, *A Revelation of the Holy Apocalyps* (London, 1610), 27: "They be shallow who hence gesse that Antichrist commeth of Dan"; and also: "The *Antichrist*, by imitation of idoles, is *Dans* childe" (328). For Trapp's knowledge of Hebraic traditions, see *Theologica Theologiae*, 346. The crossing of the Genesis and Revelation texts is common. See, e.g., John Marbeck, *A Booke of Notes and Commonplaces, with Their Expositions* (London, 1581), 277; John Napier, *A Plaine Discouery of the Whole Reuelation of Saint John* (Edinburgh, 1593), 119; Franciscus Junius, *The Apocalyps, or Revelation of S. John* (Cambridge, 1596), 83; David Pareus, *A Commentary upon the Divine Revelation of the Apostle and Evangelist John*, tr. Elias Arnold (Amsterdam, 1644), 144; and John Downame et al., *Annotations upon All the Books of the Old and New Testament* (London, 1645), 1: annotation for Genesis 49.16–17. Often in the seventeenth century, the Book of Judges is another of the crossing threads. See, e.g., Francis Rollenson, *Twelve Propheticall Legacies: or Twelve Sermons upon Jacobs Last Will and Testament* (London, 1612), 141–53; Thomas Cartwright, *A Plaine Explanation of the Whole Revelation of Saint John* (London, 1622), [95 (misnumbered 25)]; Joseph Mede, *The Key of the Revelation*, tr. Richard More (London, 1650), 74; Theodore Haak, *The Dutch*

Annotations upon the New Testament (London, 1657), note for Revelation 7.7; and John Lightfoot, "A Sermon Preached at Hertford Assize, March 13, 1663. Judges, XX.27, 28," in *The Whole Works of the Rev. John Lightfoot, D. D.*, ed. John Rogers Pitman (13 vols.; London, 1821–1825), 6:278. It should also be noted that, especially in the seventeenth century, whereas the Revelation commentators would place a negative construction on Jacob's prophecy, the Genesis interpreters tended toward positive formulations. See, e.g., Henry Ainsworth, *Annotations upon the First Book of Moses* ([London] 1616), annotation to 49.16–18; Andrew Willet, *Hexapla in Genesin, That Is, A Sixfold Commentarie vpon Genesis* (London, 1605), 453–54, 459; and George Hughes, *An Analytical Exposition of the Whole First Book of Moses, Called Genesis* (n.p., 1672), 593–94. Cf. Gervase Babington, *Certaine Plaine, Briefe, and Comfortable Notes, vpon Euery Chapter of Genesis* (London, 1596), 349–50; and William Whately, *Prototypes, Or, The Primarie Precedent Presidents Ovt of the Booke of Genesis* (London, 1640), pt. 2, 130–37. Although Whately's point is that all of Jacob's sons are "guilty of beguiling . . . with purposed fraud and guile" (pt. 2, 130), he resists including Samson in the general condemnation, citing him instead among the good examples of how to effect a marriage (pt. 1, 251).

49. John Diodati, *Pious Annotations upon the Holy Bible Expounding the Difficult Places There: of Learnedly and Plainly* (London, 1643), 35 (first pagination).

50. John Trapp, *A Clavis to the Bible. Or a New Comment upon the Pentateuch* (London, 1650), 378; and *A Commentary . . . upon All the Epistles and the Revelation*, 233.

51. Diodati, *Pious Annotations*, 73 (fourth pagination).

52. John Goodwin, *Apolutrosis polutroseos or Redemption Redeemed* (London, 1651), 365.

53. John Trapp, *Gods Love-Tokens, and the Afflicted Mans Lessons* (London, 1637), 60.

54. Henoch Clapham, *A Briefe of the Bibles History*, 4th ed. (1603; rpt. London, 1639), 63, 207. Or as Trapp remarks in an annotation for the verse in Judges: "although they lived in Gods good Land, yet because not by Gods good Laws, nor had at this time any supream Magistrate, therefore all was out of order, and their *Anarchy* begat a general *Ataxy*"; see *Annotations upon the Old and New Testament*, 1:109 (second pagination).

55. Henry Hammond, *A Paraphrase, and Annotations upon All the Books of the New Testament: Briefly Explaining All the Difficult Places Thereof*, 5th ed. (London, 1675), 756, 895. I deliberately cite Hammond again in order to emphasize that, despite the seventeenth century interrogation of the Samson story, the then orthodox reading of it persists. By 1675, however, this orthodoxy no longer prevails.

56. Henry Hammond, *A Practical Catechism* (1644; reprint, London, 1715), 108.

57. Ibid., 108.

58. If a matter of dispute during the sixteenth and seventeenth centuries, the notion of reading Samson in Dan persists, both in Jewish and Christian tradition; see, e.g., W. Gunther Plaut, *The Torah: A Modern Commentary* (New York: Union of America Hebrew Congregations, 1981), 309; and Robert Renney, *The Prophetic Blessings of Jacob and of Moses, Respecting the Twelve Tribes of Israel* (Philadelphia, 1832), 64–69. Menahem M. Kasher uses the idea that the twenty words of the original Hebrew prophecy signify the twenty years of Samson's judgeship to sanction this tradition. He also arrays the different senses in which Samson is a serpent and various reasons why Samson is no savior; see *Encyclopedia of Biblical Interpretation* (9 vols.; New York: America Biblical Encyclopedia Society, 1953–79), 6:186–89. Carl Friedrich Keil and Franz Delitzsch enlist venerable tradition to make their case: "the later Targums (*Jerusalem* and *Jonathan*) interpret these words as Messianic, but with special reference to Samson, and paraphrase . . . thus: 'Not for the deliverance of Gideon . . . and not for the redemption of Samson . . .; but for the redemption of the Messiah . . . my soul waits'"; moreover, "while the Targumists and several fathers connect the serpent in the way with Samson, by many the serpent in the way is supposed to be Antichrist"; see *Biblical Commentary on the Old Testament*, tr. James Martin (10 vols.; Peabody, Mass: Hendrickson, 1989), 1:404, 405. The fullest discussion of this tradition during the early modern period is provided by Rollenson, *Twelve Propheticall Legacies*, 135–57, though Rollenson, even as he represents this tradition, disassociates Samson from it, aligning him instead with the saints and heroes of Revelation. Rollenson obviously remembers the declaration of St. Jerome: "[Samson] surely reminds us of Jacob's prophecy"; see "Against Jovinianus," in *A Select Library of Nicene and Post-Nicene Fathers: St. Jerome*, ed. Philip Schaff and Henry Wace (14 vols.; Grand Rapids, Mich.: Eerdmans,1983), 6:363. Jerome, in turn, is probably following the three Chaldee paraphrasts: Onkelos, Jonathan, and Jerusalem.

According to Martin Luther, Samson and Dan are irrevocably involved in Jacob's prophecy, which is given a highly positive interpretation; see *Luther's Commentary on Genesis*, tr. John Theodore Mueller (2 vols.; Grand Rapids, Mich.: Zondervan, 1958), 2:356. On the other hand, John Calvin thinks this prophecy, both particular and general, refers to Samson in only one of its aspects and, though "no judgment is expressly passed, whether this subtlety of Dan is to be deemed worthy of praise or of censure," still refers to him in such a way as to allow for censure; see *Commentaries on the First Book of Moses Called Genesis*, tr. John King (2 vols.; Edinburgh, 1847–50), 2:462–63.

Finally, Simon Patrick represents a third interpretive possibility, that of acknowledging the tradition and of tracing it to Onkelos, but not crediting it, or crediting it only as a general prophecy in which Dan means *Dan*; see *A Commentary upon the First Book of Moses, Called Genesis* (London, 1695), 622. See also Henry Ainsworth, *Annotations upon the Five Books of Moses* (1616; reprint, London, 1639), 168; Willett, *Hexapla in Genesin*, 395; John Richardson, *Choice Observations and Explanations upon the Old Testament* (London, 1655), note for Genesis 49.16–17; John Lightfoot, "A Chronicle of the Times, and the Order of the Texts, of the Old Testament," in *The Whole Works of the Rev. John Lightfoot*, ed. John Rogers Pitman (13 vols., London, 1821–25), 2:106, 150; John Gill, *An Exposition of the Old Testament* (6 vols.; Philadelphia, 1810–17), 2:373–75; George Hughes, *An Analytical Exposition of . . . Genesis*, 593–94; Thomas Pyle, *A Paraphrase with Short and Useful Notes on the Books of the Old Testament* (4 vols.; London, 1717–25), 1: pt. 1, 293–94; 3:323–28; and David Durrell, *The Hebrews Text of the Parallel Prophecies of Jacob and Moses Relating to the Twelve Tribes* (Oxford, 1763), 80–83.

59. John Trapp, *Annotations upon the Old and New Testament*, 4:602; 2:24 (second pagination).

60. It is generally assumed today that, as the first Nazarite, Samson is an obvious point of reference in Amos's prophecy; some were more dubious in the seventeenth century. Cf. William Rainey Harper, *A Critical and Exegetical Commentary on Amos and Hosea* (New York: Charles Scribner's Sons, 1905), li–lii, 56–57; and Sebastian Benefield, *A Commentarie, or Exposition vpon the Second Chapter of the Prophecie of Amos* (London, 1620), who thinks that "*S. Matthew* had respect to the *Nazarites* of the *old Testament*, as to the types of Christ, may well be deceiued" and, further, that with "reference to *Samson* . . . [as] a *Nazarite* by Gods singular ordination" there is "no soliditie" to the opinion — "no ground" (268).

61. John Trapp, *A Commentary, or, Exposition upon the XII. Minor Prophets* (London, 1654), 233.

62. Trapp, *Gods Love-Tokens*, the title-page epigraphs and the epigraphs on 1 and 109; see also 62–63, 140–41, 163.

63. Ibid., 42, 113, 114.

64. Trapp, *Annotations upon the Old and New Testament*, 1:84, 86, 90, 91, 81 (all second pagination); 5:595; cf. 4:57. That Trapp intrudes the Samson story upon his gloss for Rev. 7.3 in 1662 is curious; why he does so is uncertain, although elsewhere he does contrast the shortness of Samson's wedding feast (seven days) with the "continual" feast of the martyrs (*A Commentary or Exposition upon the Proverbs of Solomon*, in *Solomonis !anápetos: Or, A Commentarie upon the Books of Proverbs, Ecclesiastes, and the Song of Songs* (2 vols.; London, 1650), 1:169. Here is the 1662 version of the Revelation note in full:

Reprobates oft fare the better for those few righteous that are among them; they are therefore singularly foolish for seeking to rid them, and root them out. . . . These resemble the Stag in the Embleme, that fed upon the leaves which hid him from the Hunter; and Sampson-like, by pulling down the pillars, they bring the house upon their own heads. (5:983).

Cf. an earlier version of this same note (1647) from *A Commentary or Exposition upon All the Epistles and the Revelation of John the Divine*: Reprobates oft fare the better for those few righteous that are amongst them: they are therefore singularly foolish for seeking to rid them, and root them out, as the Heathen Emperours did. . . . (518)

65. See Trapp, *A Commentary or Exposition upon the Proverbs*, 1:64–65, 69, 233–34; *A Commentary or Exposition upon Ecclesiastes*, 2:12, 138 (see also 132–33); *A Commentary or Exposition upon the Canticles*, 2:270; cf. 271 — all in *Solomonis !anápetos*.

66. Grotius's *De Juri Belli Ac Pacis* was published in Paris, 1625, and Frankfurt, 1626. A second edition of the work, emended and enlarged, is published in Amsterdam, 1631; a third edition of this foundational text of international law appears in 1632. The 1642 edition adds annotations by the author; that of 1699, edited by John Christopher Becmano, is a "variorum" of annotation; and yet another (Lugduni Batavaorum: E. J. Brill, 1939), based on the edition of 1631, includes variant readings of 1625, 1632, 1642, and 1646, plus notes by later editors. The Samson passage is added to book 2, chapter 20, section 8, at page 294 of the 1631 edition. This passage does not appear in Grotius's *Of the Law of Warre and Peace with Annotations*, tr. Clement Barksdale (London, 1655), which, while following the Paris and Frankfurt editions, has been described as "a small and worthless abridgment" by Jesse S. Reeves, "Grotius, *De Jure Belli Ac Pacis*: A Bibliographical Account," *American Journal of International Law* 19 (1925): 251. But the Samson passage is available in the translation by William Evats, Grotius, *His Three Books Treating of the Rights of War and Peace* (London, 1682), 367; another translation by Antoine de Courtin, *Le Droit de la Guerre et de la Paix, par M. Grotius* (3 vols.; Amsterdam and The Hague, 1688), 2:465; as well as the translations by both John Morrice, *On the Rights of War and Peace*, 2:454–55, and by J. Barbeyrac *The Rights of War and Peace* (London, 1738), 410. The passage is excluded from *De Juri Belli Ac Pacis*, published in The Netherlands, 1696, which contains only the first five chapters (up to section 7) of the crucial second book of the work (this project was terminated by the author's death); but is available in the edition by John Christopher Becmano (Frankfurt, 1699), 846. For Henrici de Cocceii's commentary on Grotius's invocation of Samson both here and in book 2, chapter 19, section 5, see Grotius, *De Jure Belli Ac Pacis* (5 vols.; Lausanne, 1751–52), 3:256, 342. And for Grotius's own citation of book II,

chapter 20, section 8, see *Opera Omnia Theologica* (3 vols.; Amsterdam, 1679), 1:115.

67. See Jesse S. Reeves, "Grotius, *De Jure Belli Ac Pacis*: A Bibliographical Account," *American Journal of International Law* 19 (1925), 251; see also 253.

68. I am grateful to my colleague Alan Fishbone for pointing out the reading in the Vulgate Latin.

69. See Edward Dumbauld, *The Life and Legal Writings of Hugo Grotius* (Norman: University of Oklahoma Press, 1969), 67.

70. See Barksdale, tr., *Of the Law of Warre and Peace* by Grotius, 16, 306–07, 385. Barksdale's translation and abridgment follows the earliest editions of Grotius's work, those without the later revisions and enlargements. On Ehud, see ibid., 169; cf. 15–16.

71. Morrice, et al., tr., *Of the Rights of War and Peace* by Grotius, 2:455–57. When quoting from the revised and enlarged edition of this work, especially long and difficult passages or arguments, I will use this translation by John Morrice, which is usually regarded as the best early translation of Grotius.

72. Ibid., 2:464–66, 467. See also Joan D. Tooke, *The Just War in Aquinas and Grotius* (London: SPCK, 1965), esp. 196–200.

73. See Grotius, *Opera Omnia Theologica* (Amsterdam, 1679), 1:115. All translations of this work and used in this book are by Alan Fishbone of The Greek and Latin Institute, The Graduate Center, The City University of New York. See also Grotius, *Of the Rights of War and Peace*, tr. Morrice et al., 2:219–20.

74. Thomas Goodwin (1600–1680), "The Folly of Relapsing After Peace Spoken," in *The Works of Thomas Goodwin, D. D.* (12 vols.; Edinburgh, London, and Dublin, 1861–66), 12:419–20. Like Milton, Goodwin attended Christ's College (1616); he was also leader of the "dissenting brethern" and in 1650 served with Milton on a commission to investigate the records of the Westminster Assembly. Finally, Goodwin attended Cromwell on his deathbed.

75. Thomas Goodwin, "Three Several Ages of Christians in Faith and Obedience," in *Works*, 7:508–09.

76. Thomas Goodwin, "The Return of Prayers," "The Folly of Relapsing After Peace Spoken," and "Of Christ the Mediator," all in ibid., 3:390, 419; 5:152.

77. Jonathan Richardson, *Explanatory Notes and Remarks on Milton's "Paradise Lost"* (London, 1734), 479.

78. See the anonymous tract, *The Cloud Opened; Or, The English Heroe* (London, 1670), 13.

79. Peter Martyr, *The Common Places of the Most Famous and Renowned Diuine Doctor*, tr. Anthonie Marten (London, 1583), pt. 2, 550.

80. See Thomas Goodwin, "The Folly of Relapsing," in *Works*,

12:419–20, and Jackson, "The Humiliation of the Son of God," in *The Works of Thomas Jackson* (12 vols.; Oxford, 1844), 12:82.

81. Trapp, *Theologia Theologiae*, 19.

82. Rachel Speght, *Mortalities Memorandvm, with a Dreame Prefixed, Imaginarie in Manner, Reall in Matter* (London, 1621), 29.

83. Euripides, *The Bacchae*, 2nd ed., tr. Michael Cacoyannis (New York: Meridian, 1982), 18.

84. John Mayer, *Many Commentaries in One* (London, 1647), 153.

85. Willet, *Hexapla in Genesin*, 444, 453–54, 459; cf. 458, 460.

86. Golda Werman thus describes the Talmud in "Milton's Use of Rabbinic Material," *Milton Studies* 21 (1985): 41.

87. Frank McConnell, ed., "Introduction," *The Bible and the Narrative Tradition* (New York and Oxford: Oxford University Press, 1986), 11.

Notes to Chapter 3

1. David M. Gunn, "Joshua and Judges," in *The Literary Guide to the Bible*, ed. Robert Alter and Frank Kermode (Cambridge, Mass.: Harvard University Press, 1987), 118.

2. *The Old Testament Pseudepigrapha*, ed. James H. Charlesworth (2 vols.; Garden City, N. Y.: Doubleday, 1983), 2:357.

3. Ibid., 2:357. Pseudo-Philo also draws parallels between the births of Moses and Samson, and numbers those slain in the temple catastrophe at 40,000.

4. Thomas Vincent, *Fire and Brimstone from Heaven. From Earth. In Hell* (London, 1670), 136–37.

5. From *Testaments of the Twelve Patriarchs*, in *Pseudepigrapha*, ed. Charlesworth, 1:808–10.

6. *Hebrew-English Edition of the Babylonian Talmud: Nazir*, tr. B. D. Klein, ed. I. Epstein (London: Soncino Press, 1985), 4a, 12b; see also 4b, 7a–11a.

7. *Hebrew-English Edition of the Babylonian Talmud: Kethuboth*, tr. Samuel Daiches and Israel W. Slotki, ed. I. Epstein (London: Soncino Press, 1971), 23b. See also ibid., *Yebamoth*, tr. Israel W. Slotki, ed. I. Epstein (London: Soncino Press, 1984), 118a, 120a.

8. *Hebrew-English Edition of the Babylonian Talmud: Yebamoth*, ibid.

9. *Hebrew-English Edition of the Babylonian Talmud: Berakoth*, tr. Maurice Simon, ed. I. Epstein (London, Jerusalem, and New York: Socino Press, 1972), 12b.

10. *Hebrew-English Edition of the Babylonian Talmud: 'Erubin*, tr. Israel W. Slotki, ed. I. Epstein (London: Socino Press, 1983), 18b; ibid., *Baba Bathra*, tr. Maurice Simon and Israel W. Slotki, ed. I. Epstein (2 vols.; London, Jerusalem, and New York: Socino Press, 1972), 1:91a.

Samson's mother is named Eluma by Pseudo-Philo (see _Pseudepigrapha_, ed. Charlesworth, 2:356). John Mayer lists those who held Delilah to be Samson's wife; see _Many Commentaries in One_ (London, 1647), 163. See also _Hebrew-English Edition of the Babylonian Talmud: Nazir_, tr. Klein, ed. Epstein, 4a.

11. John Mayer, _Many Commentaries in One_ (London, 1647), 154.

12. _Hebrew-English Edition of the Babylonian Talmud: Sanhedrin_, tr. Jacob Shachter and H. Freedman, ed. I. Epstein (London: Socino Press, 1969), 105a.

13. See Origen, _Commentary on the Gospel According to John Books 1–10_, tr. Ronald E. Heine (Washington, D. C.: Catholic University of America Press, 1989), 201; and Grotius, _Political Maxims and Observations_, tr. H. C. S. T. B. (London, 1654), 27.

14. Jeffrey Shoulson, _Milton and the Rabbis: Hebraism, Hellenism, and Christianity_ (New York and London: Columbia University Press, 2001), 138.

15. Hugo Grotius, _His Sophompaneas, or Joseph. A Tragedy. With Annotations. By Francis Goldsmith_ (London, 1652), B2v (the front matter has its own set of signatures).

16. See Hugo Grotius, _Opera Omnia Theologica_ (Amsterdam, 1679), 2, pt. 2: 1058–59: "_Plena est talium exemplorum tota Scriptura. . . . Qui omnes afflatu Divino excitati sunt ad regendum vindicandumque populum, unde & Prophetae Iosepho vocantur. Huic afflantui paruere per fidem. . . . Ibidem invenies cur neque Gedeon neque Sampson credendi sint in Legem peccasse._" All translations are by Alan Fishbone of The Greek and Latin Institute, The Graduate Center, The City University of New York.

17. Ibid., 1:115 (translation by Fishbone): _Neque jus naturae, neque jus gentium prohibet se ulcisci; sed quia modus excedebatur, deinde etiam nè ex quavis causa rixae orirentur, prohibuit id Ius civile, quale est etiam Ius Hebraeis à Deo quidem, sed valde ad modum legum humanarum, datum, quo Iure de extraneis ulcisci se nemo prohibetur: de civibus non prohibetur, nisi in rebus minoribus & quotidianis. Alia est ratio sermonis per crucem sanciti, in quo sicut rerum aeternarum aperta est sponsio, ità & rerum caducarum, ex quibus ultio oritur, contemtus exigitur. Malè haec consundunt multi, minùs nocentes si legi Hebraeae plusquam satìs est tribuant; magìs verò, si ex istis temporibus ad nostra Dei indulgentiam extendant. Heroes apud Homerum & Graecos alios, ut notatum Scholiastis, dediti amoribus, dediti irae. Alios Heroas nobis dedit Euangelii lux, de qua dicam cum sene Terentiano_, Nunc hic dies aliam viam adsert, alios mores postulat.

18. Hugo Grotius, _Of the Rights of War and Peace_, tr. John Morrice et al. (3 vols.; London, 1715), 2:465, 466, and 466–68.

19. See the annotation by Henrici de Cocceii (tr. Fishbone) in Hugo

Grotius, *De Jure Belli Ac Pacis, Cum ... Commentaries ... Henri[ci] de Cocceii ... Samuelis de Cocceii* (5 vols.; Lausanne, 1751–52), 3:342.

20. Ibid.

21. Grotius, *Opera*, 2, pt. 2: 1183: *Sed annumeratur hîc Levi, quia in Christo ea Tribus ad par jus habebat cum caeteris. Omittur verò Dan, quia jam olim ea Tribus jam olim ea Tribus ad unam familiam Hussim reciderat, ut ajunt Hebraei, quae ipsa familia bellis interiisse videtur ante Esdrae tempora. Nam in Paralipomenis, ubi posteritas Patriarcharum memoratur, Dan omittitur. Et fortè id praedicitur apud Amosum VIII, 14. Ex Danis tribu puacos supersuisse, esoque in Phoenicem profugisse, narrat Iohannes Antiochenus.*

22. See, e.g., the annotation by Henrici Cocceii (tr. Fishbone) in Grotius, *De Jure Belli Ac Pacis* (1751–52), 3:256.

23. J. Barbeyrac, tr., in *The Rights of War and Peace* by Hugo Grotius (London, 1738), 399–400.

24. Grotius, *Of the Rights of War and Peace*, ed. Morrice et al., 2:454.

25. Ibid., 2:456.

26. Ibid.

27. Ibid., 2:457, 448.

28. See Grotius, *Opera*, 1:73, 114.

29. Ibid., 1:115.

30. Ibid., 2, pt. 2:1058–60.

31. Ibid., 2, pt. 2:1059.

32. Lancelot Andrewes, "A Sermon Genesis xlix.5–7," in *Ninety-Six Sermons by ... Lancelot Andrewes*, ed. J. P. Wilson (5 vols.; Oxford and London, 1840–43), 4:185–200.

33. The phrase is taken from a supposedly impartial and judicious commentator, who chooses to remain anonymous, *The Cloud Opened: Or the English Heroe* (London, 1670), 18. But on Cromwell himself speaking out against plundering and excessive violence, see *The Writings and Speeches of Oliver Cromwell*, ed. Wilbur Cortez Abbott et al. (4 vols.; Cambridge, Mass.: Harvard University Press, 1937–47), 1:368. See also *The Common Books of the Bible*, ed. A. Cohen (New York: The Sonico Press, 1996), where the point is made that the Philistines keep their promise not to kill Samson, only blinding him, and that "Even Delilah would not betray Samson to such an extent to endanger his life" (280).

34. See Christopher Hill, *God's Englishman: Oliver Cromwell and the English Revolution* (New York: Dial Press, 1970), 90–91; and Grotius, *Of the Rights of War and Peace*, tr. Morrice et al. 1:46–47. On Cromwell as a stern disciplinarian, see Charles Firth, *Oliver Cromwell and the Rule of the Puritans in England* (New York and London: G. P. Putnam's Sons, 1900), 92, 259.

35. *The New Testament of Jesus Christ* (Rheims, 1582), 713.

36. Theodore Beza, tr., *The New Testament of Our Lord* (London, 1582), says "He skipped Dan: & reckeneth Leui" (f. 390); see also *The New Testament of Our Lord Jesus Christ* (London, 1583), 319v (actually 311v).

37. See both Edward Vaughan, *A Method, or Briefe Instruction; Verie Profitable and Speedy, for the Reading and Understanding of the Old and New Testament* (London, 1590), 56; and John Napier, *A Plaine Discouery of the Whole Reuelation of Saint John* (Edinburgh, 1593), 119. The tradition that regards Dan as the tribe of Antichrist — and sometimes Samson as the fulfillment of Jacob's prophecy — is traced generally to the Grecians, the ancient writers, the church fathers, the papists, and the Jesuits, and specifically to Irenaeus, Ambrose, Augustine "& diuerse others"; see Francis Rollenson, *Twelve Propheticall Legacies or Twelve Sermons upon Jacobs Last Will and Testament* (London, 1612), 150. Oleaster, Hippolytus, and Prosper are often included in such lists. According to Ambrose, *Seven Exegetical Works*, tr. Michael P. McHugh (Washington, D. C.: Catholic University of America Press in association with Consortium Press, 1972), 260: "The simple interpretation is this, that the tribe of Dan also supplied the judge in Israel. Granted, . . . the judges of the people were from various tribes. However, Samson was from the tribe of Dan and he judged for twenty years. But the prophecy does not mean him, but the Antichrist, a cruel judge and savage tyrant who will come from the tribe of Dan and will judge the people." For the countertradition represented by Jerome, Rupertus, Lyranus, see Rollenson, *Twelve Propheticall Legacies*, 149. In the early twentieth century, R. H. Charles comments pertinently: "the true explanation [for the exclusion of Dan in Rev. 7] as well as the most ancient is propounded by Irenaeus," according to whom "Dan was omitted because Antichrist was to spring from Dan. The same statement appears in Hippolytus, and later in Andreas." And Charles continues: "this tradition is pre-Christian and Jewish" and "was generally accepted in the Early Christian Church; for in addition to Irenaeus and Hippolytus, it was supported by Eucharius, Augustine, Jacob of Edessa, Theodoret, Arethas, Bede. This interpretation is accepted by Holtzmann, Johannes Weiss, Selwyn, Moffatt and others"; see *Studies in the Apocalypse*, 2nd ed. (Edinburgh: T. and T. Clark, 1915), 116–17.

38. *The New Testament of Our Lord Iesvs*, tr. L. Tomson (London, 1610), 257–[58]. Cf. John Napier, *A Plaine Discovery of the Whole Reuelation of Saint John* (Edinburgh, 1593), 119.

39. Cf.: *The Bible Translated According to the Ebrew and Greeke* (London, 1608), 160v, with both George Arthur Buttrick et al., *The Interpreter's Bible*, 12 vols. (New York and Nashville: Abingdon Press, 1952–57), 11:371–72; and Jacob M. Myers, *The Anchor Bible: 1 Chronicles* (Garden City, N. Y.: Doubleday, 1965), 54.

40. See John Downame et al., *Annotations upon All the Books of the Old and New Testament* (London, 1645), annotation to 1 Chronicles 7:13.

41. See Matthew Poole et al., *Annotations upon the Whole Bible* (2 vols.; London, 1683, 1685), 1: annotation to 1 Chronicles 7.12.

42. William Whiston, *An Essay on the Revelation of Saint John, So Far As Concerns the Past and Present Times* (Cambridge, 1706), 151.

43. See James Brocard, *The Revelation of S. Ihon Reueled* (London, 1582), f. 92v; and cf. Augustine Marlorat, *A Catholike Exposition Vpon the Reuelation of Sainct John* (London, 1574), f. 108: "the trybe of Dan is lefte quite out. The reason wherof . . .: namely that Antichrist should be borne of the tribe of Dan."

44. William Fulke, *Praelections vpon the Sacred and Holy Reuelation of S. John*, tr. George Gifford (London, 1573), f. 46.

45. Junius, *The Apocalyps, or Revelation of S. John* (Cambridge, 1596), 83.

46. Gifford, *Sermons vpon the Whole Booke of Revelation* (London, 1599), 147–48.

47. See Broughton, *A Revelation of the Holy Apocalyps* (London, 1610), 27, cf. 328; Rollenson, *Twelve Propheticall Legacies*, 149–50; Brightman, *The Revelation of S. John Illustrated with an Analysis and Scholions* (Leyden, 1616), 320–21; Cowper, *Pathmos: Or, A Commentary on the Revelation of Saint John* (London, 1619), 291; and Cartwright, *A Plaine Explanation of the Whole Revelation of Saint John* (London, 1622), who refers to the aforementioned interpretive tradition as "the Papists dreame" (40).

48. Pareus, *A Commentary upon the Divine Revelation of the Apostle and Evangelist John*, tr. Elias Arnold (Amsterdam, 1644), 143–44. It needs to be emphasized that for Pareus (and it is Pareus whom Milton twice cites as his authority on Revelation as tragedy, once in his preface to *Samson Agonistes*) this scriptural book is doubly a tragedy: first, aesthetically, in that it conforms to the dramatic structure of tragedy with its acts, scenes, and choruses; and second, conceptually, in that Revelation figures *"the Tragedie of Antichrist"* (my italics, but Pareus is equally emphatic through repetition; see 23, 25, 26 [first pagination]), with John himself here numbered among the "Tragedie writers" (27).

49. William Perkins, *A Godly and Learned Commentary on the Three First Chapters of the Revelation* (London, 1606), 71.

50. Elizabeth Avery, *Scripture-Prophecies Opened* (London, 1647), 5, 7; see also 33.

51. William Whately, *Prototypes, Or, The Primarie Precedent Presidents Ovt of the Booke of Genesis* (London: 1640), pt. 2, 130–31.

52. Ibid., pt. 2, 131.

53. Ibid., pt. 2 (marginal glosses), 132.

54. See *The Early Lives of Milton*, ed. Helen Darbishire (1932; reprint, London: Constable, 1965), 74, 176, 270; see also 177, 269, 271.

55. John Goodwin, *Apolutrois polutroseos or Redemption Redeemed* (London, 1651), 323, 324.

56. Ibid., 324.

57. Ibid., 325, 326. See the provocative essay by Abraham Stoll, "Milton Stages Cherbury: Revelation and Polytheism in *Samson Agonistes*," in *Altering Eyes: New Perspectives on "Samson Agonistes*," ed. Mark R. Kelley and Joseph Wittreich (Newark: University of Delaware Press, and London: Associated University Presses, 2002), 281–306.

58. Goodwin, *Apolutrois polutroseos*, 146, 329, 332–33, 336, 343 (see also 335–37).

59. Ibid., 349, 355 (see also 344–49).

60. Ibid., A2.

61. George Kendall, Θεοκρατία: *Or, A Vindication of the Doctrine . . . Concerning Gods Intentions of Special Grace and Favour to His Elect in the Death of Christ* (London, 1653), pt. 3, 77.

62. Daniel Tuvill, *Asylum Veneris, Or a Sanctuary for Ladies* (London, 1616), 21–22.

63. Thomas Pierce, *A Decad of Caveats to the People of England, Of General Use in All Times, but Most Seasonable in These* (London, 1679), 176.

64. Thomas Pierce, *The Divine Philanthropie Defended* (London, 1657), 65; and Pierce, *A Decad of Caveats*, 181, 290–91 (see also 297).

65. Stephen M. Fallon presents a cogent analysis of "Milton's anti-Calvinist discussion of perseverance," while remaining always sensitive to the complexities and nuances of Milton's positions as they unfold in the different genres of theological treatise and epic-prophecy; see Stephen M. Fallon, "'Elect above the rest': Theology as Self-Representation in Milton," in *Milton and Heresy*, ed. Stephen B. Dobranski and John P. Rumrich (London and New York: Cambridge University Press, 1998), 104.

66. Kendall, Θεοκρατία, pt. 1, 31.

67. Ibid., pt. 1, 55, 87–88 (see also 86).

68. Ibid., pt. 1, 183.

69. Ibid., pt. 2, 2.

70. George Kendall, *Sancti Sanciti. Or, The Common Doctrine of the Perseverance of the Saints: . . . Vindicated from the Attempts Lately Made Against It, by Mr. John Goodwin* (London, 1654), chap. 2, 68, chap. 4, 84; chap. 7, 101.

71. Richard Resbury, *Some Stop to the Gangrene of Arminianism, Lately Promoted by M. John Goodwin* (London, 1651), 39, 112–13. See also Richard Resbury, *The Lightless-Starre: Or, Mr. John Goodwin Discovered a Pelagio-Socinian* (London, 1652), especially 9, 59, on Arminius as a "bold corrupter of the Truth."

72. Christopher Goad, *Refreshing Drops, and Scorching Vials* (London, 1653), 82.

73. John Pawson, *A Brief Vindication of Free Grace* (London, 1652), 2, 4, 9.

74. Thomas Lamb, *Absolute Freedom from Sin by Christs Death for the World, as the Object of Faith in Opposition to Conditional, Set Forth by Mr. John Goodwin* (London, 1656), see A²–a, and also 34, 97–98, 100, 129.

75. William Twisse, *The Riches of Gods Love unto the Vessells of Mercy, Consistent with His Absolute Hatred or Reprobation of the Vessells of Wrath* (Oxford, 1653), pt. 1, 7, 22–23.

76. Ibid., pt. 1, 23–24, 24–25.

77. Ibid., pt. 1, 26 (my italics).

78. Ibid., pt. 1, 29.

79. Ibid., pt. 1, 30.

80. Ibid., pt. 1, 294; pt. 2, 49 (mispaginated); see 49v.

81. N. H. Keeble, *The Literary Culture of Nonconformity in Later Seventeenth-Century England* (Athens: University of Georgia Press, 1987), 195.

82. See, e.g., Thomas Pierce, *A Correct Copy of Some Notes Concerning Gods Decrees, Especially of Reprobation* (London, 1655), 66–67.

83. George Downame, *A Treatise of the Certainty of Perseverance* (Dublin, 1631), 277. See also George Downame, *A Treatise of Ivstification* (London, 1639), and Michael Walpole, *A Treatise of Antichrist . . . The First Part, 1613* (London, 1674) and also Michael Walpole, *A Treatise Concerning Antichrist . . . The Second Part, 1614* (London, 1674).

84. Downame, *A Treatise of the Certainty of Perseverance*, 365; see also 364, 373.

85. Richard Baxter, *The Grotian Religion Discovered, at the Invitation of Mr. Thomas Pierce in His Vindication* (London, 1658), [Bv]–B3.

86. See Nicholas Tyacke, *Anti-Calvinists: The Rise of English Arminianism c. 1590–1640* (Oxford: Clarendon Press, 1987), 174–75.

87. Robert Sanderson, *XXXIV Sermons*, 5th ed., rev. (London, 1671), 123.

88. See Hill, *God's Englishman*, 109, 123, as well as Antonia Fraser, *Cromwell: The Lord Protector* (New York: Alfred A. Knopf, 1973), 326. For Cromwell's remarks, see *The Writings and Speeches of Oliver Cromwell*, ed. Abbott et al., 2:127, 322.

89. See John Nickolls, *Original Letters and Papers of State, Addressed to Oliver Cromwell . . . Found Among the Political Collections of Mr. John Milton* (London, 1743), 92, 95, 44, 73–74. Cf. "Representation from the Lord Generall . . . in Ireland," 144–45; and "Addresse of the Alderman," 151–52.

90. For opposing arguments, see John T. Shawcross, *The Uncertain World of "Samson Agonistes"* (Cambridge: D. S. Brewer, 2001), 100; and Robert T. Fallon, "*A Second Defence*: Milton's Critique of Cromwell,"

Milton Studies 39 (2000): 167–83. Shawcross displays the better instincts here.

91. See both Hill, *God's Englishman,* [217], 227, and Firth, *Oliver Cromwell,* 180–81. For the actual passage, see *The Writings and Speeches of Oliver Cromwell,* ed. Abbott et al., 1:543. Cromwell speaks of "glorious dispensations" (1:699), "wonderful dispensations" (2:340), "marvellous dispensations" (3:53, 60). *Dispensations* are his obsession: 1:545; 2:236, 398; 3:434, 435, 579, 591; 4:46, 473.

92. See *The Writings and Speeches of Oliver Cromwell,* ed. Abbott et al., 2:483; 3:64.

93. Georg Wilhelm Friedrich Hegel, *Hegel on Tragedy,* ed. Anne and Henry Paolucci (1962; reprint, New York and London: Harper Torchbook, 1975), 139.

94. See *The Writings and Speeches of Oliver Cromwell,* ed. Abbott et al., 4:148; 2:82; and cf. 1:340.

95. John Owen, *The Doctrine of the Saints' Perseverance Explained and Confirmed,* in *The Works of John Owen, D. D.,* ed. William H. Goold (24 vols.; 1850–55; rpt. London and Edinburgh, 1862), 11:23, 93.

96. John Owen, *The Exposition of the Epistle to the Hebrews,* in ibid., 24:184, 186–87.

97. Owen, *Of Temptation,* in ibid., 6:101 (see also *A Discourse Concerning the Holy Spirit,* in ibid., 3:150).

98. Owen, *The Doctrine of the Saints Perseverance,* in ibid., 11:314, 256, 261, 263 (see also 498).

99. Samuel Cradock, *The Apostolical History* (London, 1672), 392.

100. Peter Damian, *Letters 31–60,* tr. Owen J. Blum (Washington, D. C.: Catholic University of America Press, 1990), 45, 160.

101. George Whitehead and William Penn, *A Serious Apology for the Principles and Practices of the People Call'd Quakers* (London, 1671), 43.

102. Ibid., 44.

103. Katherine Philips's poem is reprinted in *Women Writers of the Renaissance and Reformation,* ed. Katharina M. Wilson (Athens and London: University of Georgia Press, 1987), 586.

104. Ibid.

105. Eleanor Douglas, *Samsons Fall, Presented to the House 1642* (London, 1649), 3–4, 7, 10.

106. Gerald J. Schiffhorst, *John Milton* (New York: Continuum, 1990), 157.

107. Jane Lead, *A Fountain of Gardens Watered by the Rivers of Divine Pleasure* (3 vols.; London, 1696–1701), 1:G2v, 428; see also 42–45 for Lead on Samson and Delilah. For other references (some more conventional) to the Samson story, see 1:159; 2:132 (noting here the dragon/eagle imagery on 128–29, 134–36); 3, pt. 2:19. See also Lead's

The War of David, and the Peacable Reign of Solomon (1700; reprint, London, 1816), 166, where St. Samson and St. Paul ascend together, as well as The Revelation of Revelations (London, 1683), where Samson emblematizes "the eternal Spirit" ([A3]). On the other hand, Lead seems more comfortable with the analogy afforded by "the united force of Barak and Jael together" (A Fountain of Gardens, 2:500); see also Lead's The Heavenly Cloud Now Breaking (London, 1681), 10.

108. William Walsh, A Dialogue Concerning Women. Being a Defence of the Sex (London, 1691), 80–81.

109. Richard Crashaw, The Delights of the Muses (1646), in The Poems English Latin and Greek of Richard Crashaw, 2nd ed., ed. L. C. Martin (1957; reprint, Oxford: Clarendon Press, 1966), 171. But see also Crashaw's epigram on Samson in Steps to the Temple, in ibid., 102.

Notes to Chapter 4

1. Galileo to his student Benedetto Castelli in a letter dated 21 December 1613 as quoted by Dava Sobel, Galileo's Daughter: A Historical Memoir of Science, Faith, and Love (New York: Walker and Company, 1999), 63.

2. Francis Rollenson, Twelve Propheticall Legacies. Or Twelve Sermons vpon Jacobs Last Will and Testament, Recorded by Moses (London, 1612), 153. In his defense of Bellarmine, Michael Christopherson [actually Michael Walpole] reports that "the tribe of Dan is omitted, which seemeth to be done in hatred of Antichrist. This opinion is very probable" as "Jacob seemeth to speak litterally of Sampson"; yet Walpole also allows that, from Bellamine's point of view, "it is an errour to say, that Antichrist shall come of the Tribe of Dan" (see Michael Walpole, A Treatise of Antichrist [1613; reprint, London: Scolar Press, 1974], 224–25, 387; cf. 226–27, 230–33, 385–86). Thus, John Trapp credits Bellarmine with "see[ing] thorow . . . and dis-claiming" such interpretations, perhaps because elsewhere Bellarmine conforms to relatively conventional thinking concerning Samson; see Trapp, A Commentary or Exposition Upon All the Epistles and the Revelation of John the Divine (London, 1647), 518. For example, Bellarmine also remarks that "Often we have seen . . . men otherwise so captivated by love for the beauty of women . . . that they prefer the love of human beauty to . . . their dignity, . . . their parents, even to life itself and their eternal salvation. Well known are the stories in Sacred Scripture about David, Solomon, and Samson. History is full of similar examples"; see Robert Bellarmine, "The Minds Ascent to God by the Ladder of Created Things," in Spiritual Writings, tr. and ed. John Patrick Donnelly and Roland J. Teske (New York and Mahwah: Paulist Press, 1989), 74.

3. John Mayer, *Ecclesiastica Interpretatio: Or the Expositions vpon the Difficvlt and Dovbtfvl Passages of . . . the Revelation* (London, 1627), 327–28, 329, 330.

4. Arthur Dent, *The Ruine of Rome. Or, an Exposition vpon the Whole Revelation* (1603; reprint, London, 1633), 108.

5. John Diodati, *Pious Annotations vpon the Holy Bible Expounding the Difficult Places There: of Learnedly and Plainly* (London, 1643), 103 (sixth pagination).

6. John Richardson, *Choice Observations and Explanations upon the Old Testament* (London, 1655), annotation for Genesis 49:16–17.

7. John Lightfoot (1602-1675), *The Whole Works of Rev. John Lightfoot, D. D.*, ed. John Rogers Pitman (13 vols.; London, 1821–1825), 4:74–75, 258; 7:356–57; cf. 2:150, 162; 3:337.

8. J. W. Peterson, *A Scriptural Exposition and Demonstration of the Millenarian Reign* (Frankfurt, 1692), [A5], 63.

9. See William Guild, *The Sealed Book Opened. Or, A Cleer Explication of the Prophecies of the Revelation* (London, 1656).

10. See Joseph Mede's enormously important (and popular) commentary, *Clavis Apocalyptica* (1627, 1632) translated by Richard More as *The Key of the Revelation* (London, 1643) — hereafter cited as More but following the edition of 1650. Other translations: 1649, 1650, 1831, 1833. Because it offers the smoother translation, I am quoting from R. Bransby Cooper, *A Translation of Mede's Clavis Apocalyptica* (London, 1833) — hereafter cited as Cooper, but will also cross-reference the long and crucial quotations to the translation of More. For the passages cited above, see Cooper, 53, 54, 80, 130–31 (and More, pt. 1, 74). Henry More follows Mede; see *Apocalypsis Apocalypseos: Or the Revelation of St. John the Divine Unveiled* (London, 1680), 64–66, 274.

11. Cooper, *A Translation of Mede's Clavis Apocalyptica*, 132, 133 (and More, tr. *The Key of the Revelation* by Joseph Mede, pt. 1, 76, 78). Elsewhere, too, Mede is emphatic: the judgment falls not on this or that person but on everyone — "upon the Heads of the whole Tribe," both those "who commit an evil act," and those who aid and abet them; see Joseph Mede, *Diatribae, Discourses on Divers Texts of Scripture* (London, 1647), 346.

12. Cooper, *A Translation of Mede's Clavis Apocalyptica*, 133; cf. More, tr., *The Key of the Revelation* by Mede, pt. 1, 76.

13. Cooper, *A Translation of Mede's Clavis Apocalyptica*, 122.

14. Joseph Wittreich, *Interpreting "Samson Agonistes"* (Princeton: Princeton University Press, 1986), 42.

15. Poole et al., *Annotations upon the Holy Bible* (2 vols.; London, 1683, 1685), 1: annotation to Judges 13.23, and Pierre Allix, *Reflexions upon the Books of the Holy Scripture* (2 vols.; London, 1688), 2:3.

16. Lightfoot, "Horae Hebraical et Talmudicae," in *Whole Works,*

ed. Pitman, 11:406; Patrick Forbes, *An Learned Commentarie upon the Revelation of Saint John* (Middlebury, 1614), 160; John Bale, *The Image of Both Churches*, in *Select Works of John Bale*, ed. Henry Christmas (Cambridge, 1859), 334; John Trapp, *A Commentary or Exposition upon All the Epistles and the Revelation of John the Divine* (London, 1647), 495; Cooper, tr., *Clavis Apocalyptica* by Mede, 205; James Durham, *A Commentarie upon the Book of the Revelation of St. John* (London, 1659), 423–24, 455, 460; William Hickes, Ἀποκάλψς Ἀποκάλψως, *Or the Revelation Revealed* (London, 1659), 233; Sampson Price, *Ephesvs Warning Before Her Woe* [Rev. 2.5] (London, 1616), 52; William Perkins, *Lectures upon the Three First Chapters of the Revelation* (London, 1604), 272; William Guild, *The Sealed Book Opened*, 65, 292 [actually 192]; Hezekial Holland, *An Exposition Or, A Short, but Full, Plaine, and Perfect Epitome of the Most Choice Commentaries upon the Revelation of Saint John* (London, 1650), 91; Thomas Cartwright, *A Plaine Explanation of the Whole Revelation of Saint John* (London, 1622), 95 (misnumbered 25), and see also 116. The crossing of the Judges and Revelation texts through the stories of Sisera and Armageddon is particularly common; see also Thomas Wilson, "A Dictionary, for that Mysticall Booke, called the Reuelation of Saint Iohn," in *A Christian Dictionarie* (London, 1612), 8; *The Works of the Great Albionean Divine . . . Mr. Hugh Broughton*, ed. John Lightfoot (London, 1662), pt. 1, 21; pt. 3, 691; and H. K., *Apocalyptical Mysteries Touching the Two Witnesses* (London, 1667), pt. 2, 29.

  17. William Guild, *Anti-Christ Pointed and Painted Out in His True Colours* (Aberdeen, 1655), 26.

  18. E. H., *A Scriptural Discourse of the Apostasie and the Antichrist* ([London] 1653), 40.

  19. Henry More, *An Explanation of the Grand Mystery of Godliness, Or, A True and Faithfull Representation of the Everlasting Gospel* (London, 1660), 184; cf. Cooper, tr., *Clavis Apocalyptica* by Mede, 80. On eagles as "*open raveners*," see also Henry Hammond, *A Paraphrase and Annotations upon All the Books of the New Testament, Briefly Explaining All the Difficult Places Thereof* (London, 1681), 124.

  20. John Bale, *The Image of Both Churches*, in *Select Works of Bishop Bale*, ed. Christmas, 331.

  21. David Pareus, *A Commentary upon the Divine Revelation of the Apostle and Evangelist John*, tr. Elias Arnold (Amsterdam, 1644), 136, 137. William Guild, *The Sealed Book Opened*, 43; cf. 46. For more favorable readings of the four angels, see John Mayer, *Ecclesiastica Interpretatio*, 324–26, and James Durham, *A Commentarie upon the Book of the Revelation*, 382. "[W]hether good or evil angels, the Doctors are divided," says John Trapp, of these "Ministers of indignation," in *Annotations upon the Old and New Testament* (London, 1654–1662), 5:983.

22. More, tr., *The Key of Revelation* by Mede, pt. 1, 74.

23. J. H. Hexter, *Reappraisals in History: New Views on History and Society in Early Modern Europe*, 2nd ed. (Chicago and London: University of Chicago Press, 1979), 248.

24. Matthew Poole et al., *Annotations upon the Holy Bible*, 1: annotations to Judges 14.9, 16.30.

25. See, e.g., Nicholas Gibbons, *Qvestions and Dispvtations Concerning the Holy Scriptvre* (London, 1601), 360, 236.

26. See Thomas D'urfey, *A New Collection of Songs and Poems* (London, 1683), 27; and [Simon Patrick?], *A Further Continuation and Defence. Or, a Third Part of the Friendly Debate* (London, 1670), 347, 346.

27. John Goodwin, *Anti-Cavalierisme, Or, Truth Pleading As Well the Necessity, As the Lawfulness of This Present War* (London, 1642), 1–2.

28. Ibid., 2, 1. See also John Goodwin, *Right and Might Well Met. Or, A Briefe and Unpartiall Enquiry into the Late and Present Proceedings of the Army under the Command of . . . Lord Fairfax* (London, 1648), 6. In the latter work, Goodwin considers whether, and in what circumstances, commissions should be given (in this instance, by Parliament) for men "to act against themselves, or in a destructive way" and, further, in what circumstances God's laws may or may not be suspended.

29. Edmund Stanton, *Phinehas's Zeal in Execution of Ivdgement. Or, A Divine Remedy for England's Misery* (London, 1645), Av, A2, 21.

30. Robert South, "A Sermon Preached Before King Charles the Second . . . January 1662–3 . . . Judges 19.30," in *Sermons Preached upon Several Occasions*, new ed. (7 vols.; Oxford, 1823), 3:416, 438–39, 416 (again), 439, 431 (cf. 416, 420); and 416 (yet again). See also John March, *A Sermon . . . on the 30th of January 1676–7 [Judges 19.30]* (London, 1677) where it is explained of "this horrid Tragedy," "a publick Tragedy," that the wickedness of Judges is "much out-done" by the wickedness of the current age with Charles I again cast as the great martyr-hero and "the monstrous Rebels" again identified as the perpetrators of this "audacious Villany" (25, 20, 11, 15).

31. South, "A Sermon Preached Before King Charles," in *Sermons Preached upon Several Occasions*, 3:423.

32. Edmund Staunton, *Rupes Israelis: The Rock of Israel. A Little Part of Its Glory* (London, 1644), 10.

33. C. F. Burney, *The Book of Judges with Introduction and Notes* (London: Rivingtons, 1918), xxxvi.

34. Gerhard von Rad, *Old Testament Theology: The Theology of Israel's Historical Traditions*, tr. D. M. G. Stalker (2 vols.; New York: Harper, 1962–[75]), 1:334.

35. Milton values differently than South and, let us say, Thomas

Wright, *The Glory of God's Revenge . . . Expres'd in Thirty Modern Tragical Histories* (London, 1686) where the parts of the chief actors are "writ in Characters of Blood" (2).

36. South, "A Sermon Preached Before King Charles," in *Sermons*, 3:439; see also 423, 436, 439.

37. Jacob Boehme, *Mysterium Magnum or an Exposition of the First Book of Moses Called Genesis*, tr. J. Ellistone and John Sparrow, ed. C. J. B. (2 vols.; 1654; reprint, London: John M. Watkins, 1924), 2:916. Boehme's commentary dates from 1623.

38. William Hicks writes: "I desire not to rake up the faults of the Saints, which are not left upon record to encourage to sin, but to be presidents of the grace of God, and as examples for encouragement unto repentant sinners." And later: "The repentance of *David* and *Solomon* for their Adultery and Idolatry, stayed God's hand against them." Hicks also remembers Hebrews 11 (Samson is not cited, but others are) for "everliving examples of faith and godlines, for imitation to all generations to come"; see Ἀποκάλγς Ἀποκάψως 113, 119, 160 (misnumbered 190).

39. Hugh Broughton, *The Works of the Great Abionean Divine*, ed. Lightfoot, pt. 3:690, (see also pt. 1, 15, 416, 22; pt. 2, 515–17, pt. 3, 609, 656.

40. For Leonard Hoar's explanation, see *Index Biblicus Multijugus: Or, A Table To The Holy Scripture*, 2nd ed. (London, 1672), 17. For another more ingenious explanation, see Richard Simon, *A Critical History of the Old Testament*, tr. H. D. (London, 1682), pt. 1, 133: "where it is twice said that *Sampson* was Judge 20 years, . . . the *Talmudists* took occasion to say that he was Judge 40 years, to the end they might make an Allegory."

41. See David Masson, *The Life of John Milton: Narrated in Connexion with the Political, Ecclesiastical, and Literary History of His Time* (6 vols.; 1881; reprint, Gloucester, Mass.: Peter Smith, 1965), 2:519.

42. Ibid., 5:75.

43. John Lightfoot, "A Sermon, Preached at Hertford Assize, March 13, 1663. Judges, XX.27, 28," in *Whole Works*, ed. Pitman, 6:278; see also 2:36, 147–49. On disrupted chronology in both Genesis and Judges, see Richard Simon, *A Critical History*, pt. 1, 41–42 and pt. 2, 31, where of Judges Simon argues: "the Chronology . . . is not at all exact."

44. Lightfoot, "A Sermon, Preached at Hertford Assize," in *Whole Works*, ed. Pitnam, 6:277.

45. Lightfoot, "A Sermon, Preached upon Judges, XI.39," in ibid., 7:151.

46. Lightfoot, "A Chorographical Century," in ibid., 10:178.

47. Lightfoot, "A Chronicle of the Times, and the Order of the Texts, of the Old Testament," in ibid., 2:150, 161–62; and "A Sermon Preached Upon Dan. XII.12, 13," in ibid., 7:221–22.

48. Thomas Playfere, "A Sermon Preached before the Kings Maiesty... 1605," *The Whole Sermons Of That Eloquent Divine* (London, 1633), 145.

49. William Perkins, *Lectures upon the Three First Chapters of the Revelation* (London, 1604), 272. When Perkins's commentary is revised "at the request of M. Perkins Executors, by Thomas Pierson, Preacher," the passage quoted above from the 1604 edition, is revised into a cliché: "[Samson is] a most excellent figure of Christ, and did most notably represent him in his death, wherein hee killed more than in his life." For this revision, see *A Godly and Learned Exposition or Commentary upon the Three First Chapters of the Revelation* (London, 1607), 172. On Samson, see also Robert Hill's dedicatory epistle, [A6]. And for another example of this clichéd typology in Perkins's writings, see "A Reformed Catholike... [Reuelat. 18.4]," in *The Works of That Famous and Worthie Minister of Christ... W. Perkins* (Cambridge, 1605), 701; and cf. *The Poetical Works of George Sandys*, ed. Richard Hooper (2 vols.; London, 1872), 2:[481]. What is lost in Pierson's conversion of Perkins's remark into a cliché is, first, Perkins's insistence that the "theater" for the contest between Christ and the devil is "this present euill world" where "the actors are Satan and euery Christian," and the spectators or "beholders are men and Angels" with God himself as "vmpire and judge" and, second, the obvious contrast between Samson who presumably hated his enemies and Christ who loved his enemies more than his own life. See also William Perkins, *The Combat Betweene Christ and the Diuell Displayed: Or a Commentary vpon the Temptations of Christ* (London, 1616), 4.

50. Thomas Taylor, *Moses and Aaron, or the Types and Shadows of Our Saviour in the Old Testament Opened and Explained* (London, 1653), 48–54.

51. Richard Bernard, *A Key of Knowledge for the Opening of the Secret Mysteries of St. Johns Mysticall Revelation* (London, 1617), 76.

52. Ibid., 75, 76, B2, 34–36, and see also B8, C.

53. Thomas Jackson, *The Humiliation of the Sonne of God, By His Becomming the Son of Man* (London, 1635), 271 (my italics).

54. Lancelot Andrewes, *Ninety-Six Sermons by... Lancelot Andrewes*, ed. J. P. Wilson (5 vols.; Oxford, 1840–43), 4:248.

55. See ibid., 1:191 (271); 4:351–52.

56. Ibid.; see respectively 1:324, 211, 75; 2:172 (cf. 2:329), 354 (my italics).

57. Jackson, *The Humiliation of the Sonne of God*, 271.

58. John Guillory, *Poetic Authority: Spenser, Milton, and Literary History* (New York: Columbia University Press, 1983), 173, 174.

59. James Nalton, "Fear of Missing Salvation: or, the Way to Obtain Salvation," in *Twenty Sermons Preached upon Several Texts* (London, 1677), 155.

60. Herbert Thorndike, *Of the Covent of Grace*, in *The Theological Works of Herbert Thorndike* (6 vols.; Oxford, 1844–66), 3, pt. 2:676–77.

61. See also Herbert Thorndike, *Just Weights and Measures: That Is, The Present State of Religion Weighed in the Balance*, in ibid., 5:179.

62. See Dewey D. Wallace Jr., *Puritans and Predestination: Grace in English Protestant Theology 1525–1695* (Chapel Hill: University of North Carolina Press, 1982), 121, 130–32. If the Anglicans complement the sectarian Arminians, the latter group parallels the earlier "free-willers." Lancelot Andrewes and Thomas Jackson are important precursors of the sectarians, while George Fox, John Goodwin, and Milton are among their radical representatives.

63. Christopher Hill, *Antichrist in Seventeenth-Century England* (London, Toronto, and New York: Verso, 1971), 126–27.

64. Hugo Grotius, *Christs Passion. A Tragedie. With Annotations*, ed. George Sandys (London, 1640), 1, 32.

65. From the annotations by Sandys, ibid., 113–14.

66. Thomas Taylor, *Christs Combate and Conqvest: Or, the Lyon of the Tribe of Jvdah* (London, 1618), 36.

67. James Nalton, "Fear of Missing Salvation," in *Twenty Sermons*, 158.

68. Mieke Bal, "Dealing/With/Women: Daughters in the Book of Judges," *The Book and the Text: The Bible and Literary Theory*, ed. Regina M. Schwartz (Cambridge, Mass. and Oxford: Basil Blackwood, 1990), 34.

69. Lightfoot, "A Sermon . . . Dan. XII. 12, 13," in *The Whole Works*, ed. Pitman, 7:215, 216. The sermon probably belongs to the 1660s. Lightfoot's other sermon on Daniel is dated 1661.

70. William Lilly, *Monarchy or No Monarchy in England* (London, 1651), 81.

71. The possibilities for a neotypology are firmly in place by the sixteenth century as the quotation indicates; see *The Newe Testament of Our Saviour* (London, 1581), sig. Mmiiii.

72. See "On Mr Milton's 'Paradise Lost'," in *Andrew Marvell: The Complete English Poems*, ed. Elizabeth Story Donno (1972; reprint, London: Penguin Books, 1974), 192.

73. Martin Luther, *Luther's Works*, ed. Jaroslav Pelikan et al. (55 vols.; St. Louis and Philadelphia: Concordia Press, 1955–76), 26:109; 4:104 and 5:257 (see also 2:258; 22:273–74); 8:281–82.

74. See Edmond Calamy's unpaginated preface to Samuel Clark, *The Marrow of Ecclesiastical History*, 3rd ed. (London, 1675).

75. See Luther, *Luther's Works*, ed. Pelikan, 52:126.

76. Luther, *Luther's Works*, ed. Pelikan, 5:311, 325–26; 2:375–76; 3:30–31; 45:104; 46:83; 54:79.

77. John Calvin, *Calvin's Commentaries*, tr. William B.Johnston, ed.

David W. Torrance and Thomas F. Torrance (12 vols.; Grand Rapids, Mich.: Eerdmans, 1963), 12:182; 9:41; 7:231.

78. John Calvin, *Institutes of the Christian Religion*, tr. John Allen (2 vols.; Philadelphia: Presbyterian Board of Christian Education, 1928), 1:48; 125; 2:94–95.

79. John Todd, *A Question Book: Embracing the Books of Joshua and Judges* (Springfield, Mass., 1862), 75; see also 114.

80. Richard Hooker, *Of the Laws of Ecclesiastical Polity*, in *The Folger Library Edition of the Works of Richard Hooker*, ed. W. Speed Hill (7 vols.; Cambridge, Mass.: Belknap Press of Harvard University Press, 1977), 1:48-49; see also 1:42. Cf. Thomas Fuller, *Good Thoughts in Bad Times and Other Papers* (Boston, 1863), 210–11.

81. See the anonymous tract, *An Answer to the Book, Intituled, The Doctrine and Discipline of Divorce* (London, 1644), 31; and for others remarks on Milton and St. Paul, see Wittreich, *Feminist Milton* (Ithaca, N. Y. and London: Cornell University Press, 1987), 20, 67, 68, 76, 107, 141, 164.

82. Stephen Greenblatt, *Shakespearean Negotiations: The Circulation of Social Energy in Renaissance England* (Berkeley and Los Angeles: University of California Press, 1988), 35.

83. Joan Bennett, *Reviving Liberty: Radical Christian Humanism in Milton's Great Poems* (Cambridge, Mass. and London: Harvard University Press, 1989), 100. See also the important statement by Norman T. Burns, "'Then Stood up Phinehas': Milton's Antinomianism, and Samson's," *Milton Studies* 33 (1996): 27–46 (a special issue of *Milton Studies*, under the title *The Miltonic Samson*, edited by Albert C. Labriola and Michael Lieb).

84. John Goodwin, *Cata-Baptism: Or New Baptism, Waxing Old, and Ready to Vanish Away* (London, 1655), h2.

85. [Cyriak Skinner,] "The Life of Mr. John Milton," in *The Early Lives of Milton*, ed. Helen Darbishire (1932; reprint, London: Constable, 1965), 29; and Edward Phillips, "The Life of Mr. John Milton," ibid., 75 (my italics except for titles).

86. Wallace, *Puritans and Predestination*, 158.

87. John L. McKenzie, *The World of the Judges* (Englewood Cliffs, N. J.: Prentice-Hall, 1966), 154.

88. Ibid., 158.

89. Archibald Symson, *Samsons Seaven Lockes of Haire: Allegorically Expounded, and Compared to the Seaven Spirituall Vertues* (St. Andrews, 1621), 12, 63. Although he does not give so strong an accent to them, Symson attributes the same infirmities to those mentioned in Hebrews 11:32 as does John Lightfoot.

Notes to Chapter 5

1. I am here adapting what Sternberg says of scriptural narratives to the Samson story as it is unfolded in Milton's poem; see Meir Sternberg, *The Poetics of Biblical Narrative: Ideological Literature and the Drama of Reading* (1985; reprint, Bloomington: Indiana University Press, 1987), 250.

2. Both Medley's illustrated edition of *Samson Agonistes*, and his portfolio of lithographs, are in the collection of the Henry E. Huntington Library. For a catalogue of the many Samson images, see Andor Pigler, *Barockthemen* (3 vols.; Budapest: Kiádo, 1974), 1:122–32.

3. The play contains 78 question marks, 31 of which belong to Samson himself, 17 to the Chorus, and 16 to Manoa. Its interrogative spirit is finely focused by Stanley Fish, "Question and Answer in *Samson Agonistes*," *Critical Quarterly* 11 (1969): 237–64.

4. See John Penn, "Milton's *Samson Agonistes*," in *Critical, Poetical, and Dramatic Works* (2 vols.; London, 1796–98), 2:261.

5. Christopher Hill, *The World Turned Upside Down: Radical Ideas During the English Revolution* (New York: Viking, 1972), 326.

6. Nancy Armstrong and Leonard Tennenhouse, *The Imaginary Puritan: Literature, Intellectual Labor, and the Origins of Personal Life* (Berkeley, Los Angeles, and Oxford: University of California Press, 1992), 101.

7. Hugo Grotius, *Of the Rights of War and Peace . . . in Which Are Explained the Laws and Claims of Nature and Nations*, tr. John Morrice et al. (3 vols.; London, 1715), 3:306.

8. Archibald Symson, *Samsons Seaven Lockes of Haire: Allegorically Expounded, and Compared to the Seaven Spirituall Vertues* (Saint Andrews, 1621), 9, 58, 64.

9. See, for example, the intriguing essay by N. H. Keeble, "'The Colonel's Shadow': Lucy Hutchinson, Women's Writing and the Civil War," in *Literature and the English Civil War*, ed. Thomas Healy and Jonathan Sawday (Cambridge and New York: Cambridge University Press, 1990), 228–29.

10. The first term, credited to Blair Worden, is appropriated by Barry Coward as a crucial aspect of his own portrait of Cromwell; see Barry Coward, *Cromwell: Profiles and Power* (London and New York: Longman, 1991), 2; and, similarly, Austin Woolrych, *Commonwealth to Protectorate* (London: Phoenix, 1982), 397. For a far less critical representation of Cromwell, see Tom Reilly, *Cromwell an Honourable Enemy: The Untold Story of the Cromwellian Invasion of Ireland* (1988; reprint, London: Phoenix Press, 1999), esp. 93–130, 169–96.

11. See Woolrych, *Commonwealth to Protectorate*, 391; and Coward, *Cromwell*, 165.

12. Sir Henry Vane, as quoted in John Nickolls, Jr., *Original Letters*

and Papers of State, Addressed to Oliver Cromwell... Found Among the Political Collections of Mr. John Milton (London, 1743), 73; and Cromwell, as quoted in *The Writings and Speeches of Oliver Cromwell,* ed. Wilbur Cortez Abbott et al. (4 vols.; Cambridge, Mass.: Harvard University Press, 1937–47), 1:314.

13. John Birkenhead, *Two Centvries of Pauls Church-yard* (London, 1653), 14–15.

14. Richard Garnett, *Life of John Milton* (London, 1890), 184–85.

15. Thomas Newton, *Paradise Regain'd... Samson Agonistes* (London, 1785), 211.

16. See, e.g., Roger L. Cox, "Tragedy and the Gospel Narratives," in *The Bible in Its Literary Milieu: Contemporary Essays,* ed. Vincent L. Tollers and John R. Maier (Grand Rapids, Mich.: William B. Eerdmans, 1979), 298–99.

17. Thomas N. Corns, "'Some Rousing Motions': The Plurality of Miltonic Ideology," *Literature and the English Civil War,* ed. Healy and Sawday, 110.

18. Stephen M. Fallon, "'Elect Above the Rest': Theology as Self-Representation in Milton," in *Milton and Heresy,* ed. Stephen B. Dobranski and John P. Rumrich (Cambridge and New York: Cambridge University Press, 1998), 96.

19. See James Holstun, *Ehud's Dagger: Class Struggle in the English Revolution* (London and New York: Verso, 2000), 337.

20. George Fox, *Concerning Sons and Daughters, and Prophetesses Speaking and Prophecying, in the Law and in the Gospel* (n.p., n.d.), 16.

21. See *The Famous and Memorable Workes of Josephus,* tr. Thomas Lodge (London, 1602), 120, 121.

22. See Flavius Josephus, *History of the Jews,* ed. Alexander Murray (3 vols.; London, 1874), 1:455; cf. Ginzberg, *The Legends of the Jews,* tr. Henrietta Szold (7 vols.; 1909–38; reprint Philadelphia: Jewish Publications of America, 1968), 6:205.

23. See Hugo Grotius, *Opera Omnia Theologica* (3 vols.; Amsterdam, 1679), 2, pt. 2: 823.

24. See James Nalton, "Mans Petition and Gods Compassion" (1657), in *Twenty Sermons Preached upon Several Texts* (London, 1677), 13, and in the same volume, "Walking in Christ, the Mark of our Receiving in Christ" (n.d.), 111. In the first of these sermons, Nalton makes it clear that in his reading of the Samson story, the central, crucial episode is the encounter with Dalilah: now Samson, betraying his conscience, is betrayed to Satan (22, 25).

25. "A Dialogue of Comfort Against Tribulation" (1553), in *The Complete Works of St. Thomas More,* ed. Louis L. Martz and Frank Manley (15 vols.; New Haven and London: Yale University Press, 1963–1986), 12:140–41.

26. Ibid.

27. Ibid., 393.

28. Holstun, *Ehud's Dagger*, 345.

29. John Goodwin, *The Divine Authority of the Scriptures Asserted* (London, 1648), 332–33 (also 234, 336). Cf. John Goodwin, *The Saints Interest In God* (London, 1640), 157–58.

30. John Goodwin, *Apolutrosis Apolutroseos or Redemption Redeemed* (London, 1651), A2.

31. Ibid.

32. John Goodwin, *Pleroma to Pneumatikon: Or, A Being Filled with the Spirit* (London, 1670), 132.

33. See John Goodwin, *Hybristodikai. The Obstructours of Justice* (London, 1649), 123, also 97; and *Redemption Redeemed*, 303–04, 332–33, 336–37, A2–A2v.

34. Michael Lieb, *Milton and the Culture of Violence* (Ithaca, N. Y. and London: Cornell University Press, 1994), 235–36.

35. See Du Moulin, *Clamor*, YP, 4, pt. 2: 1078, and also Augustin Calmet, *Taylor's Edition of Calmet's Great Dictionary of the Bible* (4 vols.; Charlestown, Mass., 1812–14), 4:76: "Samson is said to beat, to beat to pieces his enemies, *cutat.*"

36. As quoted by Joseph Wittreich from Samuel's previously unpublished position paper, in *Interpreting "Samson Agonistes"* (Princeton: Princeton University Press, 1986), 296.

37. Francis Barker, *The Culture of Violence: Tragedy and History* (Chicago: University of Chicago Press, 1993), 110.

38. See Richard Trexler, *Sex and Conquest: Gendered Violence, Political Order and the European Conquest of the Americas* (Ithaca: Cornell University Press, 1995), 18. For further contextualization of this line from Milton's tragedy, for a representation of the circumcised as the circumciser and, finally, for a very different interpretive application of this material, see Michael Lieb, "'A Thousand Fore-Skins': Circumcision, Violence, and Selfhood in Milton," *Milton Studies* 38 (2000): 198–219 (a special issue edited by Albert C. Labriola and Michael Lieb entitled *John Milton: The Writer in His Works*). If the Circumcision and the Passion are parallel events and if, as I think, *Christ suffering* and *Samson Agonistes* are parallel texts, their chief parallelism lies in their mutual assault on the violence evident in both the temple catastrophe and the Crucifixion. *Paradise Regain'd*, published along with *Samson Agonistes*, reinforces this point, affording not a contrary vision but an interpretive context for Milton's tragedy.

39. Once again, this and all subsequent quotations of *Christos Paschon* (the translations by Alan Fishbone based on the Bramb edition cited in chap. 1, fn. 2, of this book) are given by line number parenthetically within the text.

40. See Hugo Grotius, *Christs Passion. A Tragedy. With Annotations*, tr. George Sandys (London, 1640), 14.

41. Ibid., 55, 119.

42. Ibid., 46–47.

43. See my discussion in Wittreich, *Interpreting "Samson Agonistes*," 110–15.

44. See Regina M. Schwartz, *The Curse of Cain: The Violent Legacy of Monotheism* (Chicago and London: University of Chicago Press, 1997).

45. Grotius, *Christs Passion*, tr. Sandys, 108 (Sandys's annotation), 49, 58, 53; cf. 50, 52.

46. This reading in no way precludes the one advanced by John N. King who reads in the scene of Jesus returning to his mother's house an allusion to "religious observances at private houses in violation of the Conventicles Acts of 1664 and 1670, which banned congregational meetings at locations other than established churches"; see *Milton and Religious Controversy* (Cambridge and New York: Cambridge University Press, 2000), 189–90.

47. See anon., *Reflections on Sir Richard Bulkeley's Answer to Several Treatises, Lately Publish'd, on the Subject of the Prophets* (London, 1708), 53. The remark refers specifically to Judges 13.24–25.

48. See Joost van den Vondel, *Samson, or Holy Revenge*, in *That Invincible Samson: The Theme of "Samson Agonistes" in World Literature*, tr. and ed. Watson Kirkconnell (Toronto: University of Toronto Press, 1964), 79–80.

49. I quote from *The Complete Greek Tragedies*, ed. David Grene and Richmond Lattimore, 7 vols. (1955; reprint, New York: The Modern Library, 1956), 5:151, 152, 166, 170 (my italics). A more recent translation alters the idiom only to underscore the independency of an action: thus the first of the aforementioned examples reads, "I need no order" (106); the second, "I . . . give freely, not under compulsion" (107); and in the third, Eurystheus, the Messenger explains, had "no wish to come," but was forced to do so and thus made "to bow his neck to what must be" (116); see *The Children of Heracles*, in Euripides, *Alcestis and Other Plays*, tr. John Davie, ed. Richard Rutherford (London and New York: Penguin, 1996).

50. John R. Knott, *The Sword of the Spirit: Puritan Responses to the Bible* (Chicago and London: University of Chicago Press, 1980), 124; see also 128–30.

51. Origen, *Commentary on the Gospel According to John*, tr. Ronald E. Heine (2 vols.; Washington, D. C.: Catholic University of America, 1993), 2:324, and also 322–23.

52. See *The Bible Translated According to the Ebrew and Greeke* (London, 1608), 485.

53. Theodore Haak, *The Dutch Annotations Upon the New Testament* (London, 1657), annotation to John 11.50.

54. See Matthew Poole et al., *Annotations upon the Holy Bible* (2 vols.; London, 1683, 1685), 2: annotation to John 11.51.

55. See Erasmus, *The Paraphrase of Erasmus upon the Newe Testamente* (2 vols.; London, 1548–49), 1 (fourth pagination): [lxxx] verso. Calvin, *Commentary on the Gospel According to John*, tr. William Pringle, (2 vols.; Grand Rapids, Mich.: Eerdmans, 1956), 1:453. Michael Lieb proposes other biblical sites for this idiom, which Lieb also interprets differently; see "'Our Living Dread': The God of *Samson Agonistes*," *Milton Studies* 33 (1996): 15–16. This special issue of *Milton Studies* is printed under the title, *The Miltonic Samson*, ed. Albert C. Labriola and Michael Lieb.

56. Augustine Marlorate, *A Catholike and Ecclesiasticall Exposition of the Holy Gospell after S. John*, tr. Thomas Timme (London, 1575), 424; and John Pawson, *A Brief Vindication of Free Grace* (London, 1652), 10–11.

57. See Joseph Hall, *A Plaine and Familiar Explication (by way of Paraphrase) of All the Hard Texts of the Whole Divine Scripture* (London, 1633), second pagination, 121; and Grotius, *Opera Omnia Theologica*, 2, pt. 1: 535.

58. Hutcheson, *An Exposition of the Gospel of Jesus Christ According to John* (London, 1657), 230–31.

59. Peter Martyr (Pietro Martire Vermigli), *The Common Places of the Most Famous and Renowmed Divine Doctor*, tr. Anthonie Marten (London, 1583), pt. 2, 418.

60. Martyr, *Another Collection of Certeine Diuine Matters and Doctrines of . . . Peter Martyr* (bound with ibid.), tr. Anthonie Marten (London, 1583), 108.

61. See Grotius, *Opera Omnia Theologica*, 1:115, as well as Grotius, *His Three Books Treating of the Rights of War and Peace*, tr. William Evats (London, 1682), 142 (my italics); cf. Grotius, *Of the Rights of War and Peace*, ed. Morrice et al., 2:219–20: "either of their *own accord* . . . or are by *Force* so scattered."

62. Sir Richard C. Jebb, "*Samson Agonistes* and Hellenic Drama," *Proceedings of the British Academy* 3 (1907–08): 342.

63. See George Fox, *Some Principles of the Elect People of God in Scorn Called Quakers* (London, 1671), 34.

64. Martyr, *Common Places*, tr. Marten, pt. 3, 263. For a counter argument concerning figures of faith not bound by the prescription of the law, see the fine essay by Norman T. Burns, "'Then Stood up Phinehas': Milton's Antinominianism, and Samson's," *Milton Studies* 33 (1996): 27–46 (a special issue edited by Albert C. Labriola and Michael Lieb under the title, *The Miltonic Samson*).

65. See Vondel's *Samson*, in *That Invincible Samson*, tr. and ed. Kirkconnell, 92, 104.

66. See Augustin Calmet, *Dictionary of the Bible*, 1 (no pagination): "Dagon."

67. See Hugh Broughton, *A Revelation of the Apocalyps* (London, 1610), 262, 327.

68. Jacob Boehme, *Mysterium Magnum Or An Exposition of the First Book of Moses called Genesis*, tr. J. Ellistone and John Sparrow, ed. C. J. B. (1654; reprint, 2 vols.; London: John M. Watkins, 1924), 2:868–918, esp. 915–18. This commentary was written in 1623.

69. See Ginzberg, *The Legends of the Jews*, 6:201, 144, 147; 4:48; 6:208; and Henry Ainsworth, *Annotations upon the First Book of Moses, called Genesis* ([London] 1616), annotation to 49.16–17.

70. Martyr, *Common Places*, pt. 3, 177.

71. See the annotation by Sandys, *Christ's Passion* by Grotius, tr. Sandys, 81.

72. Thomas Fuller, *A Pisgah-sight of Palestine and the Confines Thereon* (London, 1650), 214.

73. This issue has been addressed by Joan S. Bennett, "'A Person Rais'd': Public and Private Cause in *Samson Agonistes*," *Studies in English Literature 1500–1900*, 18 (Winter 1978), 155–68. It was also at the center of the Samson debate in the seventeenth century, both of the following examples belonging to the year 1657. One commentator remarks that "we must not look upon Samson as a private man revenging his own quarrel, *but* as a Judge of Israel, called and appointed by God , to deliver his people . . . and to avenge them on their enemies: Otherwise these his resolutions could not have been lawfull, seeing the nations of the Philistims had not given unto him in particular any just cause"; see John Downame et al., *Annotations upon All the Books of the Old and New Testaments*, 3rd ed. (2 vols.; London, 1657), 1: annotation to 15.7. On the other hand, Edward Sexby speaks of Samson's "private injuries" and of his "mak[ing] war upon the *Philistins*, being himself but a private man, . . . as they did unto him, so had he done unto them" even as he enlists Milton as an authority: "I answer with learned *Milton*"; see *Killing, No Murder: With Some Additions* (1657; reprint, London, 1659), 10, 11.

74. See Joan S. Bennett's two essays, "A Reading of *Samson Agonistes*," in *The Cambridge Companion to Milton*, ed. Dennis Danielson (Cambridge and New York: Cambridge University Press, 1989), 237, and "Asserting Eternal Providence: John Milton Through the Window of Liberation Theology," in *Milton and Heresy*, ed. Dobranski and Rumrich, 239.

75. See Oliver Cromwell, *The Writings and Speeches of Oliver Cromwell*, ed. Wilbur Cortez Abbott et al. (4 vols.; Cambridge, Mass.: Harvard University Press, 1937–47), 1:315.

76. See Grotius, *Of the Rights of War and Peace*, ed. Morrice et al., 2:477; but see also 1:96–98; 2:466–67, 473.

77. See Madlyn Millner Kahr, "Delilah," in *Feminism and Art His-*

tory: Questioning the Litany, ed. Norma Broude and Mary D. Garrard (New York: Harper and Row, 1982), 120.

78. Grotius borrows the phrase from Juvenal to describe Socrates; see *Of the Rights of War and Peace,* ed. Morrice et al., 2:448.

79. Vondel, *Samson,* in *That Invincible Samson,* tr. and ed. Kirkconnell, 95.

80. W. A. Scott, *The Great Judge: or the Story of Samson, the Hebrew Hercules,* 2nd ed. (San Francisco, 1858), 310.

81. Erich Segal, "Introduction," *Euripides: A Collection of Critical Essays,* ed. Segal (Englewood Cliffs, N. J.: Prentice-Hall, 1968), 9, 23.

82. Georg Wilhelm Friedrich Hegel, *Hegel on Tragedy,* ed. Anne and Henry Paolucci (1962; reprint, Westport, Conn.: Greenwood Press, 1978), 100. For portraits (without blemishes) of both Samson and Hercules, see John Mulryan, "The Heroic Tradition of Milton's *Samson Agonistes,*" *Milton Studies* 23 (1983): 217–34.

83. Northrop Frye, *The Great Code: The Bible and Literature* (1981; reprint, New York, London, and San Diego: Harvest Book, 1983), 169.

84. Grotius, *The Rights of War and Peace,* ed. Morrice et al., 2:487, 513.

85. Ibid., 3:306; compare the last of these quotations from *The Rights of War and Peace,* tr. Evats, xvii, with ibid., 1:29.

86. See Nickolas Lockyer, *A Memorial of God's Judgments, Spiritual and Temporal* (London, 1671), [A6]; and John Tillotson, *Sermons Preach'd upon Several Occasions* (London, 1671), 301. As Blair Wordon reports, the dissenting minister Lockyer remarked "that 'there wants but the jawbone of an ass' to overthrow the Restoration Monarchy"; see "Milton, *Samson Agonistes,* and the Restoration," in *Culture and Society in the Stuart Restoration: Literature, Drama, History,* ed. Gerald MacLean (Cambridge and New York: Cambridge University Press, 1995), 130. But in *A Memorial of God's Judgments,* Lockyer also laments that "Many thousands were killed by the Sword and Pestilence, but few (I fear) made spiritually alive by either" ([A5]).

Notes to Chapter 6

1. The epigraph is from Balachandra Rajan, "Milton Encompassed," *Milton Quarterly* 32 (December 1998): 88.

2. On "Dan," see Augustin Calmet, *Taylor's Edition of Calmet's Great Dictionary of the Bible* (4 vols.; Charlestown, Mass., 1812–14), 1 (no pagination): "Dan."

3. Ibid.

4. Lancelot Andrewes, *Ninety-Six Sermons,* ed. J. P. Wilson (5 vols.; Oxford, 1841–43), 4:248–49.

5. Arnold Williams, *The Common Expositor: An Account of the*

Commentaries on Genesis 1527–1633 (Chapel Hill: University of North Carolina Press, 1948), 166.

6. Jacob Boehme, *Mysterium Magnun or an Exposition of the First Book of Moses Called Genesis*, tr. J. Ellistone and John Sparrow, ed. C. J. B. (2 vols.; 1654; reprint, London: John M. Watkins, 1924), 2:917, 918 (Boehme's commentary was written in 1623); cf. John Salkeld, *A Treatise of Paradise. And the Principall Contents Thereof* (London, 1617), 215.

7. J. P., *Independency Accused by Nine Severall Arguments* (London, 1645), A2v.

8. See George Sandys, tr., *Christs Passion. A Tragedie* [by Hugo Grotius]. *With Annotations* [by Sandys] (London, 1640), 119.

9. See Peter Gaunt, *Oliver Cromwell* (1996; reprint, Oxford and Malden, Mass.: Blackwell Publishers, 1999), 238.

10. Walter MacKellar, ed. *A Variorum Commentary on the Poems of John Milton: "Paradise Regained,"* ed. MacKellar et al. (5 vols.; New York: Columbia University Press, 1975), 4:85. John T. Shawcross identifies the "Worm" in *Paradise Regain'd* as a "snake" and, in a note to *Samson Agonistes*, associates the dragon image with the "serpent in the way" of Jacob's prophecy; see *CP*, 527, 618.

11. Ad de Vries, *Dictionary of Symbols and Imagery* (Amsterdam and London: North-Holland Publishing Co., 1974), 127, 508. Similarly, John Weemes reminded Milton's century that the signatures of the tribes are found in their colors and, specifically, that the signature of "*Dan* [is] a serpent" in parallel with Ezekiel where one of the angels "appeare[s] with the face of . . . an Eagle"; see *The Christian Synagogue* (London, 1623), 214.

12. Alexander Ross, *Mystagogvs Poeticvs, or The Muses Interpreter*, 2nd ed. (London, 1648), 130.

13. Moyse Charas, *New Experiments upon Vipers* (London, 1670), 2, 151. It was also conjectured that inasmuch as "The devouring of a Serpent . . . [was] thought to produce a Dragon," the whole process should be construed not as a conquest and victory but, instead, as the production and unleashing of a monster; see anon., *The Cloud Opened; Or, The English Heroe* (London, 1670), 9.

14. Edward Phillips provides this gloss; and John Carey and Alastair Fowler, additional commentary in *The Poems of John Milton*, ed. Carey and Fowler (London: Longmans, 1968), 330–31. See also *Milton: Complete Shorter Poems*, 2nd ed., ed. Carey (London and New York: Longman, 1997), 349.

15. On displacement, see Sigmund Freud, *The Interpretation of Dreams*, tr. A. A. Brill (New York: Modern Library, 1950), 81–88, 196–200.

16. See Edward Rogers, deriving material from John Rogers, as cited in *The Writings and Speeches of Oliver Cromwell*, ed. Wilbur Cortez Abbott et al. (4 vols.; Cambridge, Mass.: Harvard University Press, 1937–47), 3:616.

17. See Laura Lunger Knoppers, *Constructing Cromwell: Ceremony, Portrait, and Print, 1645–1661* (Cambridge and New York: Cambridge University Press, 2000), 167, and also 20, 47, 67–68, 178–79.

18. See Joseph Wittreich, "'Reading' Milton: The Death (and Survival) of the Author," *Milton Studies* 38 (2000): 37 (a special issue edited by Albert C. Labriola and Michael Lieb entitled *John Milton: The Writer in His Works*).

19. See *The Complete Greek Tragedies*, ed. David Grene and Richmond Lattimore (3 vols.; New York: Modern Library, 1942), 1:116, 127, 143, 147.

20. John Carey, *Milton: Complete Shorter Poems*, 2nd ed., ed. Carey (London and New York: Longman, 1997), 411.

21. See Edward Tayler, "Milton's Firedrake," *Milton Quarterly* 6 (October 1972): 7–10, as well as William Kerrigan, *The Prophetic Milton* (Charlottesville: University Press of Virginia, 1974), 232–39. Kerrigan responds with impressive learning to Tayler's injunction, joining to Tayler's observations a biblical context, then advancing an imaginative interpretation of these lines in Milton's poem. The question is finally: which traditions, and which biblical sources, are most germane to Samson and then to *Samson Agonistes*?

22. Kester Svendsen, *Milton and Science* (Cambridge, Mass.: Harvard University Press, 1956), 148–49.

23. As one example, see the essay by Carol Kessner, "Samson," in *A Milton Encyclopedia*, ed. William B. Hunter Jr., et al. (8 vols.; Lewisburg, Pa: Bucknell University Press, and London: Associated University Presses, 1978–80), 8:138–39.

24. de Vries, *Dictionary of Symbols and Imagery*, 5, and Edward Topsel, *The History of Four-footed Beasts and Serpents . . . Collected out of the Writings of Conradus Gesner and Other Authors*, 2nd ed. (1607; reprint, London, 1658), 701–16.

25. Tayler, "Milton's Firedrake," 8; cf. Kerrigan, *The Prophetic Milton*, 235–36. See also Samuel S. Stollman, "Samson as 'Dragon' and a Scriptural Tradition," *English Language Notes* 7 (March 1970): 186–89, who, using some of the same evidence I have been using, interprets it differently in order to eliminate its "pejorative" implications. Cf. Carey, *Complete Shorter Poems*, ed. Carey, 411, who, as I do, contests Tayler's reading.

26. William Fulke, *Meteors; Or, A Plain Description* (1563; reprint, London, 1670), 20–21, 22, 33. Another edition appeared in 1654.

27. See Edward Topsel, *The History of Four-footed Beasts and Serpents*, 613 [for 713], 712, 715, 706–07; see also 702, 703, 706.

28. See John Williams, quoted in *The Writings and Speeches of Oliver Cromwell*, ed. Abbott et al., 1:323–24.

29. See anon., *The Cloud Opened*, 19, 20–21.

30. See Knoppers, *Constructing Cromwell*, 149.

31. Ann Baynes Coiro, "Fable and Old Song: *Samson Agonistes* and the Idea of a Poetic Career," *Milton Studies* 36 (1998): 137.

32. John Hollander, *The Figure of Echo: A Mode of Allusion in Milton and After* (Berkeley, Los Angeles, and London: University of California Press, 1981), 95.

33. On this typology of difference, see esp. Wittreich, "'Reading' Milton," 26–32.

34. Edward Le Comte, *Poets' Riddles: Essays in Seventeenth-Century Explication* (Port Washington, N. Y., and London: Kennikat Press, 1975), 134.

35. See, e.g., Andrew Willet, *Hexapla in Genesin, That Is, a Sixfold Commentarie upon Genesis* (London, 1632), 10.

36. Elkanah Settle (?), *Uzziah and Jotham. A Poem* (London, 1690), 29.

37. See Blair Worden, "Providence and Politics in Cromwellian England," *Past and Present* 109 (November 1985), 71; but see also 78, 83, 86, 99.

38. Henry Ainsworth, *Annotations upon the First Book of Moses, Called Genesis* ([London] 1616), C3. Another edition: 1621.

39. John Downame et al., *Annotations upon All the Books of the Old and New Testament* (London, 1645), annotation to Genesis 3:1. On whales and on dragons and on both as political leaders, "great Princes," see Ainsworth, *Annotations upon the First Book of Moses*, B.

40. See, e.g., John Brinsley, *The Mystical Brasen Serpent: With the Magnetical Vertue Thereof* (London, 1653), passim; and anon., *Miscellanea*, in Jane Barker, *Poetical Recreations . . . In Two Parts* (London, 1688), 158; Jane Lead, *A Fountain of Gardens Watered by the Rivers of Divine Pleasure* (3 vols.; London, 1696–1701), 1:G2v (first pagination), and 2:128–29, 134–36. See, too, Roelof van den Broek, *The Myth of the Phoenix According to Classical and Early Christian Traditions* (Leiden: E. J. Brill, 1971), passim.

41. These images are discussed together by Svendsen, *Milton and Science*, 140–50; they can be found depicted together in van den Broek's *The Myth of the Phoenix*, pl. 9, 2 (phoenix, winged serpent, hawk); pl. 11, 1 (phoenix with another bird descending and snakes); pl. 40 (phoenix with flying dragon). Often allied with one another (399), the phoenix is said to "resemble most the eagle" (457), while the Thessalian sorceress Eryctho, according to Lucan, uses flying serpents, vipers, horned serpents, together with the ashes of the phoenix "to bring a dead person back to life" (409). On the phoenix, see (more recently) Stella P. Revard, *Milton and the Tangles of Neaera's Hair: The Making of the 1645 Poems* (Columbia and London: University of Missouri Press, 1997), 226–33; and Blair Hoxby, "At the Public Mill of the Philistines: *Samson Agonistes* and the Problem of Work after the Restoration," in *Altering Eyes: New Perspectives on "Samson Agonistes"*, ed. Mark R. Kelley and Joseph

Wittreich (Newark: University of Delaware Press, and London: Associated University Presses, 2002), esp. 236–37.

42. Hollander, *The Figure of Echo*, 74.

43. See Guy R. Mermier, "The Phoenix: Its Nature and Its Place in the Tradition of the *Physiologus*," in *Beasts and Birds of the Middle Ages: The Bestiary and Its Legacy*, ed. Willene B. Clark and Meradith T. McMunn (Philadelphia: University of Pennsylvania Press, 1989), 70, 71.

44. Nahum Tate, *A Present for the Ladies: Being an Historical Account of Several Illustrious Persons of the Female Sex*, 2nd ed. (London, 1693), 9 (the first edition appeared the year before); Bentley, *Milton's "Paradise Lost"* (London, 1732), 157.

45. William Turner, *A Compleat History of the Most Remarkable Providences, Both of Judgment and Mercy, Which Have Hapned in This Present Age* (London, 1697), 100 (fourth pagination). Turner claims that this project was begun by Matthew Poole and completed by himself.

46. Stephen Jerome, *The Haughty Heart Hvmbled: Or, The Patients Practice* (London, 1628), 14, 15. The leveling process that sometimes envelops this trope is evident in the Donnean title of Margaret Bottrall's book, *Every Man a Phoenix: Studies in Seventeenth-Century Spiritual Autobiography* (London: John Murray, 1958).

47. John Guillory, *Poetic Authority: Spenser, Milton, and Literary History* (New York: Columbia University Press, 1983), 175.

48. Francis Goldsmith, tr., *His Sophompaneas, or Joseph. A Tragedy* [by Hugo Grotius]. *With Annotations* [by Francis Goldsmith] (London, 1652), B3, 96.

49. William Burton, tr., *The Blessed Paul's Fellow-labourer in the Gospel, His First Epistle to the Corinthians* by Clement I or Clement of Rome (London, 1647), 14; and Patrick Young, *Certain Annotations upon Clement* (London, 1647), 71; also 72. Nonetheless, Young thinks that Clement might have "spared his censure" given the longstanding traditions of the phoenix — no "meer Pageant brought but the other day, upon the stage," but mentioned repeatedly by authors of old like Herodotus and Ovid.

50. I borrow the phrase from *The Poems of John Milton*, ed. Carey and Fowler, 691, but also point to the widening range of associations Fowler provides for the phoenix in *Milton's "Paradise Lost,"* ed. Fowler (London and New York: Longman, 1998), 297.

51. E. B. Elliott, *Horae Apocalypticae: Or, A Commentary on the Apocalypse, Critical and Historical*, 4th ed. (4 vols.; London: Seeleys, 1851), 1:240–41 (including pl. 10), 242.

52. For the Kerrigan and Tayler citations, see fn. 21 above.

53. Thomas Newton, *"Paradise Regain'd" . . . "Samson Agonistes"* (London, 1785), 320.

54. D. H. Lawrence, *Apocalypse and the Writings on Revelation*, ed. Mara Kalnins (1931; reprint, London and New York: Penguin, 1995), 95.

55. van den Broek, *The Myth of the Phoenix*, 400, 416, 417, 418.

56. Thomas Keightley, *An Account of the Life, Opinions, and Writings of John Milton. With an Introduction to "Paradise Lost"* (London, 1855), 322.

57. See "A Preface Written by D. Twisse," in Mede, *The Key of the Revelation*, tr. Richard More, 2nd ed. (London, 1650), [A5–A5v]. One notable imaging of this is the painting by Frans Floris (1516–1570), "All Allégorie trinitaire," no. 20746 in the Louvre in Paris, where the arms of the cross in this Crucifixion painting blur into eagles wings and where the Crucifixion, as it were, is swallowed up in Resurrection.

58. See *Catastrophe Mundi: or, Merlin Reviv'd* (London, 1683), 105. Cf. *A True Coppie of a Prophesie Which Was Found in Old Ancient House of One Master Truswell . . . Whereunto Is Added Mother Shiptons Prophesies* (London, 1642), 4, as well as *The Prophecie of Thomas Becket* (London, 1666): "*The Eagle* shall come out of the *East* with his Wings spread upon the *SUN* . . . [T]he Sonne of Man shall be Crowned" (5–6). See also Joseph Wittreich, *Visionary Poetics: Milton's Tradition and His Legacy* (San Marino, Ca.: Huntington Library, 1979), 84–85.

59. See Kerrigan, *The Prophetic Milton*, 205.

60. Flavius Josephus, *History of the Jews*, ed. Alexander Murray (3 vols.; London: Virtue, Spalding, and Co., 1874), 1:457; Louis Ginzberg, *The Legends of the Jews*, tr. Henrietta Szold (7 vols.; Philadelphia: Jewish Publications of America, 1909–38), 6:207.

61. See William Turner, *A Compleat History*, 56 (second pagination).

62. See Clement Walker, quoted in *The Writings and Speeches of Oliver Cromwell*, ed. Abbott et al., 1:462; 2:51.

63. See Knoppers, *Constructing Cromwell*, 80; see also 126. For the biblical analogies, see ibid., 52, 99–100, 107, 137, 155–57.

64. See Antonia Fraser, *Cromwell: The Lord Protector* (New York: Alfred A. Knopf, 1973), 693.

65. Wilbur Cortez Abbott, in *The Writings and Speeches of Oliver Cromwell*, ed. Abbott et al., 1:287, 9; 4:875.

66. Fraser, *Cromwell*, 423.

67. Knoppers, *Constructing Cromwell*, 120.

68. Cromwell, in *The Writings and Speeches of Oliver Cromwell*, ed. Abbott et al., 1:365.

69. See John Nickolls, *Original Letters and Papers of State, Addressed to Oliver Cromwell . . . Found Among the Political Collections of Mr. John Milton* (London, 1743), 145; *The Writings and Speeches of Oliver Cromwell*, ed. Abbott et al., 1:287, 377, (and again) 287; and see, e.g., Charles Firth, *Oliver Cromwell and the Rule of the Puritans in England* (1900; reprint, London: Oxford University Press, 1958), 106.

70. Cromwell, in *The Writings and Speeches of Oliver Cromwell*, ed. Abbott et al., 2:189–90.

71. Ibid., 2:38. On the early Cromwell as "one of those 'violent spirits' given to 'agitation' and 'asperity'," see John Morrill, "The Making of Oliver Cromwell," in *Oliver Cromwell and the English Revolution*, ed. John Morrill (London and New York: Longman, 1990), 47–48.

72. Cromwell, in *The Writings and Speeches of Oliver Cromwell*, ed. Abbott et al., 1:544.

73. The phrase belongs to John Owen and is quoted by Fraser, *Cromwell*, 295.

74. Cromwell, in *The Writings and Speeches of Oliver Cromwell*, ed. Abbott et al., 2:189–90; 3:665; 1:340, 360; 4:148; 1:365, 632, 638; 4:472–73.

75. See *Oliver Cromwell's Letters and Speeches: With Elucidations. By Thomas Carlyle* (2 vols.; London, 1845), 2:80.

76. See *The Writings and Speeches of Oliver Cromwell*, ed. Abbott et al., 1:545.

77. See *Oliver Cromwell's Letters and Speeches*, 2:11.

78. See *The Writings and Speeches of Oliver Cromwell*, ed. Abbott et al., 1:543–44.

79. Firth, *Cromwell*, 469; see also 470, 467–68. For illuminating reflection on the role of inspiration in the thinking of both Cromwell and Milton, see Geoffrey F. Nuttall, *The Holy Spirit in Puritan Faith and Experience* (Oxford: Basil Blackwell, 1947), 114–16, but also 35, 104, 109.

80. See *Oliver Cromwell's Letters and Speeches*, 2:196; 1:396, 258.

81. See Firth, *Cromwell*, 473.

82. Grotius, *Of the Rights of War and Peace . . . in Which Are Explained the Laws and Claims of Nature and Nations*, tr. John Morrice et al. (3 vols.; London, 1715), 2:530.

83. See Nickolls, *Original Letters and Papers of State*, 151–52.

84. Firth, *Cromwell*, 255.

85. *The Writings and Speeches of Oliver Cromwell*, ed. Abbott, 2:142, 170–71; 3:62; 1:652; 4:243, 622; 3:64, 434. For other recent arguments that present *Samson Agonistes* as a critique of culture, see both Laura Lunger Knoppers, *Historicizing Milton: Spectacle, Power, and Poetry in Restoration* (Athens: University of Georgia Press, 1994), 143, and John T. Shawcross, *The Uncertain World of "Samson Agonistes"* (Cambridge: D. S. Brewer, 2001), 85, 100.

86. Cromwell, in *The Writings and Speeches of Oliver Cromwell*, ed. Abbott, 3:591, 434–35.

87. See *Calendar of State Papers and Manuscripts Relating to English Affairs, Existing in the Archives and Collections of Venice . . . 1659–61*, ed. Allen B. Hinds, 32 vols. (London: Longmans and Green, 1913–31), 32:245, as quoted by Laura Lunger Knoppers, *Constructing Cromwell:*

Ceremony, Portrait, and Print, 1645–1661 (Cambridge and London: Cambridge University Press, 2000), 184; and Grotius, *Christs Passion*, tr. Sandys, 39, 41, 53.

88. Sandys's annotations in *Christs Passion* by Grotius, tr. Sandys, 107–08.

89. Jacques Derrida, *Of Grammatology*, tr. Gayatri Chakravorty Spivak (Baltimore and London: Johns Hopkins University Press, 1976), 298.

90. See *A Book of Beasts*, tr. and ed. T. H. White (1954; reprint, London: Readers Union, 1956), 126–28.

91. Coiro is one of the very few critics of this poem to take notice of the complexity — and ambiguity — of the phoenix simile; see "Fable and Old Song," 144–45.

92. William Bryan, *A Testimony of the Spirit of Truth, Concerning Richard Brothers* (London, 1795), 8–9.

93. Don Cameron Allen, "Milton and the Descent to Light," in *Milton: Modern Essays in Criticism*, ed. Arthur E. Barker (1965; reprint, London and New York: Oxford University Press, 1967), 179.

94. I borrow the phrase from Derrida, *Of Grammatology*, tr. Spivak, 304.

95. Goldsmith, tr., *Sophompaneas* by Grotius, 54.

96. Weld speaking before the High Court of Justice, Norwich 21 December 1650, as quoted by Nickolls, *Original Letters and Papers of State*, 38.

97. Derrida, *Of Grammatology*, tr. Spivak, 310.

98. Meir Sternberg, "Time and Space in Biblical (Hi)story Telling: The Grand Chronology," in *The Book and the Text: The Bible and Literary Theory*, ed. Regina M. Schwartz (Cambridge, Mass. and Oxford: Basil Blackwell, 1990), 100.

99. Thomas N. Corns, "'Some rousing motions': The plurality of Miltonic ideology," in *Literature and the English Civil War*, ed. Thomas Healy and Jonathan Sawday (Cambridge and New York: Cambridge University Press, 1990), 113.

100. Donald F. Bouchard, *Milton: A Structural Reading* (Montreal: McGill-Queen's University Press, 1974), 171.

101. Here I transfer Andrew Robert Fausset's description of the biblical Samson to Milton's Samson; see *A Critical and Expository Commentary on the Book of Judges* (London, 1885), 245.

102. Frank Kermode, *The Genesis of Secrecy: On the Interpretation of Narrative* (1979; reprint, Cambridge, Mass. and London: Harvard University Press, 1982), 40.

103. See Roland Barthes, "The Greek Theater," in *The Responsibility of Forms: Critical Essays on Music, Art, and Representation*, tr. Richard Howard (New York: Hill and Wang, 1985), 63–88.

104. As quoted by Jeremy Collier, *A Farther Vindication of the Short View of the Profaneness and Immorality of the English Stage* (London, 1708), 20.

105. See Grotius, *Of the Rights of War and Peace*, tr. Morrice et al., 3:17.

106. Victoria Kahn, "Political Theology and Reason of State in *Samson Agonistes*," *South Atlantic Quarterly* 95 (Fall 1996): 1088.

INDEX

Aeschylus, 10, 28, 58, 63
Ainsworth, Henry, 234–35, 258
Aldam, Thomas, 273
Allen, Don Cameron, 280
Andrewes, Lancelot, 54, 94, 112, 171–72, 245
Antichrist: Catholics on, 116–17; Guild on, 155; Mayer on, 145–46; Pareus on, 117–18; Protestants on, 117; scholars on, 116–17; source of, 119, 148, 150, 171; theory of, 57, 116; tragedy of, 59
Apocalypse, 4, 9, 40, 59–60, 148, 154
Apology Against a Pamphlet, An (Milton), 4, 202
apostasy, 124
Areopagitica (Milton), 14, 20, 119, 249
Aristotle, xxviii, 3, 18, 27–28, 62, 92, 183
Armageddon, 152
Arminian theology, xii, 53, 62, 127–34, 137, 175, 185, 197, 203–04
Armstrong, Nancy, 195
Artis Logicae (Milton), 14, 202
Ascham, Roger, 30–31
Astell, Mary, 77
Aston, Walter, 5
Atheists, 159
Atonement, 11, 57, 60–62, 65
Avery, Elizabeth, 119

Babylonian Talmud, 102
Bacchae, The (Euripides), 2, 28–29, 39–40, 98, 199, 214, 240
Bale, John, 152, 155
Barbeyrac, J., 108–09
Barker, Francis, xxi–xxii, 9
Baxter, Richard, 49, 133
Bellarmine, Robert, 145

Benjamites, 159
Bennett, Joan S., 188
Bentley, Richard, 261–62
Bible. *See also* Hebrew Bible, New Testament, Old Testament, Scripture: Christian, xxi–xxii, 106; commentary on, xii, 106; Hebrew, xxi–xxii; hermeneutics of, 282; interpretation of, 1–3, 71, 280; King James Version of, xxxi; poetry of, 265; themes of, 29, 66, 258–59; tribes of, 114
Bird, Samuel, 78
Boehme, Jacob, 246
Book of Common Prayer, 273
Bouchard, Donald F., 282–83
Bramhall, John, 81
Brightman, Thomas, 117
Broughton, Hugh, 117
Bryan William, 279
Buchanan, George, xxiv, 2–3, 16, 31, 57, 65
Burnet, Bishop Gilbert, 270
Burney, C. F., 161
Burton, William, 265
Bushnell, Rebecca W., 63

Caesar, Augustus, 271
Calmet, Augustin, 23
Calvin, John, 83, 147, 181–83, 186, 224
Calvinism, xxiv, 28, 119, 126, 134, 225
Cartwright, Thomas, 117, 152
Catholicism, xxiv, 117, 145
charity, 63, 133, 137, 228
Charles I, King of England, 121, 141, 161–62, 180, 277
Charles II (King of England), 5
Christ: Crucifixion of, 7–8; and faith, 145; Passion of, 55; and Samson,

263, 282; and temptation, 267;
typology of, 180–81
Christianity: and art, 259; and
charity, 63; and ethics, 180;
interrogation in, 63–64; and
Milton, 9–11, 58, 215; mythology
of, 35; theology of, xxvi, 8, 11, 61,
149; tradition of, xiv,1–3, 217, 260
Christos Paschon (Nazianzeni), 2,
18–19, 28, 40–44, 47–48, 61–63,
69, 174, 214
Christs Passion (Grotius), 49–50, 60
Christus Patiens (Grotius), 2, 5, 43–
44, 51–52, 246, 277
Chronicles: Dan in, 114–15; teachings
of, 184, 280
Clapham, Henoch, 87
Clavis Apocalypticae, 268–69
Clement I, 265–66
Cocceii, Henrici de, 106
Constantinople, 267–68
Corinthians, 40–41, 96, 208, 265–66
Corns, Thomas N., 201, 282
Cowley, Abraham, 25
Cradock, Samuel, 139–40
Crashaw, Richard, 262
Creation, 3, 72–73, 219 244
criticism: definition of, xi; of Milton, xi,
xvii, xxii–xxiii, 8, 40, 72, 180, 284
Cromuele tragedia, Il (Graziani), 6
Cromwell, Oliver,: actions of, 197,
275–76; and Charles I, 277; critics
of, 273–74; death of, 277; Firth on,
275–76; Fraser on, 271; Grimston
on, 270; Hill on, 134–36; ideology
of, 134–35; and Ireton, 135; Ireton
on, 24, 35, 198–99; Knoppers on,
272; Lamb on, 128; Milton on, 5,
180, 197, 241n79, 270–71, 277; and
Owen, 135, 137; and Revolution,
137–38, 269–70, 274–77; rhetoric
of, 162; and Samson compared,
270–74; theology of, 214; Vane on,
198–99; Walker on, 270; and
Walton, 272; and Wharton, 272–73
*Cromwell's Conspiracy, A tragy-
comedy relating to our latter
times* (person of quality), 5
Crucifixion, 7–6, 43–46, 52, 55–57,
128, 340n57
Cumberland, Richard, 12

Dalila (character), xxviii, 30, 69, 94,
125–26, 142, 143, 189–90, 197,
207, 226, 233, 235, 240, 247, 253,
259–60, 278, 281, 283

Damian, Peter, 25, 140
Dan: in Chronicles, 114–15; and
idolatry, 80, 116–17, 148–49, 151–
52, 245; Jacob on, 86; Mede on,
152, 155; More on, 65, 154; in
Revelation, 114, 147; and Samson
compared, 146–49, 151–52, 155,
202; tribe of, 87–88, 114, 146–48,
155, 213–14
Danites, 86, 88, 148, 155, 167–68, 206
Da Vinci, Leonardo, 178–79
de Brass, Henry, 180
De Doctrina Christiana (Milton):
Scripture in, 11, 206–09, 228;
themes in, 9, 69, 96–99, 119, 124,
152, 206–07, 243, 274
De Juri Belli Ac Pacis (Grotius), 3, 51,
91–94, 104–06, 108, 226
Delilah, vi, 68, 77, 90, 95, 97, 101,
103, 107, 110, 142, 170, 172, 176,
178, 197, 231, 234–35, 330n24
Dent, Arthur, 146
Derrida, Jacques, 281
Deuteronomy, 111
Dickson, David, 78, 81–84, 91, 122
Diodati, John, 146
*Divine Authority of Scriptures
Asserted* (Goodwin), 211
Dobranski, Stephen B., 20–22
Doctrine and Discipline of Divorce, The
(Milton), 175–76, 205, 227–29, 232
Donne, John, 262
Douglas, Lady Eleanor, 141–42
Dunton, John, 77
D'urfey, Thomas, 159
Durham, James, 152

Elliott, E. B., 266
Empson, William, 11
England: Civil War in, xxiv, 4–5, 107,
113, 142, 159–60, 218; Lightfoot
on, 167–68; republic of, 197;
Revolution in, 5
Erasmus, Desiderius, 27, 68–69, 138
Euripides: classical allusions of, 11–12;
influence of, 1–3, 6, 10–12, 27, 97–98;
Michelini on, 64; Milton compared
to, xxiv, 33–34, 40, 48,; and myth-
ology, 63–64; Parker on, 29; and
Seneca, 33–35; skepticism of, 62;
Wells on, 63; works by: *The Bacchae*,
2, 28–29, 39–40, 98, 199, 214, 240;
Heracles furens, 11, 36–39, 64, 199
evil, 48–49, 110, 119, 276
*Exposition of the Epistle to the
Hebrews...., An* (Owen), 138

fable, 96–98, 189
faith, 62, 69–70, 99, 124–26, 146, 275
fall: of Adam, 197; and Creation, 3; of
    Jerusalem, 55
Ferry, Anne, 21–22
Firth, Charles, 275–76
Fisch, Harold, xii, 71–72
Fish, Stanley, xxiii, xxvii, xxx
Forbes, Patrick, 152
Fox, George, 206
Fraser, Antonia, 271
free will, 124
Fuller, Thomas, 37, 235–35

Galilei, Galileo, 145
Garnett, Richard, 199
Genesis. *See also* Old Testament, 2,
    72–73, 85–86, 114, 120, 146–50,
    258–61
Gifford, George, 116–17
Ginzberg, Louis, 234, 269
Giona profeta, 7
gloss. *See* interrogation, sermon
God: authority of, 138; and fate, 131;
    hand of, 126–27; and judgment,
    153–54; and justice, 108, 154, 272;
    laws of, 79, 177, 230–32; and
    providence, 160; as righteous, 276;
    will of, 49
Goldsmith, Francis, 19–20, 52, 281
Goldsmith, Stephen, 5
Gombrich, E. H., 7
Goodwin, John: on Repentance, 122;
    on Samson, 124–26, 129, 218; on
    Scripture, 86, 96–97, 122, 127, 139,
    159; works by: *Divine Authority
    of Scriptures Asserted*, 211;
    Obstructours of Justice, 211;
    Redemption Redeemed, 211
Goodwin, Thomas, 95–97, 156, 166
Gospels. *See* Scripture
Gouge, William, 78
Graziani, Gerolamo, 6
Great Britain. *See* England
Greek tragedy, 1–2, 10–11, 27–29, 37,
    40, 63, 284
Greenblatt, Stephen, 187
Grimston, Sir Harbottle, 270
Grotius, Hugo: on atonement, 62; and
    Barbeyrac, xxiv, 108–09; Buchanan
    on, 16, 65; Cocceii on, 106;
    Goldsmith on, 19–20, 52, 281; on
    heroism, 275; on justice, 275, 276;
    Knight on, 42; on Milton, 3, 57–
    59, 91, 196, 285; on rationalism,
    63; on Samson, 79, 92–93, 168;

Sandys on, 2, 42–43, 46–47, 50–51;
    on Scripture, 11, 105, 110–11; works
    by: *Christs Passion*, 49–50, 60;
    Christus Patiens, 2, 5, 43–44, 51–52,
    246, 278; *De Juri Belli Ac Pacis*, 3, 51,
    91–94, 104–06, 226; *Opera Omnia
    Theologica*, 4; *Sophompaneas*, 2–3,
    20, 45, 52, 60, 264, 266
Guild, William, 148, 153–55
Guillory, John, xxiii, 174, 264
Gunn, David M., 101

Hale, John K., 13
Hall, Joseph, 77, 124
Hammond, Henry, 77, 87
Hebrew Bible: covenant on, 106
Hebrew Bible. *See* Bible
Heinsius, Daniel, 19
Henriksen, Erin, 8
Henry E. Huntington Library, xxxi–
    xxxii
Heracles furens (Euripides), 11, 36–39,
    64, 199
Hercules, 7–8, 49–50, 168, 239, 263
hermeneutics: biblical, 10, 72, 188, 282;
    of Milton, 73–74, 83–84, 188, 260
heroism: definition of, 160; Grotius
    on, 275; politics of, 16–17; of
    Samson, 33, 70, 161–62, 239, 258,
    261, 264; as theme, 39; tradition
    of, 263
Hexter, J. H., 156
Hickes, William, 152, 163
Hill, Christopher, xxiii, xxviii, xxx ,
    8–9, 113, 134–36, 176, 195
History of Britain, The (Milton), 14,
    96, 98, 212–13, 221, 257–58
Hoar, Leonard, 165
Holland, Hezekial, 152
Hollander, John, 261
Holstun, James, 206
Howard, Edward, 5–6

idolatry: and Dan, 80, 116–71, 147–
    49, 151–52, 245; Dent on, 146;
    Durham on, 152; followers of, 102,
    116, 122–23, 165, 177, 226, 235;
    Gifford on, 116–17; Mayer on, 146;
    Napier on, 114
interrogation. *See also* sermon: in
    Christianity, 63–64; of Dickson,
    81–83, 128; of Goodwin (John), 86,
    139; and prophecy, 63; of Samson
    story, 22–23, 65–66, 70, 77, 81–82,
    125–26, 138, 157; of seventeenth
    century, 62, 83

Ireland, 135, 137
Ireton, Henry, 24, 135, 198–99
Israel, 167–68, 196
Israelites, 60, 113, 160, 196, 235

Jackson, Thomas, 97, 129
Jacob: on Dan, 86; in Genesis, 150;
    and Israel, 168; prophecy of, 36,
    85–86, 114, 150, 155, 157, 163, 259
Jenners, Thomas, 140
Jephthes (Buchanan), 2
Jerusalem, 43, 45, 55, 142, 147, 268
Jesuits, 146, 159
Jesus Christ. *See* Christ
Jewish: Kabbalah of, 85; law, 227–28;
    people, 44, 70; temple of, 224;
    tradition, 113, 146–47, 217, 228–
    29, 248, 260, 268
John of Patmos, 10, 28, 63, 149, 199
John the Baptist, 49
Jonson, Ben, 27, 281
The Judgement of Martin Bucer, 220
Judges, Book of. *See also* Bible, Old
    Testament, Scripture: commen-
    tary on, 2–3, 10–11, 105, 110, 151,
    160, 260, 269; message of, 98–99;
    Milton on, 70, 180; tribes in, 147
Justa Edovardo. See Lycidas
justice, 62, 108, 272, 276, 281

Kahn, Victoria, xxix, 285
Keeble, N. H., 132
Kelley, Maurice, 139
Kendall, George, 124–29
Kermode, Frank, 73, 284
Kirkconnell, Watson, 26, 48
Knell, Paul, 77
Knight, W. S. M., 42
Knoppers, Laura Lunger, xxii–xxiii,
    xxviii 272, 341n85
Knott, John R. Jr, 222
Krouse, F. Michael, xii, 77

Lamb, Thomas, 128
Last Supper (Da Vinci), 178–79
Lawrence, D. H., 267
laws, 79, 177, 227–32, 268
"A Letter to a Friend (Milton), 155–56
Levy, Primo, 45
Lewalski, Barbara, xii, xiv, xxx
liberalism, 34, 154
Lieb, Michael, xx–xxii, xxvii, xxxi, 212
Lightfoot, John, 147; on *Babylonian
    Talmud*, 102; on Milton, 165, 280;
    on Samson story, 183. 279; on
    Scriptures, xiv-xv,147, 152, 167–

70, 179–80; Sermons of, 167
Lilburne, John, 24, 79
Lushington, Thomas, 77
Luther, Martin, 83, 147, 181–82, 186,
    259
Lycidas (Milton), 125

Manoa (character), 13, 22, 70, 203,
    206, 218, 223, 225, 232, 269, 283
Manoah, 95, 131, 182–83, 206, 234
Martyr, Peter, 25–27, 96, 225–26, 228
Marvell, Andrew, 77, 97, 166, 172, 276
Mayer, John, 98–99, 145–46
McClintock, John, 75
McConnell, Frank, 99–100
Mede, Joseph, 129, 148–50, 152, 155,
    165, 268–69
Michelini, Ann Norris, 64
Midrash, 214
Milton, John: Allen on, 280; Barker
    on, xxi–xxii; Baxter on, 49; Burney
    on, 161; on Charles I, 180; on
    Christianity, 9–11, 58; criticism
    on, 8, 40, 72, 180, 284, xi, xvii,
    xxii–xxiii; on Cromwell, 5, 180,
    197, 270–71, 277, 341n79; and de
    Brass, 180; on divine illumination,
    189; and Euripides compared, 33–
    34, 40, 48, xxiv; Fisch on, 71–72;
    Fish on, xii, xxiii; on gender, 278–
    79; Goldsmith (Stephen) on, 5;
    Grotius on, 3, 57–59, 91, 196, 285;
    Guillory on, 174, xxiii; Hale on,
    13; Henriksen on, 8; hermeneutic
    of, 73–74, 83–84, 188, 260; Hill on,
    7–8, 176, 195, xxviii; Ide on, xxiv;
    imagery of, 72; influences on, 28;
    irony of, 263; Kahn on, 285, xxix;
    Kelley on, 139; Kermode on, 284;
    Kirkconnell on, 26, 48; Knoppers
    on, xxii–xxiii, xxviii; Kosofsky on,
    65; Lieb on, 212, xx–xxi; Lightfoot
    on, 165, 280; Lowenstein on, xx;
    Marvell on, 166, 172, 276; Pierce
    on, 53; poetry of, 7, 16, 72, 195,
    260, 283; and politics, xviii, xxi–
    xxii 2–3, 10–11, 16–17, 20, 160,
    188, 263, xxii; Richardson on, 96;
    Ross on, 248; Sandy on, 235, 278;
    on Scripture, 9–10, 70–72, 154,
    207; Shapiro on, 49; Shawcross on,
    xii, xx, xxvii, xxx; Sims on, 71–72;
    Skinner on, 189; Smith (Nigel) on,
    4; Staunton on, 48, 159–60; Strong
    on, 75; Taylor on, 77, 170;
    Tennenhouse on, 195; on

theology, 3, 62, 153, 157;
Thorndike on, 171, 174–75; on
tradition, 10; tradition of, 77–78;
on tragedy, 2, 10, 91, 159–60, 264,
281; Trapp on, 88–90, 97, 152;
typology of, 80–81, 87, 169;
Wallace on, 189; Walsh on, 142–
43; Weld on, 281; Westall on, 77;
Willet on, 99; Willis on, 67;
Wilson on, 77; Wood on, xii;
works by: *Apology Against a
Pamphlet, An,* 4, 202;
Areopagitica, 14, 20, 119, 249;
Artis Logicae, 14, 202; *De
Doctrina Christiana,* 9, 11, 69, 96–
99, 119, 124, 152, 206–09, 228,
243, 274; *Doctrine and The
Discipline of Divorce,* 175–76,
205, 227–29. 232; *Of Education,*
4–5; *The History of Britain,* 14, 96,
98, 212–13, 221, 257–58; "Letter to
a Friend, A," 155–56; *Lycidas,* 125;
Paradise Lost, xviii, xxiv 11, 14,
31, 34, 64, 73, 127, 149, 189, 203–
04 209, 220–22, 244, 259, 262, 265,
280; *Paradise Regained,* 8, 11, 15,
23, 47, 60, 64–66, 70, 73–74, 136,
204–05, 219, 232, 247, 264, 268;
Poems of Mr. John Milton, 14;
Pro Populo Anglicano Defensio,
125; *Pro Se Defensio,* 125, 259–61;
Readie and Easie Way, The, 125,
155, 166; *Reason of Church
Government, The,* 45, 230–31;
Samson Agonistes, 2, 6–8, 20–22,
29, 37, 49–51, 58, 70, 78, 84, 96–
99, 125–26, 140–41, 148, xviii,
xxi–xxii, 187–89, 199, 201, 235–36,
266–67 282–83; *Tenure of Kings
and Magistrates,* 121, 210, 231,
236–39; *Tetrachordon,* 73, 124,
186, 220, 227–28; *Treatise of Civil
Power, A,* 122, 125, 221
Milton and Scriptual Tradition, 8
Milton and the Christian Tradition
(Patrides), xxxvi
Milton Quarterly, xxxvi
More, Alexander, 265
More, Henry, 65, 154
More, Saint Thomas, 209
Morrison, Toni, xviii
Moses, 270
mythology: Christian, 35, 96–97;
pagan, 35, 64

Nalton, James, 174

Napier, John, 114
Nazianzeni, Gregory: influence of, 11,
18, 28, 43; theology of, 59, 61,
291n2; works by: *Christos
Paschon,* 2, 41–43, 61–62, 214
New Model Army, 24, 79, 155, 159,
269, 271
New Testament. *See also* Bible, Old
Testament, Scriptures: Chronicles,
184, 280; commentary on, 75;
Corinthians, 40–41, 96, 208, 265–
66; Revelation, 2–3, 66, 258–61,
265, 269; Timothy, 124
Newton, Isaac, 65
Newton, Thomas, 199, 267
Niemeyer, August Hermann, 75

Of Education (Milton), 4–5
Old Testament. *See also* Bible, Books
of, New Testament, Scripture:
annotations to, 111; commentary
on, 75; Deuteronomy, 111; Ecclesiasticus, 68; Genesis, 2, 72–73,
114, 258–60; Judges, 2–3, 10–11,
70, 98–99, 105, 110, 147, 151, 160,
180, 260, 269, 280; Psalms, 265
Opera Omnia Theologica: Grotius,
Hugo, 4
Owen, John: on Cromwell, 135, 137;
on Samson story, 138–39; works
by: *Exposition of the Epistle to the
Hebrews with the Preliminary
Exercitations, An,* 138
Oxford English Dictionary (OED), 239

paganism, 7, 27, 97
Papists, 116–17, 159
Paradise Lost (Milton): analogies in,
265; Knott on, 222; language in,
209; Scripture in, 149, 220–22,
244, 259, 280; themes in, xviii,
xxiv, 11, 14, 31, 39, 64, 73, 127,
189, 203–04, 247, 262, 280,
Paradise Regained (Milton): themes
in, 8, 23, 47, 60, 64–66, 70, 73,
106, 204–05, 264; Scripture in, 11,
136, 219, 232, 268, 285; Tillotson
on, 15
Pareus, David, 40, 59, 77–78, 117–18,
122, 145
Parker, William Riley, 29
Patrides, C. A., 8, 61
Pawson, John, 128, 225
Peirce, James, 76
Penn, John, xi, 58
Penn, William, 140

Perkins, William, 78–80, 91, 140, 152, 170
Peterson, J. W., 147–48
Phillips, Edward, 189
Philoktetes (Sophocles), 12
phoenix image, 261–67, 278–80, 342n91
Pierce, Thomas, 48, 76, 125
Pilgrim's Prince, A Tragedy, 6
Plato, 223
Poems of Mr. John Milton (Milton), 14
Poeticarum Institutionum (Vossius), 26
Poetics (Aristotle), 27
poetry, xxiv, 72, 259, 262, 265, 283, 285, 287n1
politics: and literature, xxii, 16–17, 279; and Milton, 2–3, 10–11, 17, 20, 160, 188, 263; South on, 160; and theology, 119, 123–24, 137–38, xxix
Poole, Matthew, 157
Porter, Thomas, 6
Presbyterian, 137
Preston, John, 133
Price, Sampson, 152
prophecy: of Amos, 86; in Genesis, 120, 157; and interrogation, 63; of Jacob, 36, 85–86, 114, 150, 155, 157, 163, 259; of John, 165; and knowledge, 266; of "Master Truswell," 269; and myth, 62; Pawson on, 225; in Revelation, 150, 157, 269; and sermon, xi–xii
Pro Populo Anglicano Defensio (Milton), 232
Pro Se Defensio (Milton), 125, 259–61
Protestantism, 74, 117, 145, 147, 262, 284, xxiii–xxiv
Psalms, 265
Ptolemy, 32
Puritanism, xxiv, 119, 129, 137, 163, 197, 200, 242, 271
Puritan Revolution, 79, 135

Quakers, 134, 185, 273
Quint, David, xxiii

rabbinical commentary, 60, 99, 269
Rajan, Balachandra, 1
Raleigh, Walter, xviii
The Readie and Easie Way (Milton), 125, 155, 166
Reason of Church-Government, The (Milton), 45, 230–31
redemption, 62
Redemption Redeemed (Goodwin), 211
Reformation, 180–81, 186–88

regeneration, 123
Religious-Rebell, The, 6
Rembrant, 178–79
Renaissance, xxiv, xxvi
repentance, 122, 123
Republicans, 137, 197
Restauration of King Charles II, The (Aston), 5
Restoration, xxii, 5, 241
Resurrection, 7–8, 43, 55, 265, 340n57
Revelation, Book of. *See also* New Testament: and Apocalypse, 148; commentary on, 2–3, 66, 148–50, 152–54, 258–61; Dan in, 114, 147; Diodati on, 146; images in, 260–61, 265; Paresus on, 59, 145; prophecy in, 150, 157, 269; tribes in, 153

Revolution: in England, 5; and Royalists, 6
Richardson, Jonathan, 96
Rolewinck, Werner, 168
Rollenson, Francis, 117, 145, 259
Ross, Alexander, 248
Royalists, 5–6, 195

salvation, 62
Samson, Of Heilige Wraeck, Treurspel (Vondel), 2, 220
Samson Agonistes (Milton): Barker on, xxi–xxii; Bennett on, 188; biblical influence in, 84; Bouchard on, 282–83; Corns on, 201, 282; criticism of, xviii, xxi–xxii, 8; Edward on, 189; emblems in, 261; epilogue to, 29; faith in, 70, 126; Ferry on, 21–22; Fuller on, 37, 235–36; Garnett on, 199; Greenblatt on, 187; Guild on, 148; Guillory on, 264; Hollander on, 261; Holstun on, 206; imagery in, 49–51, 125–26, 168, 260–62, 266–67, 274–79; interpretations of, 2, 6–7, 66, 73–74, 97–98, 197, 206, 283, 285; Keeble on, 132; Kezar on, xxii; Levy on, 45; Lieb on, xxi; Lightfoot on, 183; Marvell on, 97; Mayer on, 98–99; and Medley, xxxi–xxxii; metaphor in, 124; Newton (Thomas) on, 199, 267; Owen on, 138–39; Penn on, xi, 58; political allegory in, xxii, 20, 140–41, 263, 279; preface to, 7, 60, 96, 172, 174; Quint on, xxiii; rhetoric in, 138; Shoulson on, 8, 103–04, xiv, xxvi; Shuger on, 48, 57; simile

in, 51, 265, 267–68, 282; Skulsky
on, xxiv; Speght on, 98; Sternberg
on, 282; structure of, 259–60, 262–
64, xxix; Tayler on, 252–54, 267;
themes of, xi–xii, 18, 22–23, 59–60,
64, 70–71, 106, 123, 223–24, 244,
277, 283; transition in, 55; Trapp
on, 84–85, 94; Tuvill on, 125;
Twisse on, 83, 129–32, 268; verso to,
287n4; violence in, 7, xxii, xxviii;
Wallace on, 189; Worden on, 258
Samson Killing a Philistine
(Schiavoni), 7
Samson story: Ainsworth on, 234–35;
ambiguities in, 66, 110, 137, 268,
280; Andrews on, 54, 94; Bird on,
78; Bramhall on, 81; Bryan on, 279;
Calmet on, 23; Calvin on, 182–83;
Cartwright on, 152; Clapham on,
87; Cradock on, 139–40; and
Cromwell compared, 270–74;
Damian on, 25, 140; and Dan
compared, 146–49, 151–52, 155,
202; Dickson on, 78, 81–84, 91;
Dobranski on, 20–22; Douglas on,
141–42; as fable, 49–50, 96;
fallibility on, 119; Fox on, 206;
Goodwin on, 95–97, 124–26, 129,
156, 159, 218; Gouge on, 78;
Grotious on, 79, 92–93, 168; Hall
on, 77, 124; Hammond on, 77, 87;
and heroism, 33, 70, 161–62, 239,
258, 261, 264; Hexter on, 156; Hill
on, 176, xxiii; history of, 2–3; Hoar
on, 165; interpretations of, 73–76,
83–84, 91, 99, 151, 168, 180, 189,
258, 282; interrogation of, 22–23,
65–66, 70, 77, 81–82, 125–26, 138,
157; Kermode on, 73; Knell on, 77;
Krouse on, xii, 77; legacy of, 148;
Lightfoot on, 147, 279; Lushington
on, 77; Luther on, 182;
McClintock on, 75; McConnell
on, 99–100; misery in, 124; Nalton
on, 174; Norbrook on, xxiv;
paintings of, 7, 193–94, 265–66;
Peirce on, 48, 76, 125; Perkins on,
78–80, 91, 152, 170; Poole on, 157;
rabbinical commentary on, 99;
representations of, 266–67;
Rolewink on, 168; Saint Thomas
More on, 209; Sampson on, 152;
Sandys on, 60; in seventeenth
century, 48, 193; Shoulson on,
103–04, xiv; Smith on, 48; Spurr
on, 16, 18; Taylor on, 168; Trapp

on, 90–91; typology of, 80–81, 87,
96, 284; Whately on, 119–20;
Williams (Rogers) on, 170, 176
Sanderson, Robert, xii, 24, 134
Sandys, George: on Grotius, 2, 42–43,
46–47, 50–51, 60, 278; on Milton,
235, 278; on Scripture, 11, 50, 111
Sansone (Palma), 7
Schiavoni, Andrea, 7
Scripture. *See also* Bible, Christian
Bible, Hebrew Bible, New
Testament, Old Testament:
Ainsworth on, 258; Andrewes on,
94, 112, 171, 245; Bale on, 152,
155; Barker on, 9; Boehme on, 246;
Buchanan on, 3; Cowley on, 25; on
Creation; Diodati on, 146; Galileo
Galilei on, 145; Goodwin (John)
on, 86, 96–97, 122, 127, 139, 159,
188; Grotius on, 11, 105, 110–11;
Guild on, 153–55; interpretations
on, 10–12, 25–26, 71, 94, 264–65;
Kendall on, 124–27; Lightfoot on,
xiv-xv, 147, 152, 167–70, 179–80;
Martyr on, 25–27, 96, 225–26;
Mede on, 129, 148–50, 165 268–69;
Milton on, 9–10, 70–72, 154, 207;
Napier on, 114; Niemeyer on, 75;
Pareus on, 59, 77, 122; Pawson on,
128; Peterson on, 147–48; Pierce
on, 48; Sandys on, 11, 50, 111;
scholars on, 68, 133; Shapiro on,
61; Trexler on, 214–15; violence
in, 92, 147; Whitefield on, xv
Sedgwick, Eve Kosofsky, 65
Sejanus (Jonson), 27
Seneca: and Euripidies, 33–35;
influence of, 1–3, 6, 10–12, 27, 37,
131, 239, 281; and mythology, 63–
64; Parker on, 29
sermon. *See also* interrogation: of de
Vries, 258; and prophesy, xii–xiii
seventeenth century: consciousness
of, xix, 1-2; interrogators of, 62,
83; poetry of, 259, 262, 283;
Protestantism in, xxiv; Samson
story in, 48, 91, 193
Shapiro, James, 49, 61
Shawcross, John T., xii, xx, xxvii, xxx
Shoulson, Jeffrey, xiv, xxvi, 8, 60,
103-04
Shuger, Debora Kuller, 48, 57
Sims, James H., 71–72
sin, 122, 140, 165
Skinner, Cyriak, 189
Smith, Henry, 48

Smith, Nigel, 4, 10–11
Soggin, Alberto J., 67
Sophocles, 10, 12, 27–30, 37, 62–63, 136
Sophompaneas (Grotius), 2–3, 20, 45, 52, 60, 264, 266
South, Robert, 160
Speght, Rachel, 98
Spurr, John, 16, 18
Staunton, Edmund, 48, 159–60
Sternberg, Meir, 193, 281–82
Strong, James, 75

Talmud. *See Babylonian Talmud*
Tate, Nahum, 262–63
Tayler, Edward, 252–54, 267
Taylor, Thomas, 77, 168, 170, 178
Tennenhouse, Leonard, 195
Tenure of Kings and Magistrates, The (Milton), 121, 210, 231, 236–39
Tetrachordon (Milton), 73, 124, 186, 220, 227–28
theology: Arminian, xii, 53, 62, 127–34, 137, 175, 185, 197, 203–04; Calvinist, xxiv, 119, 134, 185; Catholic, xxiv; Christian, xxvi, 8, 61, 149; of Cromwell, 214; definition of, 61–62; Kahn on, xxix; and Milton, 3, 62, 153, 157; of Nazian, 59, 61; Pareus on, 78; and politics, xxix, 119, 123–24, 137–38; Presbyterian, 137; Puritan, 119, xxiv; of Reformation, 186–87
Thorndike, Herbert, 171, 174–75
Tillotson, John, 15, 242
Todd, John Henry, 12
tradition: biblical, 6, 16, 21, 24, 29, 66, 281; Christian, 1–3, 217, 260, xiv; of heroism, 263; Jewish, 113, 147, 217, 248, 260; Milton on, 2, 10, 159–60, 281; plurality of, xiv; and religion, 284; of Samson story, 3, 77–78, 260–61
tragedy: classical, 62; genre of, xi, xxix 1-2; Greek, 1–2, 10–11, 27–29, 37, 40, 63, 284; Milton on, 10, 91, 159–60; of Samson, 264
Trapp, John, 83–91, 94, 97, 152
A Treatise of Civil Power (Milton), 122, 125, 221

Trexler, Richard, 214–15
tribes: biblical twelve, 114, 150, 155; of Dan, 88, 114, 146–49, 155, 233–34; in Revelation, 153
Turner, William, 262
Tuvill, Daniel, 125
Twisse, William, 83, 129–32, 268
Tyacke, Nicholas, 133
typology: of Christ, 180–81; definition of, 169; of difference, 168; of Milton, 80–81, 87, 169; Patrides on, 61; of Samson story, 80–81, 87, 96, 284

The Usurper, A Tragedy (Howard), 5–6

van den Broek, Willem Palmer, 267
Vane, Sir Henry, 198–99
vengeance, 39, 107, 153, 268
Villain, The, A Tragedy (Porter), 6
Vio Cajetan, Tommaso de, 138
violence: in culture, 43; Lieb on, xxi; in *Samson Agonistes*, xxii, xxviii, 7, 48; in Scripture, 92, 147; as theme, xxix, 39
Vondel, Joost van den, 2, 220
Vossius, Gerard, 26, 28
Vries, de, 258

Walker, Clement, 270
Wallace, Dewey D., 189
Walsh, William, 77, 142
Walton, Brian, 166
Walton, Colonel Valentine, 272
Weemes, John, 62
Weld, Thomas, 281
Westall, Simon, 77
Westminster Assembly, 259
Wharton, Lord Philip, 272–73
Whatley, William, 119–20
White, Francis, 133
Willet, Andrew, 99
Williams, Roger, 170, 176
Willis, Gladys J., 67
Wilson, Thomas, 25, 77
Wood, Anthony á, 25
Worden, Blair, 258, 289n28

Young, Patrick, 265